URBAN INDIANS IN A SILVER CITY

Urban Indians in a Silver City

ZACATECAS, MEXICO, 1546–1810

Dana Velasco Murillo

STANFORD UNIVERSITY PRESS
STANFORD, CALIFORNIA

Stanford University Press
Stanford, California

© 2020 by the Board of Trustees of the Leland Stanford Junior University. All rights reserved.

This book has been published with the assistance of the Hellman Fellows Fund.

No part of this book may be reproduced or transmitted in any form or by any means, electronic or mechanical, including photocopying and recording, or in any information storage or retrieval system without the prior written permission of Stanford University Press.

Printed in the United States of America

ISBN 9781503615021
First paperback printing, 2020

The Library of Congress has cataloged the hardcover edition as follows:
Names: Velasco Murillo, Dana, author.
Title: Urban indians in a silver city : Zacatecas, Mexico, 1546–1810 / Dana Velasco Murillo.
Description: Stanford, California : Stanford University Press, 2016. | Includes bibliographical references and index.
Identifiers: LCCN 2016008088 (print) | LCCN 2016009657 (ebook) |
    ISBN 9780804796118 (cloth) | ISBN 9780804799645 (ebook)
Subjects: LCSH: Indians of Mexico—Urban residence—Mexico—Zacatecas (Zacatecas)—History. | Indians of Mexico—Mexico—Zacatecas (Zacatecas)—Ethnic identity—History. | Silver industry—Social aspects—Mexico—Zacatecas (Zacatecas)—History. | Zacatecas (Zacatecas, Mexico)—Ethnic relations—History. | Mexico—History—Spanish colony, 1540–1810.
Classification: LCC F1219.1.Z13 V45 2016 (print) | LCC F1219.1.Z13 (ebook) | DDC 305.800972/43—dc23
LC record available at http://lccn.loc.gov/2016008088

Cover images: 4-reales coin, photo by Matt Peters. Plan of Zacatecas by Joaquín de Sotomayor, 1732, from *Descripción breve de la muy noble y leal ciudad de Zacatecas*, The Bancroft Library. Cover design: Rob Ehle

Typeset by Newgen in 10.5/12 Sabon

To the people of my patio:
Paula Gallegos Casas Velasco and Jose Patricio Briones Velasco
Jose, Sara, Alberto, Rosa, Fermina, and Dora
John Patrick and Mark

Contents

List of Illustrations	ix
Acknowledgments	xiii
Introduction: Silver Veins, Urban Grids, and Layered Identities	1
1. A Tale of Two Settlements, 1546–1559	17
2. Ethnic Cohesion and Community Formation, 1560–1608	53
3. The Creation of Indian Towns and Officials, 1609–1650	87
4. Indios and Vecinos: The Maturation of Urban Indigenous Society, 1655–1739	117
5. Revival and Survival: Indigenous Society in the Mid- to Late Colonial Period, 1730–1806	159
Conclusion: From Indigenous Towns to Mestizo Barrios	199
Notes	211
Glossary	269
Bibliography	275
Index	299

Illustrations

Figures

1.1.	La Quemada: "La Ciudadela," or the "Citadel"	21
1.2.	La Quemada: Hall of Columns	22
1.3.	La Quemada: Votive Temple	22
2.1.	Exterior: Capilla of Tlacuitlapan	62
2.2.	Nahuatl and Spanish membership list, confraternity of the Santa Vera Cruz, Zacatecas, 1643	76
3.1.	"Descripción de la Muy Noble y muy Leal Ciudad," by Joaquín de Sotomayor	100
4.1.	Ethnoracial residential patterns, El Pedregoso, Zacatecas, 1633	128
4.2.	Santa Niño de Atocha shrine, Mina del Eden, Zacatecas	141
5.1.	Jurisdictional designation of the Indian towns within *cuarteles mayores* and *cuarteles menores*, Zacatecas, 1799	188
5.2.	Zacatecas and its Indian towns in 1799, by Bernardo Portugal	190
C.1.	Zacatecas: Historic center	200
C.2.	Chapel of El Niño	201
C.3.	Facade: Temple of San Diego	201
C.4.	Ex-voto to the Virgin of Solitude of Chepinque, dated 1832	206

Maps

I.1.	New Spain's northern silver mining district, c. 1650	3
1.1.	Zacatecas and its Indian towns	19

Tables

2.1.	Indigenous confraternities, Tlacuitlapan, Zacatecas	80
2.2.	Indigenous confraternities, southern communities, Zacatecas	81

3.1.	Comparative population of Zacatecas by racial categories, 1572–1608	92
3.2.	Ethnic identity of indigenous alcaldes, San Francisco (Tlacuitlapan), Zacatecas, 1611–1617	95
3.3.	Town structure of Tlacuitlapan, Zacatecas, 1686–1728	96
3.4.	Rotation of indigenous cabildo elections, Tlacuitlapan, Zacatecas, 1709–1728	97
3.5.	Evolution of indigenous towns in southern Zacatecas, 1650–1736	98
3.6.	Rotation of indigenous cabildo elections in Tonalá Chepinque, Zacatecas, 1675–1688	98
3.7.	Voting order and qualifications, alcalde elections, Tlacuitlapan, 1691	108
3.8.	Repeat alcaldes in Tlacuitlapan, Zacatecas, 1610–1700	111
3.9.	Repeat alcaldes in Tonalá Chepinque, Zacatecas, 1610–1700	111
4.1.	Civil status of adult population, San Josef, Zacatecas, 1671	123
4.2.	Ethnic identity of household composition of hacienda of Cristóbal Ramírez, Zacatecas, 1656	124
4.3.	Number and age of children, San Josef, Zacatecas, 1671	125
4.4.	Ethnic composition of hacienda of Pedro Ruiz de Quiroga, Zacatecas, 1656	126
4.5.	Ethnic composition of huerta of Juan Duarte, Zacatecas, 1656	127
4.6.	Ethnic composition, household of the alguacil mayor, Joseph de Villareal, Zacatecas, 1671, house 338	129
4.7.	Ethnic composition of the household of the factor, Roque de Arellano, Zacatecas, 1671, house 106	130
4.8.	Population, Zacatecas, 1667–1739	131
4.9.	Number of marriage petitions, Indians, blacks, and castas, Zacatecas, 1681–1740	131
4.10.	Extant population counts of Indian towns, Zacatecas, 1671–1741	133
4.11.	Province of origin of male Indian migrants, Zacatecas, 1681–1690	134

4.12.	Endogamy rates in the Indian population, Zacatecas, 1681–1740	137
5.1.	Population of Zacatecas by ethnic categories, 1754	162
5.2.	Number of male and female migrant petitioners, Tonalá Chepinque and El Niño, 1731–1780	163
5.3.	Number of adult and child migrants, male and female petitioners, Tonalá Chepinque and El Niño, 1731–1780	164
5.4.	Origin of male and female migrant petitioners, Tonalá Chepinque and El Niño, 1731–1780	165
5.5.	Composition of marriage petitioner population, 1771–1780	171
5.6.	Nonmining jobs of Indian and mulatto witnesses, Zacatecas, 1775–1777	173
5.7.	Age of female migrations at time of petition, Zacatecas, 1771–1780	174
5.8.	Number of women from marriage petitions residing in haciendas, Zacatecas, 1771–1780	174
5.9.	Mining occupations cited by male indigenous witnesses, Zacatecas, 1775–1777	175
5.10.	Number of male indigenous and mulatto marriage petition witnesses in mining occupations, Zacatecas, 1775–1777	176
5.11.	Ethnic composition of hacienda workers, Zacatecas, 1781	179
5.12.	Ethnic composition of four mining haciendas, Zacatecas, 1781	179
5.13.	Haciendas, barrios, and ranches in Zacatecas under the jurisdiction of the parish of Tlacuitlapan, c. 1750–1772	181
5.14.	Vecino status of indigenous marriage petitioners, Zacatecas, 1775–1777	181
5.15.	Extant population of Indian towns, Zacatecas, 1741–1783	183
5.16.	Endogamy rates in three Indian towns, Zacatecas	183
5.17.	Migrant and criollo status of female and male indigenous petitioners, Zacatecas, 1771–1780	184
5.18.	Originario status of female and male indigenous migrant petitioners, Zacatecas, 1771–1780	185
5.19.	Citywide population, Zacatecas, 1732–1805	189

Acknowledgments

When the Spanish encountered the peoples of central Mexico they found that the Nahuas did not have a word that readily translated as "family." For the Mexica, the family consisted of all the people who lived together in a shared residential space. The term for this kinship arrangement, *cemithualtin*, has been translated as "those of one patio." This insightful expression captures the communal nature of so many important aspects of daily life, particularly my academic endeavors. While we often think, research, and write alone (even though we should not!), our scholarship is never the product of our solitary efforts but carries input and influence from countless individuals: advisers, mentors, reviewers, colleagues, friends, and family. I have been extremely fortunate in having so many people be part of my intellectual "patio."

Throughout my career, my patio has benefited from the input of distinguished faculty, including Kevin Terraciano, Jose Moya, Robin Derby, William Summerhill, and Teofilo Ruiz. Kevin's insistence on producing careful, archivally driven history has been the fundamental basis of my scholarly work. I also want to thank Jose for his continued counsel during my time in New York in 2011 and 2012. As for Teo, anyone who has interacted with him quickly realizes that she or he is in the presence of a true humanist. Susan Deeds, Susan Kellogg, Susan Schroeder, and Cynthia Radding read drafts of chapters, proposals, and served as commentators on panels about this book. I also want to recognize the contributions and assistance of Louise Burkhart, David Cahill, John Chance, John F. Chuchiak, IV, Martha Few, Robert Haskett, Kevin Gosner, Kris Lane, Laura Matthew, Leslie Offut White, Matthew Restall, Pete Sigal, Sandra Stanley, David Tavárez, Stephanie Wood, Yanna Yannakakis, and William Beezley. Their comments on my work, advice on the profession, and general support has been invaluable. I owe them all a tremendous debt. I also had the privilege of collaborating with colleagues at my rank. Molly Ball, Brad Benton, Ben Cowan, Xochitl Flores, León Garcia, Felipe Ramírez, Pablo Miguel Sierra Silva, Zeb Tortorici, Peter Villella, and Mir Yarfitz read my papers, listened to my presentations, presented with me at panels, and traveled with me to archives. I offer warm thanks to Verónica Castillo-Muñoz, William Connell, Richard Conway, Mark Christensen, Jake Frederick, Owen Jones, Ryan Kashanipour, Mark Lentz, Margarita Ochoa, David Rex Galindo,

Robert Schwaller, and Jonathan Truitt for their professional collaborations and camaraderie.

My time as UC Presidential Postdoc at UC Irvine was a period of great production on this book, no doubt because of the support of my two faculty mentors, Steven C. Topik and Rachel O'Toole. Rachel sponsored my postdoc, and I would not hold my current position at UC San Diego without her support. As a faculty member at Adelphi University, I encountered a very supportive environment. I offer special thanks to my chair, Michael Christofferson, and to Sokthan Yeng from the Department of Philosophy. Michael believed that having a vigorous research agenda was a natural component of a liberal arts college, and he read and offered valuable input on proposals and grants for the manuscript. Sokthan made New York City seem like the friendliest place in the world and listened with a philosopher's ear to all my book plans. The History Department at UC San Diego is exceptionally collegial and supportive of junior faculty. Their professionalism and productivity is inspirational. I offer my thanks to the entire department for allowing me to develop this project in a nurturing and supportive environment. In particular, I offer thanks to the guidance of my chairs, Pamela Radcliff and David Gutierrez, as well as to my faculty mentor Natalia Molina, my weekly writing partner Jessica Graham, and fellow Mexicanist Eric Van Young. Eric's rigorous scholarship, his love of the profession, and his beautiful writing are inspirational.

This book could not have been produced without the assistance of countless individuals in Zacatecas, particularly the director of the Archivo Histórico del Estado de Zacatecas, Juan Valenciano Rojas, and his staff (especially Susana Palacios), Judith Medina Reynosa of the Archivo Parroquial de Zacatecas, John Sullivan, José Enciso Contreras, and Eustacio Cebollas. In Guadalajara, I am grateful to Robert Curley of the Universidad de Guadalajara and the *maestra* Glafira Magaña Perales, who opened the Archivo del Arzobispado de Guadalajara to the public in 2002.

Numerous institutions and organizations facilitated the research and writing of *Urban Indians*. A two-year University of California Presidential Postdoctoral Fellowship provided me with the time and resources to write this book. Grants from the Conference on Latin American History, Harvard University, and the American Philosophical Society allowed me to conduct archival research. At UC San Diego I received an Academic Senate Grant and a Faculty Career Development Program Grant that provided me with the funds and time to complete the last stages of the manuscript. I am particularly grateful to the Hellman family, whose remarkably generous Hellman Fellows Fund supported every aspect of this book's publication, from travel to research assistance. I also want to offer a particular acknowledgment to Robin Gavin of the Museum of Spanish Colonial Art and Spanish Colonial Arts Society, who secured permission of a rare ex-voto from postindependence Zacatecas for this book. Particular thanks are also due to two units of the UC San Diego Geisel Library. Lynda Claassen at Mandeville Special Collections and Peter Devine of the Interlibrary Loan Department, along with their respective staffs, met my numerous requests for images, books, articles, and other impossibly difficult-to-locate scholarly materials. I also want to mention the hard work of two doctoral research assistants at UC San Diego, Graeme Mack and Kevan Aguilar. It goes without saying that I am indebted to the hard work of the editors and staff at Stanford University Press, particularly my editor, Kate Wahl, and assistant editor, Friederike Sundaram. I also want to acknowledge Eric Brandt, who first brought the project to Stanford.

Final words belong to family and friends, those wells of emotional support and inspiration in this often-monastic profession. My parents, Jose and Paula, like so many immigrants before them, were forever stressing the value of education. In their modeling of hard work and perseverance, my siblings—Jose, Sara, Alberto, Rosa, Fermina, and Dora—made the path to academia seem possible and attainable. To Alberto I owe a special debt. He took me to libraries, museums, and his university classes, bought me books and typewriters, and showed me the beauty and power of curiosity and the written word. Family in Mexico made me feel at home after I toiled in the archives. In Zacatecas, the Velasco-Norman family enthusiastically shared their home and resources, while in Mexico City I often relied on the care of the Velasco-Cortes family. My son, John, lived every moment of my academic career, even patiently sitting hours in archives. Gratitude is also due to his father, John Murillo, who always encouraged my dream of pursuing an academic career. In the past few years, it has been a delight to share my intellectual passions and pursuits with my partner, Mark Hanna. As a scholar of early modern piracy, our debates and conversations at times evoke the old battles between Spain and England, but we both agree on the importance of promoting the history of the early modern Atlantic world, particularly its remarkable protagonists such as the native peoples of Zacatecas.

URBAN INDIANS IN A SILVER CITY

Introduction: Silver Veins, Urban Grids, and Layered Identities

In 1719, the mining town of Zacatecas, located in New Spain's northern province of Nueva Galicia, was undergoing a particularly protracted and spectacular boom in silver production. Beginning in the first decade of the eighteenth century, this boom would not lose steam until the early 1730s. During this period, Zacatecas's mines generated 25 percent of Mexico's total silver production. With this prosperity, the city reached its population apex of forty thousand in 1732.[1] The riches generated by the boom provided a lifestyle of opulence and splendor for some individuals, mainly Spanish producers and investors. But even non-Spaniards, including common workers, traders, and shopkeepers, benefited from the production and trade in silver. The scramble for resources and wealth led to inevitable contentions and challenges between different groups—miners and merchants, owners and laborers—and even between family members. In fact, in that year, 1719, a heated legal battle (which would last more than a decade) over the rights to the Los Remedios silver mine on the bluffs of the city erupted between two fictive kin, María Josefa León and Joseph de la Cruz, the godfather of her children.[2] María Josefa accused Joseph of stealing her deceased husband's 50 percent share in the mine. Joseph countered that María Josefa's spouse had never owned the mine but was merely one of its many laborers.

The quarrel between María Josefa and Joseph was not particularly novel in a city where mines often lay abandoned or changed hands frequently without proper legal procedures. What makes this case noteworthy is the ethnicity of its protagonists and how they identified themselves. Both María Josefa and Joseph were *indios*, or indigenous people. But in an attempt to demarcate their long-term resident status in the city, they also made a point of adding another word, duly recorded by the Spanish notary: *vecino*, or municipal resident. María Josefa and Joseph were two Indians living in a Spanish city fighting over ownership to a mine as they proudly declared their civic status. This episode compels us to reexamine our notions about society, ethnicity, and the construction of indigenous communities in New Spain's mining towns and cities and to consider how native peoples lived in urban centers as both indios and vecinos. It also serves as a microcosm for this book's goal of recasting the history of colonial Mexico's silver-mining district—long written as the story of Spanish miners and merchants—as one that is inclusive of the indigenous men, women, and children who lived and worked in the city and generated the wealth that fueled Spain's transoceanic and transcontinental economies (see Map I.1).

The search for riches, particularly the siren call of gold, drove the Spanish invasion of the Americas. While the desire for gold never fully disappeared, by the 1540s Spaniards had discovered the value of other forms of wealth, such as indigenous tribute and labor, as well as other types of precious metals. Silver, mined by native peoples since precontact times, was about to become New Spain's most important export, eclipsing gold as the source of the empire's fortunes.[3] In the colony silver created a small cohort of wealthy Spanish residents—*mineros* (owners of mines or refining mills), who developed production sites, and *aviadores*, who supplied or financed their projects.[4] Yet the exploitation of minerals did more than fund personal and state coffers. Silver production served as a catalyst for northern expansion, creating mining towns that led to the development of new industries, markets, population clusters, and frontier institutions. Within these towns, the need for labor, raw materials, resources and foodstuffs brought together an array of different ethnic and social groups—Spaniards, Indians, Africans, and ethnically mixed individuals, or *castas*. While Spanish "miners and merchants" usually come to mind when we consider silver mining towns, often it was non-Spanish groups that formed the bulk of the population and labor force of these new urban ventures, contributing to the survival of these sites in their boom and bust periods.[5]

In the sixteenth century, Zacatecas was one of several new Spanish urban centers (many of them northern mining towns) that depended on the labor of its immigrant workforce.[6] The discovery of silver veins in 1546 prompted prospective miners to create a town amid a barren, arid landscape then at the remote northern edge of the empire, more than 350 miles from the viceregal capital of Mexico City. The area that became Zacatecas served as one of the ancient settlement sites of a band of nonsedentary peoples known as the Zacatecos. Small in numbers, they offered the Spanish newcomers relatively little resistance and even less labor support, possessing no interest in adopting Spanish lifeways or mining ventures. Under

MAP I.I. New Spain's northern silver mining district, c. 1650

these circumstances miners in Zacatecas, unlike other places in Spanish America, such as the Andean metropolis of Potosí, lacked easy access to a coerced labor pool.[7] Faced with hills rich in ores and in need of a stable and skilled workforce, Spaniards, in a practice relatively uncommon to the period, offered incentives, wages among the most appealing of them, to encourage native peoples—men, women, and children—to migrate to the city. Freedom from draft labor and tribute requirements (through the eighteenth century) operated as additional lures or attractions, drawing large numbers of native peoples from their communities in central and western Mexico and the nearby hinterlands to the city. Indigenous immigrants arrived in Zacatecas from the late 1540s through the independence movements of the early nineteenth century. Men extracted silver from the mines, constructed the city's principal buildings, and grew and imported its foodstuffs. Women ran markets, managed properties, cleaned laborers' quarters, and cared for children. Spanish officials often commented that the city could not have survived or prospered without the labor of both its recent migrants and its long-term indigenous settlers.

In spite of the importance of Native American emigrants, the mining historiography for Spanish America has concentrated on either the roles and activities of Spaniards or the impact of silver production on global markets.[8] Studies of native peoples and silver mining are few, and primarily focused on men, their roles as temporary or coerced workers, and the hardships and exploitative conditions of mine labor.[9] But mining towns were more than sites of production or the domains of itinerant, wage-seeking men. Women, children, families, and communities of long-term residents were ubiquitous features of Zacatecas's social landscape. Moving beyond the study of mines and refining plants shifts the focus from indigenous peoples as laborers to native peoples as settlers and vecinos. Considering their experiences and roles enlarges the social footprint of New Spain's silver-mining district, adds a much-needed ethnohistorical perspective to the scholarship on mining societies, and offers greater insight into the local dynamics and viceregal influences that shaped colonial societies in northern Mexico.[10]

"Urban Indians"

Zacatecas's indigenous inhabitants were "urban Indians," native peoples who lived in Spanish cities. The ethnic category of "Indian" was a colonial construction that conflated the diverse native groups of the Americas. It was a pejorative term in the colonial period and remains so in contemporary Mexico, where the word *indígena* (indigenous) is preferred. However, in this study, the use of the term "Indian" reflects the sociopolitical realities of Zacatecas's colonial indigenous population. In areas of dense, primarily discrete native communities, indigenous peoples continued to distinguish themselves by their local ethnic affiliation, identifying, for example, as Nahuas or Tlaxcalans. As time passed, some native peoples used more collective expressions, such as *timacehualtin* (we commoners), or *titlaca* (we people), to distinguish themselves from Spaniards.[11] But in places like Zacatecas, where a significant native-language corpus has yet to appear, the word "Indian," unsurprisingly, predominates in the Spanish-language documentation. This trend speaks to the lack of Spanish interest in distinguishing the ethnic diversity of subject peoples. But it also reflects a conscious choice on the part of the native population.[12] In multiethnic urban centers, "Indian" was an especially significant legal and juridical category.[13] The appropriation of the term by the native population served as an important marker of ethnic and corporate status, affording them (theoretically, if not always in practice) certain privileges and protections from both local officials and the crown. This study's use of the term then is purposeful. In regard to methodology, it most closely retains the original language used in the documents: *indios*.[14] Yet it also employs "Indian" as an ethnic descriptor to indicate a common shared identity that derived from multiple ethnicities and cultural influences in the colonial urban context. A parallel can be drawn with Karen Graubart's work on native peoples in the Peruvian city of Trujillo. There, Graubart found that from the late sixteenth to the early seventeenth century, some native peoples had adopted the word *solarero(a)* to signal their status as urban indigenous property holders.[15] The term also may have functioned as a mechanism for creating a larger urban group identity.[16] Similarly, in Zacatecas, "Indian" was not just a Spanish administrative category but also an important marker of new and consistently evolving urban indigenous identities and institutions.

This book examines the active role that Zacatecas's urban Indian population played in the development of municipal life in a colonial town. It argues that the adaptation of Spanish-style civic identities did not lead to the erosion of indigenous societies but actually facilitated their persistence. Like other immigrants before and after them (including their Spanish counterparts), native peoples relocated to the newly formed mining town with desires of establishing their own communities. They set about building their homes and tending their fields on the edge of the Spanish *traza* (center). Over time, four autonomous indigenous towns, or *pueblos*, developed at the borders of the city, serving as bastions of indigenous society. While some non-Indians lived in the towns, they retained a primarily indigenous character through the colonial period. Within the pueblos native peoples continued to speak indigenous languages such as Nahuatl and Purépecha, even keeping records in the former, which became the indigenous lingua franca of the city. Towns organized themselves politically around municipal councils, yet often employed preconquest practices of representation and rotation to elect and appoint Indian leaders and officials. Native peoples constructed churches and founded their own religious lay societies or confraternities. They used these buildings and institutions to create and express a sense of community among the multiethnic indigenous population and to delineate their autonomy from non-Indians. In constructing bonds based on common geographic and cultural features, native peoples developed new social relations through fictive kinship and formal and informal unions. But living and laboring together facilitated more than solidarity and community among the multiethnic Indian population; it created a broad Indian identity that separated native peoples from other non-Spaniards. How Zacatecas's ethnically and linguistically plural native population successfully maintained its indigenous heritage within this colonial urban context forms the subject of this book.

We know relatively little about urban indigenous societies and communities in colonial Mexico because of a strong tradition of associating cities and towns with Spaniards. Studies have often focused on the viceregal capitals of Mexico City and Lima, on Spanish elites, and on colonial practices and institutions.[17] Spaniards rarely lived in large numbers outside of urban centers. Yet while much about the colonial city was Spanish, much else was not. Although Spaniards clearly controlled the institutions of power and imposed their cultural, social, economic, and religious practices on marginalized non-Spanish subjects, cities also were among the Americas' most multiethnic sites. Native peoples, Africans, and castas regularly outnumbered their colonizers. While many of these individuals came to cities under duress as temporary (draft) workers or coerced apprentices and servants, a greater number arrived searching for economic and professional opportunities. The colonizers' dependence on their non-Spanish subjects to meet myriad labor, commercial, and agricultural needs often created opportunities for sociopolitical accommodations and negotiations. Ultimately, native peoples did not just work in cities. They lived in them as well. In the process, they shaped their own communities and lived experiences.

This book recognizes that "urban Indians" had a genuine and natural desire to take part in greater city life. Native peoples, particularly Zacatecas's immigrant population, were no strangers to towns and cities.[18] Accounting for their long history of urban traditions and lifeways allows us to frame their actions and experiences as more than just the products of coercion and acculturation. The creation of native towns in Zacatecas, in an area with no preconquest sedentary indigenous communities, was the direct result of the cataclysmic changes generated by colonial rule, particularly those driven by Spanish economic interests. The grim realities of an oppressive colonial system influenced the various political, social, and economic adaptations undertaken by the native population. Sheer necessity and survival often dictated adherence to colonial practices and institutions. But analyzing the responses of urban native peoples solely from a perspective of coercion and subjugation disregards their agendas and decisions, reducing their movements to a series of forced or perfunctory responses. Native peoples had some say in determining which Iberian institutions and practices they accepted and adopted.[19] Interpreting the experiences of Zacatecas's native population (or those of other urban native peoples) solely through the lens of Spanish domination fails to account for their active interactions with the urban environment or how their responses and approaches toward urban living, albeit in a Spanish framework, evolved over time. The development of indigenous society in Zacatecas was ultimately linked with the adaptation of Spanish institutions, organizations, and urban lifeways. But native peoples played an active role in the direction and development of their communities and institutions, taking the lead role in creating their municipal institutions—their towns, churches, confraternities, and municipal councils—and in forming them to retain indigenous features in spite of the colonial framework.

As the native pueblos grew into their civic identities, so too did indigenous peoples, who took great pride in identifying themselves as either vecinos of Zacatecas or its native towns. Vecinos or vecinas is often translated as "citizen," an appropriate reading of the term in some historical and geographic contexts. But this interpretation homogenizes the multiple, and ultimately local, social and political connotations represented by the term. Glossing vecino as "citizen" limits our understanding of the more inclusive and nuanced civic statuses that the word conveyed.[20] Who was recognized as a vecino varied in different periods and areas, with particular distinctions between Spain and the Americas, and in the latter, from one colonial jurisdiction to another. For the purposes of this study, I prefer to speak of vecinos as municipal residents, drawing on the term's local and community connotations. *Ciudadano*—the word that currently serves as the most common translation of "citizen"—was available in the period, appearing in the Royal Spanish Academy's authoritative early eighteenth-century *Diccionario de autoridades* as "vecino of a city."[21] Yet it does not define *vecino* in relation to a ciudad. Instead, it describes a vecino as "one who lives with others in the same barrio, house, or pueblo" and "one who has earned residency by having lived" there for the time determined by law, and "one who has a house and home in a pueblo and contributes to its taxes or assessments, although they do not currently reside there."[22] The Royal Academy's description of the word, with its emphasis on local, domestic, and financial obligations, aligns with the micropatriotic tendencies typical of both Spaniards and Amerindians, explaining perhaps the continued preference of both groups to self-identify as vecino over ciudadano in countless colonial documents.[23]

Framing vecino within a context of civic and residency requirements, rather than with the more formal and legally charged "citizen," allows us to understand how the term could encompass individuals from all social statuses and ethnicities. This inclusiveness diverges from scholarship that tends to equate "vecino" status exclusively with Spaniards or that defines it as the antithesis of "indigenous."[24] In many areas of New Spain *vecindad* was neither formal nor official and hence not legally restricted to Spaniards. Rather it was implicit, secured by the mere circumstance of birth for some and granted to others over time and through social consensus. Individuals earned vecindad by staying for long periods (officially around ten years, but often much less time in practice), paying their taxes, and actively participating in community and civic life (for men that could entail attending town meetings and holding office). While the conditions of vecindad varied from one location to another, nothing prevented Indians (or Afro-descended peoples, for that matter) from meeting these residency and municipal requirements. In Zacatecas, and in many other areas of the viceroyalty, native peoples adopted the term fairly early (by 1566 at least) to indicate their deep and long-standing civic identities.[25] Nor did Spaniards contest native peoples' appropriation of vecindad. Numerous documents produced by Spanish notaries or officials routinely and unremarkably record the term in association with native peoples through the colonial period. Rigid definitions of vecinos as Spanish property holders and heads of household fail to account for the activities and experiences of native men and women (and Spanish women and unmarried men) who considered themselves municipal residents and who, in participating in civic life, "exercised the full range of passive citizenship."[26]

But if native peoples could be vecinos, could they still be Indians too? As municipal residents native peoples embraced the money economy and interacted with non-Indians—personally, professionally, and commercially—at unprecedented levels, practices that even in the colonial period were seen by some as repudiations of indigeneity. New descriptions appeared for Indians who had entered the Spanish world, such as *indio ladino*, *indio criollo*, or *indio acholizado*, which certainly implied a degree of alienation and cultural change. On the surface it appeared that these Indians had left the indigenous world behind them. They spoke Spanish, wore Iberian-style clothing, cut their hair in European fashion, worked in urban occupations, labored and fraternized side by side with non-Indians, and some even lived in Spanish households. In the early seventeenth century, the indigenous chronicler Felipe Guamán Poma de Ayala, wrote disdainfully of Indian men in Lima who "dress[ed] like Spaniards" and "Indian whores . . . with skirts, high shoes, and hair nets" who did not want to "leave the city."[27] These urban dwellers received scorn not only from native peoples but also from some Spaniards, who may have had feelings ranging from uncertainty to hostility about their successful entries into certain aspects of the Spanish world.[28] For the micropatriotic, ethnocentric indigenous societies of the preconquest period, the dual processes of permanent detachment from the local community and relocation to a Spanish urban center may have appeared akin to "social death," although we still lack substantial, quantifiable evidence of what native peoples who lived in rural or discrete communities thought of their urban counterparts.[29]

Scholarly studies have often concluded that those native peoples who were removed from their discrete communities soon substituted Spanish lifeways for indigenous ones. The thought being that Iberian cultural influences quickly undermined traditional and ancestral practices.[30] The assumption that all urban native peoples became Hispanized often revolves around interpretations of the persistence or absence of certain benchmarks associated with indigenous society and culture.[31] Individuals in the sources who did not speak native languages, dressed in Spanish clothing, had short hair, and lived outside of discrete communities appeared to have forsaken their indigenous roots, integrated into the general population, and disavowed their indigenous identities.[32]

Works that included native peoples within larger examinations of cities often perpetuated the stereotype of the biologically and culturally acculturated native person. These studies did not analyze urban native peoples as a social and cultural group. Instead, they integrated them in larger discussions of plebeian and casta populations.[33] Their focus on how urban centers transformed ethnic practices and identities did not account for nuances in the evolution of urban indigenous societies. Under this model, native peoples who moved to cities quickly and frequently engaged in informal and formal unions with non-Indians. Over time, the descendants of urban Indian migrants became less and less racially pure until, biologically, they were not Indians at all.

Paradigms emphasizing the *mestizaje*, or miscegenation, of the Indian population in urban areas have had an equally long-standing and significant influence on the historiography.[34] But indigeneity, or the construction and definition of indigenous identities, involves myriad factors, of which biology constitutes one among other important cultural attributes. When considering ethnicity, it is more instructive and reflective of local realities, as Sarah C. Chambers points out, to define it along the lines of a "shared group identity."[35] Because of their small numbers and close ties to other ethnic communities, mestizos did not develop a complex common cultural identity.[36] The appearance of the term *montañés* to describe mestizos in late sixteenth-century Cuzco, perhaps speaks to the sense of otherness that might have existed for some mestizos in certain places and periods. The term's limited usage within the greater population, however, suggests the inability of (or lack of incentive for) mestizos—or other ethnic groups for that matter—to delineate a separate cultural or corporate identity for themselves.[37] Rather, their evolution as an identifiable colonial group was born of colonial legalese or scripted racial categories, often reflecting an administrative system that needed to classify individuals in order to determine their privileges (and, more often for subject peoples, their rights to *amparo*, or protection) and obligations. But in practice, mestizos developed a cultural identity in relation to other cohesive ethnic groups, such as Indians, Spaniards, or African and Afro-descended peoples.

To whom mestizos culturally adhered often depended on geography and local factors. In theory, they formed part of the *república de españoles* (Spanish republic) and some colonial policies banned them from participating in indigenous spheres.[38] In the first two generations after the Spanish invasion, some mestizo offspring of Spanish conquerors and settlers enjoyed close Iberian ties, such as Don Fernando de Alva Ixtlilxochitl and Inca Garcilaso de la Vega.[39] But by the 1560s and 1570s, changing demographics and political climates led to greater interactions between mestizos and native peoples.[40] The settlement of mestizos in indigenous communities has led scholars to argue for their role as acculturating agents, while other works have stressed tensions and conflicts between the two groups over resources.[41] But on the ground, many mestizos were firmly (and harmoniously) part of the indigenous world. In Zacatecas and throughout New Spain, mestizos lived and worked in indigenous communities and shared their cultural affinities.[42] Nor was the presence of mestizos among the native population necessarily an index of the level of biological or cultural miscegenation within a given context. In some areas, we could even speak of the "Indianization" of the mestizo population.[43]

As such, standard approaches to the study of urban Indians that solely focus on acculturation and mestizaje (cultural or biological) do not adequately convey the processes of change and persistence that ultimately shaped urban Indian identities and practices. Dramatic, large-scale cultural transformations certainly occurred among urban or dislocated indigenous populations. However, in many cities and colonial outposts, ethnogenesis, or the evolution of new social groups and ethnic identities, proved far more nuanced and complex, resisting analyses that consider attributes like language, dress, and place of residence as the litmus tests of cultural persistence.[44] The nature of urban indigenous ethnogenesis must be firmly rooted in interpretations of sources embedded in the local context. A thorough review of the documentation may reveal that native peoples continued to participate and fully identify as indigenous despite the new cultural elements of their environment and personal life. If native peoples could not determine many aspects of their new urban experiences, they were able to develop their own strategies based on their own perceptions of normativity and the resources available to them to engage in urban life.[45] The Spanish crown, after all, was unable to control every aspect of its subjects' daily experiences. As such, the impact of colonial rule, especially on the ground, was particularly uneven. For a native population whose "goals," James Lockhart points out, "were indigenous rather than Spanish in inspiration," the persistence and survival of certain preconquest features was inevitable when confronted with Spanish organizational models.[46]

Although persistence was certainly critical to the continuity and vitality of indigenous culture in Zacatecas—and the focus of my early research on the topic—it represents only half of a dynamic story of continuity and innovation within changing circumstances. Urban native peoples did incorporate Spanish practices into their lifeways. Instead of seeing these adaptations as signs of ethnic erosion, I argue for viewing them as processes of ethnic evolution.[47] Behaviors and practices, such as learning Spanish or changing dress, that are often described as Hispanization or sometimes as the "tragedy of success," were not only essential skills but also part of normative ethnic evolution in an urban context.[48] Seen in this light, social change or acculturation does not equal cultural annihilation. It illustrates how a dynamic urban Indian culture with multilayered identities successfully incorporated and appropriated Spanish-style civic life as another facet of indigeneity. For Zacatecas, native peoples' urban fluency—their ability to speak Spanish, their engagement with non-Indians, and their participation in commercial activities—speaks to the evolution of an urban Indian culture that embraced Spanish-style civic identities as it continued to develop indigenous communities, practices, identities, and associations. In arguing that native people were receptive to many social, economic, and political postconquest changes, this work seeks to complicate traditional paradigms about urban Indians and communities.[49]

The search for indigenous identities within the "Spanish city" is vital to a comprehensive understanding of the influence of colonial rule on native peoples in the postconquest period. Just as revisionist approaches such as the New Conquest History highlight how native allies were more than just auxiliaries, a growing number of recent studies on urban Indians complicate the standard narrative that native city dwellers—both long-term residents and recent migrants—arrived in cities, swiftly lost their indigenous identities, acculturated to Spanish practices, and became part of an amorphous casta or plebeian population.⁵⁰ These works are also beginning to highlight the critical contributions of native peoples to the formation and persistence of cities. Native peoples were significant economic, demographic, political, and social agents. Their communities were vibrant elements of the urban and social landscape.

This book offers an alternative understanding of how to interpret the impact of urbanism on native peoples. It concerns itself both with the larger question of how native peoples responded to colonial rule and with specific questions about the native population of Zacatecas. How did native peoples become residents (vecinos) of Zacatecas? Did becoming a vecino mean that native peoples had to abandon their indigenous heritage? How did urban institutions and practices influence indigenous lifeways and identities? How did native peoples re-create indigenous communities and retain indigenous practices? As vecinos, how did native peoples affect Zacatecas's municipal and economic development? While the book acknowledges the changes urban living brought to indigenous ethnicities and practices, it focuses on how native peoples exploited the urban milieu to create multiple statuses and identities that allowed native peoples like the quarreling miners María Josefa León and Joseph de la Cruz to live in the city as both indios and vecinos. In the process, *Urban Indians* redefines traditional notions about colonial cities, the indigenous urban experience, and silver-mining societies. In so doing, it contributes to a vibrant ethnohistorical scholarship on the native peoples of New Spain, which has cogently documented the survival and persistence of indigenous communities and local and quotidian practices after the Spanish conquest.⁵¹

This book is divided into five chapters—primarily following a narrative thread—from the city's founding in 1546 to the early 1800s. A brief conclusion reflects on the fate of the native population during the independence period, considering how their disappearance from Zacatecas's historiography resonates with trends surrounding mestizaje and migration in the contemporary period. In general, the chapters mirror the book's *longue durée* approach, reflecting the evolution of societies, cultures, and institutions that developed both slowly or rapidly depending on circumstances. Each chapter takes on the dual goal of analyzing the most important sociopolitical developments in the creation of indigenous communities in Zacatecas while also illustrating the evolution of native identities and practices during that particular period.

The first three chapters focus on the settlement and development of indigenous communities in Zacatecas. Chapter 1 considers the pivotal roles that native peoples performed in the city's foundational years as workers and settlers. It argues that the mining camp's pressing labor needs in its early years created the conditions—financial incentives, recurring indigenous immigration, and relative latitude in Spanish and indigenous relations—that led to the development of a critical indigenous population mass. Chapter 2 considers how the evolution of indigenous communities, labor patterns, and sociopolitical organizations, such as *cofradías*, or lay brotherhoods, created ethnic cohesion among the immigrant native population. As the multiethnic native community began to put down long-term roots in Zacatecas, its residents looked to Spanish institutions to unify them and to create a corporate indigenous identity. The conversion of indigenous communities from barrios, neighborhoods with the jurisdiction of the Spanish city, to towns, and the creation of an Indian leadership cohort in the early seventeenth century are the subjects of Chapter 3.

Chapters 4 and 5 examine how native peoples responded to the changing political and economic vicissitudes of the mature and late colonial periods. Chapter 4 focuses on how indigenous society and culture weathered the cultural and demographic shifts that accompanied the early eighteenth-century mining boom. The maturation of indigenous civic identities at the personal and community levels provided both individuals and officials with the skills to engage with ethnic others and the money economy as they defended their corporate privileges. Chapter 5 considers the status of indigenous society from the mid- to late eighteenth century. It analyzes the challenges migrant and long-term vecinos encountered in the wake of the city's late eighteenth-century mining revival and the implementation of the crown's centralizing political and economic policies, commonly referred to as the Bourbon Reforms.

Missing from this chapter synopsis are familiar elements of mining histories, such as sections on labor and exploitation. These omissions are by design. This book rarely speaks directly of native "agency"—preferring to use less ambiguous terms such as experiences or activities. Yet it does focus more on native peoples' active choices than on the exploitations they suffered under colonialism. As a mining town grounded in a (silver) money economy, Zacatecas epitomized some of the most dramatic changes and onerous features of colonial rule. Mine labor was among the colony's most hazardous occupations. The work above and below ground frequently caused illnesses, injuries, and even death. The absence of *repartimiento*, or draft labor, in Zacatecas spared the native population from some of the grueling and arbitrary working conditions present in other areas of New Spain such as Taxco or the Andean metropolis of Potosí. Yet Zacatecas was not without its share of problems, including attempts at coerced labor, unlawful detentions, kidnapping of young children, delays or failures to distribute wages, long hours, and grueling conditions. These episodes of abuse and exploitation appear throughout the work, but they are not the central focus of this book. Nor would my discussion of these topics move the field forward in any new or significant way, as they are well and masterfully covered by the current mining historiography. Ultimately, I seek to round out the story of native peoples and silver mining by highlighting their experiences away from the mines and focusing on the choices they made in their daily municipal lives.

A Note on Sources and Approaches

The native population of Zacatecas—during both boom and bust periods—constituted anywhere from 30 percent to 50 percent of the city's greater population. As with many other nonelite groups, their presence is not always readily apparent in the documentation. Most ethnohistories draw from a corpus of native- and Spanish-language documents. Spanish records suggest that native-language writings were commonly produced in Zacatecas. Yet the survival of only a few documents (the remainder of these sources have disappeared or were destroyed) prevents such an approach. The lack of native-language sources hides from view many large patterns and small details about the city's indigenous population. One can only speculate about the information that the minutes of an indigenous confraternity or cabildo could offer about community life, or what glimpses into gender, household, and land patterns would emerge from Nahuatl wills. Native-language documents would also bring greater insight into the trajectory and conflation of individual ethnic identities. But until such sources come to light (if they still exist for Zacatecas at all), these details and trends elude us and must necessarily fall outside the purview of this book.

Reconstructing the history of native peoples in a multiethnic urban setting involved different methodologies and sources. I followed the approaches of ethnohistorians of northern New Spain, where the majority of native peoples did not leave a large body of written records.[52] In these regions, scholars have had to re-create indigenous history, Susan Deeds explains, through the use of "dispersed, fragmentary record(s)."[53] Uncovering indigenous voices, perspectives, and activities in Zacatecas required the compilation of a source base that included a broad range of Spanish documents. This Spanish corpus presented certain challenges, particularly the mediation of indigenous voices through a notary, and in some cases also through an interpreter. Yet in spite of their limitations, these documents revealed a great deal about the social and economic circumstances of the indigenous population.[54] Many of these texts provide indirect information on the indigenous population. But a significant number of documents directly discussed or were produced by native peoples. Examples of "indirect" sources include religious and civil censuses, municipal council records, mining inventories, chronicles, and royal and viceregal reports, correspondences, and orders. Archival manuscripts that offer more direct access to indigenous voices included wills, land and property disputes, parish records, confraternity ledgers, civil and criminal proceedings, Inquisition cases, sundry notarial documents, and local and viceregal petitions. The collection of this varied documentation provided a more comprehensive and nuanced construction of the indigenous presence in the city. Examining these sources over the longue durée allowed for the recording of change over time as it established and corroborated the persistence of long-term trends and developments in the indigenous population.

The use of qualitative sources illustrated the full breadth of native peoples' experiences in Zacatecas. But this study drew on quantitative approaches, especially demography, to illustrate the extent of their presence in the city. Fortunately, record keeping that involved counting was a common practice among Spaniards. In the absence of tribute rolls for Zacatecas, ecclesiastical and civil censuses provided invaluable estimates of the size of the native population in a given period. Information from other types of mundane documents was equally quantifiable. Inventories of *cuadrillas*, or labor gangs, for example, illustrated the significant number of women working at mining complexes. Chapters 4 and 5 drew from the nearly ten thousand marriage petitions that exist for Zacatecas and its adjacent mining towns in the period from 1680 to 1780. Of these, about eight thousand alone were made by native peoples, Afro-descended individuals, and castas. These nuptial requests provided a wealth of information on individual and societal trends relating to marriage, migration, kinship patterns, interethnic exchanges, demographic shifts, and social networks. For example, since local officials did not keep records of incoming migrants, I utilized the biographical information found in the petitions to arrive at immigration patterns. By interpreting these marriage petitions and other mundane sources using quantitative approaches, I arrived at trends that were not readily apparent in qualitative sources alone. Ultimately, this quantitative and qualitative approach facilitated greater insight into different types of indigenous experiences and practices, reflecting a more nuanced and balanced depiction of native agency and Spanish influence.

1   A Tale of Two Settlements, 1546–1559

In the early conquest period Spaniards needed little more than rumors of precious metals to launch exploratory campaigns. By the mid-1540s, tales of rich silver deposits in the northern province of Nueva Galicia (New Galicia) circulated among the region's Spanish officials, settlers, and adventurers. As of then, the sparsely populated province, lacking in large sedentary native populations to exploit for tribute and labor, had proved a poor cousin to its central Mexican counterpart. But sometime in August 1546, the soldier turned explorer Juan (or Juanes) de Tolosa mounted an expedition from Guadalajara to an unsettled semidesert region in the northern central Mexican highlands that would forever change the province's social and economic landscape.[1] For below the surface of this inauspicious environment lay fabled quantities of ore. Extracted and refined, this silver bullion would yield the Spanish crown millions of pesos and underwrite the empire on both sides of the Atlantic.

Unsurprisingly, the leader of the search, Tolosa, became one of the four recognized Spanish founders of Zacatecas, the largest silver-mining town to develop in New Galicia. But should Tolosa and his Spanish associates receive the sole credit for this momentous discovery? A large number of Indians from central Mexico voluntarily traveled with Tolosa as guides or as foot soldiers. Other native peoples from distinct ethnic groups in the province also formed part of the expedition as servants and *tamemes*, or carriers. These indigenous peoples had been captured and then enslaved in numerous raids and military campaigns by Tolosa and his fellow invaders since the Spanish arrival to the area that became New Galicia in the mid-1520s. Other native peoples also played a critical role in the operation. While he was in the indigenous pueblo of Tlaltenango, for instance, several unnamed native men informed Tolosa and his party where to search for rich silver veins.² The bounty of these initial strikes attracted other Spaniards and led to the establishment of a small *real de minas*, or mining camp, which eventually became the Spanish city of Nuestra Señora de los Zacatecas. While no native people rank among the city's founders, without their assistance, Zacatecas, New Spain's premiere silver-mining center for nearly three centuries, may never have developed.

Indigenous peoples not only supported the searches for precious metals but also authored their success. The survival and continued prosperity of Zacatecas, like its discovery, was by no means an exclusively Spanish enterprise. The city did develop under auspicious conditions, with rich silver veins and relatively little Spanish-indigenous conflict, but many a silver-mining town in the Americas followed a riches-to-ruins trajectory. Booms lasting several years, even decades, often gave way to busts, economic decline, and abandonment. The longevity and success of mining towns depended as much on the availability of a stable population base and a large skilled labor force as on continued silver strikes. As Zacatecas expanded in the mid-sixteenth century from a mining camp, or *minas*, to a Spanish town, non-Spaniards, particularly native peoples, provided the city with the bulk of its labor force, settlers, and long-term vecinos.

This chapter examines the history and contributions of the city's indigenous residents in the settlement of Zacatecas from its precolonial past through the formal establishment of Spanish municipal government in the 1550s. It considers the role of Zacatecas's preconquest indigenous population in the city's early development, the impact of Spanish dependence on the foreign Indian population to meet labor needs, and the evolution of Spanish and indigenous settlements from rudimentary mining camps to urban communities. Many individuals from various ethnic groups participated in the founding of Zacatecas. But native peoples, this chapter argues, played a critical role in the city's survival and early prosperity. While the local native population, the Zacatecos, were not numerous enough to meet Spanish labor demands, their relatively peaceful abandonment of their traditional settlement sites allowed miners and laborers to focus more on silver production than on defense during Zacatecas's early years.³ Nor could Zacatecas have prospered without the large migrant Indian population from central and western Mexico that displaced the Zacatecos. These newcomers provided the necessary labor for the emerging mining economy and its subsidiary activities, and by creating indigenous communities, they brought into being a permanent and long-term labor source. But the founding of Zacatecas was not simply the story of how native peoples supported colonial projects. As the indigenous workforce established roots in the town, native peoples began adapting the Spanish urban milieu to meet their own settlement needs, exploiting Zacatecas's

MAP 1.1. Zacatecas and its Indian towns. Based on Peter Gerhard, *North Frontier*, 157.

frontier setting and labor shortages to derive some concessions, such as mobility, wages, freedom from tribute and *repartimiento* (rotary labor drafts), and the right to form their own semiautonomous neighborhoods. From its discovery and founding, the evolution of Zacatecas was the tale of two settlements: one Spanish and one indigenous (see Map 1.1).

Early Indigenous Peoples and Settlements

When Indians and Spaniards arrived at the site of the initial silver strikes in 1546, they saw no signs of complex, sedentary indigenous populations with hierarchical urban communities such as those they had encountered in their initial invasions to the south. They dismissed the Zacatecos—the small bands of nonsedentary and semisedentary peoples who sporadically inhabited the area—as barbaric and uncivilized, and of little use to their colonization projects. But the area around Zacatecas had witnessed sedentary activity more than a thousand years earlier. Little is known about these distant precontact peoples, the forerunners of the Zacatecos. These native peoples left fewer traces of monumental architecture or material culture than their Mesoamerican counterparts.[4] Yet the sites they created served as important population epicenters in the region long before Spanish contact.

Native peoples lived near the area that became the city by the fourth century C.E. In writing about preconquest cultures in the area, archaeologists note that "the Prehispanic sedentary societies in Zacatecas started relatively late and reached complexity rapidly."[5] The earliest evidence of sedentary cultural activity comes from the western part of the current state of Zacatecas. According to archaeologists, the group of peoples now identified as the Loma San Gabriel Culture practiced sedentary agriculture and created ceramics from as early as 100 C.E.[6] Over a thousand years before the Spanish conquest, several population and cultural centers of "Mesoamerican frontier farmers" developed in and around the western and southern zones of the state.[7] Of these, the largest and most influential complex, the Chalchihuites culture, was centered in the western part of the state near what later became the mining boom town of Sombrerete. Three main population sites divided the south: the Malpaso Valley, the Juchipila region, and the Valparaíso-Bolaños Basin. Scholars remain uncertain as to the evolutionary connection between these sites and the extent of their social and economic interactions.[8] Even if these settlements possessed a common foundation, regional distinctions developed over time that characterized each area. By the time of the Spanish conquest, the Cazcanes, a loose confederation of semisedentary peoples from the Juchipila area, posed the greatest challenge to Spaniards in the pacification of New Galicia. They played a prominent role in the significant indigenous uprising, the Mixton War, which engulfed the region from 1540 to 1542. Monuments and ruins of several other preconquest sedentary cultures are scattered across the state, such as the large structures of the Alta Vista/Súchil complex located near contemporary Chalchihuites, Zacatecas.[9]

Complex sedentary cultures also flourished near Zacatecas. The ruins of one of them constitute the archaeological complex of La Quemada (also referred to as Chicomóztoc), located thirty-five miles from Zacatecas in the Malpaso Valley.[10] Archaeologists believe that the La Quemada culture probably derived from a group associated with the Chalchihuites complex. Radiocarbon testing indicates that native peoples settled the site as early as 200 C.E. and that it remained populated until as late as 1450.[11] Most scholars agree that the complex went through three stages: an agricultural stage circa 450 to 600; an apogee from 600/650 to 800; and a collapse, the date of which has yet to be determined, but which occurred well before the arrival of the Spanish. Present-day ruins indicate the grandeur and size of the settlement. Among its most impressive structures are a ball court (among the largest in Mesoamerica), a majestic hall of columns, twelve pyramids, and multiple stairways that connect several terraces and patios (see Figures 1.1–1.3).[12]

La Quemada's frontier setting has stirred a debate over its purpose. Several scholars believe the city was an extension of the Chalchihuites complex or a colony of more southern groups such as Tarascans, Toltecs, or Teotihuacanos.[13] Other researchers argue for a more defensive function, with the center serving as a fort to ward off attacks from outsiders or to serve as a sanctuary.[14] However, some scholars argue for the site's ceremonial role, finding evidence of banquets, ball games, and mortuary rites.[15] In either scenario the complex served an important role as "the central place in a regional system of sociopolitical integration" in northwestern

FIGURE 1.1. La Quemada: "La Ciudadela," or the "Citadel." Photo taken by author in 2007.

FIGURE 1.2. La Quemada: Hall of Columns. Photo taken by author in 2007.

FIGURE 1.3. La Quemada: Votive Temple. Photo taken by author in 2007.

Mexico's frontier zone.[16] Three large communities of sedentary householders flanked the main site.[17] In addition, a sophisticated road system linked La Quemada to hundreds of other population clusters in the area. There is general agreement that native peoples abandoned the community around the fifteenth century, signaling the withdrawal of sedentary agriculture in the region.[18] Even after its desertion, the complex's structures and location, in a fertile valley with a large river, continued to attract indigenous groups to the area. On their initial arrival in Zacatecas, Spaniards encountered a band of Zacateco Indians living at the foot of the ruins.[19] Perhaps the site's most important function was as a population epicenter.

The Zacatecos

The decline of La Quemada did not mark the end of an indigenous presence in the region. By the 1540s, several loosely organized ethnic groups resided and intersected in the greater Zacatecas area, including Zacatecos, Guachichiles, and Cazcanes. According to scholarly classifications of native peoples these groups are considered semisedentary and nonsedentary.[20] Sedentary peoples, such as the Nahuas of central Mexico, practiced permanent intensive agriculture, developed stable and complex settlement sites (including towns and cities), and possessed dense populations and centralized political and social hierarchies that facilitated the organization of labor projects and tribute collection. Semisedentary and nonsedentary peoples, in contrast, did not have dense populations or mechanisms for forced labor drafts or tribute.[21] Both groups moved frequently and practiced hunting and gathering. But semisedentary peoples "were not nomads."[22] They practiced some form of seasonal agricultural and could have expansionistic ambitions. The Cazcanes, for example, possessed features of both sedentary and semisedentary peoples. They cultivated crops but did not employ tribute systems. These typologies of native peoples offer general guidelines. But the cultural diversity of the native peoples of northern Mexico defies general categorizations.[23]

Often semisedentary and nonsedentary peoples did not interest Spaniards because they did not serve their purposes: they lacked the political and social structures and organizations that facilitated the extraction of resources in labor or kind. Spaniards avoided settling in areas devoid of sedentary Indians unless a region, such as New Galicia, hinted at the potential for mineral wealth. Spaniards often homogenized these nonsedentary peoples, calling them Chichimecs, a term that central Mexican Indians had used to describe the native peoples who lived north or west of Tenochtitlan.[24] The word possessed both negative and positive associations for Nahuatl speakers. For Spaniards, the term ultimately developed a pejorative association. They considered Chichimecs inferior, lazy, barbaric, and uncivilized.[25] But they also perceived them to be fierce and hostile. Many of these ethnic groups did not submit to colonial policies or practices, instead retreating to their own settlements or waging war on Spaniards and their indigenous allies in retaliation for incursions and the pillaging of their communities.[26]

The majority of information on the indigenous peoples of New Galicia (and much of northwestern Mexico) comes from Spanish sources, including chronicles, viceregal reports, and letters and accounts of religious missionaries. Unlike their central Mexican counterparts, few indigenous groups in this region left written records in their own languages.[27] The region also lacked the numerous and prolific indigenous and mestizo chroniclers of central Mexico.[28] Early histories of New Galicia's native peoples are few in number, and its chroniclers wrote well after the events they documented. Moreover, they focused on Spanish conquest campaigns, and only occasionally offered ethnographic asides.[29] Mundane documents also provide very little information. Many native peoples from this region evaded the pens of Spanish officials or bureaucrats because they did not intersect with colonial institutions, such as tribute and labor draft rolls or legal petitions. When New Galicia's native groups entered the records, Spaniards often ignored important social and cultural details of their communities. In their place they documented items that served their economic interests, such as the number of their inhabitants or their resources.[30] Under these conditions, re-creating a history for the northern indigenous groups, as pointed out in the introduction, often requires assembling fragmentary Spanish sources, providing, at best, an incomplete and biased picture of their social and cultural practices.

Unsurprisingly, extant accounts often perpetuate stereotypes of nonsedentary peoples as inferior and belligerent.[31] The bishop of Guadalajara, Alonso de la Mota y Escobar's early seventeenth-century depiction of indigenous people in their "pre-Christian" state is fairly representative of these Spanish narratives. The Indians, he wrote, went around naked or wore simple cotton garb with no footwear. They were physically course and had crude personal habits and primitive living conditions. They refused to cultivate crops or establish farms and were "generally dull and lazy in regards to work."[32] Corn bread and the occasional fish or wild animal without any seasoning constituted their diet, although many liked to go hungry to prove their personal prowess. According to the bishop, they lacked a writing system or any method of recording their history. Their bellicose temperament manifested itself in their worship of a god that occasionally demanded human sacrifices. They lived to fight with each other and their neighbors, and they cherished hardship and struggle in order to prove their personal valor and harden themselves for war. This description stands in direct contrast to the bishop's portrayal of the docile, orderly, and industrious nature of native peoples living cooperatively as Christians under Spanish rule. These types of scurrilous and generic portrayals coupled with a poor source base illustrate the difficulties in generating ethnohistorical studies of New Galicia's nonsedentary and semisedentary peoples.

Given the problematic and limited nature of the source base, it is difficult to construct more than a thin ethnohistorical sketch of the Zacatecos, the native peoples who lived in closest proximity to the area that became the city of Zacatecas. Colonial records often conflated them with other ethnic groups or referred to them as Chichimecs. The chronicles provide only brief accounts of postconquest Zacateco practices. The Zacatecos or "Çacachichimeca," appear in the *Historia general de las cosas de Nueva España*, the famous sixteenth-century Spanish and indigenous ethnography of native peoples compiled by the Franciscan friar Bernardino de Sahagún.[33] Sporadic information also appears in Jesuit reports. Other sources focus on the Zacatecos's rebellious activities, such as the late sixteenth-century accounts of their participation in the frontier wars of Nueva Galicia (c. 1550–1590) by the Spanish *encomendero* (individual with rights to indigenous labor and tribute) Gonzalo de las Casas and the frontier captain and future Zacatecan alderman Pedro de Ahumada Sámano.[34]

The origins of the Zacatecos, the time period of their entry into the region, and their numbers remain unclear. The nineteenth-century cleric José del Refugio Gasca gave them a mythical heritage, asserting that after the Mexica moved through the La Quemada area on their way toward the Valley of Mexico, the most "brave and vigorous" Chichimecs remained in Zacatecas, never to be subjugated by the Nahuas.[35] Archaeologists however are unsure as to how much time passed between the collapse of the La Quemada complex and the entry of the Zacatecos into the district.[36] Population figures are equally indefinite, although the Zacatecos probably constituted a significant number of the 4,500 peoples "labeled Chichimecs" present in the greater Zacatecas area at the time of Spanish contact.[37] One count placed a settlement of five hundred Zacatecos on the Bufa (the crested mountain that flanks the city center) in 1531.[38] Overall numbers for the total Zacateco population in 1519, the year Cortés arrived on the mainland, range from twelve thousand to ninety thousand.[39]

The encomendero Gonzalo de las Casas identified the Zacatecos as one of four major Chichimec groups of the region.[40] Sources indicate that the Zacatecos organized themselves in groups of loose confederations of small seminomadic settlements, which Spaniards called *rancherías*. They dominated a large area that stretched from central Zacatecas to the northern borders of the current state, and to the northeast, close to the city of Durango.[41] The level of agricultural or political development of these settlements varied according to the area. Some rancherías, such as those that possessed permanent housing and cultivated crops, shared more characteristics of sedentary communities than others. Bishop Mota y Escobar claimed that they possessed rulers, or *caciques*. His observations may reflect Zacateco leadership practices but more probably highlight the grafting of central Mexican concepts of rulership onto nonsedentary peoples. The various bands probably shared a common ethnic base and linguistic foundation that drew from the languages of various northern peoples along with Nahua loanwords.[42]

Zacateco lifeways reflected their nonsedentary and semisedentary modes of organization. Spanish chroniclers claimed that the Zacatecos inhabited the mountains and the forests without permanent housing or settlements.[43] According to Bishop Mota y Escobar, they did not engage in agriculture, instead living from hunting, with a core diet of rabbits, hares, partridges, and doves. They supplemented their nutritional regime with mesquite and *tunas* (prickly pears). The former they harvested in Durango for two months of the year, the latter for eight months south of the city in the area around the town of Pinos. Most important, as far as concerned Spaniards, they had no historical or current interest in silver mining.

As with other Mesoamerican groups, the Zacatecos divided labor tasks by gender. Men served as warriors and huntsmen. Their appearance, according to a 1550 description of Zacateco men from the *oidor*, or judge, of the high court of New Galicia, Hernando Martínez de la Marcha, reflected their social roles. Oidor Martínez de la Marcha reported that they wore only breeches (*mástiles*). They covered their heads with leather, painted their faces like deer, and carried large bows and arrows.[44] Women transported items and cooked food, important jobs that freed men to hunt and fight. One Zacateco man informed the friar Sahagún that men could not cook because it harmed their eyesight and jeopardized their hunting skills.[45] Another Spanish official noted the importance of women's tasks, explaining that Zacateco women carried food or clothing "so the men could be nimble and ready for war and to hunt wild animals."[46] With men frequently away hunting and fighting, Zacateco women probably played an important role in the community's quotidian tasks. Studies among other northern indigenous peoples found "considerable complementarity in productive activities."[47] Tarahumara women of the Sierra Madre cultivated crops, moved belongings between locations, prepared and stored meals, cared for children, and made textiles and pottery.[48] While we lack documentary evidence, Zacateco women probably engaged in similar important tasks.

The Zacatecos first came to the attention of the Spanish in the 1530s. Several years earlier they had joined their neighbors to the south, the Cazcanes, in a rebellion against Spanish encomenderos, settlers, and clerics.[49] The Mixton War, the most direct and significant indigenous challenge to Spanish rule in New Galicia, engulfed areas of contemporary Jalisco and southern Zacatecas from 1540 to 1542.[50] During the war native peoples killed Spanish officials, settlers, and priests. They burned churches, desecrated religious objects, destroyed both Spanish and allied, or "friendly," indigenous settlements, and fortified themselves in several *peñoles*, or mountain strongholds. The war's origins lay in Spanish attempts to exploit the native population for tribute and labor. Cazcanes are credited with starting the conflagration, but several Spaniards (and later Indians) blamed millenarian-style Zacateco religious figures with instigating and participating in the war. Witnesses claimed that Zacateco messengers encouraged Indians to rebel against colonial rule, spreading anti-Christian messages, encouraging native peoples to leave their communities, and attending *mitotes* (dances) designed to spread agitation among the indigenous population.[51] How many Zacatecos participated in the two-year war is unknown, but one Spanish participant claimed that at one peñol alone there were three to four thousand Zacatecos present. Zacateco anxiety and aggression surely rested on fears of Spanish encroachment into their territories and the implementation of tribute, draft labor, and changes in leadership that inevitably followed in their wake.

In the aftermath of the war, the Zacatecos walked a fine line between evading and being drawn into colonial rule. The military campaigns to repress the rebellion drew thousands of indigenous auxiliaries as well as famed conquerors of Tenochtitlan, such as Pedro de Alvarado, and even the viceroy, Antonio de Mendoza, to the battle lines. Spaniards declared victory in 1542 at the cost of many lives and considerable resources. And the end of the Mixton War did not stem conflicts in New Galicia. An unknown number of Zacatecos faced enslavement or forced recruitment in Spanish expeditions. Others fled successfully and retreated to their settlement sites, managing to avoid Spaniards and colonial rule until the discovery of precious minerals brought larger sections of the area into the Spanish orbit. The decentralized indigenous lifeways of the Zacatecos, centered on mobility and hunting, proved even more incompatible with the implementation of colonial rule than did those of their central Mexican counterparts. The suppression of the Mixton War and the firm colonial presence in the region also probably influenced many Zacatecos to leave the area with the arrival of the Spanish. At a later date, however, a significant number of them joined other native groups in raids and attacks against colonial settlements.

Colonization and Foundation

The origin of Zacatecas's foundation lay in the same motivations that drove Hernán Cortés and his followers: the search for mineral wealth and native peoples to subjugate and organize into encomiendas. In 1521, twenty-five years before the founding of Zacatecas, Cortés, with the participation of thousands of native allies and the assistance of European diseases, oversaw the capitulation of Tenochtitlan, the largest urban center in the Americas and the capital of the Nahuatl-speaking Mexicas.[52] Cortés grabbed the lion's share of the spoils of conquest for himself, both economically and politically, in his attainment of multiple encomiendas. His exploits and his meteoric rise inspired individuals in both Spain and from within the colony to mount a series of armed expeditions seeking to copy his success.

After the conquest of Tenochtitlan a number of Spaniards, including Cortés himself, mounted armed expeditions south of Mexico City searching for both precious metals and sedentary indigenous communities to exploit for labor and tribute, as with Pedro de Alvarado in Guatemala (1524), Francisco de Montejo in Yucatán (1527), and the Pizarro brothers in Peru (1530s). Many individuals also journeyed west into the area that became New Galicia, including Cortes's kinsman Francisco Cortés in 1524, and in the 1540s Alvarado (who met his death in the Mixton War). While Cortés and the Pizarro brothers are perhaps the most familiar and infamous conquerors of the Americas, the Spanish native and latecomer Nuño Beltrán de Guzmán stands out as one of the more ambitious conquerors of the period. Guzmán, descended from a noble Castilian family with close connections to the crown, received several prominent positions in the Americas, including governorship of Pánuco (in the current state of Veracruz) in 1527 and presidency of the first Audiencia (high court) of Mexico in 1528.[53] These positions, however, failed to satisfy Guzmán's craving for the fabulous wealth in precious minerals that had eluded even Cortés. From 1530 to 1531, Guzmán used his power and aggressive personality to authorize an expedition that tore a path of destruction and terror through western and northwestern Mexico. His campaigns and those of his associates opened the area to Spanish settlers and eventually led to the discovery of silver in Zacatecas.[54]

The invasion and colonization of New Galicia created the conditions and protagonists that facilitated the founding of Zacatecas. Three of the city's four "founders" had spent time in the region, experiencing its often harsh and challenging environment. Cristóbal de Oñate, a prosperous encomendero and experienced miner, served as former governor of New Galicia. Juan de Tolosa, who supposedly first came across the site, fought in the Mixton War. Diego de Ibarra's uncle Miguel de Ibarra was a veteran of multiple Spanish-Indian campaigns and also served in several administrative posts.[55] In other words, these men match the profile of latter-day conquistadores, individuals who had arrived too late to benefit from the spoils of the initial conquest (in this case the Valley of Mexico) and had to pursue their ambitions in areas that had yet to come under the Spanish orbit.[56] Yet they were not newcomers from Mexico City or Spain but individuals familiar with the challenges inherent to life in a frontier zone—labor, resource, food, and population shortages, and hostile indigenous groups—all problems that plagued Zacatecas to some degree in its first few years. The founders drew on their resources, skills, and experiences in New Galicia as they began the task of building a settlement in Zacatecas.

With the spotlight on the four founders it is easy to overlook how the cooperation of native peoples facilitated the establishment of the city. In a broad sense, the Spanish subjugation of the area owed a great deal to the participation of thousands of voluntary and coerced indigenous allies.[57] The pacification of large areas of northwestern Mexico and the termination of the Mixton War diminished threats of large-scale and widespread indigenous assaults, thus allowing Spaniards to launch exploratory expeditions and establish new towns and settlements. Tolosa first became aware of potential silver veins while traveling in the pacified Juchipila Valley, where the Mixton War had been fought. Native peoples, both free and forced, participated in these mineral-seeking campaigns. Thirty indigenous slaves and several other native peoples accompanied Tolosa on his trek to Zacatecas. Native communities often provided lodging, foodstuffs, and resources for these trips. Tolosa received the hospitality of several indigenous communities in southern Zacatecas, which only a few years earlier had been at the center of the Mixton War. Often it was indigenous people who knew the location of ores as Spaniards in this period were unskilled in locating silver deposits or processing metals.[58] In the case of Zacatecas, as noted, reports indicated that Indians from the Juchipila area first made Tolosa and his companions aware of the potential find, showing them ores and offering to guide them to the site.[59] More than thirty native peoples were present at the initial ore collection and surely engaged in myriad tasks—carrying items, digging, making food, constructing shelter—that facilitated the expedition. The "discovery" of silver in Zacatecas owes much to the cooperation and assistance of native peoples and should be considered a joint Spanish and indigenous affair.

When Spaniards returned to the area after the initial discovery to further develop the mining site, they received no noteworthy resistance from the Zacatecos. Accounts of the encounter between these two groups come from colonial chroniclers who often highlighted the peaceful and friendly nature of these meetings. They stressed the Zacatecos's quick acceptance of Christianity and submission to the crown. The Franciscan chronicler José de Arlegui's assertion that the Zacatecos overcame their initial hesitation to descend from the hilltops to the mining camp after they saw "the goodwill and love of the priest and Spaniards" is typical of these narratives.[60] Another cleric claimed that Tolosa, in an attempt to coax the Zacatecos and mollify their anxiety, sent Cazcan interpreters and a cleric fluent in the language with promises of goodwill, peace, and the salvation of Christianity.[61] While it is impossible to reconstruct these early meetings, it is not difficult to imagine the Zacatecos's legitimate reasons for avoiding the Spanish. Some perhaps feared reprisals for their participation in the Mixton War, while others may have wanted to avoid the onerous burdens that Spaniards imposed on subjugated native peoples. Whatever their motives, the Zacatecos apparently offered no resistance within the area that became the city proper.[62]

Ultimately, the Spanish and foreign indigenous takeover of the area forced new settlement patterns and lifeways on the Zacatecos. A few remained in the city. Some left to form communities with different ethnic groups. In a 1585 report from the mining town of Fresnillo, to the northwest of Zacatecas, a crown official commented that native peoples known as Zacatecos had lived in the hillsides called Sayn (Sain) but had all left to the interior, or *tierra adentro*.[63] While some Zacatecos managed to temporarily evade Spanish rule, it appears that by 1560 the majority had been reestablished in various towns throughout the mining district, particularly in sparsely populated areas where they could supplement growing labor needs, such as in the northern mining town of Chalchihuites. The town, according to religious officials, had been established (c. 1566) as a "new pueblo of Tlaxcalteca Indians" in attempts to settle the troubled mining camps north of the city, which remained subject to attacks from Chichimec Indians until the end of the sixteenth century. There was a barrio of Zacatecos within the pueblo, but the majority were congregated into two subject communities, San Andrés (de Teul) and Santa Clara.[64] In a 1622 ecclesiastical review of the area, it was noted that in each pueblo there lived about eighty men and women called Zacatecos, with the "most bellicose" residing in Santa Clara.[65] Some Zacatecos also settled near the mining centers of Sombrerete, Cuencamé, and Parras.[66] In 1604, one hundred Zacateco families lived in the agricultural community of San Juan del Mezquital.[67]

But while many Zacatecos submitted to Spanish rule, others went on to participate in the violent conflicts that engulfed the mining district. The colonization and pacification of northwestern and northern New Spain took far longer and proved just as expensive and deadly as the conquest of central and southern Mexico. The end of the Mixton War in 1542 signaled the permanent presence of Spaniards in New Galicia. Yet it did not bring peace and stability to the province. The nonsedentary indigenous groups of the region fiercely resisted Spanish attempts at incorporation and encroachment of their territories. Sporadic rebellions and conflicts between Spaniards and different native groups occurred with frequency during the "frontier wars," which spanned the 1550s to the 1590s. The actions of Spanish settlers and soldiers often incited or aggravated these conflicts. Many individuals took advantage of weak colonial oversight in these areas to illegally kidnap and enslave native peoples and raid their properties. Indians, in turn, retaliated against these incursions on their communities by making war on Spanish colonists and settlements. Several viceroys, starting with Luis de Velasco in the early 1550s, attempted to subdue pockets of indigenous resistance and bring the area under Spanish rule, through a war of fire and blood ("guerra de fuego y sangre").[68]

During this war of "fire and blood," Spaniards, in spite of all their money, arms, and royal support, often found themselves at a disadvantage. The absence of sedentary, hierarchically organized indigenous communities frustrated Spanish attempts to capitalize on successful political and military strategies used in the conquest of central Mexican communities, such as exploiting rivalries to garner the aid of indigenous allies.[69] Spaniards also encountered a different combatant and distinct type of battle. The native peoples of Nueva Galicia often engaged in a form of guerrilla warfare with Spaniards, launching surprise attacks and raiding supply trains and settlements. Native peoples' familiarity with the terrain and their sharpened martial skills often left the colonizers on the defensive, with several Spanish settlements (including Guadalajara) vulnerable to attacks and forced resettlements.

Tensions between Spaniards and native peoples decreased significantly in the 1590s when the crown, drained of men and money, decided to abandon its military campaigns and pursue more conciliatory tactics.[70] Attempts at diplomacy through favorable treatment and subsidies became the preferred tactic for integrating nonsedentary ethnic groups into the northern provinces.[71] The cooperation of the war-weary and beleaguered native populations helped end the majority of the conflicts by the end of the sixteenth century, opening the path to the peaceful establishment of several towns and communities. As late as 1608, the crown continued to spend forty thousand ducats a year and sustained twelve Spanish captains in areas north of Zacatecas to maintain peace with various indigenous groups in New Galicia, such as the Tepehuanes and the Tepeques.[72] Zacatecas became the hub of these conciliatory gestures, serving as a location where goods were distributed, frontier captains were stationed and received their assignments, funds for salaries were collected, and supervision of administrative matters was coordinated. The city served as the base not only for Spanish diplomatic activities but for native people as well. Native peoples involved in the peace process frequently went to the city to make their requests, collect their goods, or air their grievances.[73]

The war, especially in its early years, affected Zacatecas's economic and administrative development. The settlement never came under direct assault.[74] Rather, the source of the problem was the indigenous raids that occurred near the mining camp in the 1550s and early 1560s. Attacks usually occurred to the south and west of Zacatecas on roads and primarily targeted merchants and travelers. Reports from the period attributed these assaults to Guachichiles and Zacatecos. The latter, according to a colonial official, had come together with other groups "to make war on the Spanish."[75] The sixteenth-century account *Guerra de los chichimecas* claimed that Zacatecos assaulted a group of Tarascans bringing clothes to the mines. The Zacatecos killed the indigenous merchants and took all the goods.[76] A few days after that incident, in what proved the closest attack to the mines, these same assailants struck the mule trains (*recuas*) of two of the city's founders, Cristóbal de Oñate and Diego de Ibarra, three leagues away (about eight miles).[77] The raid led to the death of a Spaniard and the slaughter of fifty of Ibarra's horses.[78] Another attack in July 1551 by Guachichiles again targeted the supply trains of Ibarra and Oñate, resulting in the death of two blacks and five Indians, and injuring several others who had managed to flee. A few months later in September of that same year, Guachichiles killed a Spanish merchant and forty tamemes, or indigenous carriers, bringing merchandise (again mainly clothes) to Zacatecas. Many other Spanish men and women in outlying *estancias* (settlements) died in raids, which included the burning of property and the stealing of livestock and grains.[79] In these assaults, indigenous and blacks workers were killed as well. In the complicated world of alliances in Spanish America, cooperative native peoples, or "friendly Indians," as they were called, were as vulnerable to violence (perhaps even more) as Spaniards. Countless numbers of native peoples and indigenous communities suffered death or destruction during the frontier wars at the hands of other indigenous groups.

Yet even in the midst of so much strife, the main threat to Zacatecas proper remained economic in nature. Violence on the roads and in the hinterlands made it difficult for its residents to procure basic necessities. Attacks on ranches decreased supplies of foodstuff and animals (particularly mules for mining production). These conditions were exacerbated by the delays and difficulties merchants and muleteers encountered as they traveled the roads around Zacatecas.[80] The oidor Martínez de la Marcha, who passed by the area on an viceregal inspection shortly after the 1550 assault on Ibarra and Oñate's supply train (the one closest to the city), seemed more concerned with the loss of "costly" provisions than with the loss of life.[81] His economic preoccupations highlight the lack of apprehension on the part of colonial officials for the security of Zacatecas or for the merchants and traders bringing the struggling mining camp its vital goods. Did the lack of interest also stem from the ethnic composition of the supply teams? In just the four attacks mentioned here, native peoples (and some blacks) suffered the brunt of the violence. While the crown was probably not insensitive to the loss of life, their main preoccupation was with silver production, which had decreased dramatically. Output would not improve until the violence had been resolved in some measure.

Yet overall, Martínez de la Marcha's bemoaning of the "great damage" inflicted by the Zacatecos proved minimal in comparison to the disruptions caused by indigenous hostilities at other Spanish and Indian settlements. Indigenous aggressions against supply lines or to the towns themselves forced several mining camps and communities in New Galicia to curtail or cease operations. In 1549, miners from Zacatecas protested against transporting their silver to the mint at Compostela (then New Galicia's capital, located in contemporary Nayarit) over seventy leagues of "rough and frightening" (i.e., hostile) roads.[82] Around the same period, Zacatecos raided Cazcan communities as they swept through northern Guadalajara. These incursions continued through the 1560s in almost every part of the region. In 1561, Pedro de Ahumada described a particularly severe attack by the Zacatecos and the Guachichiles against the northwestern mining centers of Sombrerete and San Martín, and in 1575 colonial officials executed two Zacateco leaders, Quicama and Namiguemaculichema, for their role in raids in the northern mining town of Mazapil.[83] As late as the seventeenth century, the province of Nueva Vizcaya suffered from a series of revolts that killed native and Spaniards alike and shut down mining activities.[84]

The rise and fall of mining towns and communities in New Galicia in this period often depended on the extent to which they became embroiled in Spanish and Indian frontier wars. Communities in the path of these conflicts faced abandonment and relocation. Their residents faced death or the loss of precious supplies and resources. Settlers in Zacatecas encountered many of the challenges that were common to frontier towns in their fledgling years. These included population and labor shortages, as well as a lack of infrastructure, foodstuff, and resources. However, the fledgling mining camp emerged from the frontier wars relatively unscathed. The majority of the Zacatecos relocated to other communities or made war in other places. The lack of conflict allowed the city's founders to direct labor, energy, and resources to the main task at hand—the extraction of silver and the development of a town.

Laborers and Migrants

Tolosa and his associates had not intended to establish a city in the midst of a semidesert landscape, in an area that in the late 1540s constituted the far northern periphery of the empire. But by 1548, the ongoing discovery of rich and productive silver veins guaranteed a substantial and durable Spanish presence in the area. It also promoted the rise of a more permanent settlement and a long-term, skilled, and stable workforce.[85] Resolving the labor situation became the most pressing challenge to miners in the city's early years. It caused them to offer incentives to migrant workers. These factors shaped the social and economic dynamics of the city and its constituent Indian towns throughout the colonial period. Zacatecas was not like Potosí or other mining towns that drew from seasonal workers who returned to their hometowns on the completion of their draft service. The migrant native population in Zacatecas came voluntarily and created permanent settlements. The development of Zacatecas's labor arrangements is crucial to understanding the origins and persistence of an urban indigenous society in the city.

There were three labor options in these early years: draft, enslaved, and free wage—those who worked for pay. In the mid-sixteenth century, miners in both New Spain and the Andes often used forced labor recruited from the indigenous hinterlands to work in mines or at *haciendas de beneficio*, where workers refined the ore.[86] Draft labor, however, was not a viable option in Zacatecas. At the time of its founding, Zacatecas was located in a sparsely inhabited province and, unlike its Andean counterpart Potosí, was not surrounded by large communities of sedentary native peoples. Gathering laborers from further abroad was equally impractical considering the city's location, hundreds of miles from the major population centers of central Mexico (more than 350 miles from Mexico City).

In his first letter to the crown, Cortés recommended the use of enslaved Chichimecs as mine laborers, but miners in Zacatecas quickly discovered that the local native population would not meet their needs.[87] The Zacatecos were few in number and considered poor candidates for mine labor by the Spanish.[88] Their nomadic lifestyle meant they had little experience with organized labor, and there is no indication that, unlike other indigenous groups, such as the Tarascans, they had a history of metallurgy.[89] Nor does it appear that Spanish remuneration in cash and ore drew Zacatecos, or other local indigenous groups, to the rigorous and dangerous conditions of silver production. These factors explain the absence of systematic draft labor in the city. From its founding, it proved impossible for officials, miners, and encomenderos in Zacatecas to implement the labor recruitment mechanisms of sedentary native communities in areas such as central

Mexico, parts of New Galicia, or even more locally with the Cazcanes in the Juchipila Valley.[90] Spaniards immediately set Zacatecos to work in the mines, but over the long term, they were dispersed over too large an area and were too loosely organized politically to be subject to traditional forms of Spanish labor domination.[91]

Moreover, by the mid-sixteenth century, draft labor was losing its appeal as Spaniards began to question its effectiveness. Pockets of free wage labor began to appear in cities and sparsely populated sites.[92] Silver mining, an industry that required skilled labor to succeed, was particularly vulnerable to the erratic nature of forced draft labor. Runaways were common.[93] In the central mining center of Taxco, for example, Indians absconded from draft labor while communities found more ways to decrease their work quotas, leaving the mines at the mercy of an unstable workforce.[94] Abandoning the idea of draft labor was surely not an easy or palatable decision for the city's early miners, many of whom had reaped its benefits in other areas. Cristóbal de Oñate, one of the city's founders, for example, used forced indigenous labor from the pueblo of Xalisco at his mines in Huichichila.[95] Still, miners and officials must have soon recognized the difficulty of implementing the institution in Zacatecas.

In the absence of repartimiento, miners may have initially favored slave labor until high fatalities led to a reliance on indigenous workers. In a 1563 petition to the crown, the cabildo complained of "the many slaves that have died and die daily" while extracting silver.[96] During moments of extreme labor shortages miners often petitioned the crown to send them black slaves. Over the long term, though, the use of enslaved labor, either indigenous or African, proved financially impractical. Some black slaves came with the Spaniards on their initial forays of the site. But the use of African slaves in mining production never played a leading role in Zacatecas.[97] Unlike their indigenous counterparts, Spaniards could not seize black slaves in rebellions. They had to purchase them at considerable expense from intermediaries from Mexico City (Vera Cruz being the port of entry). Africans slaves were expensive investments and mine work was dangerous.[98] Miners surely had second thoughts about exposing their investments to dangerous dust and particles, lack of circulation, accidents, and illnesses associated with high altitude.[99] Miners in this period also harbored notions that Africans were biologically unfit to work in the mines. During his 1608 inspection, Bishop Mota y Escobar noted that miners did not employ blacks underground because they could not survive the cold and damp conditions belowground, as opposed to Indians, whom he found particularly suited "to suffer the burdens of mine labor."[100] Some miners employed African and Afro-descended slaves in excavation work, but the majority worked in the refining process. More often slaves labored on agricultural estancias, in domestic service, and in other urban occupations. The free and enslaved African-descended population played a greater role in the city's labor and population base as the colonial period progressed, but in the sixteenth century they constituted a minority of the mining work force.[101]

The enslavement of native peoples by Spaniards dates from the arrival of Europeans to the Americas. The crown took various positions on the subject in the sixteenth century, often vacillating between allowing and outlawing indigenous slavery until it finally abolished the practice.[102] Slavery remained much more common in frontier areas, where lack of oversight from viceregal officials created greater opportunities to unlawfully or unjustly enslave native peoples.[103] A common ploy, for example, involved Spaniards provoking or inciting native peoples into rebellious activity by stealing their cattle or looting their property. They then took advantage of laws, which allowed them to enslave "insubordinate" Indians. Slavery became particularly widespread in New Galicia. Soldiers, officials, and settlers capitalized on the Spanish-indigenous conflicts that plagued the area during the sixteenth century to take "just slaves." Indian slaves or forced workers served as the primary labor source at many mines in western Mexico, including those around Guadalajara and Compostela.[104]

In Zacatecas, miners frequently employed Indian slaves in the first few years of its founding. Spaniards initially coerced Zacatecos and native peoples from the Cazcan area into mine labor or forced then to serve as tamemes.[105] As free wage laborers infiltrated the markets, enslaved and encomienda Indians bore the brunt of the grueling and dangerous activities related to mining production, particularly the belowground extraction of silver. But ultimately indigenous slavery, like draft labor, failed to take root in Zacatecas, in part because of the small size of the local native population. A greater enforcement of the ban on indigenous slavery in the 1550s also made it more difficult for miners to use slaves to run their operations, contributing eventually to the closure of some mining ventures in central Mexico.[106] By the mid-1550s, there was only a nominal number of enslaved Indians in the mining cuadrillas.[107] This is not to say that the occasional indigenous slave did not appear in the town after this period, but their absence from archival documents speaks to the relatively low occurrence of this practice in the city. Cases such as one from 1672 when sixty-two indigenous slaves from the Sierra Madre were found toiling in Zacatecas were rare.[108] However, incidents in which miners kidnapped Indians from the city and forced them to work in slavery-like conditions occurred throughout the colonial period. But by the end of the sixteenth century, slavery was mainly confined to individuals of African descent.

With forced labor both impractical and economically inefficient, Spanish miners turned to the hiring of free wage laborers.[109] Mining production did not necessarily require a large workforce. But it needed a skilled and permanent labor pool. Miners particularly favored the migration of sedentary indigenous peoples from central and western Mexico who were accustomed to urban environments and labor drafts. Many northern colonization schemes, for example, involved the transplanting of "friendly" or "model" indigenous peoples, most notably the Tlaxcalans.[110] In Zacatecas, Spaniards recognized the expediency of offering native peoples incentives to make the long journey and to engage in the grueling and dangerous work associated with mine labor. Offering wages in the 1550s, a period in which few Indians had access to or involvement with the money economy, proved a novel and effective magnet. However, miners sought more than just seasonal or peripatetic workers.[111] They needed settlers and colonists from which they could secure a stable and long-term labor pool.

Remuneration in cash and kind alone would not necessarily motivate native peoples to leave their communities and relocate permanently to a frontier town then at the periphery of both Spanish and sedentary indigenous societies. In other areas, the crown successfully recruited other native colonists by offering them honorific titles and the ability to carry arms, wear European dress, and ride horses. Authorities did not authorize these privileges in Zacatecas, which were usually reserved for nobles or military allies.[112] However, native peoples taking up residency in Zacatecas earned exemption from two of the most onerous features of colonial rule: tribute collection and rotary labor draft. These incentives remained in place throughout the eighteenth century for any indigenous resident of the city. Occasional archival references to encomienda Indians should not be interpreted as a change in policy. In these cases, Indians men and women, held in encomienda in other areas of the province, labored in the city under the direction of their Spanish encomenderos.[113]

Wages and exemptions served as "pull" factors for emigrants, while the combination of heavy tribute and repartimiento obligations in home communities functioned as "push" factors. The defection of tribute and draft laborers to other communities occurred frequently in both New Spain and the Andes.[114] Spanish policies and institutions placed heavy burdens on native communities. Widespread epidemics led to demographic collapse, and heavy tribute obligations disrupted community dynamics and created tensions between commoners and nobles.[115] In central Mexico, a compulsory work system called *coatequitl* existed in preconquest times. It differed from its Spanish counterpart in that native people labored on public works projects within their communities, under local supervision.[116] Spanish labor drafts, however, had no consideration for individual needs or community obligations. Repartimiento service often separated native peoples from their families, forcing them to work long hours in dangerous occupations for meager pay. In their absence, family members struggled to sustain their households and meet community responsibilities. Spouses and children traveling with draft laborers often worked extra jobs to support themselves. In addition to its disruptive financial and familial effects, draft labor also affected the community, as a smaller populace struggled to fulfill tribute requirements for absent members.

For some native peoples, wage labor in the mines, although onerous and unappealing, proved a better option than the work and tribute obligations of their home communities. Ironically, Zacatecas probably served as home to individuals fleeing repartimiento work in the mines, among the most dreaded of all the draft labor activities. This pattern was not without precedent in this period. Some native peoples working in Taxco as draft laborers permanently relocated to the mining town on the completion of their service.[117] In Nueva Vizcaya, indigenous peoples often migrated to mining towns rather than settle in adjacent missions.[118] Wage labor was not free of exploitation, but it proved attractive enough to native migrants, particularly in the sixteenth century, when Zacatecas was the site of relatively high wages, multiple employment opportunities, and tribute exemptions. Prior experience with mining in western Mexico and at mining sites in Taxco, for example, drew Tarascans to Zacatecas.[119] Over time, work and kinship networks also functioned as a magnet for drawing native peoples to the city. By the 1550s a consistent influx of indigenous immigrants from western and central Mexico flowed into the city. Sources speak of the presence of large groups of Tonaltecos, Mexicas, Cazcanes, Otomís, Tlaxcalans, Texcocans, Cholulans, and Tarascans, along with other unidentified indigenous groups.[120] In San Luis Potosí, miners hired *reclutadores* to recruit workers from Michoacán. These individuals, also known as *sacagentes*, or people takers, traveled to indigenous communities and entered into contracts with native workers, which usually included the advancing of salary.[121] Recruiters may have been involved in bringing native peoples to Zacatecas, although no evidence has been found to that effect.

Indigenous immigration in Zacatecas during the colonial period had two consistent features: it was voluntary and recurring. Labor shortages, occasioned by diseases, silver strikes at other mining sites, and inadequate pay, plagued the city at various times. Over the long term, though, Indians arrived in large enough numbers that miners found it unnecessary to resort to the migration schemes, such as the transplanting of large groups of Tlaxcalans, so common to other areas in the north.[122] Nor is there any evidence to indicate that the wage-earning native population came to Zacatecas under any form of Spanish duress.

Indios Libres

In 1550, the oidor Martínez de la Marcha specifically identified Zacatecas's indigenous migrants as free wage laborers, or *indios libres*.[123] These free Indians should not be confused with other types of indigenous wage workers, such as *yanaconas* in the Andes and *naborías* in central and southern Mexico. Both these terms possessed distinct meanings in different time periods and regions, but in general they implied more formal and coercive labor ties with Spaniards. In the Andean silver-mining town of Potosí, Indians who left their communities to work for a Spanish master, yanaconas, were exempt from tribute and labor obligations.[124] Naboría, a more common term in New Spain, served as a proxy for servant or dependent. It could also describe those native peoples who, in being relocated to meet Spanish labor needs, had become dispossessed of their property and possessions.[125] Many Indians, including those brought with Spaniards on their pacification campaigns, as well as those organized into encomiendas in their aftermath, functioned as naborías in New Galicia.[126] In Zacatecas, this word rarely appears in local documents, but more often (and even then sparingly) in viceregal writings.[127] As with encomienda Indians, some naborías in Zacatecas probably arrived at the mines with their Spanish masters.[128] But as for the local immigrant population, there is no evidence (records of draft labor, work contracts, or inventories) that indicates that the term implied the bonds of personal service or lack of mobility associated with central and southern Mexico. Rather, in his ordinances, Oidor Martínez de la Marcha made it clear that free Indians "could contract or serve whomever they chose," and he explicitly forbade any official, Spanish or indigenous, from organizing them into repartimiento.[129] Naborías as a descriptor probably never took strong hold in the city because migrants to Zacatecas were not dependents, but wage earners who developed their own settlements.

Labor in a mining town, even in the absence of repartimiento service, brought its own particular challenges and pressures. The practice of work for pay was not always followed. Common were complaints like the one in 1620 by indigenous hacienda workers that their masters often delayed their wages for one to two years or longer, paid them incorrectly, and charged them supplies at exorbitant rates.[130] The absence of repartimiento in the town did not eliminate all forms of compulsory labor among the indigenous population. Various cabildo decrees reveal local officials unlawfully pressing Indians into service to assist in such public works projects as the building of wells or the construction of monasteries.[131] Clergy and city officials also required native peoples to prepare for the city's various religious festivities and processions. Native peoples complained to viceregal officials that the Spanish cabildo forced them to make arches for the bishop's visits and pikes and fences for bull fights without pay. In 1587, the cabildo requested that one indigenous person from each cuadrilla be sent for one week to fix the stables of the *carnicería*, or slaughterhouse, a requirement reminiscent of repartimiento labor.[132] The latter episode, in particular, illustrates the continued desire of Spanish officials to coerce labor from indigenous peoples.

Spaniards made at least two failed attempts to institute repartimiento in the city. In 1596, the cabildo advocated sending a council member to Mexico City to ask the viceroy to authorize a repartimiento of Indians to drain mines that had filled with water and assist in any other tasks necessary to the system.[133] A second request entered in 1637 (discussed later) met with some success. However, in general, officials at the viceregal level forbade the Spanish cabildo from forcing native peoples to work without pay unless they volunteered. During their inspections of the city, oidores frequently reminded Spanish authorities that they could not force Indians found guilty of a crime to do personal service.[134] Nor did native peoples idly stand by and succumb to Spanish abuse. In 1609, nine Indians of diverse ethnic affiliations, led by Buenaventura de la Cruz, complained to the *visitador*, or royal inspector, Gaspar de la Fuente of their exploitation at the hands of the *corregidor* Juan de Guzmán, Zacatecas's highest-ranking colonial official. The visitador reminded de Guzmán that he could not use the services of more than one Indian per day and that he had to "share" the individual with other city officials, pay him a salary, and not force him to engage in any other kind of forced draft service.[135]

Overall, the documentation does not support a scenario of pervasive forced labor in this period. Abuses and exploitation certainly occurred, especially in the hinterlands, areas with less administrative oversight.[136] Spanish requests for draft labor ultimately fell to the lot of native peoples living outside of Zacatecas. In 1637, local officials complained to the crown of their inability to exploit mines because of the decimation of the indigenous workforce by disease.[137] Other cabildo entries verify this demographic crisis and its exacerbation by the exodus of native peoples to other mining sites, especially the boomtown of Parral to the north in Nueva Vizcaya. In response, the crown authorized the establishment of a community of Indians within two to three leagues of Zacatecas for repartimiento labor in the mines. The pueblo, called San Josef de la Isla, was composed of "Chichimecs" brought from areas within twenty to forty leagues of Zacatecas. How long these laborers worked under draft conditions is unknown. While repartimiento was never implemented among the city's indigenous population, the potential for episodes of exploitation hovered over any labor arrangement between Spaniards and native peoples.[138]

The royal ordinances of 1550 delineated specific activities for enslaved and free wage laborers. In theory slaves, African or indigenous, and encomienda Indians performed the most dangerous and grueling work, including excavation and smelting. Indios libres gathered and brought the combustibles used in the smelting process, including wood, ash, and charcoal (*carbón*), and carried metal to the *lavadero*, or the washer, where they separated the ore. They also built the small storage buildings, or *aposentos*, adjacent to the mines. Free wage Indians could not work in the foundry or in any other aspect of the refining process.[139] It is unlikely that miners or laborers strictly adhered to these regulations, but they did provide native peoples with formal opportunities for redress.

Exploitation of the indigenous labor force certainly occurred in Zacatecas and remained a constant problem for the duration of the colonial period. Oidor Martínez de la Marcha's 1550s ordinances (and subsequent viceregal measures in the 1560s) targeted several of the town's illicit activities, including abusive Spanish practices, particularly the mistreatment of the indigenous free wage laborers. The content of several of Martínez de la Marcha's mandates suggests that miners forced indios libres to engage in work designated for slaves or encomienda Indians, or they placed undue burdens on standard tasks. For example, Indians assigned to bring metal from the mines or charcoal from the charcoal makers often bore unreasonable loads. Martínez de la Marcha ordered that native peoples could not carry more than two *arrobas* (fifty pounds) per trip. Jobs involving transport were particularly vulnerable to exploitation, especially in a town dependent on imports. Long-distance native carriers, traveling over twenty leagues, were often forced to carry excessive amounts of items or foodstuffs. Viceregal officials also worried about unlawful labor practices that interfered with religious instruction. Spaniards forced Indians to work on Sundays and holidays, sending them to look for wood, sticks, and shrubs for the smelting process. Men were not alone in being subject to abuses. While very few documents mention Indian women for this period, Martínez de la Marcha complained of encomenderos who unlawfully brought indigenous women from their communities to the mines to prepare food.[140] Without documentation it is difficult to determine the extent of exploitation and how often native peoples sought compensation or amends with local or viceregal officials.

Ultimately free wage laborer Indians in this period could exercise an even more effective option than legal redress—they could leave the town or move from one employer to the other. Written labor contracts never became standard in Zacatecas (there are no extant documents to date of this nature). Miner and indigenous laborer made verbal arrangements. Some native peoples worked as part of a miner's cuadrilla for weekly earnings; others contracted themselves in *tequío*, an agreement to produce a certain amount of ores for specific wages. As Spaniards often competed with one another over laborers, native peoples could capitalize on the production boom to increase their earnings or leave an exploitative site. Nor is there any substantial indication for this period that native peoples remained tied to sites because of debt peonage, even though they often received wages in advance.[141] Rather, the practice of *sonsacar*, by which a miner enticed a native person with higher wages to leave a work site before completing his or her contract, occurred frequently in this period. Oidor Martínez de la Marcha was so concerned with the number of Indians working in the mines without binding agreements that he threatened prosecution for vagabondage and a hundred lashes to any Indian on a cuadrilla without a contract. These circumstances should not downplay the grueling labor conditions at mining complexes or the ultimate authority of Spaniards in labor and civic matters. Still, Spanish reliance on an indigenous workforce in Zacatecas offered native peoples greater flexibility and autonomy in labor arrangements than in most other areas of the colony.

How much did indios libres earn in this period? In the absence of written labor contracts, only anecdotal information remains. Viceregal officials often attempted to standardize wages in their decrees, specifying both minimum and, in boom periods, maximum sums. Whether miners or workers abided by these amounts is open to conjecture. Wages could fluctuate dramatically from one mining site to another. In 1550, Martínez de la Marcha argued that some individuals offered native peoples "excessive" wages, thus causing great harm to other owners of haciendas and mining sites. To stabilize the market he ordered that the weekly earnings of Indian laborers on cuadrillas could not be greater than three *tomines* (three-eighths of a peso), along with meals, or four tomines without food.[142] "Meals" entailed daily rations of maize and beans, the same foodstuffs given to indigenous slaves. Martínez de la Marcha ordered that workers laboring below ground (in metal extraction) be paid about one-eighth of a peso per tequío.[143]

While Indians valued their wages, the real prize in this period was the right to silver tailings known as *pepena* or *partida*. By the mid-sixteenth century native peoples no longer regarded silver as a primarily ceremonial object or the exclusive domain of the elite, but a commodity and a means to enter the money economy. In Zacatecas workers considered silver tailings part of their pay and counted on the extra revenue from the pepena to supplement their earnings. In the 1550s many laborers probably earned more income from ores than from coin. Miners, recognizing the power of remunerations in kind, often used the partida as a bargaining tool, luring native peoples away from other labor sites by offering larger shares of ores. The discontinuation of the practice in the late colonial period (discussed in Chapter 5) caused considerable outcry.[144]

Indians in Zacatecas frequently sold their tailings to Spaniards or utilized small furnaces to smelt their own silver. Native peoples smelted crushed ore in small cylindrical (*hornos*) or cupelled (*cendradilla*) furnaces with the aid of hand-operated bellows of sheep- or goatskin for air blast or by "using aboriginal blowpipes (*soplillos*)."[145] These hornos proved particularly popular among Indians and non-Spaniards during the colonial period, as they provided an accessible and inexpensive method to process silver. Small-time smelters made a brisk trade from the tailings, smelting ores in their homes or in back areas and then selling them clandestinely to interested buyers, particularly Spaniards. They also made a profit constructing cendradillas, which they sold to Spaniards and other non-Indians, including slaves.

The amount of ores processed by Indians from pepenas constituted a small percentage of the city's yield. Still, enough *plata del rescate* (silver produced outside of an official mine), as it came to be called, circulated in the city to alarm Spanish officials that too much metal was receiving the concessionary tax of one-tenth, or *diezmo*, given to legitimate mining operations, instead of the standard one-fifth, or *quinto*, usually applied to precious metals. In 1550, Martínez de la Marcha enacted a series of measures directed primarily at indigenous peoples to curtail or at least regulate the production and sale of rescate silver. He ordered that no indigenous person could refine or smelt silver with furnaces or bellows if he or she did not own a silver mine. This measure, in particular, effectively limited most non-Spaniards who lacked the means to own the machinery and resources necessary for large mining ventures. Another set of decrees targeted the source of low-scale production. He forbade the construction of any cendradilla in secrecy or near any productive mine (an active metal-extracting site). Indigenous free wage laborers and slaves (potentially African or indigenous in this period) could not rent cendradillas from Spaniards and could make them only if they resided in a Spanish home.[146] Native peoples could not even perform jobs at the Casa de Fundación, where officials registered silver. These measures aimed to control production and ultimately taxation. However, the large number of decrees and their rigid punishments speaks to the proliferation of small-scale operators. The production of rescate silver not only benefited native peoples but the nascent town as well, forming a cornerstone of the local, informal economy.

The predominance of wage over draft labor in Zacatecas profoundly influenced the development of the city. The lure of remuneration brought a steady stream of workers to Zacatecas, especially native peoples, many of whom were not just job seekers but also colonists. The town's indigenous settlers benefitted from wages in cash and kind and, in comparison to other areas in Spanish America, from greater freedom from their colonial overseers in other aspects of daily life.[147] In the sixteenth century, in particular, Spanish dependence on the foreign Indian population to meet long-term labor and demographic needs garnered native peoples certain concessions, the most prominent of which were the elimination of tribute and labor levees and, over time, limited self-government. These conditions led to the development of a permanent indigenous labor force that began to construct their own communities on the borders of the Spanish town.

From Minas to Town

The task of urban development fell to both Spaniards and Indians. But it happened gradually. The main goal in the period from 1546 to 1568 was to find silver. City building would begin in earnest only when large quantities of ore justified a permanent Spanish presence in the area. The discovery of three large veins a few miles from the Bufa, along the city's *serranía* (mountain range) in 1548 led to the development of a larger and more permanent camp.[148] From 1548 to 1549, Spaniards settled a few miles further away in Veta Grande, the site of a large silver lode.[149] The discovery of the mine of San Bernabé on June 4, 1548, prompted the construction of settlements at El Bracho, an area about one mile outside the city center, conveniently situated between the Bufa and the mines.

Evidence from other mining sites in New Spain indicates that during exploratory periods, miners and laborers probably lived close together in temporary and basic housing called *jacales*, or huts. In the 1550s, in the central Mexican real of Pachuca, for example, indigenous prospectors stayed with their Spanish employers in accommodations near the area under exploration.[150] In the years immediately following Tolosa's arrival, this was probably the state of housing arrangements between the two groups. At some point, according to the account of the early nineteenth-century chronicler Francisco Frejes, miners assigned the eastern part of the canyon at El Bracho for the "patrician Indians," or the non-Chichimecs that accompanied Tolosa.[151] The first indigenous settlements developed in 1548 around strikes along the Veta Grande and about eight miles to the north at Pánuco.[152] Multiple native barrios followed at El Bracho. The location of indigenous settlements in this period owed more to access to mining sites than to any organized plan by Spaniards to maintain separate republics.

Later, the evolution of a town with a Spanish *traza* (center) facilitated clearer demarcations between Spanish and indigenous living spaces.

As the mining bonanza continued and the population of workers increased, long-term housing became available and the first semblance of a town emerged. In 1549, the construction of Zacatecas's first permanent structure, a *capilla* (chapel), led to the establishment of the city on its current site. According to colonial chroniclers, this small chapel, built to house a venerated image of Christ, had such a strong following that Spaniards gradually relocated from El Bracho to plots of land adjacent to the small church.[153] Both native peoples and Spaniards continued to migrate south until the city moved to its present site at the foot of the Bufa. A 1549 *visita*, or vicegeral inspection, reported 250 Spanish *pobladores*, or settlers, but offered no demographic information about a certainly larger population of Indians and non-Spaniards.[154] In spite of its permanent buildings and modest population, Zacatecas still had the feel of a frontier mining camp, with undeveloped lots, weapon-carrying Spaniards and native peoples, packs of stolen horses, a healthy profiteering trade, as well as an endless number of illicit economic transactions.

In 1550, Zacatecas possessed the jurisdictional status of a *minas*, or mining camp, as opposed to a *ciudad*, or city. It lacked the prestige or urban development of its western neighbors in the province, Compostela and Guadalajara. The former served as the site of the first Audiencia from 1548 until that institution moved permanently to Guadalajara in 1560.[155] Visita reports depict Guadalajara in 1549 as a thriving town with a prosperous and fertile hinterland.[156] The oidores, or judges, of the Audiencia described the city as well designed, with a decent plaza and church bordered by orderly streets and houses. It also possessed a good *tianguiz*, or market, and a Franciscan monastery. An adjacent barrio, recently developed "in Spanish style" (presumably along urban grids), contained over five hundred houses.[157] This very favorable description of Guadalajara may have been influenced by the oidores' eagerness to relocate the Audiencia there. Still, the city's development was unquestionably superior to Zacatecas's rudimentary and haphazard urban layout.

But a report from only two years later, in 1551, on the state of mining production, the infrastructure, and the demographic composition of the town, highlighted Zacatecas's quick growth and prosperity. In that year, the oidor Martínez de la Marcha wrote to the crown of his arrival "at the rich mines of the Zacatecas," describing the "mines and silver veins, the machinery for crushing ore and smelting silver, and the houses and populations that in such short time have been constructed there."[158] By that date, there were more than 175 known (and named) silver veins in the area. Over forty-five *ingenios* (stamp mills) served to crush, process, and refine ores. The abundance of silver produced in Zacatecas, the oidor had elegantly acknowledged during a previous trip, far outstripped those of other mining sites, "like a drop of water to the ocean." He also duly noted the frustration of miners forced to send their silver to mint in distant Compostela, over seventy leagues away.[159]

Silver production in Zacatecas was beginning to outstrip those of other sites in New Galicia. For example, in 1551, the mines of Guachinango near Guadalajara (discovered circa 1543) had the same number of Spanish settlers as Zacatecas. Guachinango also had more silver veins (214) and houses for Spaniards (219). However, the number of workers' lodgings in Zacatecas outstripped those of the rival mining camp by four to one (342 to 80).[160] Guachinango's miners had a smaller workforce because they relied on enslaved labor. Other mining sites in New Spain were experiencing the effects of the viceroyalty's mid-sixteenth century mining crisis (1549–1556), which stemmed from a labor shortage, particularly the lack of Indians to work in the mines.[161] The elimination of indigenous slavery in this period crippled some mining camps to the point of abandonment. By 1605, Spaniards had deserted Guachinango and mining activity had come to a standstill.[162] But Zacatecas's ability to draw on free wage laborer migrants, among other factors, contributed to its continued production and eventual preeminence in the province at large.

By 1551, not only silver was booming. The site's urban landscape had developed as well, with five churches and over 409 houses.[163] While Zacatecas in this period still lacked many of the institutions of a proper Spanish town, in terms of sheer demographic size and structures it was no longer a mere mining camp. Housing patterns indicate that non-Spaniards constituted the majority of the population by the early 1550s. The report documented the presence of 160 Spaniards, 60 of whom were listed as *principales*, or prominent miners and officials, and the remaining as "others," or commoners. The number of Indians and slaves (probably of African descent and not indigenous) is not mentioned. However, given the number of houses for Spaniards (67), as compared to those for Indians and slaves (342), the non-Spanish laboring population was probably about five to six times the size of the Spanish one. A report from two years earlier, in 1549, mentioned over three hundred Spaniards engaged in mining, not counting the number of Spaniards in other merchant, trade, and subsidiary activities.[164] While these numbers are certainly not comprehensive (or completely reliable), they highlight the mina's early demographic trends: a small population of Spaniards living among a large group of non-Spaniards, especially Indians. The stability of both the Spanish population and the indigenous workforce confirmed that by 1551 Zacatecas was no longer an obscure mining camp in danger of abandonment, but a thriving urban center and silver producer.

As the Spanish town grew, parallel communities of ethnically and linguistically distinct indigenous migrants evolved on the outskirts. Although many native peoples continued to live at mining haciendas on the outskirts of town, by the early 1550s communities developed north of the city, probably as extensions or overflows of the settlement at El Bracho.[165] Further discoveries of silver veins closer to the city center led to the emergence of three indigenous barrios directly south of Bracho: Tlacuitlapan, San Francisco, and Mexicapan.[166] Later, a cluster of indigenous communities developed in the south between the hills and the Spanish traza. In the sixteenth century, Spaniards viewed these indigenous settlements as parishes under the jurisdiction of religious orders. Franciscans initially had the custodianship of the majority of indigenous peoples until they divided their duties with the Augustinians and other orders. Documents refer to the northern settlements as the *barrio de arriba* (the neighborhood above the convent) or San Francisco, and the southern communities as the *barrio de abajo*.

The indigenous barrios initially formed around ethnic and language groups as the various migrants groups formed ethnic enclaves, a practice typical of immigrant populations.[167] Mexicapan, for example, suggests a colony of central Mexicans. Tonaltecos probably founded the community of Tonalá. Spaniards recognized the diverse ethnic affiliation of individual communities when they referred to the indigenous population clusters in the north and the south as *parcialidades*, a term that Spaniards used to indicate autonomous entities within a larger state.[168] Although a large group could predominate in one town, such as Mexicas, barrios of other ethnic groups also resided there. San Josef and Tlacuitlapan had a strong Tlaxcalan presence. Tarascans and Tecuexes also lived in large numbers in Tonalá.[169] These communities did not remain barrios of the Spanish city, but as we shall see in Chapters 2 and 3, they evolved into autonomous indigenous municipalities.

The first indigenous and Spanish vecinos probably acquired their land without the formal approval of colonial authorities. Squatting at potential silver lodes was common.[170] Native peoples settled in plots outside the Spanish traza around mines, haciendas, or churches, in spaces large enough to support a small home and a *milpa*, or maize field. Many barrios probably formed in this sporadic and unplanned fashion. But over time, in a practice that was common to other urban centers, Indians, like Spaniards, received vacant lots from colonial authorities, either as individuals or as households.[171] For example, in 1631 a native person sold a piece of property with two houses on it in a barrio known as Lomas del Calvario, awarded to him "by a grant [*merced*] the city had made to him."[172] There is also evidence of a community-size land grant. Native peoples established the barrio of San Josef, which eventually evolved into an Indian town, with land donated to them by the city.[173] Indians initially had to ask permission of the Indian defender (an official appointed to protect indigenous interests) to sell their plots, but colonial officials eventually handed these decisions over to the native towns, allowing them more control of the size and limits of their territorial base.[174] Eventually local indigenous officials also assumed responsibility for setting aside lands and fields for native peoples who settled in the Indian towns.

The large number of Indians who lived on the outskirts and the hinterlands frequently augmented Zacatecas's indigenous population. A core population of laborers never moved to the Indians barrios in the city center but lived permanently in haciendas within the Bracho, Veta Grande, and Pánuco complex.[175] More refining plants developed as the mining boom expanded. Large haciendas were also located in the indigenous settlements of Mexicapan and San Francisco. Throughout the colonial period large numbers of native people, including entire families, lived near the rivers that bordered these refining plants and in the large agricultural complexes that developed near the city.[176] Indians living at haciendas frequented the town to run errands, procure foodstuffs, and attend religious services.

The settled vecino population was augmented by a large number of indigenous itinerants who exploited the mining economy for their own financial needs. Peripatetic laborers worked brief stints at mines or refining haciendas before moving to other strikes. The lure of the money economy also drew indigenous merchants and traders, who brought much-needed supplies. These individuals saw the opportunity for profit in the delivery and transportation of goods. Zacatecas's location, a basin surrounded by a semidesert, its sterile topography, and its focus on silver production placed the city at the mercy of imports, especially foodstuffs.[177] Although Spanish and Portuguese merchants conducted a brisk trade, the mining camp counted on native people to bring such food as chickens, fruit, fish, and grain. The latter was of such particular importance to the city that Oidor Martínez de la Marcha forbade all indigenous merchants from selling items in the tianguiz unless they also brought with them three *almudes* (or nearly eight bushels) of maize, the food staple of the indigenous labor force.[178] Other various items arrived via the services of native peoples from the hinterlands. Miguel Costantino and Miguel Álvarez Costantino (perhaps a father and son team) were native peoples from Juchimilco who traded in Spanish clothing.[179] The men complained of having to travel through hostile territory, which perhaps explains why some traders resided in Zacatecas on a temporary basis, although living in town was not without it perils as well. Martínez de la Marcha's ordinances called on their prosecution as *vagabundos* (vagabonds) if they stayed longer than three days without contracting themselves to a Spanish employer. Some Indians rented houses to conduct longer periods of business, such as Juan González, a cacique, or indigenous leader, of the southern hinterland community of Jalpa. He stayed in the city for short periods to trade tobacco and other supplies.[180]

In addition to individual merchants, communities as far as Michoacán and Aguascalientes supplied the minas with the goods and items that it could not produce, contributing to the development of the Bajío as a grain producing region.[181] However, several of the communities that supplied Zacatecas were fairly close, many in the agriculturally rich regions to the south. The town of Fresnillo, for example, located thirty-six miles from Zacatecas, sent the city meat, wheat, maize, bread, and a variety of fruits from its ranches, cattle farms, and mills.[182] Many of these agricultural enterprises operated on indigenous labor. Zacatecas's vecinos depended on these temporary laborers, traders, and harvesters, many of them Indians, to provide the minas with its basic resources.

In the 1550s, the prosperity of mining production, the stable population base, and the relative immunity from the frontier wars motivated miners and other Spanish vecinos to earnestly take up the task of city building. By 1550, the minas still lacked a permanent town hall or jail.[183] Undeveloped land was common. The 1550 *ordenanzas* took issue with the many individuals who asked for and received lots (*solares*) only to sell them without constructing houses.[184] Still, churches, plazas, and markets began to appear along hills and twisted lanes, giving the mining town a recognizable, if not rectangular, Spanish center. Zacatecas's urban layout never conformed to the perpendicular and parallel street patterns promoted in the Americas.[185] Zacatecas's haphazard and disorganized center clearly reflected the frontier setting and status of the minas. Like other mining towns in Spanish America, the city actually bore (and continues to bear) a stronger resemblance to Spain's mountainous and medieval towns.

Zacatecas's transformation from mining camp to town, however, could occur only with the establishment of the most important urban institution, the cabildo, the forum for local government. Following a long Iberian tradition dating from the Middle Ages, the founding of a town was inextricably linked with the election of local officials from among the city's vecinos.[186] These officials included an *alcalde ordinario* (municipal judge) and several *regidores*, or councilmen. From 1549 to 1553, the crown still considered Zacatecas a *minas*, or mining camp. Lacking town status, it possessed no municipal council, only an *alcalde mayor* (magistrate) and an *alguacil mayor* (constable), and both of them received their appointment from the Audiencia.

In 1553, desiring true representative government, several miners petitioned the Audiencia, still located in Compostela, for the right to elect their own officers and establish a municipal government. From Compostela the Audiencia established the Diputación de Minería by decree on September 25, 1553.[187] This local form of government authorized the mining camp's Spanish vecinos to elect *diputados*, or representatives.[188] On the first day of the New Year, the old municipal council elected four diputados from among male hacienda owners. One of these representatives served as alcalde mayor and another as treasurer. In the absence of a town hall, elections occurred near the altar of the *iglesia mayor*, or principal church. The names of the first diputados remain missing, but familiar protagonists appear among the elected officials of 1557: Cristóbal de Oñate, Diego de Ibarra, and Diego Hernández de Proaño served as representatives; Pedro Gómez de Contreras as treasurer; and Pedro Ortiz de Palencia as notary.[189] Ideally members of the Diputación convened the first Friday of every month directly after the main mass to discuss pertinent affairs.[190] Assembling after religious services proved particularly appropriate and convenient as the church functioned as the council's initial meeting place. On January 13, 1559, the Diputación ordered the construction of a new wooden building near the main church to serve as the *casa del cabildo*, or town hall, on a plaza previously reserved for bullfighting.[191] The substitution of a makeshift ring for a municipal building serves as a visual and symbolic shift in the priority of the leading vecinos of the minas and marks an important transitional moment in the city's civic development. By the close of the 1550s, Zacatecas's transformation from a mining camp to a thriving town, with a core population of Spaniards and urban institutions and infrastructure, was well under way.

. . .

The town's success clearly rested on two pillars: steady silver production and a steady labor source. The discussion of labor needs is inextricably tied to native peoples. The size and actions of the small local native population, the Zacatecos, had lasting ramifications on the city's development. The Zacatecos did not become friendly indigenous allies or even willing laborers. However, the majority of them did not disrupt the Spanish settlement of the site, which facilitated the survival of Zacatecas in its most vulnerable years of development. The city evolved relatively unscathed from the violence and disruptions of the frontier wars, allowing Spaniards and the foreign Indian population to focus their precious resources and manpower on producing silver and settling the area.

In the absence of a large, local indigenous population to exploit for labor, miners in Zacatecas came to depend on wage-seeking migrant

Indians from communities in central and western Mexico to meet labor needs. While some Spaniards longed for a coerced labor pool, forced labor brought its share of problems, including flight and resistance. Over time miners recognized the need to maintain a skilled and permanent workforce. By 1600, 60 percent to 70 percent of all workers in the viceroyalty were free wage laborers. However, in the mid 1550s, Zacatecas's native population labored under relatively unique conditions for Spanish America.[192] This elite status allowed native peoples to garner some concessions—many of which endured through the colonial period—most important among them being wages and the absence of tribute and labor draft requirements.

Ultimately, Spaniards sought not just laborers but also indigenous settlers and colonists, particularly those familiar with hierarchical organizations and urban institutions. They encouraged the migration of native peoples who would labor at mines and haciendas, help settle the city, build its jails and town halls, and provide its foodstuffs and resources. In turn, Spaniards offered financial incentives to entice Indians to stay. Under these conditions native peoples adopted Zacatecas as their new home, creating permanent communities and eventually assuming the status of urban vecinos. The presence of native peoples as residents and laborers in Zacatecas's fledgling years proved just as important as that of Spaniards in the city's development.

By the mid-1550s, a foreign native population, some settlers, others temporary lodgers, firmly established themselves in the city. According to a count from 1554, three hundred Spaniards resided in the city as vecinos, and another thousand more were itinerants.[193] The count did not include non-Spaniards, but on the basis of previous censuses there is little doubt that the number of Indians matched or outstripped that of Spaniards. Two population settlements developed concurrently, a town of Spaniards, many living with their African and Afro-descended slaves, surrounded by several indigenous communities. Zacatecas's sporadic origins, aggravated by a lack of city planning on the part of Spanish officials and an absence of clearly demarcated boundaries for the indigenous communities, meant that there would always be fluid zones of contact between Indians and Spaniards. Still, within ten years of the discovery of silver, a clear delineation of Spanish and Indian boundaries, which lasted through the colonial period, existed in the city. The parallel development of Spanish and indigenous settlements, however, was not matched in other important milestones, particularly in the evolution of institutions of governance.

The resolution of Zacatecas's labor crisis allowed Spaniards to focus on silver production and civic life. As Spaniards established their municipal government, they gave no thought to the leadership needs of their indigenous settlers, as they considered the native communities religious parishes.

But Zacatecas's foreign Indian population also possessed a long tradition of urban government and the native population would soon adapt Spanish institutions to organize themselves and remedy their lack of governance. As the 1550s drew to a close, and in spite of the lack of formal town status or officials leaders, Zacatecas was as much an indigenous as a Spanish settlement.

2   Ethnic Cohesion and Community Formation, 1560–1608

On the first day of January 1566, Zacatecas's town leaders convened their customary gathering in the city's church. Those present included the alcalde mayor, Juan de Rentería, and four diputados: Cristóbal de Argüello, Pedro de Ahumada Sámano (author of the 1562 account of the Zacateco rebellion), Baltasar de Bañuelos (one of the city's recognized founders), and Alonso Gutiérrez del Campo.¹ Among the many duties of this annual town meeting, the aldermen needed to select a *mayordomo* (foreman) for the church. The mayordomo looked after the church's needs, including the collection of *limosna* (alms). This year they named Hernando de Soto, merchant and vecino of the town, for the job. On the same day the cabildo appointed Ruy García de Ortega, a miner, and Juan de Huidobro, a merchant, as mayordomos of the *cofradías* (confraternities or mutual-aid societies) of the Santísimo Sacramento and Nuestra Señora de la Concepción.² The first recording of the appointment of confraternity officers in the town council minutes dates to 1561, but the ceremonial ritual probably occurred even earlier.³

A few months later, on April 8, the alcalde mayor participated in another ceremony just at the edge of town at the Franciscan convent. On that day Juan de Rentería appeared before the indigenous mayordomos of the *hospital* of San Francisco: Pablo Ximenez, Pedro Hernández de Uexotcingo, Martin Chalco, Juan de Michuai, Juan Aguenel, Pedro de San Francisco, Pedro Çemmac, Diego Jacobo, and Miguel de Santiago. There, in the presence of the alcalde mayor, the *vicario* (vicar) Miguel Hernández de Herrera, and the rector, Cristóbal de Argüello, the indigenous mayordomos declared their desire "to organize and institute the cofradía and *hermandad* (brotherhood) of the Vera Cruz (True Cross)."⁴ While the town possessed at least three Spanish confraternities by this period, the Vera

Cruz held the distinction of being Zacatecas's first indigenous cofradía.[5] In their constitution the *cofrades* (members) offered their motivations for founding the confraternity—to serve god and to perform penance for the many sins committed by their members. There is little doubt that religious piety informed the establishment of the lay brotherhood. But the presence of nine foremen speaks to an indigenous population with more than just religious aspirations; they also had a desire for self-government.

The origins of the lay brotherhoods date to the late medieval period (twelfth and thirteenth centuries). They proliferated in Spain and appeared in Mexico within five years of the fall of Tenochtitlan.[6] The associations functioned primarily as religious mutual-aid societies, assisting members with burial services and fees. They also organized processions and collected charitable contributions. But in mid-sixteenth-century Zacatecas, a period in which both Spaniards and native peoples sought to establish greater lines of governance, the confraternity, including the church itself, also served a political capacity. In the absence of a town hall, for example, Spaniards employed the church for their assembly. Lacking a full-fledged cabildo, the appointment of mayordomos allowed more Spanish vecinos participation in civic government and marked continued progress in the development of the minas as a proper town. Among the native population, the confraternity also operated at more than just a spiritual level. Indigenous confraternities in Zacatecas represented the preliminary stirrings of native government and community formation.

The founding of the first indigenous confraternity surely signaled a welcome trend for the native population of Zacatecas. They not only labored under grueling conditions, but no doubt contended with wrenching emotions ranging from homesickness to nostalgia to isolation. For native peoples, relocation and separation from their ancestral communities to a Spanish urban center, whether voluntary or obligatory, ranked among the most dislocating experiences of the postconquest era. Whereas the rudimentary construction and layout of the traza offered Spaniards some vestiges of an Iberian town, the minas offered native peoples few traces of the hometowns they had left behind. Absent in Zacatecas were the administrative buildings, churches, and bustling marketplaces that characterized the postconquest *altepetl*, or indigenous ethnic state.[7] Mines and the utilitarian refining mills that often bordered the Indian communities surely served as poor substitutes. Instead of living at the center of town, native peoples found themselves relegated to the outskirts. They called their largest community Tlacuitlapan, which literally means "in back of behind something" in Nahuatl, a direct reference to its geographic location behind the convent.[8] But the name was also an apt metaphor for their social marginalization. Bringing a concern to the Spanish foreman of a cuadrilla or a local colonial official instead of a traditional indigenous leader must have been daunting to both native-language and Spanish-speaking Indians. Nor could native peoples take comfort in family or hometown social networks. Large clusters of similar ethnic groups did reside in the town. However, the sharing of similar origins or cultural traits did not necessarily entail close personal or kinship bonds among the migrant population. The generic term *Mexicano*, for example, included residents from several central Mexican altepetls, such as Cholula, Tlaxcala, Toluca, and Texcoco. Even individuals hailing from the same communities probably formed connections after their arrival in the city. Daily life for Zacatecas's early Indian migrants surely proved trying and lonely.

For native peoples and communities to survive and prosper in the minas, Indians needed to pursue support across ethnic lines. They had to create new communities without the organizing structures of the *tlaxilacalli* (the altepetl's neighborhood subunits), juridical autonomy, and a hereditary and civil leadership. As indigenous barrios began to evolve on the outskirts of town, different ethnic groups became physically united by geography. With the passage of time, native peoples began to explore other means to foster indigenous associations and to unify their communities. The urban church, particularly its traditional lay societies, served as a common thread among the ethnically plural native population. In April 1566, as several "Mexicanos" and other unidentified ethnic groups gathered around their indigenous leadership cohort to form their confraternity, Zacatecas's native population took its first steps toward formally establishing themselves as an ethnic and corporate entity.

This chapter explores the factors and conditions that facilitated ethnic cohesion among the ethnically diverse native population from the mid- to late sixteenth century. By the 1550s, the migrant indigenous population was actively adapting to the Spanish urban environment, seeking avenues for community formation and representation within colonial institutions. The evolution of a *república de indios*, that is, barrios of native communities on the outskirts of the city, created spaces in which native peoples could practice both indigenous and Spanish lifeways. Shared housing and labor arrangements further unified the native population through personal and professional ties. The establishment of indigenous confraternities allowed native peoples to develop formal social and political organizations. Rather than becoming completely integrated into the Spanish city, indigenous migrants adopted and negotiated colonial spaces and institutions to re-create central Mexican–style indigenous communities and to establish a corporate Indian status, allowing them to draw on the concessions and protective measures afforded to native peoples under colonial rule. These were small but important first steps toward the development of indigenous civic life in a Spanish town. Yet even as native peoples established roots in the city and began assuming the role of urban vecinos, they continued to identify with their ancestral heritage.

Zacatecas's Repúblicas de Indios

By the early 1560s civic life in the Spanish republic was well under way. The traza was a Spanish stronghold. Spaniards could participate in municipal council meetings, attend services at the parish church, join a confraternity, seek assistance at the hospital, and gather in the main square, the *plaza pública*. A further sign of order could be found in the existence of a probably much-needed jail located on the main street leading up to the Franciscan convent.[9] Still, in a petition from 1563, the cabildo conceded that the population remained "very small and new."[10] The town still lacked a proper town hall, or *casa de cabildo*, although the cabildo decided that year to rent homes in the plaza pública from one Eugenio Díaz de Cisneros for that purpose.[11] The buildings needed improvements. Diputados petitioned for the right to the sale of certain public offices, such as *pregonería pública* (town crier), *almotacén* (inspector of weights and measures), and *correduría* (broker) "to repair and ennoble" crumbling structures.[12] Yet for all its Iberian features, the Spanish city also contained several multiethnic neighborhoods.

Many native peoples lived within indigenous or multiethnic barrios that fell under the jurisdiction of the Spanish city. A criminal case from 1567, for example, describes a residential block in which three Spanish-speaking Mexicas (two men and one woman) occupied adjacent houses.[13] This block probably lay at the edge of the Spanish traza in a barrio that marked the convergence of several ethno-racial groups. These barrios were often the product of population growth, as individuals of all ethnicities acquired and settled on vacant or geographically undesirable land. For example, just to the southeast of Tonalá Chepinque, the waste of the slaughterhouse probably offers some explanation for why this land was still undeveloped in the late seventeenth century and why Spaniards avoided the area.[14] While Indians lived with Spaniards, castas, and Afro-Zacatecans near the traza, these residential arrangements were not always reciprocal.

As Spaniards struggled to build their town, native peoples took advantage of colonial policies to create their own communities. The beginnings of municipal life for native peoples under colonial rule resided in a Spanish imperial policy that envisioned a world of two republics in the Americas, one indigenous and another Spanish.[15] Implemented in New Spain by the 1530s, the repúblicas de indios y españoles, in theory, reinforced the social hierarchy and, most important, from the crown's perspective, protected Indians from Spanish exploitation and the dangerous and degenerate influences of castas, the empire's large population of ethnically diverse individuals.[16] To that effect the Spanish crown enacted a series of measures designed to protect native communities from the intrusions of outsiders.[17] Even with these decrees, segregating ethnic groups in certain social spaces proved impossible. Nonetheless, native peoples living in urban centers took advantage of the ideas and rules governing the repúblicas to develop their own barrios and towns near Spanish cities.[18] While these communities were particularly vulnerable to intrusion from non-Indians, some of these barrios and pueblos found more success in retaining their indigenous character and composition than others. This proved the case in Zacatecas, where, as the Spanish town grew, a república de indios, in the form of several resilient indigenous neighborhoods, evolved on its borders.

Much remains to be known about the origins of Zacatecas's indigenous communities. But as the previous chapter discussed, it appears that as miners, merchants, and officials began the earnest construction of a permanent traza, native peoples settled around the outer perimeter of Spanish construction, ultimately behind the Franciscan convent, a space of about a mile from the main church. This distance, negligible by contemporary urban planning standards, satisfied the Spanish population's desire for an adequate amount of separation between the two republics. Colonial officials often highlighted the native communities' distance and separate geographic space from the traza by using words such as *extramuros* (outside the walls) to describe their location.[19] Still, there was plenty of interaction between both repúblicas. Native peoples often went into town for their own and for their employers' errands, and miners and merchants frequently conducted business and pleasure in the indigenous barrios.

Because neighborhoods developed around mines and mining haciendas, the location of the native settlements also owed a great deal to the discovery and exploitation of silver. In 1587, for example, the cabildo sought to establish a population of workers near a series of newly discovered mines rich in ore. They authorized a decree asking the crown to settle native peoples on the border of the city (*en la comarca*—near mining sites) to assist with silver production.[20] A few years later, another appeal was made for two thousand indigenous laborers.[21] Under these conditions, the location of indigenous settlements probably reflected more circumstance than choice.[22] Ultimately, native communities developed at a distance from the Spanish town, not only because of notions of separate republics but also because it was more convenient for miners to have them settled in the hillsides and near rivers bordering silver refining plants. But while Spaniards wanted some space between themselves and their indigenous workers, they ultimately sought immigrants with long-term plans to reside in the city. In their appeals for additional labor, Spaniards requested "indios vecinos" and asked that the crown "settle" native people in the city ("pueblen indios").[23]

Religious structures also drew individuals, with large indigenous communities forming around convents and hospitals. In the sixteenth century, the Franciscans possessed sole jurisdiction over all native settlers north of the city center. This religious order constructed its church and convent in Zacatecas between 1567 and 1580.[24] The attractions of the Franciscans to the urban native population should not be discounted. Unlike other orders in Zacatecas, the Franciscans retained good relations with their indigenous parishioners throughout the colonial period. The friars would have encouraged their indigenous flock to settle near them. Doing so provided native peoples with some protection from Spanish miners and officials while also offering them religious services and opportunities for social and political organization absent at mining camps and haciendas, such as the hospital the Franciscans established (c. 1558–1564).[25] The hospital not only offered care to the ill and injured but also provided leadership opportunities for indigenous peoples in the form of mayordomos and other functionaries.

A significant number of indigenous communities—Mexicapan, San Francisco, and Tlacuitlapan—developed north of the Spanish traza around the Franciscan convent.[26] Chroniclers credit Mexicapan as the city's first Indian pueblo in the city.[27] Its name reflects the significant presence of central Mexican colonists in the initial migration waves to the city. But of these three, Tlacuitlapan, located in the northwest, developed into the city's largest indigenous community.[28] As mentioned earlier, Spaniards considered this area (now firmly part of the contemporary city's core) quite far from the traza during the colonial period.[29] The barrio served as home to several central Mexican colonists, with neighborhoods of Tlaxcalans, Mexicas, and Texcocans.[30] But these northern communities were not solely central Mexican strongholds. Tarascans settled near the convent as well. The town's name alone bore witness to the ethnic diversity of its neighborhoods. Preconquest tlaxilacalli typically had a name that referred to an ethnic association, such as Mexicapan, or a geographic characteristic.[31] Recall that the Nahuatl term *Tlacuitlapan*, "behind something," literally referred to the site's location behind the convent, but it also speaks to a community that could not describe itself by a specific ethnic affiliation.

The northern barrios mirrored a group of indigenous communities to the south. Religious institutions may have served as the impetus for native peoples to congregate to the south of the traza. Like the Franciscans, the Augustinians developed an indigenous parish (*doctrina*) on their arrival to the area in 1575.[32] A hospital was established fairly early in this period, but it is unclear whether it served the indigenous or the Spanish population.[33] By 1584, two native communities existed on the southern edge of the city, Tonalá (a community of Tarascans) and El Niño (also known as Dulce Nombre de Jesús), founded by Texcocans. Another indigenous settlement (San Josef) developed in the early seventeenth century in the southeast.[34] Of the three settlements, Tonalá (also called San Diego Tonalá) remained the most populous. The much smaller community of El Niño played the role of satellite barrio to Tonalá for most of the colonial period. Known as Tonalá until the late seventeenth century, the name suggests that a group of Tonaltecos founded the community. The Tonaltecos, among the earliest groups to migrate to the city, probably numbered among the many indigenous auxiliaries forced to accompany Spanish expeditions into New Galicia.[35] Tarascans and Tecuexes may also have been among Tonalá's earliest settlers.[36] No doubt the barrio shared its space with several other ethnic groups, as reflected in the town's various name changes. By the mid-sixteenth century a prominent neighborhood of Tlaxcaltecans dominated the Indian cabildo, proudly calling the town the "pueblo de Tlaxcala." Around the same period the community became known as Tonalá Chepinque. The term *Chepinque* may be Nahuatl in origin, referring to rain or something very wet.[37] Like its northern counterpart, the reference to a natural element speaks to the pueblo's multiethnic base.

By the end of the sixteenth century, Zacatecas had a thriving república de indios. Native barrios proliferated to the north and to the south from the main church to the hillsides of the serranía (mountain range). These locations had some advantages. Water apparently flowed in abundance above the monastery of San Francisco, close to the northern settlement of Tlacuitlapan, and in the south a river fronted the communities of Tonalá Chepinque.[38] Both the southern and northern communities were located near the main *caminos* (roads) leading in and out of the town, facilitating travel to other mining sites and allowing for easy access to the various merchants that plied the highways. At this point in time, these native communities were barrios subject to the jurisdiction of the Spanish cabildo. It would not be until 1609 that these communities would become self-governing towns.

Urban Life in the República de Indios

The barrios and neighborhoods within Zacatecas's república de indios reflected new urban realities for their indigenous inhabitants. In this period their communities had no juridical autonomy. Many native peoples lived on small plots of land in unconventional household arrangements or at haciendas. They labored at mines and worshipped at small chapels or in open spaces without even a "decent altar."[39] Non-Indians frequently crossed their path, and facets of Spanish culture were pervasive. However, over time, native peoples became skillful at adapting Spanish urban customs and practices as they maintained native spaces and identities. The república de indios in Zacatecas looked different from its central Mexican counterpart, but it retained an indigenous character. Non-Indians did not live in significant numbers in the native communities, and the migrant population successfully re-created some of the features of their hometowns.

The native peoples who settled in the indigenous barrios were colonists with the same desire as their Spanish counterparts to establish long-term roots. Consequently, unlike draft laborers in other parts of the empire who lived in rented lodgings, Zacatecas's native settlers, like proper vecinos, sought to own lots and build houses. On the basis of the haphazard development of the Spanish traza, it seems doubtful that colonial officials played much of a role in the creation of the native communities. Rather, individual land grants (along with squatting) were standard practice in the chaotic period of urban development that followed the founding of the minas. A 1609 proclamation from the visitador of Nueva Galicia, Gaspar de la Fuente, reflects a typical allotment. He ordered the cabildo to provide Indians seeking to settle in the city with comfortable sites with sufficient space to "live and make maize fields."[40] Average plot size varied by period and location. In 1631 Francisco Domingo petitioned to sell half his landholdings in the Altos de Calvario, an indigenous neighborhood near Mexicapan. The lot for sale, representative of a typical plot size in the seventeenth century, amounted to seventy *varas* in length and seventy varas in width (an approximate area of 4,900 square Spanish yards).[41] In this early period, local and viceregal officials distributed grants under favorable conditions. Zacatecas possessed a small population and an abundance of vacant land. However, tensions and conflicts over property and boundaries between native peoples, Spaniards, and castas often ensued when mining booms generated a rush for land.

New urban indigenous colonists with no possession of ancestral land understood the importance of having their lots, purchased or received, recognized by Spanish officials. Many native people had some experience with these legal procedures in their home communities. Those who procured vacant lands petitioned the cabildo for permission to build and register, while savvy sellers and buyers understood the necessity of maintaining paperwork related to land transactions. In a will from 1601, Juana Ana stated that she had maintained all the documents related to the ownership of her lands, even though these efforts "caused her much poverty."[42] The Nahuatl-speaking executors of Juana Ana's will requested that the documents they presented be translated into Spanish by two *nahuatlatos* (interpreters of indigenous languages) so its provisions would be clearly understood. Similarly, before he sold his home in 1631, Domingo García was quick to receive his *carta de venta*, or bill of sale. In a land dispute from 1667, Ana de Aguirre, an indigenous vecina of the city, submitted the *escritura de ventas* (bill of sale) to the Spanish corregidor in support of her claims, including the documents of both Ana María, the Indian woman who sold her the house, and of Juan Bautista, the previous owner before her.[43] Native vecinos' preoccupation with securing their property through Spanish administrative procedures illustrates their fluency in the management of urban properties.

On these lots native peoples built small, humble dwellings. Their adobe, clay, or even straw buildings constituted the majority of the barrios' infrastructures. When speaking of their houses, Indians and Spaniards referred to them using a Spanish term, *jacal*, derived from the Nahuatl loanword *xacalli*.[44] The earliest description of an indigenous structure suggests that Indians built their houses in a style similar to those in the Valley of Mexico. In 1602, the owner, Pablo Miguel, a migrant from Texcoco, stated that the house had an entrance of cut stone fashioned "a lo Mexicano."[45] As in central Mexico native peoples organized house complexes around separate single story living quarters or aposentos, small and narrow rooms of about four to six feet.[46] Houses might include a stable, a cultivable field, and a *tunal*, a plot of land containing cactus bearing prickly pears. In spite of differences in size and composition, these living structures bore a resemblance to those of their home communities.

These humble settings do not necessarily speak to socioeconomic conditions particular to native peoples. Some wealthy mine owners maintained elegant city dwellings on urban lots in the principal parts of town, near the main church and the casa de cabildo.[47] But there appeared to be no significant difference between indigenous houses and those of the urban nonelite. The majority of middling Spaniards and castas, like native peoples, resided in single-story adobe homes, usually attached to a shop. In addition, many miners lived at haciendas de minas in conditions that were similar to those found in the Indian communities.[48] Living conditions in Zacatecas were comparable or even better than those of other mining towns. In Potosí, native peoples resided in indigenous neighborhoods or rancherías, in humble circular dwellings made of adobe and straw called *buhíos*.[49] Repartimiento laborers occupied quarters where, according to the chronicler Bartolomé de Arzáns Orsúa y Veloa, between "twenty and thirty indios lived in rooms so tiny that they barely held a bed, a hearth, and eight to ten drinking vessels."[50] Arzáns Orsúa y Veloa's snapshot of housing accommodations offers a striking example of the different environments under which itinerant workers and permanent settlers operated. As vecinos, Indians in Zacatecas had the opportunity and incentive to acquire their own houses, lots, and planting fields.

Initially both the northern and southern barrios, like the Spanish traza, lacked much in the way of urban infrastructure aside from houses. In this period the most significant buildings, the convents and hospitals, belonged to the religious orders. But over time each barrio built its own capilla. The large ornate churches that dominated towns and villages in central and western Mexico never appeared in Zacatecas's native pueblos. Those chapels and ruins that remain today show the small and humble composition of these early edifices (see Figure 2.1). In general, native peoples constructed their capillas of stone or adobe with unadorned facades, a few small windows, and a simple bell tower. The structures had equally sparse and plain interiors. Mexicapan's chapel, for example, consisted of one long, narrow worship area with one side altar and a small loft for the choir. While humble architectural structures, the capillas later became the center of each community, serving as proxies for town halls.

In the sixteenth century, the marketplace constituted the center of urban living. In 1575, the Spanish cabildo officially designated a site for the "tiangui[z] y mercado" (marketplace) of the minas in the plaza pública.[51] Ostensibly, Zacatecas's tianguiz could not compare with the large fabled markets of central Mexico, such as the one at Tlatelolco made famous by the Spanish conqueror Bernal Díaz del Castillo. Still, at these venues native

FIGURE 2.1. Exterior: Capilla of Tlacuitlapan. Photo taken by author in 2007.

peoples sold foodstuffs, particularly grains, chicken, and fruits; mundane merchandise; cloth; and even items directly used in mining, such as wax. While men certainly worked at the tianguiz, Inés García, a migrant from Mexico City who traded in grain, was one of many indigenous women in Zacatecas who peddled their wares there.[52] In a broader sense, commercial centers served as the social nexus for the indigenous population. Even Spaniards recognized the market's important function as a central indigenous meeting place. They ordered the announcement of all official proclamations there by a nahuatlato in *mexicano* and *tarasca* (terms Spaniards used to refer to Nahuatl and Purépecha).[53]

The indigenous barrios themselves also functioned as sites of commercial, often clandestine, activities. Native peoples were active participants in the informal markets that flourished in Zacatecas, engaging in resale commerce or hawking contraband items. They also conducted a brisk exchange in wine, merchandise, and foodstuffs in their barrios and on the roads to the mines. Homes were hubs of commercial activities. Indians often sold goods out of their houses. In 1567, authorities accused Francisco Soto, a migrant from central Mexico living near the traza, of selling maize to Indians and castas from his house.[54] Merchants often brought their wares directly to the homes of native peoples and slaves, and even to the mines themselves. The oidor Hernando Martínez de la Marcha attempted to control the amount of merchandise being sold privately and to cuadrillas by forbidding any transactions outside the tianguiz.[55] The oidor's concern lay in the large number of items circulating without *postura*, the authorized price of an item assigned by the authorities.

The circulation of legal items constituted only a small sector of the informal economy in the república de indios. Some shops, especially those located on the road to the mines, functioned as places where native people and blacks sold and traded items prohibited by colonial authorities, such as wine and small amounts of ore. It was there too that indigenous peoples could buy silver and mercury without paying the royal tax. Other illegal activities included the pawning of silver, gold, and other stolen items. Spanish authorities, mindful of lost profits and excises, periodically tried to prohibit the establishment of shops beyond the city center, but there is no evidence that these directives met with much success.[56] Being located in the "back" of town and away from the eyes of colonial officials had its benefits. All this commercial activity illustrates how the urban indigenous population not only quickly adapted to the money economy but also exploited it to their advantage.

As they walked through the markets or the native towns, Indians, Spaniards, and individuals of African descent heard a variety of indigenous languages. For native peoples one of the most tangible changes of urban life involved the prominence of Spanish over native languages in secular proceedings, religious functions, and social settings. However, city living did not necessarily require native peoples to learn Spanish or to stop using native languages. Recent studies suggest that the social and economic conditions of colonial rule provided incentives for individuals of all ethnicities to become fluent in several languages.[57] Sixteenth-century Zacatecas remained a multilingual town in spite of the fact that Castilian served as the official language of the traza and at the haciendas de minas. Of the many indigenous languages that were spoken in the town, Nahuatl and Purépecha, not surprisingly, prevailed. The pervasiveness of these two languages in the town reflected the dominance of migrants from central and western Mexico in the late sixteenth century. By this time, Nahuatl (or Mexicano, as it came to be called) had already become the indigenous lingua franca of the multilingual province of New Galicia. In a report to the crown in 1576, a local official from the hinterland town of Fresnillo noted the diversity of languages among "the indios Chichimecos," but claimed that they all mainly spoke "la mexicana."[58] Writing in the early seventeenth century, the Spanish chronicler Domingo Lázaro de Arregui insisted that the majority of Indians in the province either spoke or possessed familiarity with the "mexicano" language.[59]

The persistence of a large group of native peoples who spoke only Nahuatl necessitated the town's continued use of interpreters. Spanish dependence on translators dates to Tolosa's use of Cazcanes to communicate with the Zacatecos. During the city's early rush and initial founding, other native peoples served as unofficial interpreters in ecclesiastical matters, at mining sites, and in interactions with colonial authorities. For example, in a criminal case from 1567, local officials asked the husband of a witness, a mestizo who spoke Nahuatl, to act as the official interpreter for the accused, the aforementioned Mexica Francisco Soto.[60] Other studies indicate that individuals of mixed ancestry played critical roles in translating or serving as cultural mediators between native peoples and Spaniards, particularly in more peripheral areas.[61] In Zacatecas, a growing Indian population that took an active role in Spanish activities and legal transactions called for a more formal approach. In 1577, the Spanish cabildo appointed Francisco Jiménez as the town's first official interpreter to assist in the "Indian cases that ordinarily occur in these mines."[62] Pedro Francisco Granados took over the role after Jiménez. The municipal council unceremoniously fired Granados in 1609, only to grant him a reprieve and reappointment in 1619. In the interim, the cabildo, still in dire need of a translator, hired Alonso Carreño to serve as the city's nahuatlato.[63] Municipal records indicate that the Spanish cabildo employed a native-language interpreter through the 1650s, a sign that a large segment of the population lacked fluency in Castilian (*castellano*) or spoke only Nahuatl, and that new native-language migrants continued to arrive in the city in substantial numbers.

Spaniards and native peoples alike employed interpreters in transactions that related to official or private affairs. An Audiencia decree from 1563 required the presence of two interpreters at the testimony of all indigenous witnesses.[64] *Pregoneros*, or town criers, such as Francisco, described as an Indian Ladino who spoke both "castellano" and "mexicano," served as interpreters.[65] He and men like him announced local and viceregal decrees in Spanish and Nahuatl in the traza and in the indigenous barrios.[66] Interpreters stood in attendance at Spanish visitas and reviews of Indian confraternities and town councils. They also kept busy translating documents and constitutions created by these groups. Native peoples utilized translators to record any proceedings needing approval from the Spanish cabildo. Translators also presided at more mundane events such as the execution of wills or the sale of houses. The majority of official nahuatlatos were Spaniards. How accurately they conveyed indigenous statements and concerns is unknown. Yet the presence of interpreters allowed native peoples, particularly those Indians with little or no Spanish fluency, greater participation in the civic life of both their communities and the Spanish city.

There is little documentary evidence that Spanish officials accommodated Zacatecas's other native language groups. From the 1550s to at least 1577, in response to the large number of individuals from western Mexico, royal officials had authorized the services of a nahuatlato to announce important proclamations in Nahuatl and Purépecha.[67] But in 1577, in a trend that continued through the colonial period, the cabildo charged Jiménez, the first official interpreter, only with faithfully translating from Mexican to Castilian. Yet significant numbers of native peoples from Michoacán continued to arrive and reside in the city, and a report from 1608 noted the continued presence of Tarascan speakers.[68] Whether religious and civil officials possessed fluency in other native languages remains unknown. Spanish officers perhaps relied on unofficial translators such as other native peoples to help them communicate with speakers of other languages such as Cazcan and Tecuexe. Probably several indigenous individuals or low-level Spanish officials served as language liaisons to native-language speakers. These interpreters, while lacking official status, were not without influence, and they created, as Yanna Yannakakis has argued for similar settings, "spaces for intercultural mediation."[69]

The lack of multilanguage interpreters speaks to the perseverance of spoken Nahuatl among the city's native population. Nahuatl became an especially useful and effective lingua franca, providing another means to unite the town's ethnically plural indigenous population.[70] More Nahuatl than Spanish speakers walked Zacatecas's streets in the sixteenth century. Indigenous peoples who spoke other native languages could probably settle into their job sites and communities just as easily if they learned Spanish or Mexicano. This would not be the case as society matured in Zacatecas and as native peoples who sought social and economic advancement needed fluency in Castilian. But incentives also existed for Spaniards to learn native languages.[71] In a document from 1602, two Indian executors of a will requested the city's Spanish *alcaide* (jailer) as one of their translators. According to the executors, the alcaide "understood very well the Mexican language."[72] In the early seventeenth century the large size of the indigenous population offered a compelling motivation for Spaniards, who came into daily contact with Indians, to attain some fluency in native languages. In this period of high labor demands, for example, miners and foremen could speak directly to workers or new recruits. Ultimately, while only a small number of Spaniards learned Nahuatl, their efforts signal their awareness of the large number and integral presence of native peoples in both the Spanish and the Indian repúblicas.

Labor and Ethnic Cohesion

For the majority of native peoples in the república de indios daily life revolved around mining production or an urban occupation. In Zacatecas, living in town went hand in hand with working in town.[73] These jobs provided native peoples with the income opportunities necessary to support themselves and their families. Urban labor brought Indians into more frequent and prolonged contact with ethnic others. At job sites, Indians often worked side by side with enslaved Africans, castas, or middling, as in nonelite, Spaniards. Participation in the money economy brought Indians into the Spanish orbit. Remuneration in wages often forced Indians to procure goods and resources in the city's urban markets. But urban labor arrangements also served to unify the greater indigenous community in this period. In particular, mines and refining plants, often considered acculturating institutions, served as vehicles for ethnic cohesion.[74] In sixteenth-century Zacatecas, the sheer number of native peoples and their dominance in certain areas of the workforce promoted social and professional ties among the ethnically diverse indigenous population.

Silver-mining plants proliferated around the city. Some were located within the indigenous communities. In 1562, thirty-four haciendas de minas operated in Zacatecas. Men owned the majority of these complexes, but the records note the presence of two female Spanish *hacenderas*, Teresa de Morales and Doña Ana del Corral.[75] Haciendas de minas varied in size and condition. Modest or thriving enterprises usually consisted of a series of structures and patios or courtyards within a walled quadrilateral compound near a stream or a river. The main structure usually consisted of a long narrow building divided into multiple sections. The hacienda was not solely a commercial site; it also served as home to owners, overseers, workers, and their families. The running of the complex required adequate sleeping quarters, offices, and kitchens for the large number of individuals it housed (at some sites, over one hundred people). Around the main building a series of smaller structures served as storage sheds for tools, equipment, and machinery. Stables abutted the buildings. There, several corrals housed the hacienda's animals, including the horses and mules necessary to the refining process. Around these buildings, workers refined ore in patios or washed metals in lavaderos. Outside the complex some miners built small chapels so their employees and families could attend religious services near the grounds.

While mining complexes were owned and operated by Spaniards, they were primarily indigenous sites. In the mines men served as excavators (*barreteros*) or carriers (*tenateros*). Barreteros located and cut ores with a crowbar or pick. Tenateros hauled the extracted metal in large bags up ladders and shafts to the surface. At haciendas native men prepared the ore for the reduction process, pulverizing it, processing it in the mill, preparing the amalgamation mixture, and later washing the metal.[76] Indigenous carpenters and craftsmen made and serviced tools and machinery. Native women were present throughout the mining complex as well. Market women frequented mining sites, selling food and other products. While haciendas often counted women as members of cuadrillas, there is no archival evidence that native women in Zacatecas worked below ground in the mines.[77] In Potosí indigenous women refined ore in small furnaces. Along with children they also worked in refineries straining pounded metals and searching for any leftover pieces of ore near mine entrances.[78] In Zacatecas women may have engaged in similar activities, but the majority of them labored at the hacienda itself, cleaning the living quarters and preparing food for the workers and their family members.

Wives often accompanied their spouses to their work sites, with entire families often settling at mining complexes. Single women did not constitute as significant a segment of the workforce in the sixteenth century as they did in the late eighteenth century, but widows frequently remained in the city on the death of their husbands. For example, a 1623 *padrón*, or census, of the marital status of "Indian naboríos" in the nearby mining real of Pinos offers a more detailed description of the number and civil status of women residing at the town's fifteen haciendas.[79] According to the count, more than half (178, or 54 percent) of the Indian laborers were married. Along with these spouses, the census taker also included in the count eight widows living at the hacienda of El Espíritu Santo, bringing the total number of women to 186, or more than a third (37 percent) of a total population of 510. In Zacatecas, a 1622 ecclesiastical census of fourteen mining haciendas adjoining the city found a total of 644 men and women working in the cuadrillas of the haciendas and the mines.[80] In contrast, documents from this period do not indicate a substantial presence of Afro and Afro-descendent women at mining haciendas.

The urban core also provided occupational opportunities for native men and women to interact.[81] Indian tailors, shoemakers, carpenters, and ironsmiths catered to both indigenous and casta populations.[82] Indians frequently occupied themselves with new construction and repairs in and around the Spanish traza. For example, in 1577, Indians received three reales a day for hauling rocks to construction sites.[83] They also found work related to municipal operations, serving as town criers or letter carriers (*indios correos*), transmitting important information between officials in Zacatecas and Guadalajara.[84] A significant number of native people also labored on the outskirts of town. In 1608, a colonial official reported that several Indians worked of their "own free will" in cattle ranches, where they earned fifty to seventy pesos a year.[85] Women offered laundry and food services, and labored as day domestics in Spanish homes.

While other ethnoracial groups labored in the city, native peoples constituted the largest population employed in mining (and hence the overall workforce) from the 1550s to the 1630s. Recall that although some miners had initially placed black slaves to work in the mines, from an economic standpoint it was preferable to use slaves in agricultural work, domestic servitude, or the less dangerous refining process.[86] With a large number of black slaves occupied in nonmining tasks, the burden of silver extraction and reduction fell on native peoples. A 1597 inspection of the greater Zacatecas district (the city and eleven of its larger satellite mining centers) highlights the predominance of native peoples in mining production. In the Zacatecas-Pánuco zone, indigenous peoples constituted close to 90 percent of the workforce (88 percent or 1,014 of the 1,144 total).[87] Slaves accounted for only 11 percent (130 of 1,144) of all mine workers. The demographic superiority of the native population is reflected in an earlier population count from 1572 in which Indians outnumbered their black counterparts by three to one. While these estimates are not always reliable, that earlier count reported 1,500 Indians, 500 black slaves, and 300 Spaniards.[88] Even taking into account the number of blacks employed outside mining production, the 1597 report illustrates the continued demographic imbalance between the two population groups.

The indigenous composition of the workforce in Zacatecas was typical of the late sixteenth century. Within the Zacatecas district, ten other mining sites demonstrated a preference for indigenous laborers. Slaves dominated the workforce only in the northwestern mining town of Nieves. At four mines there was no slave labor at all.[89] In the Guadalajara area, indigenous workers outnumbered slaves 83.6 percent to 16.4 percent. Of the fifteen centers in the Guadalajara district that listed information, only one site, Chiametla, had more slaves than indigenous workers. Three had no slaves, and six had fewer than ten.[90] In the same report, seven mining sites in the Guadiana district in Nueva Vizcaya reported no slave labor.[91] Enslaved labor was probably not as needed in areas near Guadalajara and Nueva Vizcaya, where forced labor practices existed. Nor did miners in Zacatecas appear concerned with bringing more slaves to the area. In the same report from 1597, when asked about labor needs, miners requested an additional 776 indigenous laborers, but no slaves or repartimiento Indians.[92] Only the combined mining complex of Charcas and La Habana, which at the time had only one enslaved worker, indicated a preference for slave labor.[93] Little evidence, in fact, exists of systematic, planned importation of slaves to Zacatecas aside from a 1637 letter from the crown acknowledging Spanish complaints of unexploited mines because of the lack of indigenous laborers and African slaves. The crown responded by ordering that four hundred black slaves from Veracruz be sent to the city and divided among owners for mine work. Officials also promised to send more slaves at a later date.[94] There is no evidence that these slaves ever arrived in the city. Instead, the majority of slave trafficking in Zacatecas occurred on a small or individual level. Numerous notarial records document the buying and selling of one, perhaps two, slaves per transaction.[95] Thus, labor arrangements in many mining districts in this period facilitated the bringing together of large groups of native peoples.

In certain colonial settings, the ethnic composition of the workforce facilitated interethnic exchanges. Work sites "exposed" individuals to peoples of diverse backgrounds, encouraging cross-cultural exchange and ultimately mestizaje.[96] But mines, refining plants, and urban markets were also sites of indigenous peoples and practices. Censuses and inventories point to a mining labor force (and overall population) dominated by native peoples. Indians labored side by side, depending on one another as they completed dangerous or tedious mine work. Many lived together at haciendas, places with significant populations of Indian women and children. This is not to say that harmony existed among all groups or individuals. Fights based on ethnic or work rivalries, as will be discussed in Chapter 3, occurred with some frequency. Still the common experience of laboring together created some solidarity. And the limited or smaller presence of other ethnic groups created space for the perpetuation of indigenous practices and languages, particularly Nahuatl. Urban labor arrangements, although exploitative, did foster ethnic cohesion, much as another Spanish institution, the cofradía, or confraternity, also facilitated more official bonds between native peoples.

Cofradías and Community Organization

Native communities and urban labor arrangements created indigenous spaces in a Spanish town and promoted ethnic cohesion among the city's diverse indigenous groups. Yet indigenous communities and solidarity did not translate into official recognition of indigenous jurisdictions or privileges. In this period, the native barrios were subdivisions of the Spanish city, not municipal entities in their own right.[97] Moreover, within the multiethnic urban context, native peoples risked being grouped together with mestizos, African slaves, and castas, amorphous groups within Spanish society with few rights and little protection.[98] Native peoples wanted to become urban vecinos, but they also sought to maintain their indigenous identities and rights. To do so, they needed to develop an "Indian" identity—to be recognized as a corporate group—in the eyes of colonial officials. Taking a cue from their Spanish counterparts, they founded an exclusively indigenous confraternity, thereby adopting a colonial institution to engage in civic life as urban vecinos and to delineate their ethnic status from among the nonindigenous population.[99]

Many of the central Mexican immigrants in the minas may not have belonged to a cofradía in their hometown. Indian confraternities evolved more slowly in central Mexico, often at the insistence of religious officials.[100] However, this institution developed more quickly in the periphery or in urban areas where there were weak mechanisms of governance and society.[101] In these environments—peripheral, urban, or both—confraternities functioned as much as sociopolitical as religious organizations.[102] It is unsurprising that the institution had such a strong appeal in Zacatecas, which in the sixteenth century remained a fringe area composed of indigenous migrants lacking the cohesion of an ethnic state. In Zacatecas it was the native population from western Mexico that took the lead in founding an exclusively indigenous sodality, finding in the adoption of the Spanish institution a means to unify and re-create indigenous communities and identities in a colonial urban context. In the time period from 1554 to 1609, when there were no formal native towns or official indigenous leaders, the confraternity of La Santa Vera Cruz provided Zacatecas's migrant population with a vehicle to form a corporate identity, assume governance positions, present group petitions, and continue to use Nahuatl for social and administrative purposes. The institution also provided prospective native leaders with the experience and training that they later required to serve on indigenous cabildos.[103] As the colonial period progressed, these powerful sociopolitical organizations would continue to play an important role in indigenous government.

The founding of the indigenous confraternity of La Santa Vera Cruz occurred in conjunction with the religious activities of the Franciscan order.[104] Some early accounts claim that a few Franciscans accompanied Tolosa's expeditionary party.[105] But archival evidence places them in the city around the late 1550s. In the midst of the early rush and then chaotic settlement, miners and local officials showed little interest in the spiritual needs of their labor force or the development of religious instruction, organizations, or institutions. The religious presence was limited to a few secular clerics.[106] The Franciscans established their parish near the native settlements that became the pueblo of Tlacuitlapan, taking over the preaching and administration of the majority of Zacatecas's indigenous residents.[107]

In other areas of northern Mexico, often violent and coercive religious efforts to convert indigenous subjects to Christianity and Spanish lifeways destabilized and destroyed the lifeways of the autochthonous native populations.[108] But in Zacatecas, the Franciscans catered to an indigenous population experienced with both Christian doctrine and urban living. They focused their efforts on encouraging their members to be good Christians by attending church and following religious teachings. The disparate ethnic and linguistic base of the indigenous population probably posed the greatest challenge to the friars. Unlike the Valley of Mexico, where the existing altepetl served as the basis for parish organization, in Zacatecas the jurisdiction of the Franciscan doctrina encompassed several distinct indigenous settlements as well as laborers residing at nearby mining haciendas.

The indigenous population collaborated with the Franciscans and utilized religious institutions, such as hospitals and confraternities, to build community.[109] The exact date of the founding of the hospital of San Francisco is unknown, but it was probably operating by the late 1550s.[110] The hospital catered to the needs of the local population, attending to routine illnesses along with injuries arising from mine labor. But hospitals functioned in more than a medical capacity. In some areas of New Spain, these institutions became the first mechanisms for community organization.[111] In Zacatecas, the hospital developed into a mutual-aid association, replete with an indigenous administration and hierarchy. By 1564 the hospital possessed a leadership group and kept membership records in a manner similar to a formal organization.[112] It provided a site where native peoples could meet, air their grievances, or ask for assistance from fellow community members.

The hospital provided the impetus for the development of an avowed mutual-aid society.[113] In 1566, with the support of the Franciscans, native peoples founded Zacatecas's first exclusively indigenous cofradía, La Santa Vera Cruz, in the barrio of Tlacuitlapan, at that time widely referred to as San Francisco. La Vera Cruz was a classic "hospital cofradía," developing in relation to and maintaining connections with the hospital.[114] Although the role of the Franciscans in establishing the confraternity cannot be discounted, the impetus and creation of the organization was an indigenous aspiration and project. A fragment of a membership list from the summer of 1564 suggests that native peoples established the brotherhood before receiving the formal approval from or recognition of secular Spanish authorities. A few years later, in 1568, native peoples established another indigenous confraternity, Limpia Concepción, in Tlacuitlapan.

The cofradías' constitutions reflect the cooperation and solidarity that had developed among Zacatecas's diverse ethnic groups. Limpia Concepción was established by Mexicas, Tlaxcalans, Tarascans, and native peoples from other areas of New Galicia.[115] Ethnic migrants from Jalisco, the Tonaltecos, founded the Vera Cruz. Tonaltecos were among the first indigenous groups to migrate to the city of Zacatecas and were familiar with the Franciscans and their institutions. While the Tonaltecos played a seminal role in establishing the cofradía, the organization did not remain the domain of one exclusive ethnic group. Migrants from central and western Mexico quickly swelled the membership ranks, such as Juan, from Toluca, and Francisco, from Michoacán. The constitution declared that "the cofradía accepted all the *naturales* [Indians] who wished to become *cofrades* [members] whether they be Tarascans or Tonaltecos" (again, notice the focus on groups from western Mexico).[116] The surviving member list from the official founding year of 1566 indicates that individual ancestral identities did not seem to be a barrier to membership, as it was rarely noted. When the records noted ethnic identity, it represented the three regions associated with indigenous migration in this period: central Mexico, Michoacán, and Guadalajara.[117] There is evidence to suggest that over time, some cofradías became strongholds of certain groups.[118] By 1595, Limpia Concepción was run by Tarascans, while the Santa Vera Cruz, as we shall see, and another indigenous confraternity, Nuestra Señora de la Asunción, were under the control of Mexicas. Still, while certain ethnic groups dominated individual confraternities, they remained fairly open to other native people. The cofradía was inclusive only in relation to the native population. Membership in this period was closed to individuals of Spanish, African, or mixed descent.[119]

The multiethnic membership shows how Zacatecas's confraternity had a different function and purpose from those of central Mexico. In central areas, native peoples formed cofradías to assist with burial costs and to promote ethnic solidarity among a primarily homogeneous population.[120] But Zacatecas's cofradías, following the patterns of lay brotherhoods in peripheral areas, focused more on the living than the dead. The organizations strove to promote an inclusive membership policy to unify and create a corporate indigenous body.[121] In Zacatecas's urban context, cofradías re-created aspects of the preconquest tlaxilacalli, serving as proxies for the support systems (e.g., municipal councils, kinship networks) found in migrants' hometowns that remained undeveloped in Zacatecas in this period. The operations of the Santa Vera Cruz illustrate how cofradías played a critical role in creating community among the ethnically diverse native population.

The inclusive membership policy meant that the Santa Vera Cruz drew from a wide range of indigenous society, with no restrictions based on sex, age, or class. The cofradía welcomed into the organization women such as María and Luisa in 1567, and children, often listed on the rolls as "un niño" (a child). In Mexico City, according to Jonathan Truitt, a constitution from 1552 mentioned the appointment of four women "cihuatepixque (women in charge of people)" who may have been mirrored by four male deputies.[122] In Zacatecas, the documents have yet to reveal whether women possessed any official roles in the Vera Cruz.[123] The constitution allowed them to participate in processions as long as they did not flagellate themselves. However informal their roles, women proved indispensable to the survival of the sodality. In 1566, they constituted 50 percent of the new members for that year (twenty-seven of fifty-four) and archival fragments from the years 1629 to 1630 indicate that they composed one-third of the new members' ranks.[124] Women of all ages and civil statuses joined the organization. Married women enrolled in the cofradía, such as María, "wife of Simon." In 1566, two-thirds of the female cofrades were single or widowed, including several mother and daughter couples like "Ana and her mother." The sodality provided a social network for the female population, providing recent migrants with a sense of community; assisting widows coping with the loss of a loved one to a mining fatality or epidemic; and offering support to wives, mothers, and sisters during the temporary sojourns of husbands, sons, and brothers to other mining sites.

The 1566 membership list also provides other insights into the social and demographic composition of indigenous society in this period. Naming patterns highlight the common, nonelite origins of the migrant population. Only one man from Michoacán, Alonso, a person who provided no surname, identified himself with the Spanish honorific title *don*. No other member had a prestigious title or surname. Most had a Spanish patronymic. Of the twenty-seven female members, two had patronymics (Juana Jiménez and Juana Gómez), and one had two Spanish first names (Marta Marina). Of the fifteen men who had two appellations, thirteen men had Spanish surnames. Only two men had a second indigenous name, Pedro Atle (whose surname meant "nothing" in Nahuatl) and Miguel Quiau (*quiahuitl*, or "rain"). The almost negligible percentages of indigenous names (two of fifty-four), along with the high number of native peoples listed without a second name (thirty-three of fifty-four), suggests a migrant population whose members discarded their indigenous names in the urban context.[125] However, it appears that indigenous surnames did not impede individuals from attaining important leadership positions within Indian organizations. Two men in the confraternity's initial leadership cohort possessed Nahuatl surnames, Pedro Çemmac and Juan Michuai[n].[126]

Because of the humble origins of the migrant population, rank did not play a significant role in the composition of the lay brotherhood. Members generally contributed the same amount of dues irrespective of social status but not gender. According to the constitution, men paid three pesos and women paid two.[127] While less social disparity existed between members and leaders in the sixteenth century, certain groups or individuals emerged as dominant figures.[128] When mentioned in the sources, the confraternity's mayordomos had names that suggest a higher status than their peers, that is they had a Spanish surname, either a patronymic or that of an important individual such as Cortés.[129] More telling, the ethnic composition of the leadership pool foreshadowed the emerging role of Indians from central Mexico in indigenous sociopolitical organization. Even though the Tonaltecos founded the cofradía, most of its leaders identified as "mexicanos" or "naturales de Mexico." The dominance of indigenous organization and institutions in Zacatecas by socially mobile Nahuas continued through the colonial period.

As native peoples assembled at the hospital, and later in their own capillas for their meetings, they often discussed and recorded community events in Nahuatl. At the official level, Castilian was the formal or public language of the confraternity. The native leadership, cognizant of the Spanish context of their environment, produced several important documents, including the constitution and lists of expenses and accounts in Castilian. However, Nahuatl remained the language of communication between members. The Vera Cruz cofradía kept its records in two distinct books, one for enrollment of members and another to log the monthly collection and expenditure of funds.[130] An account book along with a few loose *fojas* (pages) are all that remain of the Vera Cruz's proceedings in Castilian. What became of the other documents? Extant sources suggest that the native leadership recorded the confraternity's proceedings in both Nahuatl and Spanish through the early seventeenth century.[131] As late as 1618 the Franciscans, who periodically inspected the books, noted how native peoples maintained a series of ledgers with the sodality's activities in the "lengua mexicana."[132] Archival fragments speak to the continued entry of members in Nahuatl. Pasted on the rear cover of the confraternity's *libro de cofradías* is a directory of members from August to September 1564. Written entirely in Nahuatl, it predates the official founding of the Vera Cruz given in the constitution by two years, suggesting that it may date to the time of the hospital. Further fragmentary membership rolls in Nahuatl appear in the Vera Cruz's books for the years 1641, 1643, and 1644 (see Figure 2.2).[133] It is highly likely that both organizations, the hospital and the sodality, kept some proceedings in Nahuatl, particularly those produced for internal consumption just as they maintained a set of minutes in Spanish for colonial authorities. One article of the sodality's constitution, for example, stated that the cofradía had the right to translate its constitution from "the Spanish to the Mexican language."[134] This practice also explains why after 1566 there is no complete extant membership list for an entire year. The remaining reports figure among the missing Nahuatl ledgers.[135]

The use of Nahuatl within the organization reflected the membership base, as it mirrored local conditions. The majority of cofrades in this period spoke native languages, Nahuatl had become the indigenous lingua franca of Zacatecas, and central Mexicans dominated the organization's hierarchy. The continued ubiquity of Nahuatl within the local population and the recurring influx of native-language-speaking migrants explains the language's reach within the organization through the mid-seventeenth century. In the 1630s, the cofradía still paid eight pesos for the service of a notary and an official interpreter, and colonial officials continued to communicate with indigenous leaders with the assistance of a translator.[136] The native-language base of the Vera Cruz confraternity provided Nahuatl-speaking Indians, natives and migrants alike, another venue to engage in civic life within an indigenous context.

Cofradías as Civic and Governance Institutions

Although many of the brotherhood's activities were religious in nature, the administration of the sodality extended to sociopolitical matters as well. It had the structure and formality of an official organization. In Zacatecas these organizations attempted not only to unify the diverse migrant population but also to re-create the mechanisms (pre- and postconquest)

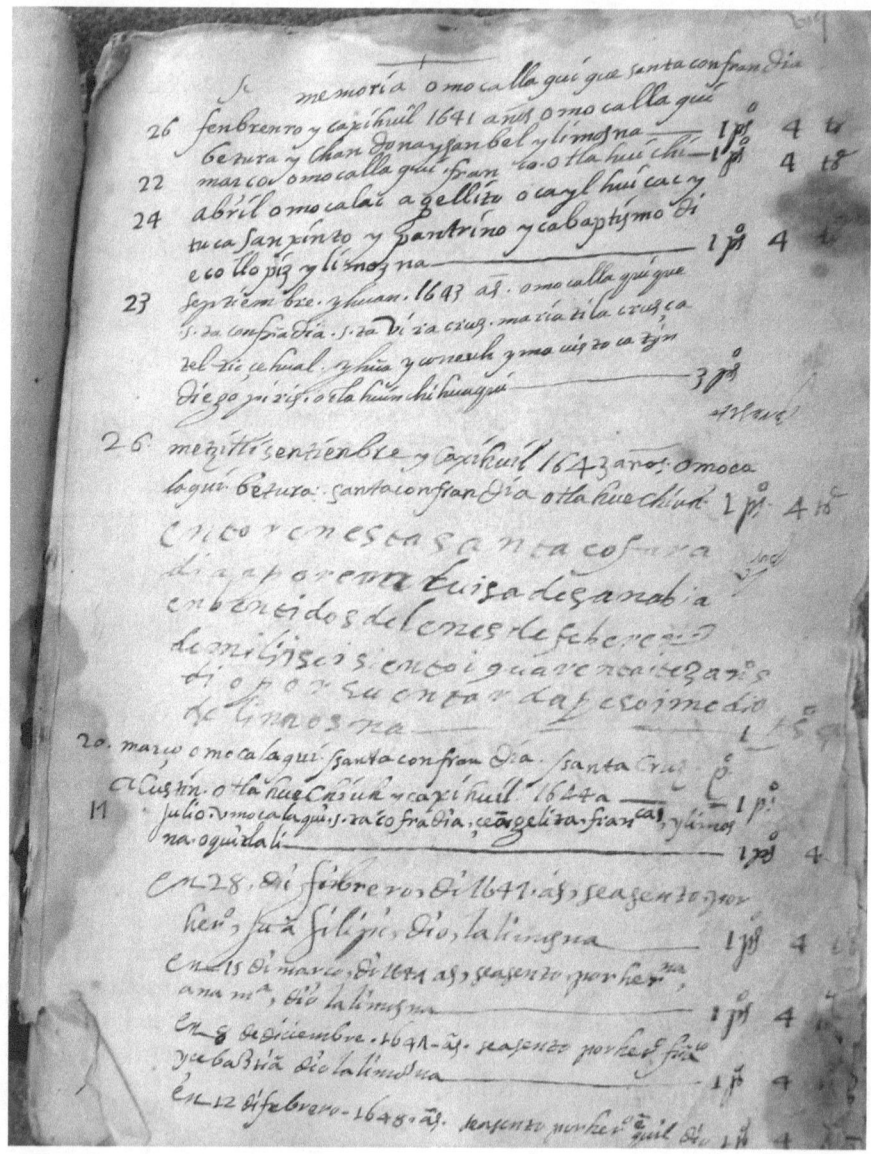

FIGURE 2.2. Nahuatl and Spanish membership list, confraternity of the Santa Vera Cruz, Zacatecas, 1643. Photo taken by author in 2007.

of the hometowns they had left behind.[137] In particular, the absence of native leaders and participation in civic life must have been extremely trying to the migrant population looking to organize its local affairs. In the place of formal civic offices, native peoples found in confraternities and hospitals the vehicles they needed to remedy their lack of hereditary nobility and governance institutions. The sociopolitical opportunities generated by these religious institutions proved extremely important and rare, as it took almost fifty years (not until 1609) for native peoples to establish civil leadership positions for themselves.

The Vera Cruz's constitution indicates that a small leadership pool led by a mayordomo had developed already around the hospital. These same men, a group of around ten, also assumed official positions in the Vera Cruz, organizing activities and resolving problems pertaining to both.[138] There is no biographical information on the leaders of either organization. However, when noted, native people from "Mexico" frequently composed the leadership of the Vera Cruz. These "mexicanos" came from the basin of Mexico, including Pedro Hernández from Huexotzinco (near Puebla) and Martín of Chalco. Why Tonaltecos or Tarascans did not assume primary leadership positions is unknown. Even during its founding year, 1566, the cofrades elected Diego Jacobo "a natural de Mexico," as mayordomo. The following year, two native peoples from Mexico City, Pedro Ruiz and Miguel, took over the position. The development of the cofradía, as mentioned earlier, illustrates a pattern typical to Zacatecas—the takeover of an organization by aspiring Nahuas from central Mexico. However, the cofradía did not become an exclusive Nahua stronghold. In 1621, when the bishop of New Galicia, Francisco de Rivera, visited the confraternity, he noted the continued presence of the founders, the Tonaltecos.[139] Nahuatl-speaking indigenous peoples lacked sufficient numbers and support to form a cohesive community without the inclusion of the many ethnically distinct native people who lived and labored among them. From the beginning, then, urban indigenous leaders needed to think and act across ethnic lines to successfully lead the diverse native population of the minas. These initial leadership experiences in the cofradía and hospital provided fertile training ground for the governance of the ethnically heterogeneous Indian towns.

Although it is not possible to identify the distinct ethnicity of all the mayordomos, as with the majority of the migrant population, they came from a commoner class. There is no evidence of Indian nobles among the immigrant population. The coveted title of *don* never appeared among the foremen. Of the founding leadership of the cofradía, seven men had Spanish surnames, and two officials possessed indigenous second names. Before 1570 the majority of these second names were Spanish patronymics such as Hernández and Jiménez. Although middling-ranking appellations—in other words, nonelite—they were fairly prestigious names for an indigenous person in this time period.[140] By the early seventeenth century, mayordomos possessed surnames such as Ortiz, Santiago, and

Díaz. Although they did not descend from hereditary nobility, Zacatecas's early Indians leaders speak to a group of aspiring social climbers who utilized the cofradía to improve their social status. These native men took advantage of the urban context and Spanish institutions to achieve levels of authority and social status probably out of their reach in their hometowns.

The intermingling of social and religious functions also was evident in the use of the hospital, and later the capillas, as election sites of religious and civil officials and meeting places for indigenous cabildos. Native peoples did not always hold dual positions on the cofradía and the cabildo. But a close connection existed between the two institutions, and confraternity officials often used the institution as a vehicle to assume governance in the indigenous barrios. These religious leadership opportunities proved especially important in Zacatecas, where the delayed development of civic officeholders left some barrios and ethnic groups without direct representation in their town's cabildo. The barrio of San Josef, for example, relied heavily on its confraternity officials to provide rulership in the years when they shared municipal office-holding positions with the pueblo of Tonalá Chepinque. In 1689, San Josef's cofradía mayordomo, Pedro de la Cruz, and his *comisario* (assistant), José de Azola, attended municipal council meetings.[141] In that same year, when the barrio decided to break with Tonalá and form its own cabildo, the community's confraternity leaders were included along with the town's alcalde, principal leaders, and elders in the decision-making process. In a city where native peoples often shared jurisdictional authority, confraternities provided indigenous communities with an additional vehicle to participate in municipal government.

Until it built its chapel, the Vera Cruz conducted the majority of its activities at the hospital and at the Franciscan convent.[142] The confraternity's mayordomos responsibilities included collecting dues, enrolling new members, balancing funds, preparing for festivals, arranging music, ordering masses, tending to the sick, and assisting with burials. Statements from quarterly fiscal reviews indicate that the cofradía usually met its yearly expenses, mainly confined to paying for masses, burials, services of religious officials, and processions. Officials also coordinated annual elections in early April (the anniversary of the confraternity's founding). According to the constitution, the event took place on the holy day of Santa Vera Cruz (the True Cross, or Good Friday). The *hermanos*, the male members of the confraternity, assembled at the hospital (and later their chapel) in the afternoon to elect their mayordomo in the presence of the vicar and the *rector de la justicia*.[143] There is little information from Zacatecas on how the native hierarchy conducted these proceedings, but it may have been similar to the one described in a constitution from an indigenous confraternity, Santo Entierro, from Pátzcuaro, in contemporary Michoacán. According to that document, the election of officials rotated between pueblos and barrios on the basis of seniority. The individual who garnered the most votes received the appointment of mayordomo.[144] The fairly consistent running of elections speaks to the high interest in the post.[145] Confraternity offices were probably not as valued in central Mexico, where native peoples had access to positions on indigenous cabildos.[146] But in Zacatecas the lack of indigenous representative government lent urgency and importance to these sociopolitical religious positions.

The leadership cohort planned and organized the sodality's religious activities, but they also acted as its watchdogs, intervening when they felt that individuals or activities threatened its livelihood or privileges. Alms collection, for example, was particularly important to the cofradía, which had limited forms of revenue outside of membership dues.[147] For a period of time the Santa Vera Cruz, among the oldest sodality in Zacatecas, could count on a certain share of the town's donations. But by 1595 the cofradía's mayordomos complained that the organization suffered from "extreme need." Part of the sodality's economic plight, while probably not as dire as the foremen claimed, derived from competition from several other confraternities. The city now had two other indigenous cofradías (Asunción and Limpia Concepción) and at least four Spanish cofradías.[148] By 1619 indigenous officials maintained that the confraternity was on the brink of dissolution.[149] During this period mayordomos frequently petitioned the bishop of Nueva Galicia to order edicts forbidding Spanish confraternities from asking for donations on the same day as the Vera Cruz. They argued that the confraternity's status as the "first and the most ancient" cofradía entitled them to exclusive rights to alms collection on Friday. They also cited the organization's extreme poverty and shrewdly pointed out that it would soon have insufficient funds to bury their dead, fund masses, or pay for priests. The petitions led to some concessions. While authorities did not ban other groups from seeking contributions on Friday, it granted the Vera Cruz the most favorable time period and location. Was the cofradía on the verge of economic collapse? The siphoning of resources to other sodalities surely affected the Vera Cruz's operations, but it is difficult to determine the true state of its finances. What is apparent from this episode is that by the early seventeenth century, a skilled indigenous leadership cohort, fluent in the structure, language, and content of petitions, existed in the city.

Native peoples used the confraternities as a training ground to hone general leadership skills. Over time mayordomos did not just serve as religious functionaries; they also utilized their positions to promote and protect the community. Throughout the colonial period, cofradía officers complained to local and viceregal authorities about labor, commerce, and property violations occurring in their barrios.[150] Often officials bypassed local authorities and addressed their petitions directly to the Audiencia of Guadalajara. The cofradía of the town of San Josef, for example, frequently complained to the high court of their abuses at the hands of Spanish employers and authorities. At the community level, confraternities and their leaders became indispensible features of local indigenous life. Mayordomos often worked in concert with Indian alcaldes.[151] A property transaction from 1735 illustrates the close relationship between a barrio and its confraternity. In that year, the mayordomo and other officials of the cofradía of San Diego purchased two houses and a stable near the traza from the Augustinians.[152] The members considered the acquisition a community affair and sought the approval of the Indian alcalde of the pueblo to which the confraternity belonged. On the day of the sale the alcalde and other members of the Indian cabildo accompanied the confraternity leaders to witness the possession of the property.[153] Their prominent role in secular society illustrates the important sociopolitical function and civic status of cofradía leaders.

As the city's indigenous population continued to grow, native peoples established more barrios and wards, neighborhoods within the barrios, many which developed their own confraternities. Within a few years of the creation of an Augustinian parish, for example, native peoples founded the confraternity of the Limpia Concepción in 1615 in the native town of Tonalá. By the end of the eighteenth century, ten indigenous cofradías operated in the native towns (see Tables 2.1 and 2.2). Four developed under the guidance of the Augustinians in the pueblos of Tonalá Chepinque and El Niño, and four more Franciscan cofradías (in addition to the Vera Cruz) formed in the town of Tlacuitlapan. Augustinians also supported the establishment of a sodality, San Nicólas, composed of Indians and Spaniards near the city center.[154] A strong cofradía, sponsored first by the Dominicans and then by secular clerics, formed in the pueblo of San Josef. Extant documentation indicates that the majority of these sodalities lasted

TABLE 2.1. Indigenous confraternities, Tlacuitlapan, Zacatecas

Confraternity	Location
Santa Vera Cruz	Capilla de la Veracruz
Jesús Nazareno	Capilla de Jesús
Limpia Concepción	Capilla de Tlacuitlapan
Nuestra Señora de la Asunción	Capilla de Mexicapan
Santísima Trinidad	Tlacuitlapan

Source: APZ, Guía de Cofradías; AHEZ, Libro de Cabildo 6, f. 314, 1686; AAG, Visitas, box 1, book 3, ff. 70v–74, 1707.

TABLE 2.2. Indigenous confraternities, southern communities, Zacatecas

Confraternity	Location	Doctrine
San Diego	Capilla de San Diego, Tonalá Chepinque	Augustinian
Nuestra Señora de la Soledad	Capilla de Soledad, Tonalá Chepinque	Augustinian
Limpia Concepción	Capilla de la Concepción, Tonalá Chepinque	Augustinian
Dulce Nombre de Jesús	El Niño	Augustinian
San Josef	San Josef	Dominican then Parish
San Nicolás	Templo de San Agustín, city center	Augustinian

Source: APZ, Guía de Cofradías; AAG, Visitas, box 1, book 3, ff. 70v–74, 1707.

well into the late colonial period, with two existing still in the nineteenth century.

The Emergence of Corporate and Urban Identities

The proliferation of confraternities in the Indian pueblos speaks to the continued use of cofradías as the primary mode of community organization. At times, it is difficult to discern whether barrios established confraternities or whether powerful cofradías evolved into sociopolitical organizations. In the period from 1550 to 1608, the confraternity served as the central unifying force of the migrant population, perhaps even reflecting continued ethnic and kinship networks. Barrios continued to develop and define themselves by their confraternities. Mayordomos played a role in the governance of the indigenous affairs. The establishment of a cofradía became as necessary to a barrio as the construction of monumental churches were to the communities of central Mexico.[155] Indigenous cofradías frequently participated with Spaniards in procession and feast-day activities, proudly displaying their banners, images, and badges in the public plaza.[156] Even colonial officials recognized the importance of these lay institutions to native people. In one instance the bishop of Guadalajara, Francisco de Rivera, threatened to bar cofradías from processions if members did not stop participating in saçemis, the popular rock fights held on the outskirts of town between rival indigenous groups.[157] Yet, as often proved to be the case in Zacatecas, colonial officials allowed native peoples substantial latitude in their own affairs as long as they did not threaten Spanish authorities or reduce the mining workforce. The use of religious organizations for community formation was one of the most successful innovations of the migrant urban Indian population. The activities engaged in by cofradías went beyond the sacred, shaping secular indigenous society. In areas where native peoples lacked mechanisms for sociopolitical organization, the church and its institutions became the central organizing force of community life.[158] The role of confraternities in the formative stages of indigenous community formation explains why the urban church remained closely tied to indigenous autonomy and corporate identity in Zacatecas at a level not seen in other areas of New Spain.

For Zacatecas's ethnically diverse population the appropriation of the colonial institution of the confraternity to organize themselves into a recognized corporate group was a particularly crucial strategy. This was especially important given the context of the wider Spanish city in which they lived. Membership was composed not only of distinct ethnic groups and classes but also of native people living outside of the city.[159] Franciscan custodianship of indigenous mine laborers on outlying mining haciendas facilitated and promoted participation by native peoples living in areas that lacked the sociopolitical infrastructure to constitute their own sodalities. For these individuals, the cofradía represented an opportunity to reconnect with indigenous people and practices.[160] Whether it was the native person living in a distant mining hacienda, the many single women residing in the barrio, or the migrant laborer just arrived from central Mexico, the cofradía provided the ethnically distinct indigenous population with some common ground, a place to foster interethnic unity in the absence of the organizing mechanisms of preconquest altepetl, and a corporate identity in relation to other ethnic groups such as Africans and Spaniards.[161]

Institutions such as cofradías assisted native peoples in establishing a corporate Indian identity in the eyes of Spanish officials. The term "Indian" often carries connotations of ethnic disintegration. But what was the other face of this colonial construction? In Zacatecas, the appropriation of this ethno-juridical designation became a central strategy in the struggle to shape and maintain viable urban Indian identities. Defining corporate status in colonial society was critical for certain groups like native peoples, as it significantly shaped their social and political life at the local level.[162] As "indios," native peoples could continue to draw on certain rights and privileges reserved for those designated "indigenous," as opposed to "mestizo" or "casta." They could establish their own towns and governance systems, control their lands, restrict non-Indians from their communities, and petition as a group. The creation of "Indian" spaces and institutions allowed native peoples to continue indigenous practices and traditions in their roles as urban vecinos.

So what did it mean to be an indigenous vecino in this period, from the mid- to late sixteenth century? Here the case of Francisco Soto is instructive. Francisco was a migrant from central Mexico. He probably lived in one of Zacatecas's indigenous barrios, between the traza and the Indian communities. Francisco vigorously engaged in the money economy, selling grains in public and, to his downfall, illegally from his home. He also frequently encountered ethnic others, hawking his products to castas and other non-Indians. In many ways Francisco was a typical, though occasionally criminal, urban vecino. But a closer examination of Francisco's lifeways indicates that he still belonged to and participated in an indigenous world. Francisco lived next to indigenous neighbors, a man and a woman who also identified as Mexica. They may have known each other before they traveled to Zacatecas—or as migrants from a similar area they more likely developed a relationship after their arrival and clustered together. Francisco also sold his products to native peoples whom he conversed with in Nahuatl. Francisco did not speak Castilian and required an interpreter—a mestizo who spoke Nahuatl—when dealing with Spanish authorities. Francisco's way of life illustrates his ability to maintain both his urban and indigenous identities, a point he perhaps makes best when he identified himself as "Mexica and vecino of the city."[163]

Markers of indigeneity in Zacatecas changed over time. But in the sixteenth century certain features and characteristics predominated. The large migrant population identified both with their ancestral homeland and their place of residence in Zacatecas. Many indigenous peoples lived and worked together in Indian communities or at mining haciendas with large native populations. Multilingual Zacatecas offered several opportunities for native peoples to engage in municipal life using native languages, particularly Nahuatl and Purépecha, at Indian barrios and even at mining sites. While Spanish-speaking Indians probably had the upper hand within the traza and at haciendas, lack of fluency in Castilian had little impact on the attainment of important positions within indigenous organizations. Most native peoples belonged to an indigenous confraternity and participated in quotidian religious functions in their local parish. The establishment of communities and confraternities, together with labor and residential patterns, promoted ethnic cohesion among the migrant population. In this formative period native people had devised multiple strategies for manifesting and maintaining indigenous identities and connections within Spanish urban mechanisms.

. . .

As native peoples consolidated their communities and established their confraternities, Spaniards continued their progress toward city building as well. On the first day of the new year of 1563, Baltasar de Bañuelos, one of the town's diputados, or civic officers, approached his fellow councilmen with a proposal. He had in his possession a series of pertinent measures and other documents related to the town's governance and requested their storage in safekeeping with the *libro de cabildo* (the book of the council's proceedings) in the community chest.[164] Among these important papers could be found the Audiencia decree from Compostela on September 25, 1553, authorizing the election of diputados and a concession from the crown on November 15, 1556, allowing the taxing of the town's silver at one-tenth instead of the standard one-fifth. Bañuelos's concern with the safekeeping of these documents is readily apparent. Together, the promulgations constituted the town's political foundation and economic prosperity.

Yet these papers did not remain the chest's most treasured contents. A few fojas dated from 1585, written on parchment, stamped with the royal seal in colored wax, attached by silk cords, and graced with the king's signature, now constituted the gem of the council's archive. Tucked away in a box secured by three locks, the fojas documented Zacatecas's conversion from minas, or mining camp, to ciudad. On October 17, 1585, in the northwestern Spanish town of Mozón, King Philip II elevated Zacatecas's status, in perpetuity, as the "ciudad de Nuestra Señora de los Zacatecas." When the paperwork arrived on December 5, 1586, the corregidor, Don Félix de Zúñiga y Avellaneda, in accordance with Spanish custom, kissed the document, placed it on his head, and pledged his obedience to its content.[165] This jurisdictional shift gave the city a certain amount of social and cultural prestige and, more tangibly, a new form of municipal government. As of 1586, the town had continued to operate under the Diputación de Minería with an alcalde mayor and four diputados. But almost exactly a month after receiving the monarch's decree, on January 4, 1587, Spanish officeholders took advantage of their new status and composed a more traditional cabildo, naming and appointing two *alcaldes ordinarios*, or local magistrates, Antonio de Salas and Alonso Fernández Bachiller, and five regidores.[166] Zacatecas's juridical elevation along with the prosperity of silver production in this period converted it into one of New Spain's most important provincial urban centers.[167] Puebla alone stood as its rival.[168]

As Spaniards celebrated their newfound city status, native peoples continued in their attempts to re-create some aspects of municipal life. While not as elaborate as those of their Spanish counterparts, they too possessed a series of books and a *cofre* (chest) where they recorded and stored their most important events. We know that the constitution of the Santa Vera Cruz figured among the documents carefully conserved in their *libro de cofradía*. Other papers included the Vera Cruz's right to collect alms at the door of the city church on Friday afternoons. One wonders about the contents of other fojas, written in Nahuatl, and now missing. Did native peoples record their assignments to religious parishes or the establishment of their hospital and the names of its first mayordomos? Did they keep lists of the elections of confraternity leaders and note when they decided to build their capilla? Unfortunately, the loss of the city's native-language corpus renders it impossible to reconstruct the proceedings of indigenous organizations with the same detail and clarity as those of their Spanish counterparts.

What remains clear is that by the end of the sixteenth century, a large and permanent native population was indispensible to Zacatecas's civic vitality and its production of silver. By 1572, Indians constituted the city's largest ethnic group, a position they retained through the sixteenth century.[169] The ethnically diverse migrant population faced many challenges in this period, adjusting to both their lack of ethnic cohesion and the absence of institutions and organizations of their hometowns, along with the daily challenges of life and labor in a Spanish city. But Zacatecas's native population demonstrated a remarkable ability to adapt to their new urban environment. Within the city, and especially in the Indian communities, they could still participate in civic life even if they only spoke Nahuatl. They built solidarity and cohesion through the creation of indigenous communities and confraternities, and even by laboring together at mining sites. The confraternity, in particular, in its attempts to re-create organizing mechanisms of the altepetl served as the primary mode of social organization.[170]

The founding of indigenous communities and confraternities in the sixteenth century demonstrates that native peoples came to Zacatecas not only to labor in its mines but also to become its vecinos. As urban residents, Indians did not differ from their Spanish counterparts in their desire for jurisdictional autonomy. As native peoples heard and celebrated Zacatecas's elevation to ciudad status and encountered officials with new civic titles, it surely reminded the indigenous population of their lack of municipal leaders and councils. Cofradías served as sociopolitical organizations, but they failed to mollify the desire for self-government in a migrant population accustomed to indigenous rulers and towns. As the mining boom continued and the Indian population both grew and developed roots in the city, native peoples began to look to another Spanish institution to fulfill their cravings for self-rule.

3 The Creation of Indian Towns and Officials, 1609–1650

In November 1608, the oidor and visitador of the Audiencia of Guadalajara, the *licenciado* Gaspar de la Fuente, embarked on a lengthy and productive yearlong visit of several towns and communities in New Galicia.[1] Among his many stops, de la Fuente toured several of the province's smaller mining towns, including Mazapil, Sombrerete, and Fresnillo. A few months later, on May 12, 1609, he arrived in Zacatecas for a stay of four and a half months.[2] The visitador had several objectives to accomplish on his inspection, including matters to do with the Real Hacienda (the royal treasury), particularly the collection of debts owed to the crown, and a review of judicial records and procedures. The crown also had enjoined the judge to assess the condition of the province's native subjects and to intervene in their welfare, if necessary. King Philip III charged de la Fuente with determining whether native peoples received proper Christian doctrine and treatment at the hands of Spanish employers and officials. By the time he arrived in Zacatecas, the visitador had witnessed enough to confirm his worst suspicions. In the northern mining town of Mazapil he had conducted a series of *interrogatorios* (interviews) with the native population. They told him of being detained against their will for receiving advanced wages in underground cells (*calabozos*) de la Fuente deemed the "roughest prisons to be found in these parts."[3]

The grievances of Zacatecas's indigenous population contrasted starkly with those of the native peoples of Mazapil. Abuse and other forms of coercion existed in the city and the native population could draw on a long list of injustices. But Zacatecas's native population escaped the more serious and extreme forms of labor exploitation found in the city's hinterlands and satellite mining towns. Moreover, de la Fuente's presence marked the potential for a more disinterested forum of justice. He had no local ties to the city or to the mining industry. On August 22, 1609, the visitador heard a series of declarations from native peoples, including those of Francisco Miguel, Luis Melchor, Jerónimo Bernardino, Pedro Martín, Diego Hernández, Cristóbal Miguel, Buenaventura de la Cruz, José Juárez, and Francisco Gaspar. These were prominent men in the community, perhaps even mayordomos of the Vera Cruz, representing areas from central Mexico such as Texcoco, Cuatitlán, and Tlaxcala, along with Tonalatecos and native peoples from Michoacán.[4] Led by Buenaventura de la Cruz, a migrant from Texcoco, the native peoples presented their concerns to the visitador. They protested against forced labor services at the hands of the corregidor, Don Juan de Guzmán, such as personal service and the making of fences for the bullfights, for which they had received no salary or other forms of compensation. Nor did de la Cruz and the others limit their complaints to labor matters. They also pointed to the lack of support from Spanish officials in granting them new settlement sites and the failure of local authorities to defend them from Spanish encroachments of their properties and goods. Buenaventura and his colleagues found a willing ally in de la Fuente, who appears to have taken seriously the crown's mandate to look out for the welfare of its indigenous subjects. To that effect, he ordered the corregidor and his subordinates to desist in their exploitative labor practices and to take particular care in providing amparo (protection) to the native population's settlements, houses, lands, and possessions.

But aside from the standard role of protector, it appears that de la Fuente possessed certain insights into Zacatecas's Indian population that local officials had failed to notice or disregarded. Unsurprisingly, he echoed long-standing Spanish concerns about the indigenous population's excessive consumption of alcohol. But he also noted the prevalence of informal ritualized fighting among the native labor force near the indigenous barrios. These fights, known as saçemis, occurred with regularity on Sundays and feast days between rival ethnic and occupational groups.[5] Protracted and intense battles, they often resulted in serious injuries and multiple fatalities as indigenous participants fought with rocks, knives, spears, bows and arrows, and firearms. Spaniards knew about the battles, at times forming part of the crowd of spectators that watched them or, on other occasions, profiting from them by selling weapons and other merchandise at the skirmishes. But the loss of life and productivity (from a weakened or diminished labor force) did not seem to disturb local officials, who made no serious efforts to prevent them until they challenged Spanish secular and religious authority in the mid-1620s. The origins of the fights remain unclear, but it is not too difficult to imagine that the presence of so many native peoples of diverse ethnic backgrounds and statuses, such as migrants versus long-term settlers, provoked tensions and fissures typical to a frontier boomtown.

The saçemis spoke to disunity among some sectors of Zacatecas's indigenous population. But the majority of native peoples lived together in orderly and populated barrios and collaborated through Indian organizations and leaders. The astute visitador recognized and encouraged this unity. In particular, he acknowledged and promoted the native population's need and interest in self-rule. His visit noted the presence of "so many Indians and no one to govern them."[6] So with the "appearance of trustworthy [and interested] individuals," he mandated the creation of indigenous leaders, one alcalde for the population clusters around San Francisco and another for those of Tonalá. By this decree, de la Fuente followed in the actions of the viceroy, who had issued a similar mandate in 1601 regarding urban native communities in other areas of New Spain.[7] A little over sixty years after the city's founding, native peoples could finally celebrate the arrival of formal indigenous rule in their communities. De la Fuente made it clear that the institution of Spanish-style governance came at the *pedimento* (petition) of native peoples, such as Buenaventura and his colleagues, and not Spaniards.[8]

This chapter examines the creation of formal indigenous towns, municipal councils, and leaders in the seventeenth century. It outlines the establishment of two Indian towns, Tlacuitlapan and Tonalá, on geographic (north-south) and parish (Franciscan-Augustinian) lines. It examines the sociopolitical factors behind the subsequent creation of two additional indigenous pueblos, San Josef and El Niño. It charts the evolution of Indian governance from the initial appointment of two native alcaldes to the development of full-fledged indigenous municipal councils modeled on both Spanish and preconquest indigenous governance practices. The chapter then considers the establishment of a nonhereditary indigenous leadership. It discusses the changing nature and role of native rulers, highlights trends in the ethnic composition of the leadership, and documents the rise of a group of professional officeholders who held multiple positions of government or exercised the same office over various terms.

In central Mexico, one historian has argued that the impetus for creating indigenous town councils came from the Spaniards "bent on spreading their own system."[9] In Zacatecas, however, it was the indigenous population, lacking vehicles for redress and governance, which petitioned Spanish officials for the right to establish the institution, just as they took the lead in the formation of confraternities. The migrant and now multigenerational resident population creatively adapted Spanish-style governance to meet personal, group, and community needs. The creation of indigenous towns and municipal councils in Zacatecas provided native peoples with a modicum of juridical autonomy over indigenous affairs. The appropriation of these institutions facilitated the establishment of Indian towns and created a civil leadership, serving as proxies for both the altepetl and dynastic rulers. The mining economy, local conditions, and municipal and viceregal ordinances played a formidable influence on the daily and long-term affairs of native peoples. While native peoples could not always control their social, political, and economic circumstances, their sociopolitical organizations provided them with some mechanisms for redress from Spanish exploitation and influences. Moreover, unlike other areas of New Spain where local officials frustrated or opposed the development of Indian governance, Zacatecas's cabildo suffered relatively little interference from Spanish officials.[10] Within the pueblos, native peoples could maintain some indigenous practices in land tenure or language and offer recent migrants a culturally familiar environment.

As with the Indian confraternities, sources indicate that native peoples kept their council minutes in Nahuatl. But the proceedings themselves remain missing. The information for this chapter is reconstructed solely from Spanish documents, particularly entries found in the minutes of the Spanish municipal council, or *libros de cabildo*. The loss of the native-language ledgers limits our understanding of urban indigenous government. Still, the extant Spanish-language documentation illustrates some of its operations and the formal nature of indigenous sovereignty. Colonial authorities recognized the authority and autonomy of Indian leaders and communities and considered their activities a separate but important aspect of the city's municipal operations. The creation of indigenous cabildos and leaders in the seventeenth century converted the native settlements into official sociopolitical entities and their residents into formal urban vecinos. The establishment of indigenous governance played a key role in the persistence of a corporate indigenous identity through the late colonial period.

The Beginnings of Civic Government

The development of indigenous municipal councils in New Spain took some time as the crown determined how to organize and govern its subjugated territories for maximum financial efficiency.[11] Over time, Indian municipalities received the designation of city, *villa*, or pueblo according to the size of their population. In the sixteenth century, the crown granted city status to a handful of indigenous communities in central Mexico, including Tlaxcala (1535), Tenochtitlan and Texcoco (1543), Xochimilco (1559), and Tacuba (1564).[12] The majority of native communities received the designation of *pueblos de indios* (juridically autonomous towns).

Within these communities, predynastic indigenous rulers continued to play a role in governance. From the fall of Tenochtitlan, Spaniards appointed native nobles to govern their former altepetl, using them as intermediaries to facilitate tribute collection and labor draft teams. Municipal council–style positions significantly predated the actual institution of cabildos. In 1530, the crown authorized the appointment of an indigenous regidor and alguacil to each community.[13] It took another fifteen years before the establishment of the first indigenous cabildo in Tlaxcala in 1545.[14] Most indigenous communities in central Mexico had councils in place by the 1580s. The native elite often dominated office holding in the early cabildos until the seventeenth century when non-nobles came to play a more substantial role.[15]

In Zacatecas, indigenous governance developed at a much slower pace. There was no hereditary nobility rallying to reassert their authority and prerogatives through colonial institutions. Spaniards recognized the native settlements as Indian barrios but showed little interest in converting them into pueblos de indios, thereby endowing them with jurisdictional autonomy and authority.[16] Although some of the indigenous communities ranked among the oldest in the city, Spanish administrators considered the barrios units within one of two religious parishes. Colonial authorities conflated any settlement of native people to the north of the Franciscan convent as the barrio of San Francisco, or *el de arriba*, while they subsumed those south of the center, *de abajo* (below), as part of the barrio of Tonalá or San Agustín, as it was sometimes called, because of its proximity to the Augustinian convent.

It is also possible that the mechanisms for governance within the confraternity system ameliorated the need for a formal leadership vehicle. The election of confraternity mayordomos had created a small cohort of indigenous leaders who also assumed roles in civil affairs. Mayordomos and *fiscales* (religious and civil functionaries) had organized, promoted, and protected the community in the sixteenth century. But they lacked the power and recognition of proper civil leaders. The majority of their duties were religious in nature. All important decisions they sought to make or promote in religious matters (and ultimately civil as well) required the formal approval of their religious guardians. Without juridical autonomy, their daily and long-term affairs were constrained and subject to the influence of non-Indians to a greater extent.

It may have been mining itself that created the conditions for the establishment of indigenous governance in the city. A surge in silver production in the late sixteenth century, which continued through the 1620s, brought with it another wave of indigenous migrants. Estimates of the extant population for this period (see Table 3.1) indicate that native peoples constituted

TABLE 3.1. Comparative population of Zacatecas by racial categories, 1572–1608

Year	Group	Number	Percentage of total population
1572	Spanish	300	13
	Indian	1,500	65
	Black slaves	500	22
c. 1602–1605	Spanish vecinos	570	20
	Indian laborers	1,500	52
	Slaves—all sexes and ages	800	28
1608	Spanish	1,500+	33
	Indian laborers	1,500+	33
	Mestizo and mulattos	1,500+	33

Source: For 1572, see Gerhard, *North Frontier*, 158–59. For 1602–1605, see Mota y Escobar, *Descripción geográfica*, 145. For 1608, see Anonymous, *Relación*, 292, 295.

the largest ethnic group in the city. At first glance, there appears to be no growth in the native population from 1572 to 1608, which appears to remain stable at 1,500 individuals. But we must take into account that the two early seventeenth-century estimates include only "laborers," and that the 1608 count adds the word *plus* (more people) to its approximates. Both counts failed to capture the significant number of native peoples working outside the mines, including indigenous women and children. The continued boom in production would have drawn more native peoples to the city. Many of the immigrants that arrived in the post-1580s period brought with them traditions of town councils and office holding firmly established in central Mexico by this period. This large urban migrant population began to seek more direct control over its barrios and affairs.

In 1609, native peoples led by the Texcocan migrant Buenaventura de la Cruz, petitioned visitador de la Fuente for self-rule. The visitador acceded to their request, authorizing the creation of two indigenous alcaldes "of good sense and vigilance."[17] One alcalde would have jurisdiction over all the native barrios above the Franciscan monastery, and the other would watch over those below the Augustinian convent. De la Fuente also ordered the appointment of several indigenous fiscales to oversee indigenous affairs in the outlying haciendas. The following year, the native leadership of the barrio of San Francisco (Tlacuitlapan) nominated Pedro Reynoso as their first alcalde, and Tonalá put forward Francisco Miguel. The Spanish notary listed Pedro as a "married Indian and vecino of the pueblo." He also described Francisco as a "married Indian, vecino of the barrio."[18] The recording of these indigenous leaders as vecinos in the minutes of the Spanish cabildo illustrates once again how both Spaniards and native peoples accepted the appropriation of this civic descriptor. Both Francisco and Miguel possessed all the appropriate attributes of a vecino. They were married urban dwellers, probably in possession of property, and obviously men of sufficiently good standing as to be trusted by their communities. For native peoples, assuming a municipal role was not incompatible with possessing an indigenous identity, but it was a necessary step to developing indigenous communities in the urban context.

Although a significant advancement, the appointment of native leaders and the creation of the indigenous pueblos constituted only the first of several phases toward self-government. To begin, the native communities had to navigate the challenges that arose when the visitador appointed only two alcaldes to represent distinct ethnic groups living in separate barrios. Spanish ordinances dictated that native pueblos with fewer than eighty homes or one hundred people receive only one alcalde, one regidor, and one fiscal.[19] It is possible that individual ethnic barrios did not possess the necessary numbers to have their own officers. But it is more likely that de la Fuente did not fully comprehend the dynamics of the native barrios. By establishing the pueblos on the boundaries of the two native parishes, he forcibly incorporated multiple barrios into two conflated juridical entities. This sociopolitical arrangement promoted conflicts of interests and limited representation for each community.

Spanish interference in the selection of Indian officers remained an intermittent obstacle to self-rule through the colonial period. This was particularly the case during the first years after the establishment of the post. In this period, the Spanish cabildo chose the alcaldes from a pool of three Indians nominated by each pueblo.[20] Viceregal and local religious officials appointed the indigenous fiscales.[21] After the pueblos submitted their nominations, or *memoriales*, the Spanish cabildo made the final selection, ratified the election, enjoined the alcaldes to perform their duties correctly, and gave them the staff of office.

De la Fuente had recognized the native population's desire for self-governance. But he also believed that the Indian communities needed supervision and that the native leadership should work in concert with Spanish officials. The visitador encouraged alcaldes to care for the poor, report any problems, and "give notice of the excesses of the Indians of the towns and the haciendas and barrios."[22] He ordered fiscales to ensure that native peoples attended church services. Spanish authorities and the indigenous vecinos of the pueblos expected the alcaldes and fiscales to uphold public order. Alcaldes had the power to interrogate, hold, and turn delinquents over to the corregidor, the highest-ranking Spanish official in the city. Fiscales regularly helped clerics prevent and disrupt saçemis that occurred near haciendas and the native communities.

However, Zacatecas's Indian leaders did not function as intermediaries between native peoples and colonial authorities at levels found in other areas of New Spain. In matters of justice and order, native officials cooperated with Spanish authorities, but they also vigorously defended their communities and their juridical autonomy. Often, the councils challenged Spanish officers, especially once they had matured in the mid-seventeenth century. Episodes of discord between leaders and subjects appear in the documentation, but there is little evidence of serious or sustained animosity between the two groups. Local conditions in Zacatecas left fewer opportunities for native leaders to exploit their subjects or to enrich themselves at their subjects' expense. The most onerous and contentious responsibilities of indigenous officials, the collection of tribute or the organization of draft labor, did not exist in the city. The fact that native leaders and residents came from similar socioeconomic backgrounds also influenced their relationship. Privileges usually accorded to native nobles, such as personal service, did not occur in the native towns.[23] While a cohort of indigenous leaders with their own ambitions and agendas did emerge over time, the absence of native nobles meant that some of the issues and tensions that erupted between commoners and elites in other areas were not as pronounced in Zacatecas.[24]

From Barrios to Pueblos

As with the early lay brotherhoods, the establishment of cabildos provided a forum for self-government, as it created and defined the municipality to both its residents and outsiders. While native settlements had existed since the founding of Zacatecas, within the Iberian tradition, communities did not evolve into official municipal bodies until they had proper municipal councils.[25] It took the development of Zacatecas's cabildos to convert their communities from barrios to pueblos. The native towns would remain subject to Zacatecas's Spanish cabildo, but that was standard practice for most indigenous communities unless they possessed city status.[26] With their own cabildos, native peoples had greater administration and say over their towns' affairs and those of its subject neighborhoods. Officials could make important decisions regarding distribution and control over their corporate lands and resources. Alcaldes also had the right of first instance in smaller crimes and misdemeanors that occurred within their jurisdiction.[27] They could also legally restrict outsiders and non-Indians from their communities. In the overall political scheme, the native pueblos operated as subject municipalities within Zacatecas's greater jurisdiction. But in general, Spaniards tended not to intervene in their administration.

Within the first few years of the establishment of indigenous alcaldes, native peoples interested in municipal life found creative ways of adapting the Spanish position to meet their needs. One of the primary challenges the indigenous leadership confronted involved providing adequate representation for the different ethnic groups and barrios present in the pueblos. In central Mexico, larger cabildos with more members allowed smaller units participation through an officeholder.[28] In Zacatecas, where the cabildo expanded slowly, native peoples achieved geographic representation through yearly alternation of one office.[29] In preconquest central Mexico, rotation of duties and responsibilities among a series of relatively equally (usually four to eight) altepetls commonly occurred. Zacatecas's native people innovated on this tradition of rotation, applying it to their leadership cohort.

In 1615, for example, the pueblo of San Francisco vehemently protested the Spanish cabildo's appointment of Angel Coyote. Spanish authorities did not realize that the three major ethnic groups present in the town, the Mexica, the Texcoca, and the Tarascans, rotated the position of alcalde. Indigenous leaders argued that Angel Coyote could not accept the office because that year it pertained to a Tarascan. To avoid problems and to maintain "peace among the Indians," cabildo members accepted the petition and ordered the change in leadership.[30] Extant information illustrates a consistent pattern of rotation among the three major ethnic groups (see Table 3.2). By alternating the office among different ethnic groups, the pueblo resolved conflicting interests, avoided dissension, and promoted equal representation. The appointment of other minor officials in this period probably followed a similar pattern.

The rotation of offices reflected the use of traditional indigenous organizational practices. It also revealed the continued diversity of Zacatecas's native communities in the seventeenth century. After 1630, individual ethnic identities were rarely noted in the Spanish cabildo's minutes. Yet Spanish ignorance or disinterest in understanding the diverse ethnic composition of the indigenous settlements does not necessarily speak to the disappearance of distinct kinship or ethnic groups. Rather the documents suggest that the pueblos consisted of a *cabecera*, a head town, and several smaller *sujetos* (subjects), or units, of ethnically distinct barrios.[31] In 1650, for example, Mexica and Tlaxcalan barrios existed in the Tarascan

TABLE 3.2. Ethnic identity of indigenous alcaldes, San Francisco (Tlacuitlapan), Zacatecas, 1611–1617

1611	1612	1613	1614	1615	1616	1617
Juan Agustín (Tarascan)	Juan Jiménez (Mexica)	Buenaventura de la Cruz (Tetzcocan)	Pedro Reynoso (not recorded)	Juan Agustín (Tarascan)	Juan Tomás (not recorded)	Buenaventura de la Cruz (Tetzcocan)

Source: AHEZ, Libro de Cabildo, 2, f. 267, 1611; 2, f. 276, 1612; 2, f. 294, 1613; 2, f. 319, 1614; 3, f. 6v, 1615; 3, f. 16v, 1616; 3, f. 13v, 1617.

stronghold of Tonalá.³² An ethnic group also could dominate one community and have barrios in several other pueblos. There was a Tarascan neighborhood in the heavily Tlaxcalan barrio of San Josef. Within these towns, the various groups vied for political participation within the limited forum for self-government.

Over time more opportunities for representation and participation developed through expanded cabildos. At that point, the emphasis for representation shifted from rotating positions among ethnic groups to controlling elections among neighborhood wards or units. From 1709 to 1728, for example, despite some omissions and missing records, a clear pattern of rotation among neighborhoods emerged in the pueblo of Tlacuitlapan. Barrios within Tlacuitlapan developed around confraternities. These organizations probably reflected continued ethnic and kinship networks (see Table 3.3). Table 3.4 illustrates how Tlacuitlapan, the cabecera of the pueblo, allowed one barrio to control the election of the alcalde, if not of the other officials as well. In 1723, a new unit, Jesús, entered the pattern.³³ After 1730, indigenous elections in Tlacuitlapan no longer specified which barrio elected the town's officers. It remains unclear whether native peoples ceased rotating office holding and elections or whether Spanish officials failed to record the information in their minutes.

Power sharing between barrios and ethnic groups evolved differently in the southern settlements clustered around the cabecera of Tonalá, a community whose earliest settlers included Tonaltecos, Tarascans, and Tecuexes. Known occasionally by its religious affiliation, San Agustín, the town's name evolved with the changing power dynamics of its barrios. By the seventeenth century, the pueblo incorporated several large barrios over a wide stretch of area: El Niño (to the southeast), Chepinque, a large settlement of Tlaxcalans (to the west), San Josef, and several smaller neighborhoods that left few traces in the historical records. Efforts to determine how to distribute office-holding positions between the town and its barrios

TABLE 3.3. Town structure of Tlacuitlapan, Zacatecas, 1686–1728

Cabecera	Barrios
Pueblo de Tlacuitlapan	Asunción
	La Veracruz
	Jesús

Source: Barrios were sites of confraternities of the same name. See AHEZ, Libro de Cabildo, 6, f. 314, 1686. The confraternity of Jesús Nazareno formed sometime between 1707 and 1723. See AAG, Visitas Pastorales, box 1, ff. 174–74v, 1728.

TABLE 3.4. Rotation of indigenous
cabildo elections, Tlacuitlapan,
Zacatecas, 1709–1728

Year	Election sites
1709	La Veracruz
1710	Tlacuitlapan
1711	Not recorded (Asunción?)
1712	Tlacuitlapan
1713	Not recorded (Asunción?)
1714	La Veracruz
1715	Tlacuitlapan
1716	Not extant (Asunción?)
1717	Not extant
1718	Not extant
1719	La Veracruz
1720	Tlacuitlapan
1721	Asunción
1722	Tlacuitlapan
1723	Jesús
1724	La Veracruz
1725	Tlacuitlapan
1726	Asunción
1727	Not recorded
1728	Tlacuitlapan

Source: AHEZ, Libros de Cabildo, 10–19, various fojas, 1709–1728.

became more contentious with time. Eventually, the two larger units separated and formed their own pueblos (see Table 3.5).

Tonalá tried to meet the needs of its diverse barrios by rotating power. In 1659, a vecino of the "community of the Mexicans" held the post.[34] Over the following few years, Tonalá divided office-holding responsibilities with the barrios of San Josef and Chepinque. Ultimately, the power-sharing strategies that worked in Tlacuitlapan failed to appease the desires of Tonalá's barrios for autonomy. In the mid-seventeenth century, a strong Tlaxcalan community began to exert its presence in the pueblo. In 1654 and 1656, election results recorded the town's name as Tlaxcala instead of Tonalá.[35] By 1674, the Tlaxcalans had split from Tonalá. With Spanish approval, they established the pueblo of Chepinque, although they had probably been electing their own leaders unofficially for quite some time.[36] Both towns were then able to vote for their own officers.

Yet after its independence, Chepinque continued to rotate office holding with Tonalá and the barrio of San Josef (see Table 3.6). Perhaps this political arrangement persisted because of Spanish insistence on following the original mandate allowing for only two Indian alcaldes for the native communities. Chepinque would not control the majority of the elections until 1686, an indication perhaps of the entrenched power of leaders loyal to

TABLE 3.5. Evolution of indigenous towns
in southern Zacatecas, 1650–1736

Year	Cabecera(s)	Barrios
c. 1650	Tonalá	Chepinque
		San Josef
		El Niño
		San Juan (c. 1615)
		San Nicolás (c. 1667)
c. 1689	Tonalá Chepinque	El Niño
	San Josef	
c. 1736	Tonalá Chepinque	
	San Josef	
	El Niño	

Source: AHEZ, Libros de Cabildo, 3–26, various fojas, 1615–1736; AAG, Visitas Pastorales, f. 6v, 1667.

TABLE 3.6. Rotation of indigenous cabildo elections
in Tonalá Chepinque, Zacatecas, 1675–1688

Year	Alcalde	Barrio
1675	Pedro Miguel	Tonalá
1676	Pedro Miguel	Tonalá
1677	Juan Francisco	Tonalá
1678	Simón Miguel	Tonalá
1679	Pedro Martín	Tonalá
1680	Juan Bautista	Chepinque
1681	Andrés Suárez	Tonalá
1685	Juan Gerónimo	San Josef
1686	José de Bonifacio	Chepinque
1687	Mateo de Gamboa	Chepinque
1688	Juan Diego	San Josef

Source: AHEZ, Libro de Cabildo, 6, various fojas, 1675–1688.

Tonalá. Chepinque, however, eventually became the predominate community. In the documentation from this period, the town's name begins to appear as Tonalá Chepinque, and by the eighteenth century, just Chepinque. Tonalá remained closely affiliated to Chepinque for at least another forty years, although the community eventually lost its equal status and became a subject unit.

Despite these attempts at power sharing, Chepinque suffered from its own fragmentation as well. The activities of the barrio of San Josef offer an example of how indigenous communities employed different strategies to meet their leadership needs, whether they were sanctioned by or reported to Spanish authorities. By 1661, the barrio had a very active governor and alcalde, even though it lacked Spanish municipal status.[37] From

1673 to 1688, San Josef's officials took an active role in the cabildo of Tonalá Chepinque.[38] By 1689, the barrio's leaders argued that though they had participated in municipal governance "with the Indians of the pueblo of Chepinque," the elections "on many occasions brought about disharmony among the two barrios." To avoid these problems and for the convenience of all, the Indians of San Josef chose to separate themselves and to appoint their own alcalde.[39]

The need for more direct control of their affairs also prompted the separation of the barrio of El Niño. Chepinque attempted to pacify the self-governing aspirations of El Niño by allowing the barrio to nominate a minor official to the town council.[40] In 1713, the cabildo added a permanent new officer, a *teniente* (a deputy to the alcalde), in this instance Juan González, to represent the barrio of El Niño.[41] The concession proved only a temporary solution. In 1736 barrio leaders petitioned the Spanish council to allow them to form their own pueblo. A year later El Niño convened its own cabildo composed of an alcalde, two regidores, a fiscal, and two minor officials, a *mandón* (a mine foreman) and a *ministro* (assistant to the alcalde).[42]

Why were Tonalá and later Chepinque unable to maintain their hold over their sujetos? The answer may lie in the connection between the church and indigenous community formation. In other areas of New Spain, religious custodians encouraged native peoples to organize themselves not only in religious orientated cofradías but also in their secular counterparts, cabildos.[43] It is possible that the religious custodians of El Niño and San Josef, both of which had strong ties to their parishes, promoted their jurisdictional separation. The establishment of confraternities also had some direct bearing on indigenous government. It is striking that documentation for two cofradías proliferated around the same period as the secession movements of their barrios. The powerful sodality of San Josef appears in 1690, a year after that barrio declared its independence from Tonalá Chepinque in 1689. The confraternity of Nuestra Señora de la Soledad developed in 1681 around the time that Chepinque began sharing power at an equal level with Tonalá in 1680. In Tlacuitlapan, stronger and more autonomous confraternities may have lessened the need for separate municipal governments.

The time period of the fragmenting of sociopolitical units coincided with a growing push for autonomy that occurred throughout central and western Mexico, as indigenous councils became more experienced and sought more direct control over their affairs.[44] The creation of two additional Indian pueblos, San Josef and El Niño, illustrates native peoples' interest and success in the most essential feature of urban life, the establishment

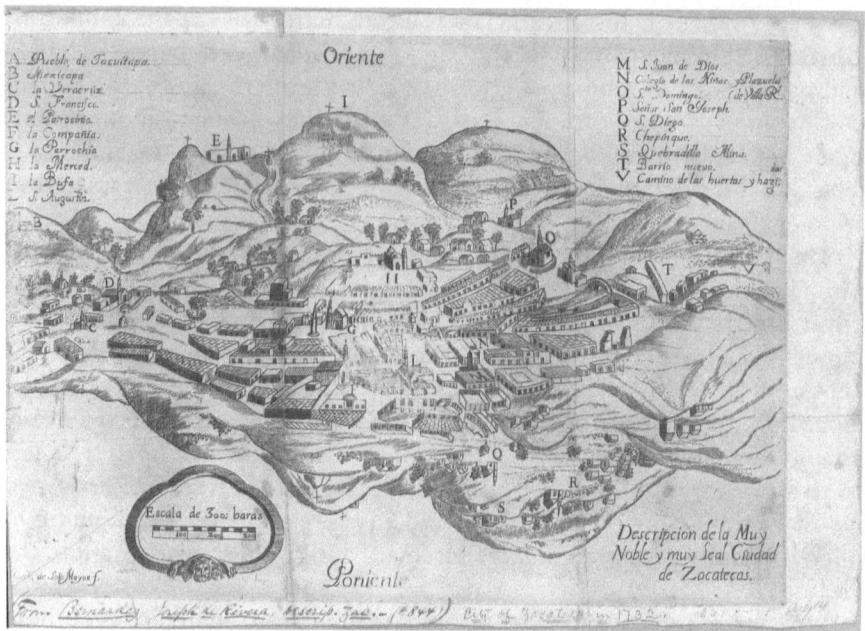

FIGURE 3.1. "Descripción de la Muy Noble y muy Leal Ciudad," by Joaquín de Sotomayor. Plan of Zacatecas by Joaquín de Sotomayor, 1732. In *Descripción breve de la muy noble y leal ciudad de Zacatecas . . . / delinéola el señor conde de Santiago de la Laguna, coronel de infantería española Joseph de Rivera Bernárdez.* Courtesy of the Bancroft Library, University of California, Berkeley.

of municipal governance. A map from 1732 (see Figure 3.1) illustrates the prominent role of the three Indian towns (El Niño had yet to separate)—Tlacuitlapan ("Pueblo de Tacuitapa") (A), San Josef (P), and Chepinque (R)—in the city's urban layout. It also illustrates several other indigenous neighborhoods, including Mexicapa[n] (B), La Veracruz (C), San Francisco (D), and San Diego (Q).

In the absence of dynastic leaders or altepetls, native peoples creatively adapted the cabildo to meet their towns' needs. Drawing on precontact practices, they shared power between individual ethnic groups for one position, rotated town council elections between cabecera and barrios, appointed officers to represent geographic districts, and sought autonomy as smaller independent units. By 1736, four Indian cabildos with a variety of officers existed in Zacatecas—a number reminiscent of a traditional altepetl with four *calpolli* (constituent political units)—a significant advance from 1609, when two alcaldes had watched over the entire indigenous population.

The Proliferation of Civic Office Holding

By the late seventeenth century the expansion of the cabildos gave adequate representation for the pueblos as native peoples remained eager to exercise their say in municipal life. The creation of new officers allowed for the consolidation of a larger, more formal leadership pool. However, large gaps of several years in the records—the product of lost, unrecorded, or destroyed election results—makes it difficult to track the expansion of the Indian cabildos and to determine when offices first appeared.[45] Even extant records are unreliable. Until the mid-1680s, Spanish notaries, or *escribanos*, recorded only the information they considered pertinent from the indigenous election results. It was not until 1686 that the notaries made greater efforts to enter the indigenous election memoriales (the minutes written or dictated by the alcalde) directly into the Spanish libros de cabildo.[46] While these notes provide detailed information on present and future officers, even the information given in these entries are not full records. Random discussions of disputes, election practices, and other commentaries suggest that the majority of the councils' internal machinations failed to be recorded or did not survive. This discussion thus focuses on the evolution of officers as they appear in the documents, keeping in mind that positions probably predated the records by several years as indigenous leadership bodies often evolved before they received formal Spanish approval.

Complete indigenous cabildos, following a standard evolutionary pattern in New Spain, took some time to develop in Zacatecas.[47] Positions arose slowly, with higher-level posts developing first and lower offices appearing with need or circumstances. The evolution of town councils depended on the size and location of the population. By the early seventeenth century, for example, most town councils in the Cuernavaca region had a governor, four alcaldes, four regidores, a fiscal, two alguaciles mayores (constables), four mayordomos, and a notary.[48] In a large community, a typical municipal council could double its number of officers to provide adequate geographic representation for its wards or units. Minor officials such as alguaciles and tenientes developed next. In Zacatecas, positions evolved slowly, some perhaps never developing at all. The cabildos themselves did not achieve maturity until the early eighteenth century, a lag of more than a hundred years in relation to their central Mexican counterparts.

For reasons I discuss below, the alcalde, not the governor, retained the preeminent position in Zacatecas's Indian cabildos. For more than fifty years the Spanish council bothered to record only the post of alcalde in their minutes. Most alcaldes served before and after their terms as regidores. Many had been confraternity mayordomos, a position that provided them with leadership experience and, in some pueblos, participation on the municipal council.[49] For example, Melchor Espinosa, the alcalde of Tlacuitlapan in 1626, had served as the mayordomo of the cofradía of the Vera Cruz nearly ten years earlier.[50] There is no biographical information on these individuals, but alcaldes had to satisfy certain prerequisites. They had to identify as indigenous and have vecino status in one of the pueblos. In other words, this coveted and important position could not be assumed by any individual, especially a non-Indian. Leaders had to be well known men of long and good standing residence in the community. Notaries usually described indigenous alcaldes in the records as married, intelligent individuals of good character, just as they would any other Spanish vecino.

The alcalde's duties included the standard law-and-order activities of other indigenous towns, the running of elections, and preparations for festivals and processions.[51] Native leaders were not responsible for collecting tribute or assigning and supervising labor drafts. They gathered household taxes.[52] Cabildos and confraternities also administered rents from homes within the pueblo's jurisdictions and authorized the sale and purchase of land within the town's boundaries.[53] These funds surely helped the cabildos pay for the various expenses incurred during religious and civic functions.[54] Cofradía inventories and vicereal inspections and censuses indicate that some municipalities had more resources than others.[55] Aside from these administrative tasks, alcaldes helped to resolve conflicts within the pueblos and sought to protect the community from exploitation. Although the Spanish cabildo appointed an indigenous protector every year, this individual often spent much of his time and energy working with native communities in the hinterlands, either tending to cries of abuse or suppressing rebellions.[56] Not surprisingly, this official appeared less frequently in the day-to-day struggles of Zacatecas's indigenous population after the establishment of the Indian cabildos. That said, the Indian protector often assisted the population with crafting legal petitions that circulated beyond the local jurisdictions of both the Spanish or Indian cabildos, such as with appeals to the Audiencia. Ultimately, at the local level, the task of defending community and individual interests often fell to the indigenous leadership. It is not known how they were compensated for their activities. A fragment from 1698 suggests the community endowed them with maize fields and property.[57]

In Zacatecas, most pueblos never developed cabildos with multiple alcaldes. In some towns, alcaldes shared power and influence with *gobernadores*, or governors. The scarcity of documents makes it difficult to determine when the position of governor evolved and the nature of his roles and duties—the office clearly postdates the institution of the alcalde.

Indian governors are not regularly noted in the records of the Spanish town council until the eighteenth century, and then only for the pueblo of San Josef, which possessed a governor as early as 1661, even though they had yet to develop a separate municipal council.[58] The existence of a governor in San Josef prior to the Spanish cabildo's formal approval of town status once again illustrates native peoples' initiative in developing and carrying out their own mechanisms of self-governance. The office is mentioned infrequently in the election results of the three other towns. The residents of Chepinque mentioned a governor in their 1688 elections, but this individual, Juan Antonio, may have represented San Josef.[59] In that period, both communities still participated in the same town council. The absence or lesser prominence of this office is easily explained. In central Mexico, the postconquest *tlatoani*, the hereditary ruler of the altepetl, assumed the role. Since neither the political position nor the dynastic figure existed in the city, there was initially little incentive or justification to develop the post.[60]

Perhaps in San Josef, as the pueblo grew in population and autonomy, the community took the opportunity to establish another leadership position, especially one associated with political sovereignty. Like the alcalde, the governor was an elected office. The post's three-year term was comparable to the position's lengthier tenure in central Mexico. However, an excerpt from an election in San Josef suggests that if the governor did not fulfill his duties, the Spanish corregidor could appoint another vecino in his place.[61] The governor never possessed more authority than the alcalde.[62] In fact, it was the newly confirmed alcalde who officially appointed the governor.[63] It appears that the two worked in concert. Since these leaders rarely appear in the documents, little is known about them or their activities.

The council's regidores (council members) were an equally elusive group in the records. Regidores do not appear in the documents until the 1690s, but these positions probably existed much earlier. The position of regidor declined by the mid-seventeenth century in central Mexico. In Zacatecas, this period marks the establishment and growth of the office, and there is no indication that this position waned as the colonial period progressed.[64] These civil servants remained important community leaders through the eighteenth century, partially because the councils rarely had multiple alcaldes like other places in central Mexico. Regidores (aldermen) played an active role in the council's elections and came from among the pueblos' principales, or influential community leaders. These aldermen were elected on a yearly basis but were rarely in jeopardy of losing their post. Once in office, these individuals usually retained their position for multiple years. The number of cabildo members depended on the size and seniority of the pueblo. By the 1720s, all three towns had four regidores, reminiscent of practices in central Mexico.[65] However, the numbers varied by time period. For example, the newly formed pueblo of El Niño had only two regidores in 1737.[66] In 1698, the pueblo of Chepinque had six aldermen, and the cabildo of Tlacuitlapan had seven councilmen. Perhaps these larger municipal councils attempted to appease other barrios or accommodate additional community members. An internal hierarchy also existed with a *regidor mayor*, a head councilman, followed by a second, third, and fourth in importance.[67]

Principales constituted another core group of vecinos who participated in town governance. These influential residents often presided at elections and other public functions, operating as a larger and more informal leadership body that derived status from their seniority. While the Nahuatl term *huehuetque* (or elders) never appears in the Spanish documents, the frequent use of the term *antiguos* conveys a similar meaning.[68] Although the extent of their influence and functions is unknown, they probably had some say in matters of importance to the community. For example, in Tlacuitlapan the election of the alcalde occurred "by the votes of the elders and the councilmen."[69]

Over time, several lower level functionaries joined the leadership cohort. Once again, there is very little information on these individuals. Archival evidence suggests that these minor officials appeared at different stages of the cabildos' expansion. Alguaciles and *topiles* (constables) developed fairly quickly as standard members of every cabildo, although the latter was not recorded as often as the former.[70] Religious functionaries such as fiscales and confraternity mayordomos also frequently participated in the council.[71] As the cabildo matured other positions evolved, such as *ministros* (men with some relationship to alguaciles), tenientes, and *justicias mayores*, men probably associated with local law and order.[72] Sometimes the appointment of minor office holders depended on local dynamics within the council. For example, San Josef made all sorts of innovations during the years it shared a joint cabildo with Chepinque. In the years when San Josef ran elections, they appointed a teniente. When Chepinque took charge, San Josef elected its own alcalde ordinario.[73] These lower-level officeholders were instrumental in providing different barrios with adequate geographic representation.

Other positions left almost no trace in the records. Although a strong tradition of native-language notaries did not develop in the city, fragments of indigenous-language records suggests their presence. It is equally unclear when Spanish-speaking notaries emerged, although it was probably sometime in the mid-seventeenth century, a period that marks the waning of Nahuatl writings. By 1709, Tonalá and Chepinque had their own notary, Andrés Martínez.[74] He was fluent in Castilian and perhaps in Nahuatl as well. The late development of this office may explain why this position, which was so prestigious and powerful in central Mexico, was rarely documented in the records. Another office that appears just as late and infrequently is that of *juez*. The term was used in the pueblo of San Josef for only a few years. It appears to have been a synonym for the word *regidor*.[75] Two lower-level functionaries, mandones and fiscales, bear further investigation because of their ties to the mining industry.

Mandones, according to royal ordinances on mining, served as overseers.[76] In Zacatecas, miners often selected fellow Spaniards to supervise their mining labor force. But records also indicate that multiple Indian mandones operated on behalf of the indigenous towns. In 1691, for example, each of Tlacuitlapan's three barrios had its own mandón. Diego Martín and Miguel de los Reyes served as the mandones respectively of the barrios of Jesús and the Veracruz. A third mandón, Jerónimo de la Cruz, while not associated with a particular barrio, probably represented the community of Asunción.[77] These men were not outsiders forced upon the indigenous community but respected vecinos elected to their positions by the Indian cabildos.[78] Mandones also served on the cabildos. For example, in 1709, four mandones, Manuel Padilla, Asensio Herrera, Salvador de la Trinidad, and Juan de la Cruz, participated alongside the regidores in Tlacuitlapan's municipal council.[79] Their post appears to have been more important than that of a typical lower-level functionary. For example, during elections, two of the three mandones voted before the confraternity's mayordomo because they had more seniority. The exact nature of their mining duties remains unclear. In other areas of New Spain, mandones collected tribute from their communities.[80] Perhaps in Zacatecas these individuals took charge of issues that affected labor forces from individual towns.

Fiscales were another set of officials associated with silver production. They often served as minor functionaries in both religious and secular organizations. At mining haciendas outside of the jurisdiction of Indian towns, fiscales may have been appointed or elected by miners or cuadrillas. They undertook religious duties, such as religious instructions to mine workers on Sundays and feast days. But they also intervened in nonreligious matters, frequently exercising low-level judicial power in a manner that exceeded those ascribed to their office. For example, during the Spanish campaigns to suppress the saçemis, local and religious authorities enlisted the support of several indigenous fiscales, enjoining them to search for and impound weapons, and to identify and report instigators and troublemakers to Spanish authorities.[81] The diligence and enthusiasm with which some fiscales undertook these duties caused great ire among the indigenous communities and led to their maltreatment at the hands of both indigenous and Spanish residents.[82] Spanish authorities eventually sided with the fiscales, promoting and protecting their activities. But it is important to remember that these officials operated on refining plants outside of the jurisdiction of the Indian towns. Yet even with the support of Spanish authorities, fiscales did not directly influence or intrude on the autonomy and authority of the native cabildos. Indeed, in the outlying mining haciendas, fiscales, as the sole representatives of Spanish and indigenous interests, may have had a more active, albeit exploitative, role than their counterparts in the indigenous pueblos.[83] More information is needed to understand whether these Indian overseers (and mandones as well) ultimately promoted Spanish or indigenous interests.

The composition of the cabildo, in both its minor and its major officeholders, reflected the unique roots of Zacatecas's indigenous communities. Important positions such as governor and notary developed late and without the prestige of their central Mexican counterparts, whereas alcaldes and regidores remained high-ranking officials. However by 1740, Zacatecas's indigenous municipal councils resembled those of central Mexico and Michoacán, although they were much smaller.[84] Indian cabildos possessed a core group of elected officeholders who served on the council for long terms of service in different capacities, supported by elders, an important unofficial leadership body, and a group of low-level functionaries. There would be variations of this model according to time period and pueblo. San Josef, for example, developed a wider variety of officers earlier than did the other towns. In general, a complete cabildo in the mid-eighteenth century possessed an alcalde, an alguacil, four regidores, a ministro, mandones, and two to three minor officials such as topiles or fiscales.[85] The expansion of the native cabildos allowed for the growth of leadership opportunities among the towns' many vecinos and addressed the challenges of representation generated by their ethnically diverse populations.

Election Patterns

By the mid-seventeenth century, the pueblos gained even more autonomy from the Spanish municipal council. By this period, they determined the number and variety of their officers, directly chose their representatives, and had more control over where and how they conducted elections. Although the proceedings could not be ratified without Spanish approval, this procedure was a far cry from the days when colonial authorities had appointed an alcalde from a list of three indigenous candidates.[86] Fortunately, several documents illustrate how the various pueblos ran their elections.[87]

Cabildo sessions and elections took place in the individual towns. Native leaders held their meetings either at the pueblo's church or at the chapel of one of the indigenous confraternities.[88] It is not clear whether the meeting place, like the office, rotated according to which barrio controlled the elections. For example, native peoples convened elections in the capilla of the Veracruz the year that barrio assumed charge of the proceedings.[89] In San Josef, gatherings occurred in the *sala*, a general dwelling allocated for the pueblo's business while residents constructed their church.[90] Officers, principales, and sometimes the local cleric gathered at these sites to vote for the alcalde and other minor officials, such as the alguacil mayor. Before they controlled their elections, indigenous leaders were assigned their offices after the Spanish cabildo selected their representatives in early January. By 1690, native peoples usually ran their elections in December and submitted their results to the Spanish municipal council for acceptance within the first week of the year.[91] Once approved, the corregidor sent their decisions to Guadalajara for final ratification by the Audiencia. There are no indications that Spanish authorities overturned their results.

A group of present and past officeholders, along with select community members, chose the alcalde and other officials. Election procedures varied by communities and time periods. In pueblos with strong ties to their parishes, such as San Josef and El Niño, the local priest played a role in running the elections, whereas in other towns the outgoing alcalde ran the meeting.[92] In San Josef, the leadership team usually nominated two to three candidates for each position. A group of no more than twenty men then elected the candidates.[93] A note from 1702 suggests that occasionally native peoples selected officials by secret vote. In 1732, when the governor and alcalde were selected from among three candidates, the former won with eighteen votes and the latter with seventeen.[94] That same year, the post of alguacil mayor went to a man who gathered twelve. A similar process occurred in Chepinque and El Niño. In Tlacuitlapan the alcalde, the regidores, and the elders nominated and chose the incoming alcalde.[95] Perhaps other community members had input in selecting the candidates for nomination. However, it appears that no more than a total of four to twenty of Tlacuitlapan's vecinos participated in the process.[96]

The casting of votes was governed by a protocol based on seniority that encompassed age and previous office holding. Records from a 1691 election in the pueblo of Tlacuitlapan provide a rare glimpse into this process (see Table 3.7).[97] As the oldest person in the pueblo and a two-time alcalde, the cabildo ceded the honor of casting the first vote to Antonio de Trinidad. Priority was then given to two past alcaldes, Mateo Hernández and Nicolás Ramos. The former had held the post three times. After the alcaldes, it becomes more difficult to determine which factor, age or office,

TABLE 3.7. Voting order and qualifications, alcalde elections, Tlacuitlapan, 1691

Order of voters	Name	Qualification(s)
First	Antonio de Trinidad	Eldest individual in the town; two-time alcalde
Second	Mateo Hernández	Three-time alcalde
Third	Nicolás Ramos	Alcalde
Fourth	Sebastián Ramírez	Capitán
Fifth	Diego Martín	Mandón of Jesús
Sixth	Jerónimo de la Cruz	Mandón [of Asunción?]
Seventh	Diego García	Elder
Eighth	Nicolás Martín	Elder
Ninth	Juan Martín	Criollo of town (and outgoing alcalde)
Tenth	Sebastián López	Mayordomo of Nuestra Señora de la Asunción
Eleventh	Miguel de los Reyes	Mandón of La Veracruz

Source: AHEZ, Libro de Cabildo, 7, ff. 328–28v, 1691.

held precedence. The three subsequent voters were a captain and two mandones, which suggests that their positions outranked the "elder" status of Diego García and Nicolás Martín. Yet these same antiguos preceded another mandón, Miguel de los Reyes, and the foreman of a confraternity, Sebastián López. Juan Martín, the current alcalde, figured ninth out of eleven. Clearly, other factors, including probably age, influenced the process. In one of his final roles in office, Juan Martín tallied the results and certified the election. In this case, Nicolás José defeated Lucas Martín by seven to five votes.

Spanish influence over the appointment of officeholders cannot be discounted in spite of viceregal and royal ordinance expressly forbidding colonial officials from interfering in indigenous elections.[98] This was especially the case in pueblos with strong parish ties. The local priest was an omnipresent figure in the election meetings of many towns, especially in the parish of San Josef, where the cleric seems to have run the elections. A 1701 entry from the town states that the priest, Fray Pedro Martínez, "had proposed" the three candidates for the positions of alcalde, alguacil mayor, and topil. Another record from 1724 indicates that the native leadership finalized their choices with the assistance of their priest.[99] The situation was similar in El Niño, another pueblo with close affiliation to its parish. In 1737, the curate assisted the town with its first independent elections.[100] The pueblo, which had been a barrio since the late sixteenth century and had participated in elections with Tonalá Chepinque, did not lack experience in civic government. However, religious interference occurred even in pueblos accustomed to running their own elections. During Tlacuitlapan's 1748 elections, the local priest proposed three individuals for alcalde. Two years later an indigenous official once again assumed the task.[101] Although religious authorities may have been invited by native leaders to participate in elections, their presence suggests an intrusive attempt on the part of the church to influence the pueblos' operations. Overall, religious in Zacatecas made rather minor sociopolitical interventions when compared to other indigenous communities in New Spain.[102]

Secular authorities also interfered with indigenous governance. In 1676, when native people failed to present officers, Spanish authorities ordered the indigenous alcaldes from the previous year, Francisco Real of Tlacuitlapan and Pedro Miguel of Tonalá, to continue in their positions.[103] Likewise, in 1657, when the pueblo of Tlacuitlapan could not agree upon an alcalde because of dissension among electors, Spanish officials appointed Pedro Sebastián, a vecino of the pueblo.[104] These examples aside, election records suggest that the frequency and level of interference by Spanish officials was minor. Authorities appointed officers but did not remove them. No matter how little they interfered in the day-to-day operations of the pueblos, Spanish officials demanded a certain level of submission, even if only on paper. In the early eighteenth century, a change in the tone and content of the election memorandums, manifested in more formal and obsequious language directed at the Spanish cabildo, speaks to tensions and power struggles between the groups that, as we shall see, became more contentious in the late colonial period.

Conflicts within the community also affected elections. Power struggles and differences between barrios were commonplace. Factions within cabildos could be equally problematic. In 1719, Tlacuitlapan's cabildo had to hold three elections before they arrived at a nominee, Miguel Reyes.[105] In addition, there were periods when office holding held little attraction for the population. Spanish cabildo records note years in which indigenous people did not submit their election results or when alcaldes had to be summoned to pick up their staffs of office.[106] In 1657, the cabildo of Tlacuitlapan stated that it had not conducted an election because it could not settle on anyone who would take the office. Individuals who were eligible to hold the post cited, among other excuses, prior service as a reason for not holding office again.[107]

This lack of interest in leadership positions occurred during a downturn in mining activity, when problems in the community, most notably epidemics, a slow economy, and depopulation, would have proved detrimental to community finances. Alcaldes probably received very little compensation for their duties, and the lack of tribute collection left them with few opportunities to extract funds from their communities. Office holding came second to basic economic needs. But the cabildos regenerated in size and prestige as the mining economy began to revive and the migrant population increased at the end of the seventeenth century. As the economic climate improved, native peoples once again used the institution as a vehicle to seek prestige and status.

Leaders and Vecinos

The native town councils were crucial to the evolution of the indigenous pueblos and to the creation of a leadership group in Zacatecas. In central Mexico native nobles often fulfilled the pueblo's core roles of governor, alcalde, regidor, and notary. There is no compelling evidence from the sixteenth or seventeenth centuries to suggest the presence of indigenous nobles in the city. This should not be surprising given the lack of incentives for elites to leave their communities.[108] In Zacatecas, a mere five recorded cases of the honorific and leadership titles *don* or *cacique* appear in reference to an indigenous person before 1690. None of these individuals possessed leadership or even vecino status. They were traders or merchants from the hinterlands traveling through the city.

In Zacatecas, socially mobile commoners assumed roles commonly reserved for hereditary elites in central Mexico. Many of these individuals were Nahuas. The Mexica, in particular, dominated religious and secular offices in the period from 1550 to 1630. Recall that in the sixteenth century the leadership of the cofradía of the Vera Cruz had been composed of "many mexicanos."[109] In the towns, the Mexica not only served as alcaldes in their own stronghold of Tlacuitlapan, but they also exercised that office four times in a nine-year period (1611–1619) in the Tarascan community of Tonalá.[110] Individuals from Tlaxcala and Texcoco also appear frequently in this period in elected positions. To what can we attribute their significant presence in the leadership ranks? Perhaps Spaniards encouraged and supported the assumption of office holding by the more ethnically and linguistically familiar groups of central Mexico. It is more likely, however, that central Mexicans, familiar with Spanish practices and policies, quickly began monopolizing colonial institutions and, as we shall see, created their own kinship leadership groups.

By 1630, it is unclear which ethnic groups dominated indigenous positions of leadership, either because of Spanish disinterest in marking individual ethnic identities or because, for some native people, especially those *criollo* (native born) to the city, their ancestral ethnic identity became less salient.[111] After this period, charting the evolution of a group of professional officeholders who repeatedly served as alcaldes or regidores offers greater insight into the dynamics of indigenous leadership than tracing positions through ethnic lines.[112] In Tlacuitlapan, four men held the position of alcalde eight times in the first eleven years of the office's existence

(1610–1621). The monopoly of this post by a few men continued through the seventeenth century. Of the sixty-six elections recorded for Tlacuitlapan between 1610 and 1700 (see Table 3.8), ten men together held the position of alcalde thirty-one times (47 percent).[113] In the same period, a slightly greater distribution of the office occurred in the town of Tonalá Chepinque (see Table 3.9). Of the fifty-nine extant elections for that pueblo, ten men together occupied the position of alcalde twenty-four times (41 percent).[114] In both pueblos several men held the office three times. In Tlacuitlapan, Antonio de la Trinidad served as alcalde a record ten times before the community barred him from the position.[115] However, he still remained on the cabildo as a regidor, a common practice among former alcaldes. In 1695, all the regidores of Tlacuitlapan had also held the post of alcalde.[116] In addition, it was not unknown for officials to occupy positions in other towns. Mateo de Gamboa and Juan Diego, for example, served as alcaldes of Tlacuitlapan and San Josef and Tonalá. Many also had held prominent

TABLE 3.8. Repeat alcaldes in Tlacuitlapan, Zacatecas, 1610–1700

Name	Years
Pedro Reynoso	1610, 1614
Juan Agustín	1611, 1615
Buenaventura de la Cruz	1613, 1617
Juan Francisco	1620, 1621, 1625
Gaspar de los Reyes	1657, 1689, 1699
Diego García	1665, 1668
Antonio de la Trinidad	1670, 1672, 1678 (and seven other unmarked years)
Melchor de los Reyes	1671, 1679, 1698
Francisco Real	1675, 1676
Mateo Hernández	1687, 1693

Source: AHEZ, Libros de Cabildo, 2–9, various fojas, 1610–1700.

TABLE 3.9. Repeat alcaldes in Tonalá Chepinque, Zacatecas, 1610–1700

Name	Years
Francisco Miguel	1610, 1615, 1618
Balthazar García	1619, 1624, 1631
Luis de la Cruz	1656, 1659
Francisco Hernández	1659, 1665
Mateo de Gamboa	1667, 1687
Francisco Miguel	1668, 1678
Juan Francisco	1670, 1674, 1677
Diego López de Lizalde	1673, 1674, 1692
Pedro Miguel	1675, 1676
Francisco López	1697, 1700

Source: AHEZ, Libros de Cabildo, 2–9, various fojas, 1610–1700.

religious offices, such as confraternity mayordomos. The consolidation of office holding could have been even higher because more than a third of the election results for the seventeenth century were lost, unrecorded, or destroyed. The trend of repeat office holding continued through the eighteenth century.

There is some evidence for the development of powerful political kinship networks in the pueblo of Tlacuitlapan. One Agustín de la Trinidad, a relative of the ten-time alcalde Antonio de la Trinidad, held the position of alguacil in Tonalá Chepinque and Tlacuitlapan (1673 and 1681, respectively). The de los Reyes trio—Melchor, Gaspar, and José—held the office of alcalde seven times; and two men surnamed de los Reyes, Miguel and Juan, served as alguaciles.[117] In 1694, the governing body of Tlacuitlapan elected Lorenzo García alcalde of the pueblo for the following year not only for his abilities but also because his father, Diego, had served in the position in 1665 and 1668.[118] In 1732, two brothers competed for the position of alcalde in the pueblo of San Josef.[119]

As these examples illustrate, the development of a small group of principales who derived their status from seniority and office holding remedied the lack of an indigenous hereditary rulership. These individuals utilized Spanish governance institutions (municipal councils and confraternities) to dominate leadership positions for themselves and others within their kinship or social networks. Under these conditions, neither the absence of indigenous elites nor the running of yearly elections made Zacatecas's indigenous cabildos more egalitarian.[120] Offices were, at first, more open in the sense that a small group of commoners had the opportunity to assume leadership positions. Over time, however, as officers accrued status through service and seniority, they began to appropriate honorific titles and mimic noble practices. By the beginning of the eighteenth century there was a titled don in the ranks of every town council, at least two indigenous alcaldes sported the title of *capitán*, and communities referred to cabildo members as principales and caciques, titles usually reserved for hereditary nobles in central Mexico.[121] Native officials even began exercising roles outside of their communities. In 1689, the Spanish cabildo named Juan Basílico, an indio principal of the town of Chepinque, Zacatecas's master builder.[122] Even Spanish officeholders recognized the importance of indigenous leaders. In 1708, during a prominent celebration, Spanish emissaries and officials invited the governors, alcaldes, alguaciles, regidores, ministers, and some of the principales of the Indian towns to accompany them, on horseback, in a parade though the city.[123] Their prominent presence in the procession was a far cry from the time when their participation in special events had been limited to setting up fences, making arches, and gathering wood.

Sources indicate that these powerful and prestigious positions remained in the hands of individuals who identified as Indian. Occasionally Spaniards identified an alcalde, such as Baltasar García in 1624, as *ladino*. But this descriptor was not particularly remarkable or incompatible with an indigenous identity. To be "ladino" in this period literally meant to be bilingual. Baltasar was a migrant from central Mexico who had surely learned Spanish in the viceregal capital.[124] Before 1650 many leaders did not speak Spanish and required the assistance of an interpreter to receive their office.[125] But by the mid-seventeenth century the majority of office holders spoke Castilian and had fluency in Spanish practices and customs.[126] While the ethnic descriptor *mestizo* never appears in association with an indigenous official in the documents, inevitably some individuals of mixed indigenous ancestry held leadership positions. Yet the retention and assumption of these important posts required that these individuals possess close ties with the indigenous sphere. In Cuernavaca, for example, Robert Haskett argues that as long as mestizos "were culturally part of the Indian ruling group," they did not face serious challenges to participating in indigenous governance. Still, Zacatecas's records do not indicate that non-Indians infiltrated the leadership ranks.[127] In the period spanning 1610 to 1736, no alcalde was identified by a nonindigenous ethnic category.[128] Nor do we encounter any records of complaints from native peoples of mestizos taking over their offices.

Other factors than ethnicity and ancestry played an equal or greater role in the selection of leaders. Cabildo members, after all, served as caretakers and guardians of their communities and the position was not likely to be bestowed on a disinterested outsider. In 1692, the cabildo of Tonalá Chepinque's nomination of Juan Francisco for alcalde offers insight into the qualities they considered necessary to hold and exercise the office. They described Francisco as a man of "ability and intelligence and of good character and talents." Equally important he was a "natural [Indian] and a vecino."[129] Records like this one indicate that vecino status was mandatory. Preference also was given to individuals who had been born in the town. Recall the indigenous alcalde Juan Martín whose "criollo" status had been listed as one of his leadership qualifications. In 1691, one of the principales of Tlacuitlapan's cabildo recommended Nicolás José for the post of alcalde because "he was a criollo of this pueblo" whom he had "known since birth and who had always behaved responsibly."[130] A few year later, in the same town, leaders cited the good standing of Matías Ramírez and that of his parents as the basis of his appointment.[131] The elections of Nicolás José and Matías Ramírez indicates that Zacatecas's native population was most concerned that its leaders identified as indigenous, possessed familial ties, were born in the pueblo, and had vecino status. Indigenous officials who rose to power probably had well-developed social networks in their towns. Indeed, as the eighteenth century progressed, identifying as criollo to the pueblo was as much a mark of status as were seniority and office holding.

The election of men with strong ties to the community was critical as they would be at the forefront of both espousing its rights and protecting it from exploitation by other corporate ethnic groups. In 1661, for example, the leaders of San Josef, governor Francisco de Ibarra and alcalde Matheo de Gamboa, wrote a petition to the crown and the Audiencia of Guadalajara to complain about Spanish miners who entered the town and forcibly removed its vecinos to labor against their will at mining haciendas.[132] These tactics, the officials lamented, injured individual community members and threatened the very integrity of the town. If the Spaniards did not cease their raids, they lamented, the pueblo soon would be depopulated. The petition illustrates Ibarra and Gamboa's understanding of colonial policies and laws, basing their request on royal orders that outlined the community's right to proper treatment and protection by Spaniards. Other entries, such as one from the cabildo of Tonalá Chepinque in 1691, indicate that Indian leaders remained "well informed of their rights and actions and what in similar cases they could and should do" in regard to their elections and other jurisdictional issues.[133] As the Indian cabildos grew in officials and power, they became even more active in defending their own corporate rights. In the late colonial period they even aroused the ire of Spanish officials by conducting patrols outside of the native towns.

One could argue that in the establishment of indigenous governance, de la Fuente created another layer of colonial authority (albeit indigenous) to oversee the activities of the native population. Indigenous officials did cooperate with their Spanish counterparts, but there is no compelling proof of strong ties between the two groups. This is not to say that the Indian pueblos were free of Spanish interference (or corrupt leaders for that matter). In Zacatecas, however, the absence of an hereditary nobility cultivated an indigenous leadership with fewer incentives to collaborate with Spaniards. Nor should we underestimate the mining economy's inveterate need for labor in encouraging Spaniards to cooperate with their indigenous labor force, especially in the administration of their towns. These conditions facilitated the Indian cabildos' ability to remain a colonial bastion of support for native peoples.[134]

In the development of the Indian cabildos we see the continued evolution of indigenous identities within Spanish institutions in seventeenth-century Zacatecas. By the 1630s, Spanish records, as I have discussed, rarely noted the individual ethnic identity of alcaldes and other officials. While this practice reflects Spanish disinterest, it also speaks to changes in the origins and affiliations of the indigenous population and a gradual fading of individual ethnicities in favor of broader, indigenous associations. The mining boom of the early seventeenth century ushered in another substantial wave of indigenous migrants with significant ties to their home communities. But both migrants and locally born native peoples displayed a preference for identifying with their vecino status in an Indian town, or as residents of the city of Zacatecas, rather than identifying with their ancestral homelands. It is in this period that the term *criollo* (locally born) emerges as an important indicator of status and legitimacy in the community. Indians frequently used both *criollo* and *vecino* when identifying themselves in the documents to indicate both local and civic statuses that complemented, not negated, their indigenous identity. Indeed, native people rarely, and even Spaniards only occasionally, employed the term *ladino* as an ethnic descriptor (i.e., to indicate a Hispanized Indian). *Ladino*, when used as a proxy for acculturation, often suggests significant levels of ethnic disintegration. But in Zacatecas, changes in cultural practices did not efface indigenous identities. Rather, as native peoples acquired fluency with Spanish institutions and customs, their practices signaled the emergence of ethnicities tied to multiple identities—ancestral, corporate, and civic—that were nevertheless indigenous.

Indian cabildos remained a distinctly indigenous institution in spite of their Spanish origins and structures. The native leadership remained the most visible symbols and active guardians of indigenous culture and practices in their town. Many leaders continued to speak only Nahuatl. The staff of office was often presented to the newly appointed Indian alcalde through the services of a translator. An interpreter was present whenever Nahuatl-speaking representatives of the Indian town councils presented petitions to the Spanish cabildo. The predominance of Nahuatl speakers in the leadership reflected the continued use of Nahuatl in religious and secular functions by the criollo population, particularly through the middle of the century. Cabildo decrees from the 1640s and 1650s required that religious officials serving the indigenous population spoke Nahuatl.[135] As late as 1640, a priest encountered trouble procuring a post in the city because, unlike his predecessors, he lacked fluency in Nahuatl. Indigenous cabildos facilitated the formation of native towns and leaders. The creation and endurance of these institutions and positions played a key role in the perpetuation of a corporate indigenous identity through the late colonial period.

· · ·

Spaniards transferred their preference for city living and institutions to the Americas. In the seventeenth century, Zacatecas represented New Spain's largest, northernmost urban outpost of Spanish and native colonists. Over time, native peoples recognized the possibility of greater input in the daily and long-term affairs of their communities through the creation of towns and cabildos. While a Spanish official initially appointed the first indigenous leaders, these actions should not overshadow native peoples' internal desire for indigenous governance or diminish their initiative in establishing Spanish-style cabildos in their pueblos. The development of Indian cabildos remedied the absence of a hereditary leadership, juridical autonomy, and ethnic cohesion, thus providing Indian vecinos with autonomy, authority, and jurisdiction—albeit limited at times—over their affairs. The establishment in the early seventeenth century of native alcaldes and indigenous cabildos converted the city's indigenous communities into official sociopolitical entities. Cabildos (and their predecessors, cofradías) enabled native people to promote indigenous interests individually and as a corporate group. Indigenous leaders protected their community from abuse and exploitation, they promoted their pueblo's interest, and they helped maintain order in and around their town. The Indian towns provided its residents official entry into municipal life within their own juridical spaces, allowing native people to exercise both civic (vecino) and indigenous identities.

In the early seventeenth century, Zacatecas's native vecinos were far from unified geographically, culturally, or even politically. The mining boom brought a steady stream of ethnically diverse migrants. Immigrants and long-term residents lived throughout the city, in the pueblos, at mining haciendas, or at ethnically diverse barrios on the borders of the Spanish traza and the Indian pueblos. In some of these neighborhoods, violent ritualized fighting took place between occupational groups on Sundays and holidays. Within the political arena, barrios separated from towns and indigenous leaders did not always agree with their subjects. Yet even with division at the individual and community level, unity and consolidation prevailed. By 1630, the basic sociopolitical features and organizations of Zacatecas's indigenous communities were in place and would remain so until the late colonial period. Mirroring an empirewide trend, native society in Zacatecas entered a mature period, one with the necessary institutions, leaders, social networks, and urban experiences to retain its indigenous identity as it weathered the economic and population vicissitudes generated by the city's booms and busts.

4   Indios and Vecinos: The Maturation of Urban Indigenous Society, 1655–1739

Following a fifteen-year mining downturn, Zacatecas reached its economic apogee thanks to a spectacular surge in silver production from 1705 to 1732. The boom ushered in waves of migrants of all ethnicities, sexes, and social levels seeking better fortunes and employment at mines or refining plants. By 1732, the city reached its colonial-era population apex of forty thousand individuals.[1] These boom years were not without their trials and challenges for officials, residents, and miners and workers. Disputes and quarrels, both personal and corporate, arose over wealth and resources. As vecinos and laborers, the indigenous population did not remain immune from the tensions and changing socioeconomic circumstances of the period.

In the spring of 1734, the corregidor Don Joseph de Ribera Bernárdez received an unusual and alarming communication from the city's native leadership. The message made it clear that if Ribera Bernárdez failed to resolve certain matters in favor of the Indian leaders and residents of San Josef, the city should brace itself for a widespread indigenous *motín*, or riot.[2] For upon hearing of San Josef's grievances, the other indigenous towns stood ready to rally to its side. Ribera Bernárdez took the warning very seriously. Rarely did Indian towns or even individuals threaten violence against the Spanish traza or local authorities. The rallying of unity among pueblos also underscored the seriousness of the situation. What event could have generated so much conflict, threatening to shatter the relatively peaceful, centuries-long coexistence between Spaniards and native peoples? Of all things, the source of contention was a custodial battle over a revered statue between a Spanish confraternity and the cofradía of the pueblo of San Josef. The image in question, heavily adorned in silver, represented a substantial financial investment. To the native community, it also represented their religious integrity and civic autonomy.

Conflictive episodes between individuals also occurred with frequency throughout the boom. In 1702, an indigenous woman, Andrea Rodríguez, filed a petition against a Spaniard, Joseph Carrasco, for abducting her two adopted children, Joseph and Antonio. Carrasco refused to return the boys, countersuing Andrea for their custody.[3] In 1719, María Josefa León and Joseph de la Cruz began a protracted and bitter case over the rights to a silver mine situated on the bluffs of the city.[4] And in 1729, two Indians from Chepinque, Joseph Antonio García and Anastasio de los Santos, filed a petition against local officials claiming that the community had taken possession of some houses and land on the edge of the city belonging to their family for several generations.[5] Such were the quarrels, among many others, over children, mines, and property that characterized the boom.

On the surface these cases may not appear particularly remarkable. But on closer inspection, they reveal both the vulnerability and the resiliency of the native population in the early eighteenth century. Andrea, for example, was not fighting to keep indigenous children from the hands of abusive Spanish miners (a common practice in the period). Her adopted children were Spaniards. The case of the rival miners stands out because the two litigants were indigenous people. Native peoples (and primarily men, not women) were usually associated with labor in the mines, not with the means of production. The petition of Antonio García and Anastasio de los Santos is equally striking. Their quarrel was with indigenous, not Spanish, officials. The two litigants sought to sell the houses to individuals from Zacatecas. Community leaders, unwilling to see the land alienated from Chepinque, refused the request. In all three examples, native peoples called on their status as "vecinos" to support their arguments and bolster their credibility. In the latter case, Antonio and Anastasio argued that because they were vecinos of Zacatecas, not Chepinque, they were not beholden to the rulings of the cabildo of the Indian town.

These cases, which I examine in greater detail in this chapter, reveal much about native society and ethnicity in this economically volatile period. This chapter spans two mining busts, from 1630 to 1670 and from 1690 to 1705, as well as two booms, from 1670 to 1690 and from 1705 to 1732. Episodes of elevated production, with their influx of migrants and merchants, often created their own microenvironments that both transformed and destabilized the status quo. Native societies and communities were influenced by the demographic, cultural, and social changes that developed in the boom's wake. One need only look to the preceding examples for evidence of native peoples' full engagement with Spanish institutions, individuals, and the money economy. Yet this period also witnessed the maturation of an urban indigenous society and culture in Zacatecas, at both the community and the individual level, which continued to develop indigenous identities, practices, and associations, even as it embraced Spanish-style civic life.

Part of the answer to how indigenous culture survived and flourished in spite of the social and demographic changes ushered in by the boom lay in the stability of native institutions and communities. By the late seventeenth century, native cabildos, communities, confraternities, and social networks had been in place for close to a hundred years. They had attained, as with other institutions in Spanish America, "a certain equilibrium," serving as cultural and political bastions of indigenous society.[6] Of equal importance, the native community was composed of long-term (many multigenerational) native vecinos who retained their associations with the indigenous world even as they acquired the skills and fluency to succeed in the Spanish urban environment. Permanent residents strengthened and renewed indigenous connections through their associations with incoming immigrants, who brought with them indigenous practices and traditions. Together, these two groups created a critical population mass that facilitated continued indigenous social and kinship networks and organizations.[7] By the early eighteenth century, native peoples had developed the strategies and institutions they needed to survive (and even prosper) as a community and ethnic group in a multicultural urban environment.

Weathering the Bust: Stability and Solidarity in Community

Zacatecas's seventeenth-century mining downturn began in the mid-1630s. It followed a spectacular twenty-year boom from 1615 to 1635. Production decline was the product of several factors, including the disruption of mercury supplies, lack of credit, and changes in administrative policies that made financing mining ventures more challenging.[8] It was not the product of a shortage of Indian laborers. Mining, though a labor-intensive industry, never required more than five thousand workers at a time.[9] Many miners, however, blamed their problems on the exodus of the labor force, particularly "la gran falta" (the great lack) of indigenous workers. By 1637, the Spanish cabildo likewise complained bitterly of the "falta de vecindad" (lack of residents) and "gente de servicio" (workers).[10] It warned of waning mining production, arguing that less and less silver was being extracted from the mines. The lack of workers also included the many urban laborers who served the communities, from butchers and candle makers to housekeepers and water carriers. And there was some truth to the cabildo's complaints. Economic busts usually produced population exoduses as workers searched for income from alternative sites or enterprises. Such was the case of Zacatecas, where some laborers and *gente de servicio*, struggling to make ends meet or seeking new opportunities, abandoned the city, searching for work and markets at other boom sites. These included strikes in the 1630s more than 350 miles to the north, at Parral in Nueva Vizcaya, as well as from 1670 to 1690 in Sombrerete. Desperate miners pleaded with the crown to give them Indians in repartimiento or to send them enslaved workers (*cafres*) from the Philippines.[11]

The decline in silver production did not affect Spanish miners and officials alone. Mine laborers, petty merchants and shop owners, female street vendors, and laundresses all fell victim to the economic and social consequences of the contracting economy. No aspect of city life, from trade and commercial enterprise to marriages and criminal infractions, remained immune from the population downturn. The scarcity of documents from 1630 through 1670 produced by officials, miners, religious figures, and laboring vecinos reflects waning commercial and civic activity, with a marked decrease in records of every genre—including criminal, civil, ecclesiastical, and personal correspondences. In both the Spanish traza and the Indian towns, confraternity leaders enrolled fewer members and collected fewer alms. The city's churches entered fewer petitions to marry. Processions and feast days lacked the opulence of previous years. The demand for interpreters declined, and notaries recorded smaller numbers of land and property transactions. Decreased tax revenues and other sources of municipal income created less administrative business for cash-strapped cabildos. Minutes of meetings were significantly shorter than for other periods. They were dominated by persistent requests to the crown for assistance recruiting laborers or the granting of concessions, such as the reduction of the *alcabala*, or merchandise duties.

The decline in the city's population cannot be ascribed solely to voluntary migration. The *gran falta* of indigenous people and other workers was also the product of a *gran mortandad*, an epidemic that caused "great death."[12] Spanish records note that the epidemic of 1634 to 1637 struck the indigenous population with particular severity.[13] This outbreak had followed relatively quickly on the heels of a series of "contagious illnesses" that killed a large number of Spaniards, blacks, Indians, and mulattos in 1629. The contagions were probably strains of a virulent *cocoliztli* (illness) or plague that struck the Valley of Mexico during the same period.[14] The combination of disease and out-migration slowed production and urban growth. Some smaller mining centers folded under such pressure, becoming "ghost towns," never to regain their prosperity.

The cabildo minutes record the frustrations of Spanish miners and officials. But what was the state of the laboring population? After all, every mine that closed not only brought possible financial ruin to its owner but also left an entire cuadrilla bereft of work. The native population in this period, hit hard by disease, had to face uncertain economic times. If we follow the paradigm that mine workers were primarily transient men, then most laborers probably left the city in search of better prospects. Flight did occur. But it was not the only response. Consider the example of Matheo de Morales, an indigenous harp instructor. He had migrated from Michoacán and continued to offer lessons through the economic downturn until illness struck him in 1656. He made his final plans to be buried at the church of San Juan de Dios.[15] A few years earlier, Isabel Rodríguez, a widow and "indigenous vecina of Zacatecas," stayed on in the city even after her son was murdered.[16] Economic realities made emigration necessary for many native peoples in this period. But seeking employment and abandoning one's community were two distinct processes. For large sections of the indigenous population, the city had become more than just a place to work. Francisco Martín, for example, was an indigenous migrant from Querétaro. But he and his parents had relocated to the barrio of Santo Domingo, a neighborhood in San Josef, and had been proud to call themselves vecinos. Rather than return to Querétaro during the downturn, Francisco, his wife, his son, and his daughter (all Zacatecas born) continued to labor cutting wood and making charcoal for the city's mines at a nearby ranch.[17] Some individuals like Francisco had lived in Zacatecas for decades. Others, like his wife and children, had never called any other place home.[18]

Many vecinos with strong ties to Zacatecas left the city but for only temporary periods. Magdalena de la Cruz and her husband, for example, departed Zacatecas in search of work in 1664.[19] But they left their son Josepe with his uncle—a significant sign that they had not cut ties with the city. Two years later, in 1666, they returned to their kin and resumed their lives in Tlacuitlapan. In another example from a later mining bust, in 1742, Mathías de Acosta returned to the pueblo of Chepinque after a five-year stay in the northern mining town of Sombrerete. According to a witness, while Mathias "had had some absences from the town, he had always returned, recognizing Chepinque as his pueblo."[20] Mathias not only returned to Chepinque but also proceeded to marry a native woman from the town. Episodes of this nature were not uncommon. Documents attest to large numbers of native émigrés who embarked on temporary sojourns only to return to Zacatecas, reestablish connections with their loved ones, and establish deeper roots in the city.

Married couples like Magdalena de la Cruz and her spouse were one of several domestic units—including families, widow-headed households, and single men and women—who provided the city with social stability in this period. The indigenous family in the preconquest period was a fundamental social institution, ensuring biological reproduction and serving as a mechanism to socialize children and reinforce gendered labored roles.[21] It has been argued that under Spanish rule, it was rural indigenous society that conserved traditional family order.[22] Qualitative and quantitative documents on indigenous family life in Zacatecas are thin, so we cannot speak with certainty on how urban living changed traditional familial practices. Yet indigenous familial structures reconstituted themselves in Zacatecas, in spite of the particular challenges inherent to mining societies.[23] Haciendas, for example, proved no impediment to family life. A study of early seventeenth-century San Luis Potosí found evidence of marriages between individuals who had previously worked for the same employer.[24] Petitions from later periods in Zacatecas illustrate similar trends. An inventory from 1656 of several mining haciendas found at least five families called haciendas their homes.[25] In 1711, one indigenous man resided with eight of his young ones at the Hacienda del Fuego.[26] Having children there not only provided additional labor support for families but also helped keep family structure intact, unlike other urban centers where indigenous children often lived and labored with Spaniards.[27]

Outside of the hacienda complex, nuclear families lived in their own homes throughout the city, alongside households of widows and groups of single women.[28] Orphans, of which high numbers appeared in Zacatecas, were often integrated into these domestic arrangements.[29] Some of these children were indigenous. But a great many were non-Indians.[30] The overall picture in Zacatecas is one of families, women, and young children. A 1671 census from the town of San Josef, for example, illustrates the family-based composition of the population. In that year, the pueblo had 132 inhabitants, with more adult women (48) than men (30). Fifty-nine percent of the adults were married (see Table 4.1), a number that would rise to 94 percent if we included widows. Children made up 41 percent of the population. At the time of the census, only five single adults resided in the town. Overall, the familial picture that emerges from Zacatecas is one of nuclear and extended units helping one another in times of need by caring for children while other members were at work, sharing homes together, and assisting with economic burdens. During these hard times, these units continued to grow, even if slowly. The 1671 census from San Josef indicated an increase of thirty-eight members from the previous count of ninety-four vecinos in 1669.[31]

TABLE 4.1. Civil status of adult population, San Josef, Zacatecas, 1671

	Married	Widowed	Single	Total
Male	23	4	3	30
Female	23	23	2	48
Total	46	27	5	78

Source: AAG, Padrones, exp. 7, 1671.

Within these families, the roles of Indian women became even more important in periods of economic slowdown. They kept the city running by serving as domestics at haciendas, laundresses, seamstresses, healers, and wet nurses.[32] They also bought and let houses. At the onset of the decline in 1633, Mariana, a single indigenous woman, rented one of her two properties in the multiethnic neighborhood of El Pedregoso to a Spanish merchant.[33] Indian women also played a critical role in keeping their communities together, particularly when economic circumstances had forced some men to temporarily leave for work. Often these women appear in the documentation without their male spouses and kin, assuming the primary role of watching out for their own interests and caring for their children and those of relations and acquaintances. In 1667, for example, Ana de Aguirre complained to the Spanish cabildo that a Spaniard, Juan Bautista Jiménez, had illegally taken possession of her land, on which she had a room and a stable, and had begun building a mill.[34] In a series of child labor abductions from the year 1666, several indigenous women, including mothers and cousins, took the initiative in recovering the young boys from Spanish miners and ranchers.[35] Where were the male heads of household? One man was away from the city, another was ill, and a third was deceased. The circumstances around the absence of the male family members—fathers, spouses, brothers, and uncles—reflect larger patterns of male circulation among the indigenous population. Men and women were traveling to and from the city for short and more prolonged labor trips, and those who remained faced the ever-present dangers involved in mining production. Recall the large number of female widows (48 percent, or close to half of the adult female population) from the census of San Josef. Surely many of these women lost their spouses to mining accidents or perhaps to another epidemic that struck in 1667. The physical absence of their husbands, the loss of loved ones, the decrease in the family's overall monetary revenues, placed heavy burdens on native women, pushing them to the forefront of their community and children's care, particularly during a mining downturn.[36]

Other sources indicate that married couples often worked as teams at mining haciendas, sometimes constituting close to half of the total indigenous labor force. It is not difficult to imagine entire families arriving at haciendas and finding some task for every member.[37] Typically men extracted and refined the silver while women completed the hacienda's numerous domestic chores, including child care, the cleaning of work and living spaces, and cooking. The household composition of the hacienda of Cristóbal Ramírez in 1656 shows the varied gender, civil, age, and ethnic status of his workforce (see Table 4.2). Seven married couples, such as Bartolomé de Zamora and his wife, Juana de la Cruz, labored together. Couples represented more than half (fourteen of twenty-five) of his workforce. Only one indigenous woman, Juana de la Cruz, appeared on the inventory without her spouse. Perhaps her husband worked in another location or was temporarily absent from the city. Four single women and three unwed men, along with three youths, rounded out the labor force. It is worth noting the overwhelmingly indigenous composition of the hacienda (a point I return to later) and that women at this site outnumbered men.

The presence of indigenous youths in hacienda inventories is a reminder that children were an important group in mining societies. Ecclesiastical censuses illustrate the substantial presence of indigenous children in the

TABLE 4.2. Ethnic identity of household composition of hacienda of Cristóbal Ramírez, Zacatecas, 1656

Bartolomé de Zamora (*Indian*), married
Juana de la Cruz (*Indian*), his wife
María de la Cruz (*Indian*)
Juan (*Indian*), youngster
Bernardina Beatriz (*Indian*)
María Magdalena (*Indian*), married
Juan Gabriel (*Indian*), her husband
Josepha de la Cruz (*Indian*)
Juana Isabel (*Indian*), married
Juan Nicolás (*Indian*), her husband
Luisa Francisca (*Indian*)
Ana (*Indian*), youngster
Juana de la Cruz (*Indian*), married
Francisca Agustina (*Indian*), married
Juan Francisco (*Indian*), her husband
Juana de la Cruz (*Indian*), married
Francisco de la Cruz (*Indian*), her husband
Francisco (*Indian*), youngster
Agustín de la Cruz (*unmarked*)
Clara Francisca (*Indian*), married
Antón de la Cruz (*Indian*), her husband
Dionocio (*morisco*)
Pedro de la Cruz (*Indian*), married
Agustina (*Indian*), his wife
Antonio (*Indian*)

Source: AAG, Padrones, 1656.

community. In the early seventeenth century, for example, Fray Pedro de Aguilar suggested at the large number of indigenous offspring in Tlacuitlapan, observing that "the newly baptized were innumerable."[38] In the San Josef census of 1671, the padrón indicated that children constituted around 40 percent of the population, with children younger than age four accounting for more than a quarter (27 percent) of the pueblo's inhabitants (see Table 4.3). Other extant counts illustrate similar trends, with children averaging around 30 percent to 40 percent of the total population.[39] Aside from natural reproduction, parish records indicate that substantial numbers of children, ranging from newborns to fourteen years old, arrived in the city as migrants. Antonio Saenz's mother, for example, brought him to Chepinque at the age of two. She remarried and raised Antonio in the pueblo, where he continued to reside at the posting of his nuptials.[40] The documentation occasionally offers glimpses into the lives of these children, highlighting the mundane but important activities that helped their families meet their economic needs.[41] Boys entered the labor force at seven or eight years of age.[42] They helped their fathers run errands from the hacienda to the traza, and young girls assisted their mothers with daily chores.[43] For the indigenous communities, children revitalized the population, serving as the basis for multigenerational families.[44]

Women and children also formed an important part of the economic and social landscape of mining societies. Some Spaniards viewed native women and children as additional sources of labor. In 1661, for example, governor Francisco de Ibarra and alcalde Matheo de Gamboa of San Josef wrote a petition to the bishop of Guadalajara. They told of the harassment of Spanish miners and vecinos against the men of the pueblo, forcing them to work against their will, paying them meager wages, and imprisoning them in prohibited prisons. They also asked that Spaniards not "force them [the men] to take their wives or children [or] to depopulate the pueblo."[45] A telling case from 1671 illustrates the vulnerability of children in lean times. For unknown reasons, an indigenous woman, María Magdalena Flores, attempted to donate her child to a Spanish couple.[46] This arrangement would have destined her son to a life of indentured servitude.

TABLE 4.3. Number and age of children, San Josef, Zacatecas, 1671

	0–12 months	1	2	3	4	Confessional age	Total
Boys	3	6	4	2	2	8	25
Girls	6	5	3	3	1	11	29
Total	9	11	7	5	3	19	54

Source: AAG, Padrones, exp. 7, 1671.
Note: The category "confessional age" contains those individuals who were listed with children and were probably from ten to thirteen years of age.

But while María Magdalena was able to relinquish her child, her parents were not. They even petitioned the Spanish cabildo of Zacatecas in their quest to keep the child with their family.[47] The efforts of Maria's parents and those of the officials of San Josef illustrate that for Indian communities women and children were valued family members as well as forces of continuity and stability, especially during lean times.

But family networks were not the only place where native peoples found support within the larger native community. Solidarity and connections also developed at work sites. By this period, censuses speak to a sizable number of castas and free and enslaved blacks at mining haciendas and ranches. However, the Indian population continued to dominate the workforce, particularly during mining downturns, with slaves and free mulatto men and women continuing to labor in greater numbers as domestic servants.[48] In addition, there was a pattern of ethnic segregation at work sites, with some ranches and refining plants primarily employing Indian and mestizo laborers, such as the hacienda of Pedro Ruiz de Quiroga, while others, such as the *huerta* (commercial farm) of Juan Duarte, employed people of primarily African descent (see Tables 4.4 and 4.5). These labor dynamics provided greater opportunities for native peoples to establish bonds between long-term vecinos and incoming migrants and men and women (note in Table 4.4 how the latter once again outnumbered the former) at their job sites.

TABLE 4.4. Ethnic composition of hacienda of Pedro Ruiz de Quiroga, Zacatecas, 1656

Owners and foremen
Pablo Ruiz de Quiroga
Lucas Ruiz
Agustín de la Peña
Laborers
Juana Cristina (*Indian*)
Ana García (*Indian*)
Magdalena (*black*)
Luis González (*mestizo*)
Pedro González (*mestizo*)
Sebastián (*Indian*)
Diego de la Cruz (*Indian*)
Juan Francisco (*Indian*)
Catalina (*Indian*), his wife
Sebastiana Micaela (*Indian*)
Isabel Juana (*Indian*)
Catalina (*Indian*)

Source: AAG, Padrones, 1656.

TABLE 4.5. Ethnic composition
of huerta of Juan Duarte,
Zacatecas, 1656

Laborers
Matheo (*black slave*)
Pedro (*black slave*)
María (*black*), his wife
Diego (*black slave*)
Domingo (*mulatto*)
Juan (*black slave*)
Lucas (*Indian*)
María Francisca (*unmarked*), his wife
Andrés de la Cruz (*black slave*)
María (*black slave*), his wife

Source: AAG, Padrones, 1656.

Labor patterns also influenced domestic arrangements, which had a significant impact on the retention of indigenous identities and practices. Wage-laboring Indians could live in their own homes in indigenous communities or with their families and other Indians at mining haciendas. The latter, in sheer numerical terms, were often indigenous strongholds. In contrast, as the primary domestic labor force, individuals of African descent often lived where they served with their Spanish patrons or owners. These residential patterns are discernible at both the city block and the household levels.

Many native peoples settled in the areas between the Spanish core and the surrounding Indian towns. Indians had been living in these spaces and identifying themselves as vecinos of Zacatecas proper since the 1550s. These neighborhoods were among the city's most ethnically fluid spaces in contrast to the more homogenous Spanish traza and indigenous pueblos. A cabildo entry from 1633, for example, illustrates a high level of ethnic integration in one of these barrios, El Pedregoso, an area just west of the Spanish center and north of the pueblo of Tonalá Chepinque.[49] In the two blocks under consideration, three Indians, three Spaniards, one with an African slave, lived side by side (see Figure 4.1). Three indigenous women, María Jerónima, Angelina, and Mariana owned property adjacent to that of Spanish occupants. Mariana even rented a separate property, a few houses down, to one Pedro de Artacha, a Spanish merchant who had established a store on the lot. But while they lived in close proximity to Spaniards and Afro-Zacatecans, many native peoples still maintained separate households.

More than thirty years later, in 1671, a census of 431 homes in the Spanish traza illustrated the distinct living arrangements between Indians and other ethnic groups. The house-by-house census found that blacks and

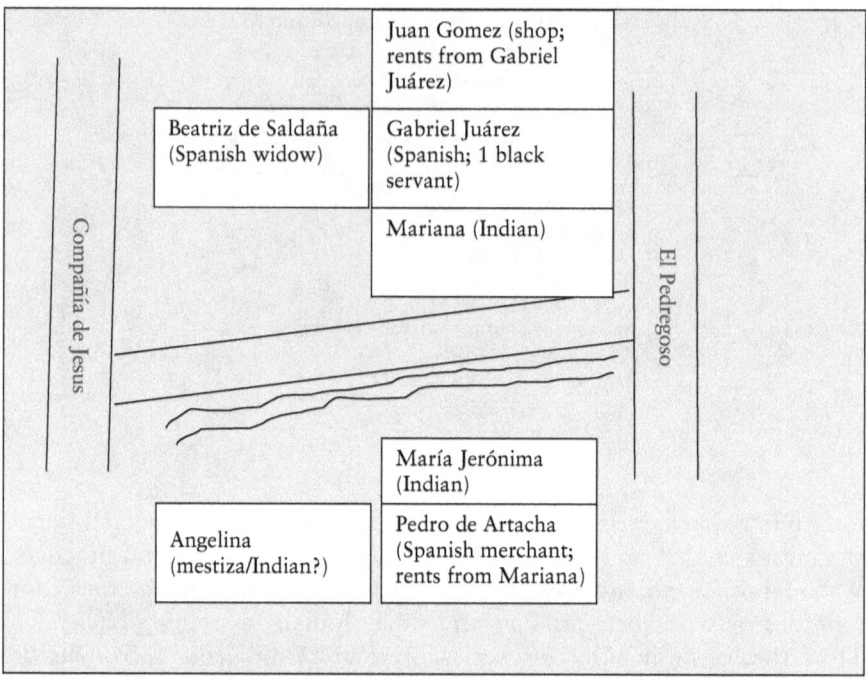

FIGURE 4.1. Ethnoracial residential patterns, El Pedregoso, Zacatecas, 1633. Based on AHEZ, Libro de Cabildo, 3, ff. 262v–265v, 1633. This figure shows a residential block abutting the barrio of El Pedregoso and the city center. All of the women owned their respective properties.

individuals of African descent lived in over one-third (37 percent) of all households in the city center, primarily as servants of Spanish residents. In contrast, Indians resided in only 9 percent of these homes and usually in relatively smaller numbers (one or two individuals). In comparison, Afro-Spanish households commonly had from three to ten black occupants. For example, in the house of the alguacil mayor at least half the servants (ten of twenty) were individuals of African descent (see Table 4.6). In addition, several individuals and children of unmarked ethnicities were probably also of mixed race descent. Only one native person, Juan, resided in the alguacil mayor's home. The examination of another household revealed a similar trend. In the house of the *factor*, or purchasing agent, Roque de Arellano, there were twenty-eight servants. Of the sixteen individuals identified by an ethnic ascription, thirteen were of African descent, two were *chinos* (individuals from Asia), and one, Miguel, was indigenous (see Table 4.7).[50]

TABLE 4.6. Ethnic composition, household of the alguacil mayor, Joseph de Villareal, Zacatecas, 1671, house 338

Spaniards	Others
Joseph de Villareal	Leonor (*black*)
Doña Josepha de Vera, his wife	Petrona (*mulata*)
Nicolás	María (*mulata*)
Teresa	Magdalena (*mulata*)
Joseph	Juan Cajeta (*unmarked*)
	Juan (*chino*)
	Mateo (*black*)
	Antonio (*black*)
	Juan (*chino*)
	Andrés (*black*)
	Manuel (*black*)
	Juan de la Serna (*unmarked*)
	Beatriz, his wife (*unmarked*)
	Juan
	Gregoria
	Diego
	Antonio
	Juan (*black*)
	Diego (*black*)
	Juan (*Indian*)

Source: AAG, Padrones, 1671.

Across the census, very few households contained both indigenous and Afro-descended servants. Only twenty-four households—about 6 percent—were composed of Indians and Africans. This census does not provide a comprehensive view of ethnic household composition. It fails to account for the ethnicity of some individuals and of children. However, it does show how, in terms of residential arrangements, native peoples continued to reside among the greater indigenous population even during times of economic hardship both in the Spanish traza and its adjacent barrios.

Living and working together provided financial, social, and emotional support for native peoples during this lean period. The years between the booms caused strain among the Indian population. Men and women left their children to seek income elsewhere. Married couples worked together at mining sites. Spanish frustrations with declining labor sources resulted in abductions of children and forced impressments of wives at levels not seen in other periods. Records indicate internal problems as well. Recall that in 1657, the cabildo of Tlacuitlapan could not find one individual to assume the position of alcalde.[51] The lack of interest in office holding speaks to a declining interest in indigenous governance, no doubt another casualty of economic malaise.

These challenges all speak to financial hard times, but they do not indicate a disintegration of indigenous social units, networks, institutions,

TABLE 4.7. Ethnic composition of the household of the factor, Roque de Arellano, Zacatecas, 1671, house 106

Spaniards	Others
Roque de Arellano	Catalina (*mulata*)
Doña Ana de Zaldívar, his wife	Antonia (*mulata*)
Doña María de Arellano	Ursula (*unmarked*)
Juan	María (*unmarked*)
Vicente	Nicolás (*chino*)
	María, his wife
	Pascuala (*black*)
	Juliana (*black*)
	Isabel (*black*)
	Ana (*mulata*)
	Antonia (*morena*)
	Agustina (*morena*)
	Joseph, unmarried (*mulatto*)
	Pedro, unmarried (*mulatto*)
	Diego (*mulatto*)
	Tomas (*chino*)
	Pascual (*black*)
	Juan de Dios
	Ignacio
	Pedro
	Bernardina (*black*)
	Nicolasa
	Miguel (*Indian*)
	Juan
	Ana
	Tomasa
	Teresa
	María

Source: AAG, Padrones, 1656.

or identities. Even before the bust ended, indigenous leaders once again assumed their posts and responsibilities and their native residents returned. Recall the case of Magdalena de la Cruz and her husband, who after a two-year absence returned to the city to reunite with their son and extended kin. The experiences of Magdalena and her family are probably typical of many native individuals and families that ultimately, and even under adverse circumstances, made Zacatecas their permanent home. Indigenous families and extended kin networks worked and lived together. This solidarity helped the general indigenous population to overcome the economic and demographic losses generated by disease and out-migration. Indigenous society, bolstered by a stable and resilient population base of returning residents, multigenerational families, and extended kinship networks, was in no danger of eroding during the city's production lulls. It was the personal and social networks that had developed from these resilient entities that made it easier for native peoples to surmount the production downturn. The challenge would come in weathering the demographic and cultural changes brought about by the boom.

Persistence in Diversity: Indigenous Population Growth and Production Upsurge

In Zacatecas, production booms and busts were the most significant catalysts for population circulation in the city, drawing in and driving away significant numbers in their wake. Extant figures illustrate the critical role of the mining economy on overall population patterns (see Table 4.8) in this time of production fluctuations. From about the closing years of one bust (1667) to the tail end of the second boom (1732) the population more than doubled before declining, almost by half, to twenty-four thousand individuals as the period of elevated production drew to a close. Marriage petitions offer another example of the influence of mining production on population cycles. Table 4.9 illustrates the nuptial activities of the non-Spanish population in this period.[52] Unsurprisingly, the fewest number of petitions were made during the decades that spanned the production decline of 1690 to 1705. With the waning of the boom in 1732, requests decreased by about 22 percent from the decade 1721–1730 to that of 1731–1740. In both cases, population decreased as fewer migrants arrived and other individuals left the city in search of better economic prospects.

TABLE 4.8. Population, Zacatecas, 1667–1739

Year	Population
1667	15,000–16,000
1732	40,000
1739	24,000

Source: For 1667 and 1739, see Gerhard, *North Frontier*, 158–59. For 1732, see Ribera Bernárdez, *Descripción breve*, 48.

TABLE 4.9. Number of marriage petitions, Indians, blacks, and castas, Zacatecas, 1681–1740

Years	Number
1681–1690	227
1691–1700	200
1701–1710	207
1711–1720	466
1721–1730	2,079
1731–1740	1,613

Source: APZ, Matrimonios, Informaciones, Indios, Negros y Castas, 1681–1740.

These population fluctuations serve as valuable indices of change. They influenced every aspect of urban life—from labor patterns to economic opportunities to the price of food—and altered the social dynamics of every ethnic group. We can arrive at a more nuanced understanding of the impact that these boom-bust cycles had on indigenous society in Zacatecas by considering the demographic restructuring that occurred during production fluctuations.

With the resurgence of mining activity in the 1670s, Zacatecas and its Indian towns began to show signs of recovery. As waves of men, women, and children arrived, they revived the city's civic and economic institutions. The migration pattern of the 1670–1690 boom differed from those of the sixteenth and early seventeenth centuries. Whereas Indian migrants from the Valley of Mexico dominated those early waves, this period witnessed a more geographically diverse immigrant population, and larger numbers of mestizos and mulattos. In part, the surge in non-Indian migrants corresponded to the overall growth of the casta population in the viceroyalty. Early eighteenth-century Zacatecas was a melting pot of ethnicities and classes, and myriad cultural ideas and practices. The mining booms of 1670–1690 and 1705–1732 certainly contributed to the "castazation" of the city, both culturally and biologically (a point discussed in greater detail later).

Yet even within this surge of demographic diversity, native peoples remained a viable overarching ethnic group. The native individuals and families who had weathered the seventeenth-century decline served as a population base. Moreover, if the boom attracted large numbers of non-Indians to the city, it also drew significant numbers of native peoples. Civil and ecclesiastical censuses, religious inspections, and marriage petitions illustrate that the Indian population would increase, sometimes in astronomical numbers, during production upsurges. For example, the average size of the native pueblos in the seventeenth century fluctuated from around 130 to 1,000 individuals. Figures from Table 4.10 indicate the extent to which the eighteenth-century mining boom elevated the native pueblos' populations to their highest colonial numbers. Tlacuitlapan had always been the largest Indian town. By 1728, its population of 724 individuals had nearly reached the levels of the previous boom in the early seventeenth century (804 individuals).[53] Such was the attraction of mining booms to the native population that within only four short years Tlacuitlapan experienced exponential growth, quadrupling in size to three thousand vecinos! Growth, though not as extraordinary as that of Tlacuitlapan's, occurred in the other pueblos as well. By 1732, Chepinque had nearly doubled its population from four years earlier from 388 to 700 individuals. San Josef's numbers increased by nearly 35 percent from a count in 1671 (200 to 132). We

TABLE 4.10. Extant population counts of Indian towns, Zacatecas, 1671–1741

	1671	1679	1728	1732	1741
Tlacuitlapan	N/A	N/A	724	3,000	677
Chepinque	N/A	N/A	388	700	188
San Josef	132	156	241	200	200

Source: Ribera Bernárdez, *Descripción breve*, 48; AAG, Visitas, box 2, ff. 172v–173, 1728; AAG, Padrones, various fojas, 1671–1783.
Note: N/A = not available.

should also consider that most of these counts failed to include children, who could account for close to 30 percent or more of the total population of an indigenous pueblo. Together, the Indian inhabitants of at least three of the four pueblos constituted 10 percent of Zacatecas's total residents (3,900 of 40,000) in 1732, a year that marked the city's colonial population apex.[54] While the production surge increased the city's ethnic diversity, it also contributed to the growth of the native population. Likewise, the decline in indigenous residents in counts from 1741 mirror the overall decrease in the city's population in the period after the boom.

Some of the demographic growth in the Indian towns was generational, but migrants continued to represent a significant number of the newcomers.[55] A series of quantifiable petitions from *libros de matrimonios* (marriage registers) exist from 1681 to 1810. Religious officials recorded nuptial petitions by ethnic groups, with a *libro* for Spaniards and another for "Indians, blacks, and castas." In their requests, both the male and the female petitioners usually noted their place of origin, their current vecino status, their age, their ethnic ascription, and the names of their parents. Each petition was accompanied by the statement of three (and on rare occasions, four) male witnesses. These individuals also provided information on their place of residence (but not birth), age, and ethnic identity. Some of the male petitioners and witnesses occasionally provided information about current or former employment. This material was not simply listed; it was recorded in narrative form. These biographical descriptions, while brief, were not formulaic. They contained personal information on mundane aspects of daily life in an indigenous voice, offering extremely valuable (and rare) insights into indigenous society.[56] But they also tell us much about native immigrants in northern New Spain, where the voluntary nature of labor arrangements often obscured their ethnic identity, social status, origins, and migration patterns.[57]

The first set of indigenous nuptial requests that exist for a production upsurge encompass the ten-year period from 1681 to 1690. During this decade there were seventy-one total male indigenous petitioners. This analysis, however, excludes twenty-four Indians who did not possess vecino status in the greater city and six individuals who failed to indicate their place of residence.[58] Of the forty-one Indians residing in greater Zacatecas, only eleven cited criollo or native-born status. Migrants, then, constituted nearly 75 percent of the city's indigenous petitioner population. The majority of them settled in barrios in the city or in the satellite mining camp of Veta Grande. Two native peoples settled in San Josef, and one relocated to Tlacuitlapan. While this figure may not necessarily be representative of larger patterns among the greater indigenous population, it suggests that immigrants played no small role in the growth of indigenous society during the boom periods.

The origins of the thirty migrants offer some insight into why Zacatecas continued to draw a large indigenous population. Many petitioners arrived from regions traditionally associated with indigenous migration to Zacatecas. One-third of the immigrants (ten), for example, came from areas associated with Purépecha sites in Michoacán. This pattern reflects historical migration trends since Tarascans were among the earliest settlers to the city. But it also suggests that social networks or recruiting operations, which would have facilitated migration between the two regions, were still in place. Individuals from central Mexico continued to stream into the city as well, with more than two-thirds of the immigrants originating from areas within central New Spain (see Table 4.11). This pool of immigrants, however, were no longer arriving from the Valley of Mexico as they had in such large numbers in the sixteenth century. They came instead from the mining towns within central New Spain's jurisdiction, such as Guanajuato and San Luis Potosí, from pueblos along the silver trunk line, such as Querétaro, or communities like San Miguel, established by Spaniards and Indians to defend and provide resources to silver-mining towns. The remaining migrants were from New Galicia (seven) and Nueva Vizcaya (one). In New Galicia the majority of immigrants came from the city's indigenous hinterlands, with only two citing the Guadalajara region (another popular sixteenth-century sending region). The small number of migrants from the northern provinces suggests that many individuals from

TABLE 4.11. Province of origin of male Indian migrants, Zacatecas, 1681–1690

Province	Number
New Spain	20
New Galicia	7
Nueva Vizcaya	1

Source: Ribera Bernárdez, *Descripción breve*, 48; AAG, Visitas, box 2, ff. 172v–173, 1728; AAG, Padrones, various fojas, 1671–1783.

this region were occupied at productive mining sites closer to home. In regards to out-migration, only one individual, Roque Antonio Durán, had moved out of the city. He had relocated to Montegrande, a mining camp in the hinterlands, probably to join his wife's family, she being an *originaria*, or native, to the area.

These migration trends continued through the eighteenth century.[59] In spite of the growing non-Indian population, Zacatecas continued to be an indigenous draw. The attraction of wages in cash and ore as well as exemption from tribute and repartimiento remained valuable incentives in this period for men and women. But other factors related to familiarity and geography also played a role. Individuals from mining towns that had developed certain skills continued to be drawn to environments where they could put their abilities to use. Cases such as that of Hilaria Paola and her daughter, who had relocated to Chepinque from her hometown of Guanajuato, were not uncommon.[60] The most significant shift in this period witnessed the predominance of migrants from the hinterlands, particularly women. By the seventeenth century, several population centers of satellite mining reales and agricultural ranches had developed, and some had evolved into sizable communities. The proximity of these sites to Zacatecas and the social and trade networks that existed between the city and these communities encouraged and facilitated migration. Thus while production upsurges increased the ethnic diversity of the city, they also drew large numbers of native peoples.

The influx of migrants during boom periods and the subsequent upswings in local markets and foot traffic presented native people with unprecedented opportunities for social and occupational interactions with Spaniards, Africans, and castas. These professional or social gatherings occurred in such common city spaces as plazas, markets, taverns, and other public institutions. Some of these exchanges led to intimate relationships such as the one between Andrés de Mendoza and Dominga de las Nieves. Andrés was a native man born and raised in the agricultural community of Teocaltiche. Dominga, identified as a "negra," was a native and resident of Zacatecas. They petitioned to marry in April 1718.[61] It is possible that the mining boom drew Andrés to the city where he met Dominga. Perhaps better work opportunities motivated Antonia Jerónima Martínez, an indigenous woman, born on a local hacienda, to leave the site and establish vecindad in the city proper. While there she met Miguel de la Rodríguez, a mulatto slave originally brought to Zacatecas from Mexico City.[62] Miguel's master was the Spanish alcalde Antonio Martínez de Murguía. Sometime during their daily routine in the city their paths crossed, and they managed to continue meeting, which led to their marriage petition in May 1720. These two cases are typical of the many intimate relations that developed between Indians and non-Indians during a period in which the city had a large multiethnic population. No doubt these formal unions reflected a large number of informal or consensual relationships as well.

Marriage patterns reflect, on the most personal and intimate level, the rate of integration within and between ethnoracial groups. Individual decisions to marry are based on myriad personal reasons, from affection and companionship to financial motivations and personal advancement. But local social factors also should be taken under consideration. Most significant for Indians, spousal selection often depended on the size and ethnic makeup of a population center. In greater northern Mexico, from Nueva Vizcaya to Texas, disease, warfare, relocation, and changing environmental conditions often impeded Indians from rebuilding or gathering together a critical population mass.[63] In Sonora, Cynthia Radding found that to reconstitute Indian communities devastated by Spanish rule, ethnic integration became a "[strategy] for physical and cultural survival" and "depended on the exogamous selection of partners."[64] These demographic circumstances also occurred in mining towns with smaller indigenous populations. For example, just a few miles from Zacatecas, in the satellite mining communities of Pánuco and Veta Grande, marriage registers indicate a greater presence of ethnoracial diversity in marriage petitions.[65]

Zacatecas's native population did not suffer from the demographic limitations of its northern neighbors when it came to selecting a mate, even during mining booms. For the purposes of this study, marriages between individuals who identified as "Indian" in the records are classified as endogamous. While these unions were not necessarily between discrete ethnic groups (for example, a Nahua man and a Nahua woman), they represent individuals who shared social and cultural affinities as part of a greater urban indigenous population.[66] Marriage trends among this larger native cohort illustrate how demographic changes generated by production fluctuations influenced their spousal selection patterns. The decade of 1681–1690 was marked by high endogamy (87 percent).[67] The following fifty years (1691–1740) were characterized by rates between 53 percent to 65 percent (see Table 4.12). These figures suggest a steep decline, with marriages between native peoples decreasing by as much as 35 percent during this overall period.

The decline in endogamous marriage petitions during the years of 1691 to 1730 speaks to the increasing diversity of Zacatecas's overall population and native people's wider interactions with non-Indians. The most dramatic drop in inter-Indian unions occurred from 1691 to 1710. After this period rates remained relatively stable, averaging about 64 percent from 1711 to 1740. Contrary to expectations, the petitions indicate that the period of greatest exogamy occurred during mining slowdowns. Native

TABLE 4.12. Endogamy rates in the Indian population, Zacatecas, 1681–1740

Years	Percentage	Production levels (approximate years)
1681–1690	87	Boom
1691–1700	56	Bust
1701–1710	53	Bust from 1701 to 1705; boom 1706 forward
1711–1720	66	Boom
1721–1730	61	Boom
1731–1740	65	Boom until 1732; bust forward

Source: APZ, Matrimonios, IINC, 1681–1740.

peoples were actually marrying Indians in larger numbers during mining booms, when we would expect to see elevated levels of interethnic integration. Yet these trends make sense when we reconsider that the boom had brought in large numbers of native migrants who served as one of the pillars of the indigenous spousal pool. Likewise, a downturn would have led to a decrease in criollos and migrants. Even with a more diverse spousal boom, older preconquest traditions regarding marriage choices may have been a factor. There is some evidence that native peoples, particularly commoners, showed a tendency to select a mate from among their local larger subdistricts, or with individuals with whom they shared a common past.[68]

Moreover, many of these interethnic unions were with mestizos, individuals with biological and social affinities to the native population. In 1718, for example, Francisco Romero Rodríguez, an indigenous widower and *originario* (native) from the mining town of Sombrerete, and probably another boom migrant, petitioned to marry one Ana María de Zaldaña. A mestiza, Ana had also migrated to the city from Aguascalientes.[69] Francisco and Ana shared the common bind of being migrants, and Ana probably had close ties to indigenous culture and society. Their petition reminds us that even those Indians who married ethnic others did not necessarily withdraw from indigenous associations and organizations. Rather, for native peoples in this period, interactions with non-Indians were a common feature of urban indigenous life.

Marriage petitions from 1680 to 1740 indicate that indigenous peoples had not been absorbed by larger casta groups by the eighteenth century but remained a viable demographic group, even at the height of an extended period of elevated mining activity.[70] The production upsurge brought in large groups of non-Indians. Yet newcomers to the population included significant populations of native people as well. While marriage petitions record a substantial number of interethnic unions among the Indian population, even at the height of the boom (1690 to 1710), on average, a 60 percent probability existed that Indians would marry within their larger ethnic group. The boom actually strengthened as much as it diluted the spousal pool. Unlike other areas in New Spain, Zacatecas's native population was able to reproduce itself through marriage with other Indians. High endogamy rates, in turn, contributed to a vibrant multigenerational population through the eighteenth century.

Civic Challenges and Community Responses

By the late seventeenth century the city's indigenous pueblos not only had stable and vibrant populations; they also had matured, with fully developed governments, infrastructures, and organizations. During this period each of the three towns—Tlacuitlapan, Tonalá Chepinque, and San Josef—possessed full-fledged municipal councils and conducted business in the pueblos' capillas. The barrio of El Niño del Dulce Nombre de Jesús would officially separate from Tonalá Chepinque and establish its own cabildo near the end of the boom in 1731. A 1728 visita illustrates the bustling state of civic life within these towns.[71] In Tonalá Chepinque a large street known as Calle de Tonalá, which began at the mines and descended through the community, was a particularly significant thoroughfare and the location of all the pueblo's primary institutions (chapels and hospitals). This was also the site where the town crier made important announcements in Spanish and Nahuatl.[72] Jails and cemeteries rounded out the towns' main structures.

Unsurprisingly, religious institutions, which had served an important sociopolitical function from the initial formation of the Indian communities, also were particularly well developed. Several small chapels, and even a hermitage in Tlacuitlapan, figured prominently among the pueblo's buildings. This was a far cry from the early seventeenth century, when the town lacked a chapel to conduct religious services or civic business. These chapels housed the pueblo's multiple cofradías: Santa Vera Cruz, Jesús Nazareno, Nuestra Señora de Asunción, and Limpia Concepcíon. Nuestra Señora de la Soledad, San Diego, and Limpia Concepcíon operated in Tonalá Chepinque, and El Niño and San Josef each had sodalities of the same name. The cofradía of San Josef owned and operated a ranch.[73] Women's roles had also evolved within these institutions. In the sodality of San Josef women served as *temachti grande* (head teacher) and as *temachti menores* (probably assistant instructors) in the confraternity of Jesús Nazareno.[74] Several cofradías continued their tradition of operating in conjunction with hospitals, a necessary community service in an environment where diseases were rampant and mining accidents occurred on a daily basis. In Tlacuitlapan the pueblo's hospital was located in front of the hermitage. According to visita records the hospital had separate rooms for men and women. Tonalá Chepinque had two hospitals; one accommodated five patients, and the other four. El Niño's hospital had three beds. The bishop encountered only one patient during his 1728 inspection of the three Indian hospitals. However, we should not measure the rate of illness or disease from the number of patients, or in this case, the lack of patients. Mining accidents and injuries, among other ailments that sent individuals to seek medical assistance, were rarely reported in the records and just as often treated at home.[75]

The transformation of the Indian communities from settlements to full-fledged towns went hand in hand with the evolution of strong civic identities. The ubiquitous micropatriotism that characterized precolonial native altepetl in central Mexico was no less fervent in Zacatecas's Indian pueblos.[76] Indians had always considered their towns to be autonomous political entities and not just peripheral barrios or religious parishes of Zacatecas. They distinguished themselves from the city by identifying proudly as vecinos of a particular native pueblo. But one could argue that the early eighteenth century also marked the "maturation" of civic identities. Native residents not only saw their towns as independent; they also saw them as an integral part of Zacatecas. Their gaze began to extend beyond their territorial and jurisdictional limits as they sought greater participation in citywide affairs, including those that occurred in the Spanish city. By 1711, a cofradía with a Spanish and indigenous branch, San Nicolás, had been established in the city center. In 1710, an indigenous man, Pedro Esteban, held the grim job of meting out punishments as the city's *verdugo*, or executioner.[77] Earlier this job had been considered inappropriate for Indians and had been assigned to individuals of African descent. Esteban was not the only native person to be entrusted with a weapon. Several native peoples participated in Spanish military campaigns. In 1702, eight individuals from San Josef, eight Tlaxcalans from Tlacuitlapan, and six from Tonalá Chepinque joined a Spanish-led expedition to assist in the suppression of rebellions to the southwest in Colotlán.[78] But it was not only native individuals who began to participate in the Spanish world but also the leadership of indigenous institutions as well. In 1735, the Indian confraternities of Tonalá Chepinque were buying land in areas outside of their pueblos. That year, the cofradía of San Diego paid seven hundred pesos for three rundown properties within the city limits.[79] Native leaders began conducting patrols on the borders of the Indian towns that sometimes brought them into contact (and conflict) with Spanish residents and officials.

This mature and more cosmopolitan civic identity, and the Spanish response to it, is illustrated in the conflict that erupted in 1734 between the cofradía of San Josef and the Spanish confraternity of the Vera Cruz. At the heart of the dispute between the two groups lay rival claims to the possession of a revered statue, the Santo Cristo de Raja Peñas.[80] The image currently resided in San Josef's main church. Its vecinos considered the Santo Cristo to be the sodality's most revered and valuable item. But in May 1734 the mayordomo of the Spanish brotherhood of the Vera Cruz, Don Gregorio de Zumalde, lodged a petition with Spanish authorities in which they claimed that the Cristo rightfully belonged to them. According to the Vera Cruz's mayordomos the statue had always belonged to them, but several years earlier in 1728—in a gesture of goodwill—they had loaned it to the Indian confraternity. In support of their claim they produced a document describing a meeting which occurred between them and the Indian leaders of San Josef, including the mayordomo, Juan Marcos Casillas, and the alcalde, Diego Vázquez Macias, at the pueblo's church to inventory the Cristo's adornments and accessories. At that meeting, the Spaniards claimed, the native alcalde acknowledged that the image belonged to the Vera Cruz and that it was kept at their church at the Spanish cofradía's leisure and discretion.

San Josef, however, had no intention of handing over the Santo Cristo. The confraternity—supported by the town council and its residents—refused the request and began a lengthy legal battle to keep the image. In their counterpetitions, the Indian officials, led by governor Vicente Ferrer Sánchez and alcalde Vázquez Macias, told a very different story. The Santo Cristo had initially belonged to one of the now deceased *hijos* (members) of the pueblo. Miguel Francisco Sánchez, an ore cutter, had received the statue, "without any obligation" from two Dominican priests resident in the church of Santo Domingo. Together, he and his wife, Francisca de Ibarra, kept the image in their house for five years until Miguel had had a fight with his overseers, who threatened to remove the statue from him. Claiming that he would rather give his life than the image, Miguel and his wife agreed to hand over the Santo Cristo to the alcalde of San Josef to ensure, according to Francisca, "that it would remain forever with her and the other Indians in the church of her pueblo."[81]

Was the pueblo's story true? Until 1708—about twenty years earlier—San Josef had been under the custodianship of the Dominicans.[82] It is not improbable that the Dominican priests gave Sánchez—a mine laborer—a religious statue to house at his work site. As an ore cutter, Sánchez worked belowground in one of the most dangerous tasks associated with mining production. Mine workers frequently established minishrines within excavation sites as a form of protection against accidents and injuries, placing crosses, images, or statues in spots where workers could make offerings and ask for intercessions. Visitors to mining sites in Zacatecas today often encounter one or two alcoves with saints' images along with several

FIGURE 4.2. Santa Niño de Atocha shrine, Mina del Eden, Zacatecas. Photo taken by author in 2007.

ex-votos—photographs or drawings created in thanks to a saint for their intercession (see Figure 4.2).[83] The statue under contention, the Raja Peñas Cristo, may have remained belowground for some time until Miguel Francisco and his wife relocated it to their home. When his overseer threatened to remove the statue the couple may have decided that the only safe place for the image was at San Josef's church.

Indigenous pueblos strongly identified with Christian figures. Each parish venerated its own particular saint, Mary, or Christ effigy. Statues were valued possessions that native people often considered the corporate property of their churches or chapels. Occasionally they even considered them personal belongings, excluding them from inventories of their parish's possessions.[84] In this case the Santo Cristo also was not without monetary value. Its head, hands, heart, crown, and four teeth were made of silver. The statue's ultimate worth, though, lay in the significance of its political and civic symbolism.

Since Zacatecas's earliest days the absence of a central organizing indigenous political unit had led to the development of a close connection between the urban church, corporate identity, and indigenous community formation. The forceful implantation of Christian rituals and beliefs on the native population ranked among the most violent and oppressive measures of colonial rule. But, as scholars point out, over time, church practices and objects evolved to the "status of legitimate symbols of identity" among the indigenous population.[85] In many ways the Santo Cristo represented the community, signaling its autonomy from both the Spanish city and the other Indian towns. San Josef's vecinos widely revered the statue, proudly parading it during processions and feast days. It was this connection between the statue and the pueblo's corporate identity that nearly embroiled the city in a large-scale, premeditated indigenous riot when Spanish authorities threatened to remove it from the town.

For the Spanish, in contrast, the origins of the conflict had more to do with procession than with possession, which explains why after so many years the Vera Cruz (if indeed they were its legitimate owners) demanded the statue's return. Earlier that year the two sodalities had engaged in a heated encounter during a local ceremony. Processions in Spanish America were choreographed events with officials, groups, and spectators parading according to their social levels.[86] As the oldest Spanish cofradía in the city, the Vera Cruz naturally would have assumed precedence over all the other groups and certainly over any indigenous organizations. In 1734 the mayordomo of the Vera Cruz, Don Gregorio de Zumalde, complained that for the previous three years the Indians of San Josef had tried to disrupt the order and protocol of the annual Holy Tuesday processions by attempting to parade the Santo Cristo in front of them. This year, he asserted, in their hurry to take the lead, San Josef's members unceremoniously raced past the Vera Cruz's followers, almost trampling him in the process. The fact that San Josef paraded with "their" Cristo surely added insult to injury. Mayordomo Zumalde claimed that it was the lack of "veneration" shown to the statue, along with the desire to avoid future "scandals" during the event that motivated the cofradía to reclaim the image.[87] The deeper source of contention, though, rested in the Vera Cruz's belief that San Josef had clearly upset the social hierarchy by trying to take precedence over a Spanish entity in a civic procession.[88]

What the Spanish confraternity encountered—or rightly recognized—was an emboldened and more confident Indian community that sought to participate fully and even occasionally take precedence in religious and municipal rituals. Indians no longer saw their role in civic life as building the infrastructure for city ceremonies—fences or props, for example—as they had done in the sixteenth and seventeenth centuries but felt entitled to participate in those events as vecinos of the greater city. In a similar manner, Spanish attempts to admonish them for overstepping their bounds by removing their prized possessions no longer had the same success as in the past.⁸⁹ In 1626, for example, threats from Bishop Francisco de Rivera to take away all the images and insignias of the Indian confraternities and to bar them from processions had proved an effective strategy in helping to end a series of indigenous rock fights that had strayed too close to the Spanish traza.⁹⁰

But by 1735, Indian leaders proved that they were not to be so easily intimidated. Over twenty Indians, led by then governor Juan Nicolás, gathered to protest the claim and entered countersuit. When it seemed that Spanish authorities would forcibly remove the image from the pueblo's church, the community took more radical action. San Josef's native leadership met with Corregidor Ribera Bernárdez within a few hours of the handover to ask him to postpone the action. The native officials argued that the order to remove the statue had occasioned great despair, tears even, in the community. Governor Nicolás assured the corregidor that while the native leadership had accepted the decision, he could not quell the anger of the native vecinos. Nor could he be held responsible if this anger and sorrow turned to violence, warning corregidor Ribera Bernárdez that he should prepare for a widespread Indian rebellion.⁹¹ The ominous announcement was not an idle threat or ruse. San Josef's vecinos had called together and shared their plights with residents from the other Indian towns. In a rare show of interpueblo solidarity, the city's native population warned that they would take to the streets in armed rebellion, if necessary, before they let Spaniards take the statue.

Not coincidentally, another reference to a potential indigenous riot in the city during the colonial period also had its origins in a religious conflict, again with the Dominican order. In 1654, the barrio of El Niño reacted strongly to attempts by the Dominicans to wrest them from the Augustinians. The latter had served as the pueblo's custodians for over seventy years. Juan Baltazar, mayordomo of the cofradía of El Niño, along with other vecinos from the pueblo, complained to viceregal officials of a three-year-long Dominican attempt to take over their administration.⁹² The struggle had recently reached a boiling point when, according to Baltazar, the priests of Santo Domingo, without any orders from the bishop, had informed the town that they were their new ministers. The pueblo deeply resented this intrusion into their affairs and informed viceregal officials that in "order to keep the peace," the clerics needed to desist from their actions. These words closely echoed those of the leaders of San Josef. Changes in religious administration that were not approved by Indian communities were considered a direct affront to their pueblo's jurisdiction and a challenge to its autonomy. El Niño's actions ultimately convinced Spanish officials to allow them to remain with the Augustinians. The heated response from El Niño may have had some bearing on another religious jurisdictional dispute in 1707. Secular clerics had been attempting to claim custodianship over the indigenous population in the city and adjacent mining haciendas, many of whom were receiving services from the friars in Tlacuitlapan. In this case, Bishop Diego de Camacho ruled in favor of the religious of Tlacuitlapan, granting them continued supervision over Indians who lived in barrios and mines adjacent to the pueblos.[93]

The forceful and coordinated response from El Nino in the seventeenth century and San Josef in the eighteenth century illustrates the close connection between the urban church and indigenous sociopolitical identity. Religious organizations and institutions often formed the base of the community's organization, influencing sociopolitical autonomy more so than in central Mexico.[94] In the case of San Josef, the removal of the image was seen as a direct assault to the town's autonomy, one that resonated with the Indian population as a whole. Unsurprisingly, corregidor Ribera Bernárdez allowed the pueblo to retain its prized possession and calm returned to the city. But the episode probably lingered in the minds of Spanish leaders who could no longer ignore the growing political and social aspirations of their indigenous neighbors. For their part the mayordomos of the Vera Cruz pursued their case, convinced that San Josef had illegally taken position of their image and overstepped their social position. The episode illustrates the maturation of the indigenous communities as it marks the evolving jurisdictional tensions between Spanish and Indian officials.[95] The native towns by this period had fully developed and embraced civic identities, considering themselves an integral part of the city's greater social landscape.

By the eighteenth century, the native communities became more outward looking in some matters, particularly in their desire to participate in some aspects of Spanish municipal affairs. Yet at the same time, they sought to maintain the indigenous integrity of their communities as the attractions of the boom drew a greater number of ethnically diverse migrants. Taking advantage of colonial policies, native officials were relatively successful in barring non-Indians from their pueblos.[96] Other ethnic groups frequented and worked in the native towns, and some non-Indians even resided in them, but overall these communities remained fairly indigenous. In a property transaction from 1747, for example, the leaders of San Josef assured local officials that they were "following the rules and not selling [property] to mulatos, mestizos, or Spaniards, but only to Indians who were good vecinos."[97] Marriage petitions from the four indigenous towns indicate that over a hundred year period, from 1681 to 1780, only thirty-seven non-Indians were vecinos of the pueblos when they made their requests.[98] Of these individuals, more than half were immigrants, perhaps an individual with close ties to a native person such as Juan de la

Fuente, a casta who worked side by side with fellow townsmen Josef Saenz at the mine and hacienda of La Chiquita.[99] The native communities also served as home to individuals who were biological mestizos, but not in significantly greater numbers than any other large Indian town in central Mexico.[100] Nor should we see these mestizos as dramatic (or traumatic) cultural catalysts since many remained culturally and socially within indigenous spheres.

Intrusions from outsiders into the native towns varied from period to period but proved particularly challenging during mining booms when large populations sought more lands and resources. During the production upsurge of 1705 to 1732, residents began to settle in greater numbers in the areas between the Indian towns and the Spanish traza. Many of these settlers, however, were indigenous. In 1709, for example, an "indio ladino," Nicolás García, sought to build a house for his family on unappropriated lands (realengas), "on a hill that descends below that of the butcher near the stream called Chepinque."[101] In September of that year he registered the site with the Spanish cabildo. About a month later, Bartolomé González, bought a smaller site close to Chepinque as well.[102] But it was not just native peoples alone who moved into vacant areas near the Indian towns. Non-Indians lived in these areas as well. In 1689, a tailor had petitioned to own property "on the road to the pueblo of Tlacuitlapan."[103] A brick maker, possibly of African descent, Lucas González, had built several homes on a sizable lot adjacent to the pueblos of El Niño and San Josef.[104] Near Chepinque, Nicolás García would have had Spanish neighbors to his right and behind his house.[105] These spaces where the lines between Spaniard and Indian were not so firmly drawn, also proved attractive to interethnic couples and individuals, whose numbers had grown during the boom. In 1736, Antonia González, a *loba* (an individual of black and indigenous ancestry), and an Indian, Nicolás Ventura, had purchased a plot some distance from the traza after their first attempts to acquire land near the city center had failed.[106] Unsurprisingly, the boom also led to the proliferation of Spanish-owned haciendas, some new and others rehabilitated, around the Indian towns. The mine known as Del Carmen was located just above Tlacuitlapan, and the mines of San Eligio and La Victora operated on Chepinque's hillsides.[107]

The increasing proximity of these multiethnic blocks and haciendas to the Indian towns made native leaders especially vigilant of protecting the lands and boundaries of their communities.[108] In 1709, for example, the cabildo of Tonalá Chepinque became embroiled in a dispute with two native men, Joseph Antonio García and Anastasio de los Santos, over the ownership of two houses located on the edge of the town.[109] Joseph Antonio and Anastasio claimed that the houses belonged to their parents and grandparents who had legally bought the property in the early to mid-seventeenth century. Now of legal age, they sought to dispose of the lots as they pleased without interference from the pueblo. Tonalá Chepinque's Indian cabildo forbade the men from selling the houses, accusing Joseph Antonio and Anastasio of attempting to alienate town lands. The men appealed to Spanish officials in Zacatecas to assist them in a suit against the pueblo, arguing their case as one of possession and legal jurisdiction. According to them, their parents had purchased the houses, as opposed to receiving them as a merced or land grant from the community. Not only did the houses not belong to Tonalá Chepinque; because they were vecinos of Zacatecas, Joseph Antonio and Anastasio were not beholden to the native cabildo's rulings. They argued that they remained under the jurisdiction of the Spanish municipal council. For that matter, they continued, all the former occupants of the house had been "subject" to Zacatecas, not Tonalá Chepinque.[110]

The evidence in the case, however, strongly suggests that Joseph Antonio and Anastasio were residents of Tonalá Chepinque. They probably identified themselves as vecinos of Zacatecas to secure a favorable ruling. Land and property dealings conducted in the pueblos were subject to the oversight of the Indian cabildos, while sales and purchases in the city required approval from the Spanish municipal council. Decisions by either assembly were typically respected and upheld by the other. Nonetheless, disgruntled individuals could attempt to manipulate matters of jurisdiction in order to secure more favorable results. In this case, the establishment of the true vecindad of the litigants would determine which side received a more favorable outcome. Locating the land (and themselves) under Spanish jurisdiction gave the men the ability to base their case on colonial concepts of Spanish private property, which were not always followed in the native pueblos.

For their part, the Indian leaders of Chepinque argued that the houses belonged to the pueblo and that the lands were community property. They also took pains to trace the history of the litigants' vecindad in the town. The native leaders pointed out that the ancestors of the litigants had been granted occupation of the houses for themselves and their families because they were vecinos who worked for the benefit of the town. Their families had been allowed to stay in the houses as long as they contributed to the pueblo's well-being and obeyed its rules. Even the witnesses brought forward on Joseph Antonio and Anastasio's behalf, they argued, had acknowledged that the men's parents had been subject to the pueblo's rents and taxes. The native leaders also brought forward evidence to prove that the petitioners belonged to their community, reminding the men that their parents had baptized them and their siblings in the town's church. The alcalde Miguel Angel concluded that Joseph Antonio and Anastasio's actions were "malicious and seditious" and that they deserved punishment for disturbing the peace. It is not known which petition prevailed. The corregidor eventually passed the case to the Audiencia.

Another dispute from 1719 illustrates the continued challenges that native peoples faced in maintaining their lands during the boom. In that year, officials from San Josef entered a petition with the Spanish municipal council for the removal of a mulatta that they claimed was living on land that pertained to their town.[111] The defendant, Nicolasa González, insisted that she had inherited the property from her father, who had formally registered the land with the Spanish cabildo fifty years earlier. The year of the alleged original sale, 1670, marked a transition between a bust-boom period. San Josef's smaller population at the time (see Table 4.10), may have emboldened the Spanish cabildo to sell vacant space at the edge of the pueblo to incoming boom migrants. Colonial officials eventually sided with Nicolasa despite San Josef's assertions that they held the property's titles.

Land and property transactions during the production fluctuations of 1670 to 1732 illustrate the effects of Zacatecas's shifting social and demographic environment on the native towns. A growing non-Indian population lived near their borders. Lands and lots were vulnerable to alienation from the Spanish cabildo or from native residents themselves. Yet these cases also illustrate how the native towns attempted to maintain their corporate and ethnic integrity during a period of significant demographic and cultural change. Indian cabildos utilized both Iberian legal customs and concepts of vecindad and land-tenure practices that bore a close resemblance to those of indigenous communities in central Mexico to defend their communities.[112] Leaders actively blocked non-Indians from intruding into their towns, taking aggressive action against any individual, even native peoples, who threatened the ethnic integrity of their communities. It was this combination of indigenous and Spanish practices that explain how the native towns weathered the land and population pressures of the early eighteenth century, and how they emerged from the boom with their indigenous character and composition intact.

Weathering the Boom: Fluent Vecinos

The survival of the city's Indian communities depended on their ability to maintain a viable population base from which to draw on indigenous practices and social networks. Unlike other areas in northern Mexico, they did not depend on other ethnic groups to survive or to regenerate. Even under adverse economic conditions, as we have seen, native peoples in Zacatecas managed to maintain group solidarity. They relied on large and deep social networks and affiliations of families, fictive kin, and work associates to constitute a critical demographic mass. Within their communities, they had created their own forms of municipal governance and religious organizations. By the early eighteenth century, these institutions had stabilized and matured, becoming bastions of indigenous society in the city.

But to credit the persistence of indigenous culture alone to mature indigenous institutions and individuals leaves the story only half told. This narrative does not adequately account for the dynamic and inclusive nature of indigenous culture in this period. Native peoples did not retreat into indigenous strongholds or shy away from non-Indians. Indian men and women sought and desired exchanges, social and economic, with other ethnoracial groups. Many even lived and labored in highly ethnically integrated sites. Rather than viewing these interethnic interactions as signs of indigenous integration into the general population or the disavowal of indigenous identities, they should be considered evidence of the ethnogenesis of a mature urban Indian culture, one that successfully incorporated urban practices into indigenous culture. To be an urban dweller, a vecino, was not a repudiation of indigeneity, but another facet of indigenous identity.[113]

How would we describe an Indian vecino in this period? A vecino could be a longtime indigenous resident, such as Matías Ramírez of Tlacuitlapan. By 1712 he had already become a career politician, serving for the previous five years on the municipal council, once as alcalde and four times as regidor. But a vecino could also be a recent migrant, such as María de Amaya, a widower who labored as a servant at the mining hacienda of San Pedro.[114] In other words, there is no generic description for a native vecino although we might be tempted to describe Matías as more acculturated than María, the latter having spent less time in the city. Yet Matías was a member of the town council, a select group with a history of defending indigenous interests. Thus simply classifying native people as "acculturated," a process that traditionally implies cultural loss, is ultimately misleading, failing to capture the complex dynamics of ethnogenesis that occurred among indigenous people as they layered Spanish practices to their native lifeways. Indigenous ethnicity in the urban context was much more nuanced, with individuals developing various urban skills and attributes according to their personal situations and socioeconomic contexts. While lifestyle, linguistic, sartorial, and occupational changes had an acculturative impact on indigenous identities; they did not convert a native person into a Spaniard or make them any less of an Indian. In other words, you could be "urban" and an "Indian." For example, let us turn to the city's vecinos with the greatest urban fluency, those native peoples often identified in the documentation as "ladinos." Ladinos were bilingual Indians.[115] More often they were bicultural as well.[116] These individuals had developed the skills and attributes to move with the greatest ease and breadth within the urban context. In most cases these native peoples usually spoke Castilian, were long-term residents, and had social connections with Spaniards. Yet as the following cases illustrate, these more fluent or culturally adaptable urban Indians always remained firmly within the indigenous sphere.

The heightened mining activity generated by the boom provided more opportunities for non-Spaniards to access individuals and resources associated with production. Some Indians, still the dominant labor force in the city's mines and haciendas, saw an opportunity to become mine owners rather than workers. In this period, a minero, or miner, denoted an individual who owned some stake in silver production, such as a mine or a refining plant.[117] Indian mine workers had used homemade hornos to smelt and sell silver since the city's founding, but these were small operations when compared to the large ventures produced by Spaniards using the amalgamation process.[118] Even Spaniards faced difficulty maintaining profitable operations. Fortunes from production typically lasted only one or two generations. Silver-mining ventures often required the formation of a *compañía*, a group of partners (*parcioneros*) who each owned a certain area of a mine measured in varas (about thirty-three inches). Ideally, partners shared labor and equipment expenses.[119] The pooling of resources could lead to spectacular successes or prolonged and bitter civil suits. Partnerships of two or four mineros were among the most common in Zacatecas. Spanish men formed the largest demographic from this pool, but women and native peoples occasionally emerged in the documentation. A series of legal petitions spanning 1719 to 1735 provides some insight into four indigenous peoples—Joseph de la Cruz and his wife Ignacia de la Cruz, as well as Diego de León and his wife María Josefa—who claimed ownership of twelve varas, or about half of a mine in addition to an undefined stake in a refining hacienda.[120]

María Josefa was the spouse of Diego de Leon, an indigenous miner and mine worker of the Hacienda de Leones.[121] Maria Josefa claimed that Diego had owned a 50 percent stake in a mine known as Los Remedios (which had been renamed El Angel at the time of the petition), which was located in the hillsides east of the city near a series of mining haciendas along the Veta Grande. In 1697, as he lay on his deathbed, María Josefa claimed that Diego asked Joseph, his *compadre* (godfather or fictive kin), to operate his share of the mine for the benefit of her and their two sons, neither of whom lived to their majority. In the period before her sons' deaths, it appears that Joseph worked the mine, occasionally providing

María Josefa with some of its profits. Formal litigation began in 1719 when María Josefa heard a rumor that Joseph offered twelve of the mine's varas to a local Spaniard, Martín de Ursua. As the last surviving member of her family, María Josefa argued that the mine belonged to her and petitioned for the return of its *títulos* (titles) and for any profits during the twenty-two years since her husband's death. For his part Joseph insisted that the mine had always belonged to him. Diego, he contended, had never owned Los Remedios. Instead, he had been only one of the many native peoples who labored at the site.

Conflicts over rights to a mine were not uncommon, especially during a boom period when there was more exploration and excavation than colonial officials could supervise. Initial forays into silver production often involved haphazard searches and the establishment of many informal claims until a mine proved that it merited serious exploitation, at which time the claims would be registered. During this exploratory period, which could last years or decades, frequent changes in ownership were common. Various partners worked and then abandoned mines, leading to serious problems over ownership rights. In spite of ordinances outlining steps to register, work, and relinquish a claim, individuals often exploited and abandoned mines without following official procedures.[122] Usually disputes over ownership rights involved Spaniards. How did María Josefa León and Joseph de la Cruz and their respective partners get involved? Answering this question reveals some of the skills, attributes, and connections of native peoples that successfully transitioned from worker to owner. But on a broader level, their experiences illustrate how Indian vecinos maintained indigenous identities as they operated with fluency in more culturally Spanish spheres.

As the city's oldest and largest labor source, native peoples would have been among those individuals with the greatest physical access to working mines. They would also have had contact with persons involved in exploration or the exploitation of metals, or with individuals interested in making investments. Documents show that at least three of the four native peoples had ties to a silver refining plant, the epicenter of production. Joseph had labored at several different mining haciendas. At the time of their partnership, Diego had worked for a Spaniard, Nicolás de Mendiosa, as a barretero and *repasador* (refiner) at the Hacienda of the Leones. Working (and perhaps even living) at the hacienda exposed both native men to the various steps and processes involved in mining production. As both an ore cutter and the more skill-based repasador, Diego possessed the necessary abilities to run a small mining operation. In town he was widely known as El Tarasco, which referred as much to his ancestral background as to his capacities as a metalsmith, because Tarascans had been famous, since preconquest times, for their skills in metallurgy.

Hacienda work not only taught people the silver-mining trade but also served as an avenue to form connections and opportunities. Native peoples were ubiquitous at mining sites, often working at least six if not seven days a week. Under these conditions it is not difficult to imagine Spaniards congregating with experienced native laborers—prospectors who knew the location of veins, and barreteros and repasadores with the requisite skills— and offering them partnerships in exploratory ventures. This would have allowed Indians entry into the world of production. Joseph and Diego met as fellow laborers at the site and, according to María Josefa, it was during her husband's tenure at the hacienda that he met a Spaniard, don Joseph de Urquiola, with whom he entered into a joint venture to exploit and work the site (Los Remedios). Over the following several years, according to her account, María Josefa and Diego held the mine in partnership with several different Spaniards.

Indian women did not work below ground in the mines. In general, they rarely participated in mining at the production level, no doubt a product of their limited access to miners and creditors as well as prescriptive gender roles. There were a few examples of single Spanish women who owned mines. Perhaps there were more than the documentation indicates. More commonly, Spanish and indigenous women held mines in joint possession with their husbands. In the dispute from 1730, the notary listed Ignacia de la Cruz as co-owner with her husband (Joseph) of twelve varas, which amounted to their total holdings.[123] Stakes were also obtained or claimed, as in María Josefa's case, through bequests or inheritance. Still, many women like María Josefa resided in haciendas, preparing food for male laborers and performing basic housekeeping activities in the complex's working and sleeping quarters. Like their spouses, daily routines and interactions around mining sites provided Indian women with valuable social opportunities and material knowledge that could advance their husbands' projects.

Fluency in Castilian facilitated movement within a predominately Spanish world of silver production. Colonial authorities identified Joseph and María Josefa as "indios ladinos en lengua castellana." While the city possessed a long history of monolingual native-language laborers, knowledge of Spanish would have been crucial to any indigenous person looking to participate in a mining operation. Fluency in Castilian enabled social and economic transactions between Indian miners and Spaniards, who remained the key players in the various stages of production, from refining to minting. It allowed for direct communication on such matters as the brokering of partnerships, the purchase of materials, contract negotiations, and the establishment of social connections, particularly patronage ties.[124] Spanish-speaking Indians had more strategies at their disposal to defend their interests. In addition to a greater understanding and perhaps access to the legal system, they could also employ informal channels that evaded monolingual native-language speakers. For example, on discovering Joseph's plan to give varas to Martín Ursua, María Josefa initially took her objections to Martín's wife, Josepha Moran. Although Josepha declined any knowledge of the matter, María Josefa nonetheless was able to communicate with her directly. Spanish fluency facilitated Indian access to the world of Spanish mining at production sites and in social and economic arenas.

Perhaps even more important than residency or language skills was the social capital Diego, Joseph, and Maria Josefa had acquired from their long-term tenure in the city as vecinos. María Josefa, for example, identified both as a vecina of the hacienda de los Leones and of the ciudad (Zacatecas). Joseph went even further identifying himself in the fashion of most Spanish miners as "vecino and minero of the city." The petitions do not indicate whether they were born in Zacatecas or when they arrived, but Joseph and María Josefa's residence can be traced to the early 1690s, whereas Diego may have been born or brought there as a child. It is no coincidence that his last name is the same as that of the hacienda (Leones), where he labored and lived with his wife and children. Being long-term vecinos provided Indians with a certain edge. They were known quantities in a city continuously flooded by migrants and itinerants of all ethnicities, especially during a boom period. Any native person could arrive in Zacatecas and quickly find employment as a mine worker, but a stake in mining production required economic and social capital. Long-term residents had more opportunities to amass resources and, as evidenced by Joseph and María Josefa's witness pool, to develop connections from diverse social and ethnic groups. Witnesses included miners, merchants, and laborers, as well as Spaniards, Indians, and people of African descent. Vecinos could capitalize on their known membership in the community to garner them favors and concessions. To meet his share of mining operation expenses, for example, Joseph received a series of loans totaling over three hundred pesos from a Spanish merchant.[125] This was an incredibly large sum of credit, clearly beyond the reach of the average indigenous laborer.

Ultimately María Josefa lost her case. Joseph retained title to the mine. But he did not secure sole ownership. His crippling debts, furthermore, made his victory rather hollow. Nevertheless, the case overturns traditional paradigms of native peoples and silver mining. Not all native peoples worked in the extraction of silver. Nor was silver production exclusively the domain of men. By the early eighteenth century, certain native peoples capitalized on their ability to speak Spanish, their long-term vecino status, and their experience with mining to form compañías with Spaniards. The dispute between María Josefa and Diego illustrates native peoples' full engagement with commercial institutions, the money economy, and their numerous social connections with ethnic others.

Interethnic interactions during the boom, however, were not limited to commercial matters. A custody dispute from 1702 between an indigenous woman and a Spanish man highlights the complex and intertwined relationships between native peoples and non-Indians. The population dynamics of silver-mining cities such as Zacatecas often created conditions that led to interethnic familial units. Recall that men and women of all ethnicities often left the city for short periods of time to work at other production sites. During these absences, children remained in the care of mothers, relatives, or servants.[126] The itinerant nature of the population along with its lax social environment often produced large numbers of displaced and abandoned children.[127] Although their numbers evade quantification, orphans appear frequently in extant documents, reflecting both general trends for other Spanish cities and the socioeconomic conditions endemic to many mining towns.[128] Unlike other major urban centers, Zacatecas did not have institutions such as orphanages and foundling homes that cared for displaced children.[129] In other words, there was a large population of children of diverse ethnicities circulating in the city, especially during boom periods. Living and laboring near mining haciendas, it is not difficult to imagine how indigenous women came to informally adopt or care for children abandoned by itinerant miners, workers, and illicit couples, indigenous or otherwise.

In the early morning of January 19, 1690, Andrea Rodríguez, who identified herself as a widow and vecina of Zacatecas, welcomed a newborn boy into her home.[130] The baby was not her child. A Spaniard from the nearby satellite mining community of Veta Grande delivered the infant along with a desperate plea from the boy's mother, an unmarried Spanish woman, to take him into her care. The Spanish woman could not raise him, he explained, because of the threat it posed to her reputation. The young boy would not be the last infant to arrive at Andrea's home under enigmatic circumstances. Five years later her sister, María, brought her another Spanish infant. María had also found this other newborn one morning at her door, keeping him for only fifteen days before handing him over to Andrea.[131] As with the first child, his parentage remained unknown. Andrea considered these infants *expósitos*, or orphans, and she reared the boys through their early childhood years, tending to their material and spiritual needs.[132] Within days of their respective arrivals, Andrea baptized both boys. She invited her partner, Diego Carrasco, an impoverished Spaniard, to serve as the *padrino*, or godfather, for one of the boys.

But in the summer of 1702, a man named Joseph Carrasco, the brother of Andrea's then-deceased partner, arrived on the scene. According to Andrea's version of events, Joseph and two of his relatives conspired to successfully remove the children from her care. A distraught Andrea filed a petition asking the corregidor to order the return of her children and to prohibit Joseph from any future attempts to wrest them from her custody. She based her right to the children on her *caudal*—or her economic investment—namely the goods, property, labor, and affection she had bestowed on them over many years. In response, Joseph entered a countersuit to have the boys (then twelve and seven years of age, respectively) remitted to his guardianship. They were, he claimed, his nephews by custom, if not by blood. Andrea, he argued, had no legal claims to the boys, caring for them only in the capacity of servant under the orders and at the expense of his brother. As the case progressed from Zacatecas to the Audiencia of Guadalajara, Joseph used Andrea's ethnic status as a means to discredit her fitness as a guardian and caregiver. The boys, he argued, would have more opportunities for advancement under the care of Spaniards than with an indigenous widow of no *calidad*, or social standing.[133] Ultimately, Joseph prevailed and Andrea lost custody of the two children.

Andrea's custody dispute offers insight into the relationship between ethnicity and guardianship, but it also illustrates how indigenous identities and associations persisted even as native peoples developed social and occupational connections with ethnic outsiders. Andrea had clearly cultivated both intimate and casual relations with several Spaniards. At the house level, she was raising two Spanish children and living in some type of informal union with a Spaniard. Her intimate relationship with Diego Carrasco brought her into contact with several other Spaniards, including his friends, acquaintances, and family. Andrea's occupation as a washerwoman also meant that other non-Indians crossed her path. Of the six witnesses she brought forward in her defense, five were Spanish vecinos, many of whom were miners, and all of them testified to her good character and her diligent care of the children. She also sent the boys to a school near her home run by a Spaniard, Pedro Vizcarrio. And she surely had some relationship with at least one of the mothers of the boys. Perhaps she met the women through her sister María, who, in her capacity as wet nurse, probably interacted with several Spanish woman. In other words, Andrea, like several other Indians in this period, had substantial social connections to and interactions with ethnic others, particularly Spaniards, at both the personal and the professional level.

Yet for all her connections and associations with Spaniards, Andrea was still tied to an Indian world with indigenous affiliations. Her sister María was identified as mestiza, and another sibling lived in the indigenous pueblo of San Josef. Andrea's jacal, a term typically associated with indigenous residences, was near the convent of San Francisco in the huerta of Barrito, an area adjacent to Tlacuitlapan and the site of several indigenous neighborhoods.[134] The house was located near a mining hacienda—a work site that was typically staffed by indigenous people.[135] Indeed, Andrea may have been one of these workers, washing clothing and attending to some of the other hacienda's household needs, a job common to indigenous women. Ultimately, no matter how involved she was with Spaniards, Andrea's daily life continued to involve indigenous peoples, occupations, and neighborhoods. The same could be said of Joseph de la Cruz, our litigious Indian "vecino and minero" from the previous case. He was married to an indigenous woman, served as godfather to indigenous children, lived in an indigenous barrio of the city, and worked at a mining hacienda with indigenous coworkers. The mere fact that Indians interacted closely or frequently with Spaniards or ethnic others—raising their children, or engaging in intimate relations or business ventures—does not necessarily mean that they disavowed their indigenous identities or associations. Among the native population, vertical ties, at the personal and occupational levels, remained as important as horizontal ones.

However, throughout the case, Andrea's use of language illustrates her concerns that associations with an indigenous or casta identity could jeopardize her claims to the children. She never identified by any ethnic affiliation and downplayed her non-Spanish status, emphasizing her Spanish connections and relationships. She often reminded authorities that she was a vecina of the Spanish city, as opposed to a resident of Zacatecas's Indian towns. Andrea's petitions made no reference to indigenous peoples or communities, stressing instead how she had reared the boys in a Spanish environment. But Andrea's attitude and position were less about her attempts to disown her indigenous identity. Rather, they were part of a legal strategy to win her petition in light of Joseph's attempts to cast doubt on her ability to raise the children. Joseph stressed that Andrea was indigenous ("india"), and hence, according to the colonial hierarchy, ethnically inferior to Spaniards.

Indios ladinos like Andrea and the Indian miner Joseph de la Cruz were deeply involved in the Spanish world. Debate exists as to whether bicultural individuals like them had abandoned their indigenous identities and were trying to "pass" as mestizos.[136] Indeed, even in their own time, determination of a person's ethnic identity was subject to the impressions of local community members, some well known, but others less so.[137]

Assessments were often based on visible benchmarks associated with dress and occupation. But a better sense of an individual's ethnic identity lies, as others scholars have cogently argued, in an examination of their social networks.[138] Andrea and Joseph were both highly fluent urban vecinos, yet in their personal, labor, and living arrangements they remained indigenous (as they did in the eyes of Spaniards as well). Nor were they or other bi-cultural native peoples necessarily the feared "agents of Hispanization."[139] Andrea and Joseph de la Cruz's experiences remind us that becoming a vecino in Zacatecas was less about passing as mestizo or non-Indian and more about becoming a resident—an individual with an occupation, home, and familial and social connections—who engaged in civic and commercial life.

. . .

For the native population the sharing of city space with a massive influx of immigrants of different ethnicities was one of the many daily changes they faced during the production booms of the late seventeenth and early eighteenth centuries. Revitalized mines and trade networks drew them further into the money economy and into greater interactions with ethnically diverse producers and consumers. Migrants and newcomers crowded into the city, settling near indigenous communities and laboring at mines and refining plants. Non-Indians passed through the indigenous towns. They sought to buy goods in their shops or stalls, and they found amusement and company in the pueblos' plazas and patios. While these interactions were good for trade, they also affected indigenous culture. How did native societies and identities persist in the face of such unprecedented interethnic contact and influences?

Native society weathered the production bust, surviving, and even growing, through the boom period. It did so in great measure because of the resilience of indigenous communities and institutions and a continued critical population mass, which facilitated indigenous associations and connections. As a group, native peoples had emerged from colonial society as "new peoples," developing a corporate identity based on certain shared attributes, including not being of Spanish or of African descent, residing in an Indian town or neighborhood, participating in indigenous organizations and institutions, and maintaining indigenous associations.[140] But indigenous culture also persisted because of its malleability and adaptability. Ethnogenetic processes, according to Stuart B. Schwartz and Frank Salomon, involve "fission, readaptation, and recombination."[141] The native population, in what was perhaps its most innovative strategy, grafted Spanish-urban practices onto their indigenous identities. Over centuries, these processes in Zacatecas led to an urban Indian culture that fully engaged institutionally, commercially, and personally in Spanish urban life even as it remained firmly within the indigenous sphere. This fluency in urban practices, which is often described as acculturation, was another facet—not a repudiation—of their indigenous identities.[142] By the eighteenth century, native people managed to live in the city as indios because they had become apt vecinos.[143]

As the mining boom drew to a close and the city experienced yet another paralyzing economic downturn, native vecinos would play a critical role in the revival of Zacatecas. At the same time, they experienced greater challenges in navigating the economic and cultural changes of the late colonial period.

5 Revival and Survival: Indigenous Society in the Mid- to Late Colonial Period, 1730–1806

The night of February 12, 1806, promised to be one of great celebration and camaraderie for the pueblo of El Niño. A wedding welcomed a new couple to the community and local officials had secured permission for a *fandango*, or dance, to commemorate the nuptials. As the merrymaking drew to a close, a large group of people assembled at the mouth of the alley of the street known as Juan de San Pedro. But the presence of Perfecto Hernández, the Indian alcalde of El Niño; his alguacil mayor, or constable, Máximo Juárez; and other indigenous officers among the crowd, suggests that this after-gathering had little to do with the festivities.

As the leader of his town, Hernández's presence at the event had both ceremonial and civic functions. One of these was the maintenance of public order in the small community. But that particular evening the indigenous official was less concerned about trouble from lingering revelers as he was by the arrival of Don José Ramón Gómez, the Spanish alcalde of one of Zacatecas's four subdistricts, along with his other Spanish associates, as well as some Indian officials from the pueblo of San Josef. Their arrival came as no surprise to Hernández. Much to the annoyance of the indigenous leadership—and indeed the entire town—Gómez and his crew had taken advantage of new jurisdictional changes enacted by the Spanish crown to justify making rounds in the native pueblos. According to the Indian officials, the Spanish alcalde was meddling and causing trouble, not maintaining law and order. In testimonies taken during a formal inquiry into the episode, the native officials claimed that Gómez and his accomplices were intoxicated, belligerent, and insulting—the Spanish alcalde especially so—calling the Indian leaders *alcahuetes* (instigators or troublemakers).[1] Fearing their volatile and drunken state, Alcalde Hernández argued that he had little choice but to arrest them for the good of the pueblo and the greater community. He declared, "In the name of the King, tie Don José Gómez and whoever else who accompanies him and tries to resist."[2] The Indian officials then stripped Gómez of his cane, hat, and cape, and tied his arms tightly with ropes. While he was bound, they led him and his minister, who suffered the same fate, to the *carcel pública* (public jail), where they remained until the following morning.

Four days later Gómez initiated a suit (*demanda*) against the indigenous officials seeking reparations for the injuries to his person and the affronts to his honor and his office. In a vastly different account from those of the native alcaldes, Gómez claimed that he had been arrested unjustly. He argued that within a matter of seconds after the encounter, and with no provocation from him or his colleagues, he had been accosted by the "entire pueblo," a mob of more than a hundred people, and then forced to languish ignominiously in prison. As for the cruel authors of his disgrace, the indigenous officials of El Niño, they remained unpunished and "triumphant" over their actions. Despite these impassioned accusations, the native officials maintained their version of events, although they did admit that Gómez's arrest was not solely the product of this one confrontation. It was also the culmination of long-standing grievances against the Spanish official for consistently interfering in their pueblo's governance and activities. This dispute, which this chapter returns to later, illustrates the frequent jurisdictional conflicts between Spaniards and Indians in Zacatecas in the late colonial period. It also captures the complex nature of indigenous society in the post-1730s boom period, which sought to protect its corporate identity and the autonomy of its institutions as it became increasingly drawn into Spanish society.

After the virulent and widespread *matlazahuatl*, or epidemic, receded in the early 1740s, New Spain's indigenous population began a steady demographic increase that lasted through the late colonial period.[3] This population surge occurred in urban centers as well. A study by Claudio Esteva Fabregat, based on figures from 1789, found that Indians represented 59 percent of the total population of a sampling of ninety-five cities from across New Spain.[4] John Chance, for example, points out that "in purely numerical terms, Antequera [Oaxaca] became a more 'Indian' city during these years," with native people constituting 27.9 percent of the total population by the end of the eighteenth century.[5] In Esteva Fabregat's study mining towns also emerged as sites of large indigenous populations. Of the thirty-eight centers under consideration, Indians accounted for 52 percent of their residents.[6] Zacatecas's population exhibited similar trends. In 1799, native peoples accounted for 29 percent of its total inhabitants.[7] These numbers confirm that late eighteenth-century cities and reales de minas remained sites of large populations of urban Indians. But what was the state of native societies and communities in these Spanish urban centers?

In Zacatecas, the period between 1730 and the start of New Spain's independence movements in 1810 witnessed dramatic economic and political changes at the local and viceregal level. Some changes were familiar, as the city once again fell prey to a commercial and demographic boom-bust cycle. The spectacular early eighteenth-century production upsurge that lasted nearly thirty years (from 1705 to 1732) could not be sustained. Zacatecas then experienced another prolonged forty-year downturn, with most mines being abandoned until the resurgence of mining activity in the late 1760s. This mining boom brought the city and its native residents economic relief. Yet new and unfamiliar challenges made daily life more difficult, from working conditions to struggles to maintain indigenous institutions, organizations, and towns. Across the empire, administrative projects designed to centralize authority and increase economic productivity— often referred to as the Bourbon Reforms—altered the political, social, and even geographic boundaries of both Spanish Zacatecas and the Indian towns.[8] These new policies touched the heart of indigenous society, affecting native lands and resources, religious organizations, and systems of governance. This chapter considers how indigenous society and culture fared during this period, as indigenous peoples strove for both the city's revival and their own survival. It argues that native societies and institutions remained fairly vital through the mid-1770s, but that social, economic, and demographic changes during the last decades of colonial rule (1775–1810) weakened and undermined indigenous communities and institutions to the point that they eventually ceased to function as autonomous units in the postindependence period.

Indigenous Migration: A Demographic Basis

In the 1730s, the city's population continued to swell with working men and women eager to capitalize on the trade and commerce generated by the great mining boom. But the great days of plenty were numbered. Problems with production, resources, and financing soon left the city in the grip of another protracted downturn.[9] The mining bust spanned the entire mid-eighteenth century, from 1732 to 1770. The decrease in production led to fewer employment opportunities and market activities, contributing to a citywide population decline as individuals left Zacatecas in search of better opportunities and wages elsewhere. The city's population gradually fell from its colonial peak in 1732 of 40,000 individuals to its eighteenth-century nadir in 1770 of 16,260.[10]

How did Indians respond to these new circumstances? As in previous episodes of economic contraction, some native peoples left the city in search of better economic opportunities elsewhere. But many Indian vecinos remained—more so, if a 1754 padrón is to be believed, than any other ethnic group. The census captures a moment well into the bust period. It indicates that native peoples constituted close to half of Zacatecas's total population of 21,250 individuals (see Table 5.1). From 1750 to 1780, Indians were probably the city's largest ethnic group. The stability of the Indian population during a severe decline in silver production, a period in which there could have been a massive exodus to other more prosperous mining sites, speaks to the strength of the long-term roots that many native vecinos had established in the city. It also explains their strong demographic presence and corporate vitality in the late colonial period.

Some studies argue that indigenous migrants accelerated the destabilization of Indian communities. Others highlight the role of immigrants in perpetuating indigenous practices, arguing that migrants served as links to traditional Indian communities and contributed to the restructuring of indigenous society in the areas where they settled.[11] In Zacatecas, for example, references to Nahuatl-language interpreters resurge during migrant booms. In 1752, the priests of Tlacuitlapan had a license to administer the sacraments and confess men and women in both "the Castilian and Mexican languages."[12] The continued use of Nahuatl in religious functions was directly related to the large influx of migrants to the city from 1720 through 1745. What impact immigrants had on other daily cultural practices is less clear. But in terms of sheer numbers, marriage petitions illustrate that the continued influx of indigenous migrants helped regenerate the Indian communities. Highlighting the settlement and creation of social networks among the migrant population brings some balance to scholarly arguments that cast the native migrant pool almost exclusively as male, itinerant (or *vago*), and ultimately connected to their home communities.[13]

Marriage petitions from two Indian towns—Tonalá Chepinque and El Niño—illustrate how migrants directly affected their demographic vitality

TABLE 5.1. Population of Zacatecas by ethnic categories, 1754

Group	Number	Percentage of total population
Spanish	7,000	33
Indian	9,950	47
Others	4,300	20
Total	**21,250**	

Source: Gerhard, *North Frontier*, 158–59.

during an economic slowdown. From 1731 to 1780, the native vecinos of Tonalá Chepinque and El Niño submitted 193 petitions to marry. Of the total 386 petitioners from this period, 17 percent (66) were migrants. These were individuals who indicated a place of origin distinct from that of the Indian pueblos or the Spanish city. Of these sixty-six individuals, there were forty-one men and twenty-five women (comprising 11 percent and 6 percent of total petitioners, respectively). Dividing the migrant population into ten-year sets illustrates that 44 percent of the migrants arrived in the period 1731–1740, a decade that had yet to feel the full impact of the economic downturn (see Table 5.2). However, it also indicates that individuals were still migrating to Zacatecas even during leaner economic years.

Tonalá Chepinque and El Niño continued to remain indigenous strongholds for men and women. Sixty-two of the town's new vecinos (94 percent) identified as indigenous in their petitions. All of the men identified themselves as Indian, except one who described himself as a mestizo. Twenty-two women (88 percent) identified as indigenous; one woman described herself as a mestiza, the other as a *coyota*, an individual of Indian and African descent. Although Table 5.2 illustrates that men outnumbered women, female migrants still constituted more than a third (38 percent) of the immigrant petitioners. Of the eleven female petitioners who indicated that they migrated to Zacatecas as adults, four may either have left to follow partners or they moved when their husbands died. For more than half the women, the decision to leave their communities was not necessarily based on family circumstances.

Female immigrants brought a certain demographic and social stability to their communities. Children, who constituted a significant sector of the immigrant population, did so as well.[14] Of the fifty-two immigrants who reported their age at migration, half were brought to the city as children (between birth and fourteen). Nearly 70 percent (eighteen of them) migrated between the ages of two and twelve, and another 30 percent

TABLE 5.2. Number of male and female migrant petitioners, Tonalá Chepinque and El Niño, 1731–1780

Years	Men	Women
1731–1740	19	10
1741–1750	7	3
1751–1760	8	5
1761–1770	3	6
1771–1780	4	1
Total	41	25

Source: APZ, Matrimonios, IINC, box 67, carpeta 2, exp. 194, ff. 1–263, 1731–1780.

TABLE 5.3. Number of adult and child migrants, male and female petitioners, Tonalá Chepinque and El Niño, 1731–1780

Years	Adults	Children
1731–1740	13	6
1741–1750	2	6
1751–1760	5	7
1761–1770	3	6
1771–1780	3	1
Total	26	26

Source: APZ, Matrimonios, IINC, box 67, carpeta 2, exp., 194, ff. 1–263, 1731–1780.

reported coming as *niños* and *niñas* (boys and girls). The age range of the adult migrants fell between sixteen and twenty-eight. Adults predominated in the period marked by a rise in silver production, whereas children began to appear more frequently in years of economic decline (see Table 5.3). These figures suggest a greater movement of families seeking more permanent residence in the pueblos rather than itinerant laborers. These youthful migrants augmented the population and formed the basis for future generations, particularly during the long bust years. Most child immigrants had lived in the pueblos for an average of eight to ten years at the time of their petitions. Migrants raised in the pueblos often established strong ties to the communities and were more likely to return to the towns after brief labor spells at other mining sites.

Where were migrants journeying from during these lean years? Fortunately, marriage petitions requested both their vecino status and the applicant's place of origin. In-migrants continued to arrive from the traditional sites noted in Chapter 4 for the late seventeenth century, particularly from areas around Guanajuato, Guadalajara, and Michoacán. Pedro Sánchez, for example, migrated to El Niño from Michoacán because the death of his father had left him with few resources in his home community.[15] The most significant change in regard to place of origin was the large number of migrants from the New Galicia hinterlands. Women in particular were arriving in greater numbers from this area than from central Mexico. In the pueblos, close to half of both the female and male migrants (45 percent) were from the city's hinterlands (see Table 5.4).[16] The heavy migration of people from the hinterlands to Zacatecas suggests that declining silver production had been detrimental to commerce and trade in local markets. These short-distance migrants may have been more likely to establish long-term roots in the community. They had familiarity with the area and probably had existing social, kinship, and trade networks in the city.[17]

TABLE 5.4. Origin of male and female migrant petitioners, Tonalá Chepinque and El Niño, 1731–1780

Province	Men	Women
New Spain	16	4
New Galicia	20	17
Nuevo León	0	1
Nueva Vizcaya	1	0
Nuevo Santander	1	0
Unknown	2	3
Total	40	25

Source: APZ, Matrimonios, IINC, box 67, carpeta 2, exp. 194, ff. 1–263, 1731–1780.

While the need for wages was a powerful motive, it was not the only driving factor in determining a destination. The frequent practice of choosing individuals from their home communities as witnesses suggests that social networks played a key role, with individuals traveling to sites with an established support base. Important changes in family life, such as the death of a spouse or a marriage, often served as the impetus for movement. María Alba, for example, migrated to Zacatecas from another mining camp on the death of her husband.[18] A significant number also became engaged to native vecinos. Nearly a third (29 percent) of all the pueblos' marriage petitions involved an immigrant. In fact, all sixty-six migrants were engaged to a current resident of either Tonalá Chepinque or El Niño. Seventy percent petitioned to marry an originario (a native to the pueblo), whereas 30 percent planned to wed a fellow immigrant. Only one Indian migrant married a non-Indian, a mestiza who was nonetheless an originaria and vecina of the pueblo. The substantial rate of formal unions (marriage) and informal networks (witnesses) between migrants and Indian vecinos indicates a group of immigrants with more personal and permanent ties to the community.

The selection of witnesses also illustrates a migrant population closely connected to the Indian community in the greater city. Three witnesses (and occasionally four) added their support to each marriage petition. Only 28 of 171 witnesses were individuals from other ethnoracial groups (16 percent). In those cases the witness was often a known individual, a connection from the petitioner's place of origin. The majority of witnesses were Indians, primarily vecinos from the pueblos (141, or 82 percent). The selection of spouses and witnesses from among fellow vecinos in the towns reflects the strong ties that immigrants made with fellow community members and challenges the idea that migrants rarely established long-term ties with their new communities.

The steady flow of immigrants, including women and children, to Tonalá Chepinque and El Niño during a period of mining decline illustrates that Zacatecas drew Indians interested in establishing roots in the community, not just those capitalizing on mining bonanzas. As vecinos, native immigrants—men, women, and children; married, single, or widowed—contributed to the persistence of a critical demographic mass. In lean years they rounded out the indigenous and the city's smaller population base, and in boom times they furthered the persistence of indigenous society, creating a greater indigenous pool of spouses, acquaintances, fictive kin, and work colleagues. Overall, marriage petitions along with other qualitative sources indicate that the decline of indigenous people as a demographic, corporate, or social group had yet to occur before 1775.

Yet as native peoples revitalized the city's population base, changes in colonial policies at the viceregal level and shifts in attitudes of local authorities brought unprecedented pressures to indigenous individuals and communities. The mid- to late eighteenth century marked a time of growing challenges to indigenous rights and institutions from the city's non-Indian population. Some of these challenges originated from empirewide policies that destabilized the organization of jurisdictional units at the local level. On the ground, circumstances related to production and population surges strained the fragile relationships between Indians and Spaniards and led to jurisdictional conflicts between the two groups. Native peoples' struggles to assert their rights as vecinos and Indians during this period met with varying levels of success.

Changes in Religious Life

In 1700, the end of the Hapsburg line led to the ascendancy of French-descended Bourbon rulers. The Bourbon crown, influenced by a blend of absolutist and Enlightenment principles, sought to restructure Spanish America at both the viceregal and local levels through a series of political, economic, and military policies. These reforms arrived in two waves. The first set, often considered less dramatic, was implemented from the 1700s to the 1760s.[19] The changes of the late colonial period (circa 1760 to independence) were even more invasive. Still, even before the implementation of the later reforms, the entire populace, Indians as well as Spaniards, experienced some changes in their daily lives under Bourbon rule.

As part of their attempts to centralize power and consolidate assets and resources, the Bourbons sought to curb the role of the church in the colonies by replacing more autonomous units—particularly mendicants and Jesuits—with secular priests. The expulsion of the Jesuits in 1767 was the most dramatic manifestation of the eighteenth-century religious reforms. But the Jesuits were not the only victims of Bourbon policies. Around mid-century, the crown issued a series of decrees aimed at limiting the power of the mendicant orders. The most drastic of these was the secularization of their parishes.[20] The process occurred in two waves: the first, from 1749 to 1755, and the second, between the 1760s and the 1790s.[21] Local factors contributed to the uneven execution of this measure in New Spain, with its implementation primarily occurring in areas with lucrative benefices or large populations of diocesan clergy.[22] Because mining towns with their money economies had always been considered coveted posts, it is not surprising that all of Zacatecas's Indian doctrinas (parishes) eventually came under the control of secular priests in 1773.[23]

Secular priests had descended quickly on the city after its initial settlement in 1548.[24] But they did not attract a large following. Religious life in the early years of their custodianship was improvised, sporadic, and informal. The immigrant indigenous population, accustomed to worshipping in their own churches, found themselves forced to attend services with blacks and Spaniards, often outdoors around makeshift altars.[25] Repeated directives from viceregal authorities admonished miners and regidores for their lack of effort in instructing their laborers in the faith. This suggested that they forced native workers (and slaves) to work on Sundays and feast days.[26] Not all native peoples desired an active religious life. Indeed, many took advantage of religious days to engage in social events or to work on their own commercial enterprises.[27] But as we saw in chapters 2 and 4, the role of the urban church in providing a platform for indigenous social organization and in creating ethnic cohesion should not be underestimated. Ultimately, only a few labor gangs composed of Indians working in nearby mining haciendas were granted to parish clerics. The majority of the native population preferred the structure and familiarity of the religious orders.

Motivated by profits derived from fees associated with sacraments and sundry religious functions, the city's secular priests frequently attempted to wrest custodianship of the Indian population from the brotherhoods.[28] In what was common practice in the Spanish empire, native people in Zacatecas paid fees for sacraments, burials, and the registration of marriage petitions, and indigenous communities compensated priests for services such as sermons, masses, vespers, and processions. Although Indians had lower fees than Spaniards, their large numbers made them a coveted group. Disputes and other complaints suggest that secular priests were less concerned with the spiritual needs of the Indian population than with securing their share of religious fees.[29]

The change in clergy went far beyond who officiated mass or administered sacraments. It ended more than two hundred years of close ties between native peoples and the Franciscans and Augustinians. In other areas of northern Mexico, the imposition of Christian practices on non-empire peoples had brought about changes that went far beyond religious beliefs. Chapter 2 discussed how the organization of native peoples in mission complexes where they were directly supervised by friars dramatically altered their lifeways. Coercive and exploitative living and labor arrangements within missions often created animosity between friars and their subjects. But in Zacatecas, several factors contributed to more harmonious than contentious relations between the orders and their indigenous parishioners. By the time of Zacatecas's founding, the majority of the migrant pool had been exposed to Christianity and was generally accepting of its practices and institutions. Moreover, in Zacatecas the regular orders could not blatantly exploit their parishioners to meet religious and personal needs through repartimiento or tribute. An ecclesiastical review from 1708 offers some evidence of the amicable relations between the Franciscans and their wards. In December of that year, Spanish officials charged a brother from the convent of San Francisco with insubordination and then imprisoned him. The Indian leaders of Tlacuitlapan not only spoke on the friar's behalf but also sheltered him for one night in the pueblo's capilla after he escaped from Spanish authorities. This friar, a witness later proclaimed, "was much loved by the Indians."[30]

One town had already come under the control of secular priests. San Josef had had a particularly contentious relationship with their religious custodians, the Dominicans. In 1704, principales from the cabildo and the cofradía set out for a routine meeting with a newly arrived priest. He was scheduled to say mass and attend to other religious functions on the feast day of the pueblo. Arriving at the order's monastery, the visit quickly turned sour when the priest became incensed at their request that he accompany them to their church. He not only ran them out but he also called them "vulgar and disorderly names."[31] According to the indigenous leaders, money was the source of the cleric's discontent. The priest, who had been paid twenty pesos in anticipation for his services, claimed that he deserved more money. He also let it be known that attending to the pueblo was not his paramount concern. The incident eventually led colonial authorities to remove the pueblo from the Dominican's supervision, entrusting it to diocesan clergy.[32] San Josef peacefully acquiesced to the change. Whether other native parishioners responded to the change in guardianship with similar feelings is unknown. There is no strong evidence that native peoples vehemently opposed secularization.[33]

Over the long term, the turnover of the Indian parishes to diocesan priests had more than spiritual implications. It affected even such diverse aspects of daily life as labor. For example, in 1801, an Indian, Manuel de la Cruz, who had taken shelter from an oppressive master in a nearby convent was quickly handed over to local authorities.[34] This complicity between religious custodians and authorities was a far cry from when the Franciscans purposefully undermined colonial authorities in support of their indigenous parishioners, such as during the saçemi suppression campaigns of the early seventeenth century.[35] As time passed, secular clerics, with a long history of exploiting the Indian population for financial gain, sided with elite interests to their detriment. A decree from 1835 illustrates the deteriorated relations between the church and its humble parishioners. Siding with mine owners and city officials, ecclesiastical authorities agreed that the number of religious feast and saint days significantly "disrupted and delayed" the exploitation of the mines.[36] As a consequence, religious officials reduced the number of days given to laborers to celebrate feast days from ten to fourteen depending on the area.[37] They conceded that laborers could attend mass on those other days, but only if they returned promptly to their job sites. This change in policy marks a dramatic shift from the Hapsburg period, when colonial authorities instructed clergy to ensure that workers and slaves were released from their labors at the mines and taught doctrine on feast days.[38] But it aligns with Bourbon practices from the late colonial period that sought to undermine the power of local religious entities and promote economic efficiency.

Changes in guardianship were also accompanied in the mid- to late eighteenth century by the dissolution of several native confraternities and the reorganization of others into larger archconfraternities. Cofradías were another aspect of religious life in Spanish America that gradually became incompatible with crown attitudes and policies. The organizations were considered too autonomous. The rituals, ceremonies, processions, and possessions they sponsored on their behalf were deemed wasteful and superstitious.[39] Measures were taken to decrease the number of brotherhoods and bring their practices in line with Bourbon positions of moderation, economy, and efficiency. In Mexico City, over one-quarter of the viceregal confraternities had ceased to exist by the end of the eighteenth century.[40] Poor administration and badly managed finances served as grounds for their closure.

In Zacatecas, several smaller confraternities were absorbed into larger entities. In Tlacuitlapan, the cofradías of Jesús Nazareno and the Vera Cruz had merged with Tlacuitlapan's most prominent sodality, Limpia Concepción, by 1746.[41] By 1798 the confraternity of San Nicolás was extinguished, along with El Niño's sodality, Nombre de Jesús.[42] The bishop of Guadalajara, Juan Cruz Ruiz de Cabañas, advocated further closures during his inspection of Zacatecas's cofradías in the late summer of 1798. Following Bourbon practices, Bishop Cabañas found fault with the records and accounts of three cofradías—San Diego, Limpia Concepción, and San Josef—and advocated further reform.[43] He encouraged Chepinque to demolish the chapel near its main church and relocate its members to the capilla of Concepción. He proposed similar measures for Tlacuitlapan. He advised that all cofrades congregate in the largest capilla of the town and that the other chapels be closed. Other signs of reforms appear in this period as well. Tonalá Chepinque had a tradition of carrying deceased vecinos under a cross through the city to the church of the convent. This practice disturbed some secular ecclesiastics who petitioned viceregal officials to halt the processions.[44] The move to modify elements of baroque religiosity had a substantive impact on native peoples, both living and dead.

However, even with these changes, the native population once again illustrated its resiliency and adaptability. Indigenous peoples continued to worship in the churches of their pueblos. But by the early 1770s, they were joined by a greater number of castas who attended services and received rites in the indigenous barrios.[45] But more ethnically diverse congregations were not particular to this period. Castas, particularly mestizos, had attended services in the Indian parishes long before their secularization.[46] Some native cofradías also persisted. For example, San Diego remained viable through at least 1802. Nuestra Señora de la Soledad still served the pueblo in 1832.[47] San Josef was in existence as late as 1856.[48] It is possible that these larger organizations provided a means by which to consolidate members and support, a strategy reminiscent of the formation of the first indigenous cofradía, the Vera Cruz. Native peoples also appear to be behind the establishment of a new brotherhood. In 1763, barreteros established the cofradía of the Santísimo Sacramento in the convent of Nuestra Señora de la Merced in the Spanish traza.[49] Ore excavation was a job traditionally assumed by native peoples and the evidence indicates that the majority of members were indigenous.

Still, changes in religious practices, policies, and caretakers in this period ultimately undermined indigenous society and institutions. The merging of smaller cofradías into archconfraternities was certainly a loss to the independence of subject communities. The consolidation of chapels eliminated (literally) indigenous spaces and the opportunities for civic participation that they represented. Unlike the Franciscans or Augustinians, secular clerics often failed to understand the use of religious organizations by native people as expressions of sociopolitical autonomy. Native peoples had to weather these changes in religious life as they contended with the new urban realities generated by the late eighteenth-century mining boom.[50]

The Indigenous Revival of Zacatecas

From 1732 to 1770, problems with production, resources, and financing contributed to an economic downturn.[51] The bust led to an eventual decline in employment opportunities, market activities, and population. But beginning in the late 1760s, the city underwent what David Brading described as a "revival," an increase in silver production, economic activity, and population growth that spanned the years 1767 to 1809. Brading credited this boom to a series of Spanish men who, with the assistance of crown concessions, reinvested in old mines and revitalized the industry. He also argued that the mining recovery was "heavily dependent upon outside capital" to support the infrastructure and technology needed to refurbish many of the abandoned mines. While there is little doubt that silver production resurged because of the efforts of colonial entrepreneurs and crown incentives, ordinary native men and women, the city's local "human capital," also played a role in Zacatecas's production and population revival.

The late colonial boom had its own distinct dynamics, but mining production in Zacatecas remained dependent, as it had been from its origins, on access to an available labor pool to staff its mines and to serve in other urban occupations. The silver revival of the late colonial period drew individuals from every element of colonial society. Even with an increasing number of non-Indians, Zacatecas's native population still constituted a significant sector of the population and the labor force. By century's end, the city's population recovered to around thirty thousand. Indians accounted for 29 percent of those inhabitants.[52]

Marriage petitions from the boom's first ten years, separated by greater ethnoracial groups, mirror the city's overall population trends (see Table 5.5). Indians constituted the largest group in the petitioner population, averaging at 33 percent between men and women. The figures also

TABLE 5.5. Composition of marriage petitioner population, 1771–1780

	Men		Women		Total	
	Number	Percentage	Number	Percentage	Number	Percentage
Indians	382	35	340	31	722	33
Mestizos	318	29	361	33	679	31
Spaniards	309	28	325	29	634	29
Mulattos	81	7	61	6	142	6
Undeclared	4	0	5	0	9	0
Other castas	10	1	12	1	22	1
Total	1,104	100	1,104	100	2,208	100

Source: APZ, Matrimonios, IINC, 1771–1780; APZ, Matrimonios, Españoles, 1771–1780.

illustrate the city's growing casta population. Non-Indians totaled about 38 percent of the petitioner population. But in this period this was still a highly "indigenous" casta population, with mestizos comprising about a third (31 percent) of the population. As the boom began, Indians and their mixed-raced descendants, individuals who often maintained strong ties to the indigenous sphere, remained the city's most populous vecinos, constituting around two-thirds (64 percent) of the city's inhabitants. Miners, merchants, traders, store owners, and ordinary residents relied on these non-Spaniards to continue to meet the city's numerous labor needs.

The mining and population recovery of the late colonial period created jobs throughout the city for both Indian men and women. However, native peoples were not simply working below ground or at refining haciendas, but in many other jobs that provided important services to the urban population. Biographical statements from the marriage petition witness pool offer a window into male Indian jobs (and those of their mulatto counterparts) outside the mining complex in the initial years of the boom from 1775 to 1777 (see Table 5.6). In that period, there were a total of 546 witnesses. About 50 percent of the witnesses identified as indigenous (269). Mulattos accounted for 12 percent (sixty-five) of them. Of the 261 native men who listed an occupation, sixty-eight (26%) worked in some activity that supported the urban economy.[53] Indigenous farmers provided needed foodstuffs prepared by bakers and confectioners. Indian muleteers and truck farmers (produce vendors) brought needed resources to the city. Hatmakers, tailors, and weavers dressed the general population. Carpenters, masons, and brick makers worked on new construction and maintained weathered buildings that were often in need of maintenance. And mining production would have come to a halt without the products crafted by candle makers and blacksmiths. Associations between ethnicity and occupations continued in this period. There were more Indian weavers, bakers, and muleteers, while more mulattos labored as shoemakers. These occupations and the people who performed them are often overshadowed by the roles of miners and other high-level functionaries. But these urban workers kept both mining production and the city functioning.

Marriage petitions from 1771 to 1780 offer some information on the presence of Indian women in the labor force. They indicate that a sizable number of women migrated to Zacatecas, almost at the same pace as that of men: 16 percent to 18 percent.[54] Their voluntarily migration to the city—at a similar pace to that of their male counterparts—indicates that there was a continued demand for their labor in other sectors of the mining economy. Since the registers record their age only at the time of their petition, it is not clear at which period of their lives the women arrived to the city. But a survey of the age of the female migrants indicates that the

TABLE 5.6. Nonmining jobs of Indian and mulatto witnesses, Zacatecas, 1775–1777

	Indians	Mulattos
Alms collector	0	1
Baker	10	0
Blacksmith	1	2
Blanket maker	2	0
Brick maker	4	2
Candle maker	1	1
Carpenter	3	2
Confectioner	2	0
Farmer	1	0
Farmworker	2	1
Grill maker	0	1
Hatmaker	2	0
Mailman	0	1
Mason	1	0
Muleteer	7	1
Provision dealer	1	0
Ranch hand	1	0
Saddle maker	1	0
Server (of legal orders)	1	0
Shoemaker	6	10
Stonecutter	0	1
Straw or hay collector	3	0
Street vendor	5	0
Surveyor	1	0
Tailor	1	3
Tanner	2	0
Truck farmer	1	0
Water seller	0	5
Weaver	9	3
Total	68	34

Source: APZ, Matrimonios, IINC, 1771–1780.

great majority (87 percent) probably migrated in their teens and twenties (see Table 5.7). The movement of women from within this age group suggests that mining towns were as attractive a draw for females as their male counterparts and that they considered relocation to a mining town a viable strategy for meeting economic needs. For example, thirty-year-old Maria Estafana Vázquez, a widow of five years at the time of her petition, probably arrived in the city between 1772 and 1776, at the start of the boom. She had lived with her former husband, Alejandro Dolores Elías, for five years in the nearby mining town of Real de Ángeles.[55] Zacatecas's proximity to her former residence may have been the reason for her relocation or, alternatively, she had developed skills that were well suited to working in a mining town. María Josefa Nuin was a native of Chihuahua. Identified as an "india mapache," she had probably worked at one of the region's reales de minas.[56]

TABLE 5.7. Age of female migrations at time of petition, Zacatecas, 1771–1780

Age	Number	Percentage
10–14	1	2
15–19	25	45
20–29	23	42
30–39	3	5.5
40–49	3	5.5
Total	55	100

Source: APZ, Matrimonios, IINC, 1771–1780.

TABLE 5.8. Number of women from marriage petitions residing in haciendas, Zacatecas, 1771–1780

Type	Indians	Non-Indians
Mining	11	3
Agricultural	5	2
Total	16	5

Source: APZ, Matrimonios, IINC, 1771–1780.

During the late colonial boom, Indian women continued to be very active at mining complexes and agricultural haciendas, perhaps with an even more visible presence than in previous periods. Indigenous women, ranging in age from fifteen to forty, constituted a majority of this workforce (see Table 5.7). Of the twenty-one women who identified a hacienda as their place of work and residence, slightly more than three-quarters of them (sixteen) identified as indigenous. Sixty-nine percent of these Indian women worked at mining haciendas, and 31 percent worked at agricultural ranches (see Table 5.8). One woman worked at a stone quarry complex. As with men, hacienda work for women may have been a trade that passed from generation to generation. Fifteen of the sixteen women were born at the haciendas where they labored and resided. Within the haciendas, women cleaned, cooked, hauled water, and cared for the many laborers, families, children, and visitors who worked and resided at the haciendas. An 1826 account by the English traveler George F. Lyon found women involved in the refining process. Lyon commented on the presence of *apuranderas*, older women assigned to carry off and rewash the ore after its initial mixture with quicksilver.[57] It is not known when women took on this task.

The significant number of single women who lived and worked at mining haciendas also speaks to larger changes in indigenous society. Inventories of cuadrillas from earlier periods included women. But the majority of the women were part of marital units (see Chapter 4). On average, there were only about one or two single Indian women per cuadrilla. Larger pools of single women at haciendas in the 1770s reflect the feminization of the city as women began to demographically outstrip men and sought work in the mining industry to meet economic needs.[58] By the late colonial period, the world of silver mining was as much a part of women's lives as it was that of men's.

Thus, despite greater ethnic diversity in the city, indigenous men and women continued to dominate the mining labor force in the late colonial period. The witness pool, once again, offers insights into the activities Indian men performed at these sites. Of the 261 indigenous witnesses that listed an occupation, 74 percent worked in the mining sector. Of these individuals, many engaged in nonspecialized or general labor jobs. However, at least a quarter of this cohort worked in some of the more skilled sectors of extraction or refining. Twelve men identified themselves as miners, a relatively small percentage, which follows larger trends in which most Indians were relegated to labor rather than ownership (see Table 5.9). The dominance of native people in the mining industry becomes even more apparent when comparing their presence to other ethnic groups such as mulattos. Native mine laborers composed 74 percent of the total indigenous workforce, while slightly less than half of Afro-descended laborers (48 percent) worked in mining (see Table 5.10). These numbers indicate that the core of the labor force, at least at the start of the boom, remained indigenous. Indians had been the largest group to remain in the city during the bust. This allowed them to take advantage of new employment opportunities as they arose. Moreover, the Spanish preference for hiring indigenous labor also continued in this period. Over the course of multiple generations native

TABLE 5.9. Mining occupations cited by male indigenous witnesses, Zacatecas, 1775–1777

Occupation	Number
Assayer	13
Charcoal maker	4
Driller or blaster	2
Furnace stoker	1
Laborer	78
Miner	9
Ore carrier	1
Ore cutter	33
Refiner	41
Smelter	1
Stamp mill operator	8
Woodcutter	2
Total	**193**

Source: APZ, Matrimonios, IINC, 1775–1777.

TABLE 5.10. Number of male indigenous and mulatto marriage petition witnesses in mining occupations, Zacatecas, 1775–1777

	Indians	Mulattos
Assayer	13	0
Charcoal maker	4	0
Driller or blaster	2	0
Furnace stoker	1	1
Laborer	78	13
Miner	9	0
Ore carrier	1	2
Ore cutter	33	7
Refiner	41	8
Smelter	1	0
Stamp mill operator	8	0
Woodcutter	2	0
Total	193	31

Source: APZ, Matrimonios, IINC, 1775–1777.

peoples had developed skills in the extraction and refining of silver; trades that probably even ran along family lines. At this point, Afro-Zacatecans may not yet have developed such a strong mining tradition. The majority of the individuals of African descent had served in domestic service, on estancias, or in other urban occupations.

Changes in Labor Practices and Conditions

The boom stimulated jobs for native women and men in both mining and its subsidiary economies. But the empirewide population resurgence also created a larger labor pool. Native peoples contended not only with greater competition for jobs but also with the more oppressive labor environments and conditions that characterized Bourbon Mexico. Mine owners took advantage of the initially depressed job market, and later the surplus workforce, to lower wages in the face of rising commodity prices.[59] The absence of labor contracts and inventories makes it difficult to speak systematically about remuneration practices in the city beyond describing larger trends. Mine workers typically engaged in informal contracts with owners, were commonly paid in advance, and received compensation in coin and in kind.[60] In the period before the mining recession of the mid-1700s, their wages included food, accommodations, and the right to silver tailings. Pick and blast men, for example, averaged six reales a day and were allowed to keep a quarter of the metal (pepena or partido) they produced.[61]

During the late boom, compensation practices, although they varied by site, illustrate the erosion of mine workers' wages. In 1769 the average mine laborer made seven pesos a month and received eight quarts of maize and ten pounds of meat. However, they no longer received any partido, or shares of ore.[62] Attempts to eliminate the partido or pepena were one of several strategies, according to John Monteiro, to "'rationalize' the mining economy," or to make it more efficient and cost effective. Miners, he argued, even tried to justify reviving systems of coerced labor "couched in the Enlightenment rhetoric of 'social utility.'"[63] Metal sharing had already disappeared much earlier in other areas. In Chihuahua, miners attempted to eliminate the pepena as early as the 1720s. They met with violent opposition from laborers who left their jobs and threatened death and destruction on the town. But despite their actions, ore sharing appears to have disappeared there by the 1740s.[64] Conflicts between laborers and miners throughout New Spain speak to the growing exploitation of mine workers in the eighteenth century. At sites in central Mexico, Guanajuato, and Michoacán, Spanish miners requested more draft laborers, imposed longer work schedules, and reduced wages.[65] Unsurprisingly, communities responded with protests, legal recriminations, and even violent resistance. Among the most dramatic of these labor uprisings were those that occurred in 1766 at Real de Monte near Pachuca in central Mexico.[66] There, over a series of tense months, labor walkouts, riots, and even homicides occurred over attempts to limit workers' selection and take of the partido.

In Zacatecas, metal sharing continued in the eighteenth century but decreased dramatically over time. These changes were exemplified by the case of the famous mine owner José de la Borda. Credited with initiating the boom, de la Borda took advantage of the unemployment caused by the depressed economy in 1775 to reduce workers' wages to four reales a day and to limit their share of metal production to one-eighth.[67] In a similar trend, in the 1780s, the owner of the Malanoche mine allowed his workers to keep only one-sixth of the metal they produced. By 1809, workers were no longer allowed to take metal as part of their daily wage. This policy remained in place in the postindependence period. During his 1828 visit to a Zacatecan mine, English traveler George F. Lyon observed that overseers and clerks "carefully examined" men and women engaged in washing the metal "upon leaving the place, to see that they have secreted no Pella [pepena] about their persons."[68] Equally detrimental, many miners began to pay wages in goods and not in currency, even though this practice was unlawful.[69]

Mine labor had always been a dangerous, grueling, and exploitative occupation. Yet the indigenous population recognized its compensations and attractions. Since the city's founding, native peoples had been the preferred laborers, facilitating their employment at haciendas or mines with fellow Indians. They also had enjoyed some latitude in the terms and tenure of their employment. Wage sharing in particular offered a steady source of supplemental income as native peoples sold or refined tailings in both the formal and informal economy.[70] But this late boom found native peoples competing with other ethnic groups for jobs and working at less ethnically homogeneous mining sites. The decrease in wages, along with the practice of compensation in kind, left many native people more vulnerable to debt peonage. The removal of the partido was probably the most devastating blow, representing a dramatic loss in overall income. This decline in real wages was not particular to Zacatecas or to mining; it also occurred in other areas and sectors of the colony.[71]

Anecdotal evidence, in the absence of quantifiable information on salaries, suggests that basic living standards decreased among the Indian population as the eighteenth century drew to a close.[72] In 1796, a Spanish official claimed that the poverty of the vecinos—or "wretches," as he termed them—living in the city's barrio was "notorious."[73] Conditions appear to have been even worse in the hinterlands. There, documents not only speak of decreased wages but also hint at the resurgence of repartimiento-like practices. In 1790, viceregal officials, responding to reports of episodes of draft labor, reminded local authorities that forced labor was illegal.[74] It is not difficult to imagine how worsening economic circumstances forced native peoples into more exploitative labor arrangements just to meet daily subsistence needs. The situation of an indigenous woman, Juana Cosme, from the tributary town of San José de la Isla, offers the most dramatic example of the strained conditions facing some indigenous communities. In 1801, she claimed that her inability to feed her children had forced her to give them away as indentured laborers. One of her sons, Emiterio Seledonio Vanegas, was forced to work for an abusive charcoal maker.[75]

Declining wages and reduced ore sharing were not the only dramatic labor changes that native peoples had to face. As the mining boom progressed, mines and refining works became more ethnically diverse. Findings from a census from 1781, ten years well into the boom, indicate that while Indians remained the primary labor force in the city's haciendas (34 percent), they had been joined by a large number of mestizos and mulattos (see Table 5.11).[76] One study argues that mestizo laborers even outnumbered indigenous workers.[77] The composition of workers at four haciendas offers greater details on the integrated nature of these labor sites (see Table 5.12). Of a total population of 558 workers, Indians, at 40 percent, still constituted the largest group in the workforce. However, unlike previous periods, no hacienda had an exclusively or even predominantly indigenous labor force. Indians were the largest group at only two of the four sites. At the Hacienda de Bernárdez, native people worked with a

TABLE 5.11. Ethnic composition of hacienda workers, Zacatecas, 1781

Group	Number	Percentage of workers
Indians	423	34
Mestizos	346	28
Mulattos	303	24
Spaniards	175	14
Coyotes	3	>1
Total	1,250	100

Source: AHEZ, Padrones y Censos, 1781.

TABLE 5.12. Ethnic composition of four mining haciendas, Zacatecas, 1781

Hacienda	Indian	Mestizo	Mulatto	Spanish
Bernárdez	60	50	0	9
Sauceda	94	38	97	15
San Juan Trancoso	40	1	34	1
Santa Trinidad	31	34	41	13
Total	225	123	172	38
Percentage of total labor force	40	22	31	7

Source: AHEZ, Padrones y Censos, 1781.

mestizo population of almost exactly the same size (sixty and fifty workers, respectively). Mestizo and mulatto mine workers actually outnumbered Indians (135 to 94) at the Sauceda complex.

The increase in the non-Indian population at haciendas does not necessarily reflect a diminishing indigenous presence in the city but rather the demographic growth of the casta population (and Indian as well) that characterized the late colonial period. A greater presence of mestizos and mulattos at these sites has been offered as proof that these groups dominated the mining labor force in the eighteenth century.[78] Indeed, many mining towns operated with ethnically diverse cuadrillas because they lacked a large indigenous base.[79] In 1785, for example, Chihuahua's Indian residents numbered 6 percent of the population as compared to a combined casta population of nearly 60 percent.[80] But this was certainly not the composition of all mining towns. In Zacatecas gone were the days when Indians worked exclusively with each other. But mine work had not been taken over by castas. Native peoples still represented a sizable segment of the workforce.

As the Bourbon period progressed, native peoples had greater exposure to the influences and practices of other ethnic groups, conditions that surely affected indigenous traditions and customs. But to speak of a general "castazation" of the city's population in this period neglects important nuances, especially in regard to indigenous society. The growing casta population, as hacienda inventories and other counts indicate, had a predominantly mestizo base. Mestizos were often the descendants, siblings, or spouses of native peoples, and they had strong ties to the indigenous world. Even without adding mestizos to their numbers, the Indian population remained large and vital in the late eighteenth century. Yet the growing number of mestizos marks the beginning of their ascent as an ethnic group in the city and their eventual predominance as an ethnoracial group in the nineteenth century. At that time, however, colonial authorities did not associate mestizos with Indians or with the persistence of indigenous society. Grouping mestizos together with the general casta population, they would use their growing numbers as a means to discredit native peoples.

The Diffusion of Indigenous Communities

Chapter 4 discussed how native peoples began to live in increasing numbers in the areas between the Spanish traza and the Indian towns. Demographic data indicates that this trend accelerated in the mid- to late eighteenth century. An analysis of the vecino status of male marriage petitioners from 1751 to 1760 indicates that during this time frame about a third of the native population lived in three core areas.[81] Thirty-one percent of the indigenous petitioners lived in the Indian pueblos. A slightly greater number of native people (36 percent) cited the Spanish city as their place of residence, and another third (32 percent) lived in Indian settlements no more than a few leagues from the city (see Table 5.13).[82] In the mid-eighteenth century, then, around two-thirds (68 percent) of the city's Indian population lived outside of the pueblos. Still, while the communities outside the Indian towns were more ethnically heterogeneous, many remained heavily indigenous. For example, of the 524 vecinos of the outlying settlements listed in Table 5.13, only five petitioners (less than 1 percent) did not identify as indigenous, with four of those individuals residing at one site, the Hacienda de la Polvorista.

The preference for settling with greater frequency in native communities that had developed outside of the Indian towns gained momentum during the first years of the boom. An examination of male and female indigenous residency patterns from 1775 to 1777 illustrates the continued settlement of native peoples in barrios that fell within the jurisdiction of Spanish Zacatecas (see Table 5.14).[83] In these years the strains on indigenous society brought about by the boom and political reform began to manifest themselves. Table 5.14 illustrates that 78 percent of the petitioner population claimed vecino status in Zacatecas, whereas only 18 percent resided

TABLE 5.13. Haciendas, barrios, and ranches in Zacatecas under the jurisdiction of the parish of Tlacuitlapan, c. 1750–1772

La Quebrada de la Maneche
La Plazuela de García
Barrio de Olivas
Calle de San Diego
Calle de San Francisco
Puesto de la Cruz de Moya
Calle de San Josef
Puesto de San Francisco
Barrio de Nava
La Hacienda de García
La Cuesta de Menchaca
La Hacienda de Bracho
Puesto Cañada
Puesto de la Acevada
La Hacienda de Olivas
Hacienda de los Leones
La Hacienda de Mitre
La Hacienda Chica
Rancho Guadalupito
Hacienda de la Polvorista
Hacienda de Gil
Hacienda de Plata
Rancho de Ortega
Hacienda Nueva
Cerro de Mala Noche
Hacienda de Jove
Capilla de Guerreros

Source: AGI, Guadalajara, 348, n. 4, ff. 1025v–1026v, 1772.

TABLE 5.14. Vecino status of indigenous marriage petitioners, Zacatecas, 1775–1777

Location	Men	Women	Total	Percentage of total Indian petitioners
Zacatecas (city center)	126	118	244	78
San Josef	15	13	28	9
Chepinque	7	8	15	5
Tlacuitlapan	0	1	1	0
El Niño	3	3	6	1.5
Ranches	4	2	6	1.5
Haciendas	7	7	14	5
Total	162	152	314	100

Source: APZ, Matrimonios, IINC, 1775–1777.

in the Indian towns. Over one-third of these vecinos were migrants who had settled in the city rather than the Indians towns. Out-migration was also occurring. In the two years under consideration, thirteen individuals migrated from the pueblos to the city center.

Over time, the diffusion of indigenous peoples to neighborhoods within the city contributed to smaller populations in the Indian towns. However, it does not necessarily speak to a decline in indigenous communities. Native peoples had resided in Indian neighborhoods within the jurisdiction of the Spanish city in significant numbers since Zacatecas's founding. In fact, in the previous sample, over two-thirds of the native petitioners from 1775 to 1777 claimed originario status, meaning that their parents probably were vecinos of the city in the 1750s and 1760s. Generic references in the petitions to "vecino of Zacatecas" often occluded the names of heavily populated indigenous barrios and haciendas that had evolved between the traza and the Indian pueblos. In Chapter 4 we saw how these communities had been steadily growing since the late seventeenth century. Juridically, these communities belonged to the Spanish city but had strong affiliations with the native towns and fell under the control of the Indian parish of Tlacuitlapan (see Table 5.13). Neighborhoods on the border of the Spanish traza also represented an opportunity for native peoples to connect with one another. In other words, the Indian towns were not the only bastions of indigenous cultures and peoples. The growth of these neighborhoods should not be taken as evidence of the disintegration of native peoples as a biological or corporate group. Rather, this trend speaks to the diffusion of Indian neighborhoods throughout the city. Spaniards and castas intruded upon native lands, but native peoples also encroached upon non-Indian spaces.

Indigenous settlement outside of the native pueblos undermined their population base. Still, by the late 1770s, about 18 percent of Zacatecas's native population lived in Indian towns. An ecclesiastical census from 1772 reported that Chepinque had fifty-six houses with 209 individuals. The cleric of the 1772 count admitted that the figure might have omitted children.[84] Recall that previous counts illustrated that children could compose from 30 percent to 50 percent of the population. Four years later, in 1776, Chepinque had probably received some migrants from the boom, as its numbers grew by 161 individuals (see Table 5.15). In the same census from 1772, Tlacuitlapan's population, while smaller than the previous count, remained a viable size. In 1772, the town and its adjacent barrios had 628 individuals and 179 houses.

Other vital statistics from the censuses speak to continued signs of strong family life. Children constituted about 30 percent of the population of Tlacuitlapan's padrón, averaging three per household.[85] In the five-year

TABLE 5.15. Extant population of Indian towns, Zacatecas, 1741–1783

	1741	1752	1772	1776	1777	1783
Tlacuitlapan	677	827	628	495	473	N/A
[Tonalá] Chepinque	188	188	209	370	N/A	219
San Josef	200	N/A	N/A	354	N/A	N/A

Source: AAG, Padrones, various, 1741–1783.
Note: N/A = not available.

period from 1767 to 1772, seventy-three baptisms and twenty-three marriages took place in Chepinque.[86] The reference to twenty-seven deaths also speaks to natural population loss. The pattern of marriage between native peoples in these towns continued to remain high. San Josef and El Niño had endogamy rates of over 90 percent, illustrating little change in rates over a forty-year period (see Table 5.16). Although Chepinque had higher numbers of endogamous unions, its percentage still remained slightly higher than those of the city. Thus, in the first decade of the boom, despite general population decrease, community and family life continued in the indigenous pueblos.

Native institutions and organizations also illustrated continued vigor in this period. Indian officials, as we will see, continued to exercise their duties. Despite the dual blows of secularization and the merging of cofradías, indigenous religious organizations continued to operate in the community. In 1777, the main chapel of the pueblo of Tlacuitlapan was a small building constructed of adobe with a wooden roof and a tower with three bells. Inside, the church had a sacristy, a baptistery, and three altars.[87] The pueblos' confraternities continued to be invested in their churches, spending large funds to make repairs. In 1783, for example, the confraternity of Soledad in Chepinque took three hundred pesos from its account to paint the church white.[88] In 1798, San Josef spent over two hundred pesos in the repair of a cupola and a bell.[89] Indeed, the cofradía of San Josef remained very active. In 1770, the brotherhood reported that it spent about a hundred pesos a year on sundry religious functions. These expenses were paid through the collection of alms and the sale and rental of properties owned by the confraternity.[90] By 1798, San Josef collected income from the ranch Jaramillo, eleven houses, a well, stables, forty heads of cattle, and

TABLE 5.16. Endogamy rates in three Indian towns, Zacatecas

Town	1741–1750	1771–1780
San Josef	95%	94%
[Tonalá] Chepinque	97%	79%
El Niño	100%	94%

Source: APZ, Matrimonios, IINC, 1741–1750, 1771–1780.

forty-three horses.[91] Other cofradías had significant assets as well. San Diego yielded income from the rental of two homes and three teams of oxen. They also had three plots of land. Tlacuitlapan's archconfraternity had five houses and one lot on San José Street.[92] Many of these properties were located outside the jurisdiction of the Indian pueblos. Native institutions, like native peoples, had also diffused into the urban core.

Migration Trends and Population Decline in the Indian Towns

By the close of the century Spanish officials claimed that the pueblos were depopulated, only serving as home to a small casta population. These accusations were part of a larger campaign to dissolve the Indian towns. While the native towns were far from depopulated, unlike other booms, the late eighteenth-century production upsurge failed to draw a dramatic number of new vecinos to the Indian pueblos. Marriage petitions from 1771 to 1780 indicate that of the 722 indigenous peoples who entered petitions to marry, an overwhelming majority (around 82 percent) were native to the area (see Table 5.17). From the general age pool of the criollo petitioner population, these individuals were most likely descendants of settlers who had remained or retained roots in the city during the protracted population and production downturn of 1732–1767.

Migrant women and men constituted about 16 percent of the total petitioner pool, arriving from areas encompassing the contemporary states of Zacatecas, Aguascalientes, Michoacán, San Luis Potosí, Jalisco, Querétaro, Chihuahua, Mexico, and Guanajuato. These movements conform to some traditional migration patterns. The city continued to draw native peoples from its hinterlands and from regions with past migration ties, such as the areas surrounding Aguascalientes and San Luis Potosí, suggesting that the city's economic recovery motivated those individuals who had kinship and or economic ties with Zacatecas to return or remain in the greater area.

The familiarity of a mining center attracted both women and men, with 55 percent of the former and 59 percent of the latter originating from

TABLE 5.17. Migrant and criollo status of female and male indigenous petitioners, Zacatecas, 1771–1780

	Women	Percentage	Men	Percentage	Total	Percentage of total indigenous petitioners
Migrants	55	16	66	18	121	17
Criollos	277	83	309	82	586	82
Not recorded	4	1	1	0	5	1
Total	336	100	376	100	712	100

Source: APZ, Matrimonios, IINC, 1771–1780.

TABLE 5.18. Originario status of female and male indigenous migrant petitioners, Zacatecas, 1771–1780

	Women	Percentage	Men	Percentage
Mining town	30	55	39	59
Agricultural site	24	44	26	39
City	0	0	1	2
Unknown	1	1	0	0
Total	55	100	66	100

Source: APZ, Matrimonios, IINC, 1771–1780.

another mining town (see Table 5.18). A substantial group of women (44 percent) and men (39 percent) arrived from agricultural communities from the hinterlands to the south and west of the city. As a whole, men from these towns and villages migrated from further distances; some even journeyed from the fertile plains of the Bajío. More women arrived from agricultural communities than men, but not at a significant rate. They did, however, arrive from within a closer range, perhaps suggesting that they had fewer resources or support networks to stray too far from their home communities. Indian women from mining towns traveled further distances. Men came from an ever wider variety of mining sites.

The petitions also illustrate some migration trends distinct to the late colonial period. Unlike the sixteenth and seventeenth centuries, very few migrants traveled from afar. José Manuel Rodríguez, from Mexico City, was the southernmost migrant, and María Josefa Nuin, a native of Chihuahua, was the northernmost immigrant. While the city had never drawn many individuals from the far north, the absence of Indians from central Mexico was a marked change. Nor were men or women arriving from more traditional sites in western Mexico, such as Michoacán and the Guadalajara region.

By this period, these regions offered their own compelling magnets and pulls. Guadalajara had boomed from what Eric Van Young describes as a "small, dusty town" in the sixteenth century to a large economic hub, undergoing a "sixfold" population increase in the eighteenth century.[93] Guadalajara's census of around eight thousand individuals in 1738 paled in comparison to Zacatecas's 1739 count of twenty-four thousand inhabitants. But by 1770, Guadalajara's population outstripped that of Zacatecas by almost 6,000 individuals (22,394 to 16,260 respectively).[94] Guadalajara's development from a moderate sized administrative town to a bustling site of trade, commerce, and industry, servicing a wide market base, was accompanied by a parallel growth in rural production. In earlier times many native migrants from or near this area would have migrated to Zacatecas in search of work and wages, but in this period they could encounter similar economic opportunities closer to home.

A similar argument could be made for the Bajío region, which initially had developed in response to the agricultural needs of Zacatecas and its satellite mining towns. But this area too had developed vital economies and markets, particularly at Guanajuato and Querétaro. Spaniards had been operating relatively small mining ventures at Guanajuato since the late 1550s. Guanajuato had always lagged behind Zacatecas in population, trade, and production. But in the late 1770s, Guanajuato became New Spain's top silver producer and retained that position until the early nineteenth century, when droughts, rising costs of production, and independence movements caused a serious decline in the industry.[95] Large, productive sites like Guanajuato (and later Catorce in the San Luis Potosí jurisdiction) drew its own local Indian population—on order of close to forty thousand by 1791—and those of its hinterlands.[96] Querétaro would have been the other draw in this area. By this period it had become the site of a brisk textile trade in need of laborers.[97]

Despite these competing economic poles, Zacatecas remained a vital component of the near north's economy, especially as the mining recovery of the late colonial period began in earnest. The boom attracted individuals from smaller mining towns within the region. But native peoples were no longer arriving in the same numbers. Nor were they settling in the native towns at the same rate. These two trends undermined the Indian towns' traditional population sources, contributing to both their decline in size and vitality.

"Nothing but a Bunch of Castas"

As part of its broad and sweeping political organization of its Spanish American colonies, the crown added jurisdictional units know as intendancies to the Hapsburg system of viceroyalties. In 1786, in recognition of its long-standing importance as an administrative and commercial center, Zacatecas became one of several intendancies established in New Spain. The creation of these jurisdictional units reflected Bourbon interests in centralizing judicial and economic functions in the hands of a few key administrative figures, mainly *peninsulares*, or individuals born in Spain. In Zacatecas, royal authorities eliminated the position of corregidor, appointing in his place an intendant. The intendant became the highest-ranking official of the city and the greater region. The changing political climate once again intruded upon the autonomy and rights of indigenous peoples and towns.

In the late 1790s (c. 1798?) the infamously corrupt and unpopular viceroy, the Marquis de Branciforte, revoked the indigenous population's most prized possession—tribute exemption.[98] Under these new terms, Indians in Zacatecas were registered on tribute roles and forced to pay this onerous fee. One can only imagine the anger, frustration, and despair this decree occasioned among the native population. Overall, the total funds raised from tribute were small in comparison to those generated by silver production. In 1810, Indian tribute amounted to 24,061 pesos, or 3.8 percent of the income of Zacatecas's Royal Treasury.[99] But for native peoples, the new royal assessment, coupled with the reduction or in some cases the elimination of the pepena and accusations of repartimiento-like labor practices, significantly affected their daily and long-term living conditions. Late colonial policies and practices stood in stark contrast to the labor arrangements and incentives of the sixteenth century and may explain why indigenous migration to Zacatecas declined in this period.

Yet even as native peoples were entered as "Indians" on tribute roles, officials were actively working to deprive them of their rights and privileges. In 1799, Intendant Don Francisco Rendón authorized Joseph Fernández Moreno to compose a series of ordinances that would serve as the basis for the city's political and juridical organization. The division of the city into districts was part of the same bureaucratic campaign of economic and civil efficiency that had governed the reorganizing of larger units into intendancies. In Zacatecas, Spanish officials availed themselves of the political reform to incorporate the indigenous towns into larger city districts. Fernández Moreno was one of the most prominent officials in the movement to eradicate indigenous towns and leaders. His justifications for these measures drew on Bourbon principles of efficiency. The majority of the Indian population, he argued, lived in the city center and the native pueblos had decreased in populace and territory.[100] The incorporation of the Indian pueblos into citywide districts in a royal ordinance from 1799 had a significant impact on the indigenous pueblos, placing them within jurisdictional units (*cuarteles*) that encompassed areas outside the native towns. The royal ordinances divided the city into four major districts known as *cuarteles mayores*. Tlacuitlapan formed part of the second cuartel. Chepinque belonged to the third district. And El Niño and San Josef came under the jurisdiction of the fourth.[101] Each major district contained two minor units, or *cuarteles menores* (see Figure 5.1).

Under this configuration, social and political decisions that affected each district did not necessarily reflect indigenous interests. The existence of a Spanish district alcalde, as we saw at the beginning of this chapter, further intruded upon the towns' juridical autonomy. The district alcalde provided an indirect but official vehicle for Spanish officers to interfere in the day-to-day operations of the indigenous communities, thus exacerbating tensions between Spanish and indigenous officials. Article 26 of

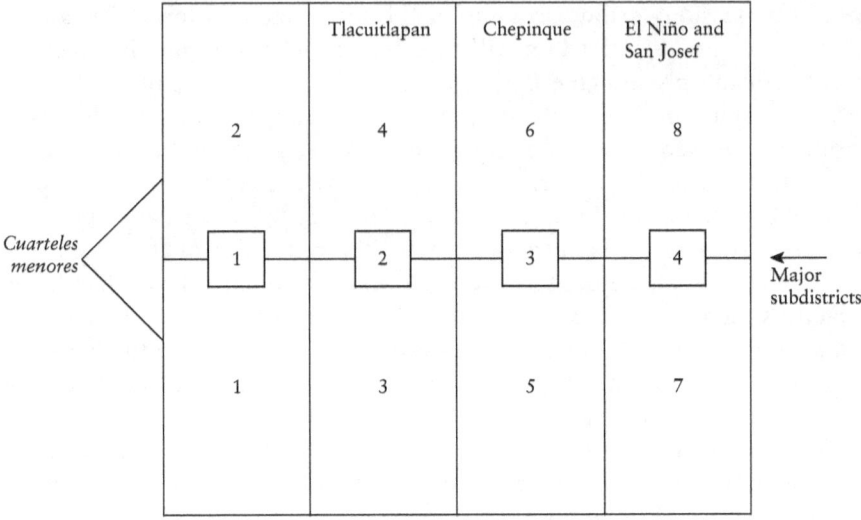

FIGURE 5.1. Jurisdictional designation of the Indian towns within *cuarteles mayores* and *cuarteles menores*, Zacatecas, 1799.

the ordinances establishing the new cuarteles ordered the Indian towns to present the district alcalde with a census of the pueblo and cautioned native people to be "mindful" of his presence and authority.[102]

These jurisdictional changes reflected relatively recent sentiments on the part of some Spanish officials and vecinos to dissolve the Indian towns and annex them to the city. Spaniards had basically left the Indian pueblos to manage their own affairs since their establishment in the early seventeenth century. But evolving sociopolitical dynamics led to this new more oppressive stance. The production upsurge and the population boom it engendered created a healthy competition for resources. From the late seventeenth century, the growing need for land resulted in the natural (and inevitable) expansion of the Spanish city toward the boundaries of the Indian communities. This process had been a slow one, but over many years neighborhoods had developed in the empty spaces between the traza and the pueblos. Changes in the terms Spaniards used to describe the geographic location of the native pueblos reflect their perceptions of the increasing proximity between the Spanish city and the Indian communities. Previously, Spaniards had chosen words such as *extramuros* (outside the walls) to highlight their distance and separate geographic space from the Spanish core. By 1799, officials and vecinos described the pueblos as "adjacent to the city." In 1806, one Spaniard claimed that they "embrac[ed] the majority of the capital."[103]

But the move to dissolve the Indian towns was not simply motivated by population density and resource scarcity. Zacatecas's population had increased citywide. But the earlier eighteenth-century boom had actually witnessed a greater demographic upswing. Even with a population of thirty-three thousand individuals in 1799, the city still had seven thousand fewer vecinos than it did during the 1705–1730 boom (see Table 5.19). Yet the earlier eighteenth-century demographic upsurge sparked no movements to incorporate or dissolve the Indian towns. Two extant eighteenth-century city maps raise further questions about potential land shortage. Composed at the height of the early boom, Joaquín de Sotomayor's 1732 plan illustrates that the traza's urban sprawl had already come fairly close to the outer limits of the Indian communities (see Figure 3.1). The second map was designed by Bernardo Portugal in 1799 to accompany the ordinances of that same year (see Figure 5.2). A comparison of the Sotomayor map with the 1799 plan shows a small increase in urban infrastructure. Portugal's map looks to be heavily based on its predecessor—a mirror copy in some areas—suggesting that the encroachment of the Spanish city on the native towns predated the current boom. Recall how Chapter 4 discussed the development of vacant lands between the Spanish city and the Indians towns during the early eighteenth century. Competition for land and resources were certainly at stake in the late colonial period, but then it appears they had already been so for well over seventy years.

We must look beyond the population boom to discern late colonial motives for doing away with the pueblos. There is little doubt that Spaniards and individuals of all ethnicities were eager to appropriate the lands and resources of the native towns. But the deeper issue resided in issues of jurisdiction and power. Spaniards did not simply seek to incorporate the towns into the city. They wanted to dissolve them along with the native leadership. While non-Indians (and native peoples) had attempted to settle

TABLE 5.19. Citywide population, Zacatecas, 1732–1805

Year	Population
1732	40,000
1790	22,495
1798	32,720
c. 1799	33,000
1805	33,000

Source: For 1732, see Ribera Bernárdez, *Descripción breve*; for 1790–1799, see Gerhard, *North Frontier*, 158–59; for 1805, see José María Bustamante, *Descripción de la serranía de Zacatecas* (México: Imp. de Galván a cargo de Mariano Arévalo, 1834), 4.

FIGURE 5.2. Zacatecas and its Indian towns in 1799, by Bernardo Portugal. Archivo General de la Nación, México, Intendencias, vol. 65, f. 13, 1799. Reprinted with permission.

or expropriate land from the native towns in the past, this period marks the first time that Spaniards seriously moved to abolish the indigenous communities. Colonial officials focused their efforts on discrediting the viability of the towns, questioning the ethnic composition of their residents, and attacking the abilities of their native leaders.

Spanish challenges to the legitimacy of the pueblos included claims that native people no longer inhabited them. In 1796, several Spanish officials collecting a *donativo* (charitable money for the crown) declared that the native pueblos were no longer viable communities; rather, they were run down and depopulated.[104] The officer in charge of the collection, Joseph Fernández Moreno, asserted that the barrio of Chepinque was uninhabited, with only a few houses of no more than twenty families. The majority of the town's vecinos, according to him, had moved to Zacatecas proper. They had settled in the "interior" of the city.[105] Their "frail" buildings, he observed a few years later, were rundown or ruined.[106]

But to take over the Indian communities Spaniards had to do more than simply prove they were uninhabited. The latter might speak to a poor use of urban space, but it did not constitute a legal justification. Rather, colonial officials understood that they had to invalidate the corporate status of the native population by casting doubts on the indigenous composition of their pueblos. It comes as no surprise, then, that by 1806 another official not only critiqued the conditions of the pueblos but also questioned the indigenous identity of their residents. He claimed that only a few people living in the Indian towns could "consider themselves legitimately indigenous, as the majority were mulattos, lobos, or of some other degenerate casta ancestry."[107] Castas were also subjects of the crown but, unlike Indians, they were not entitled to any specific corporate rights and privileges, such as the ability to establish their own towns. By leveling accusations that the Indians living in the pueblos were really castas, Spanish officials based their arguments on both moral (i.e., the vicious and degenerate behaviors associated with castas) and legal grounds. These accusations looked to deprive native peoples of their status as indios and vecinos.

The campaign to convert the Indian towns into barrios of the city also entailed the dissolution of the indigenous municipal councils, as one entity could not exist without the other. One official insisted that although the vecinos of the Indian settlements called their communities pueblos, they were really barrios of the Spanish city. Others also claimed that the native cabildos no longer functioned as viable institutions. Indians, one official alleged, were no longer interested in office holding because of the demands it placed on their time. The annual elections, he claimed, marked the limits of the councils' activities.[108] In the eyes of these Spanish officials, native leaders deserved to be deprived of their jurisdictional privileges because they had no legitimate body to govern (i.e., towns). Their inactivity also spoke to their lack of respect and enthusiasm for the office.

But complaints and accusations by colonial authorities about the activities of native officials from the mid-eighteenth century to the early 1800s strongly contradict their claims of moribund cabildos. The 1799 ordinances, for example, enjoined the Indian alcaldes not to bother Zacatecas's vecinos and to give notice immediately to the appropriate officials when they imprisoned a city resident.[109] These decrees reflected past and current problems. One Spanish alcalde accused the native leadership of refusing to cooperate with Spanish authorities. Indian leaders, he complained, only occasionally offered assistance to the alcalde mayor, and only when asked. No one, the official argued, had been able to "restrain" them.[110] Another official echoed similar statements, claiming that "too much tolerance" had been shown to the activities of the native alcaldes, who he believed needed to confine their duties to their own jurisdiction.[111] He complained, for example, that they imprisoned individuals from the city in the Indian pueblos for the smallest misdemeanor, often leaving them in the stocks for the entire night.

These sentiments and grievances on the part of Spanish officials speak to motives for abolishing the native pueblos that had less to do with urban planning, such as the ineffective use of developed spaces, and more to do with power and authority. As Chapter 4 pointed out, by the eighteenth century indigenous officials had evolved into a formidable leadership body that no longer felt confined to exercise their roles and responsibilities only in their towns. Under their own initiative they increased their jurisdictions, conducting rounds within their pueblos and in the multiple indigenous barrios adjacent to the Spanish traza. They also frequently took action against Spaniards and castas who committed crimes or disturbances or other delinquencies in their pueblos, apprehending and at times even imprisoning them. As the city's limits and the towns' boundaries came closer together, the existence of both Indian and Spanish officials in one area inevitably led to jurisdictional conflicts over watches, seniority, and detentions.

In earlier periods, Indian leaders had confined themselves to exerting their authority over their indigenous residents. But by the mid-eighteenth century, native leaders had taken to detaining any individual—indigenous, African descendent, or Spanish—who committed an infraction in their pueblo. In 1759, for example, the alguacil mayor of Tlacuitlapan, Felipe Zacatecas, apprehended a mulatto, Marcos Joseph, as he passed through the town. According to alguacil mayor Zacatecas, Joseph was imprisoned for a debt of ten pesos that he owed to a Spaniard. Joseph was held for three days and released on the condition that he pay one peso a week toward his debt and twelve reales for the cost of his prison stay. But after agreeing to these terms, Marcos protested his sentence on the basis of illegal jurisdiction. He complained to the corregidor that he deserved a new sentence from Spanish authorities because he was a vecino of the city, not one of the native pueblos. Why, he argued, should he be vexed by the Indian leadership or pay them a prison fine? Joseph found a sympathetic ear in the corregidor. He reprimanded the Indian officials, reminding them that they had no right to exert jurisdiction over vecinos of the city. He singled out Zacatecas, scolding him and accusing him of "acting in an excessive manner."[112] In response, the indigenous officials adamantly declared that they had done nothing wrong. Zacatecas admitted that the mulatto had been detained without the corregidor's consent. But he stood by his decision to incarcerate him, adding that his actions had pleased Joseph's Spanish creditor.

The more aggressive stance by Indian leaders—their willingness to police non-Indians—often led to tensions between them and Spanish officials. In Joseph's case, his status as a vecino of the city did not offer him immunity from Indian justices. Rather, his frequent visits to the town left him open to disciplinary action from indigenous officials. Spanish authorities, however, did not welcome this more active and assertive native leadership. The corregidor, more annoyed with the actions of the native leadership than with Joseph's relatively petty debt, scolded them for overstepping their authority. While this episode was a relatively minor affair, it offers insight into the nature of Spanish animosity against indigenous leaders in this period. These types of contentious episodes formed the basis of Spanish desires to eradicate indigenous cabildos, and thus rid themselves of local challenges to their authority.[113]

The integration of the native towns into cuarteles under the oversight of a district alcalde presented significant challenges. Shrewd native leaders, however, utilized the 1799 ordinances to maintain their juridical privileges and to assert their authority, particularly their ability to elect their own leaders, a practice that continued through the early nineteenth century.[114] Multiple documents from the period illustrate vital native cabildos composed of a full set of officers and several minor officials. The 1806 arrest of the Spanish alcalde Don Jose Gómez, by his indigenous counterpart, Perfecto Hernández, which opened this chapter, illustrates both the challenges that beset native leadership in this period and their resilient responses.

The ordinances reorganized the city into four greater districts and eight subdistricts. El Niño and San Josef were part of the fourth district and the eighth ward. These multiple jurisdictions brought native people under the supervision of several Spanish officials, the most immediate being the alcalde of their subdistrict, in this case, Gómez. Officials such as Gómez and his superiors had the opportunity to meddle in indigenous concerns and activities at greater levels than before. The ordinances forced native officials to seek approval for both official and mundane activities that heretofore would have required only the consensus of the indigenous cabildo. It is not difficult to imagine how the indigenous leadership, which had become more autonomous and emboldened over time, deeply resented these intrusions into their local affairs.

The scheduling of a dance or fandango after a wedding, for example, required approval from a district official. According to their version of events, Hernández and other members of the Indian cabildo followed established protocol and searched for a Spanish official to request a license. They received permission from Gómez who directed them to hold the fandango around 10:30 p.m. Later, another Spanish official allowed them to commence the event at 9:30, a time more to the community's preference. Before the cuartel system, the fandango would have been a local event. Under the new political terms it had evolved into a time-consuming administrative affair. Native leaders no doubt were already irked that they had to hunt down Spanish officials and seek their permission for a small gathering. Under these circumstances, is it unsurprising that their annoyance quickly turned to anger when the alcalde Gómez once again appeared on the scene. Adding insult to injury, he brought with him a group of Spaniards and Indian leaders from San Josef and proceeded to publicly disparage the El Niño leaders in front of a large number of its vecinos.

The antagonism that existed between Indian and Spanish officials prior to this period was exacerbated by the cuartel system. Further statements from both indigenous officials suggest that Gómez had become an ubiquitous figure in the pueblo. The ordenanzas gave Gómez oversight over the entire fourth district to which El Niño belonged, and according to the Indian leadership, the Spanish alcalde consistently intruded upon their rights and privileges. Gómez not only undermined Indian officials by consistently making rounds in the pueblo (a charge he admitted) but also created further enmity between the two groups by bringing in outsiders who did not have official credentials. On the night in question, for example, Antonio Carrion, a Spaniard of no authority, also participated on the watch.[115] In his statement, Hernández pointed out that the latter, an individual with no official title or position, had no justification to meddle in the pueblo's affairs or give orders to him or the other indigenous officials.

Gómez further antagonized El Niño's leadership by inviting the indigenous alcaldes of San Josef with him on his patrols of the town. Alcalde Hernández reported that officials from San Josef (which also belonged to the fourth district) had accompanied Gómez on his watch on the three consecutive nights before the fandango. Overall, genuine goodwill and cooperation existed between indigenous towns and officials. But each sociopolitical entity strove for and vigilantly guarded its own political autonomy. San Josef's officials were well aware that El Niño's leader would not easily tolerate their making rounds in their pueblo, with or without Spanish officials. The presence of San Josef's leaders speaks to tensions between indigenous communities in this period that remain hidden in the absence of documentation. But the favor shown to San Josef's leaders suggests that the jurisdictional changes implemented by the Bourbon Reforms facilitated the playing out of intercommunity antagonisms and rivalries.

Gómez's attempt to offer the Indian alcaldes of San Josef some control over El Niño's activities—and seniority over its officials—offers some explanation for the deep and long-standing resentment the Spanish alcalde had engendered among its leadership. The large crowd that had gathered to witness his arrest and imprisonment also speaks to the anger it had generated among its vecinos. A Spanish witness, Don Josef María Moreno, asserted that he had heard a rumor that a large group of Indians had assembled premeditatedly, lying in wait for Gomez early in the evening.[116] Another Spaniard, Don Bonifacio Caballeros, stated that on hearing a commotion outside of his store, he was surprised to discover that a mob of over a hundred people had formed. He also declared that an Indian had told him that they were "determined to see if the alcalde [Gómez] arrived because if he did, they were going to bind him and take him to jail."[117] The indigenous officials of El Niño, and no doubt the entire pueblo, found it highly offensive that the Spanish alcalde, among many other grievances, brought Indians from other towns with him on his rounds to do his bidding in their community.

While the actions of the indigenous leaders were not exonerated, Spanish officials recognized that there were some legitimate grievances against Gómez. Initially, his superior, Don Josef de Robledo, did not take any significant action against the indigenous alcalde or his alguacil but stated that he for one had been "satisfied" with the indigenous leaders' explanation that they had taken action "to calm down the many resentments against Gomez."[118] Given the potentially volatile situation, the assault on the Spanish alcalde had been relatively mild, especially in light of the violent reactions of other native communities to the policy changes brought about by the Bourbon Reforms.[119]

Gómez, outraged by what he considered a blatant disregard by local authorities to his plight, pursued the matter with viceregal authorities, drawing on the general animosity of Spaniards toward indigenous governance. The leaders of El Niño, in his opinion, were ill suited to execute their jobs. In his view, they were individuals of base birth who had no sense of prudence or respect for the law or noble people. He cited various examples of their "temerity" in regard to legal and criminal matters.[120] Many times, it was commonly acknowledged, they had been corrected for their excesses with censures. In some instances incarceration had been the only means to make them respect and acknowledge the superiority and authority of Spanish officials. On one particularly infamous occasion in the past, one that certainly resonated with Gómez, another set of officials from El Niño had arrested and imprisoned a Spanish alcalde in the prison of their pueblo.[121]

Gómez, however, did not limit his attacks to the shortcomings and problems of indigenous leaders. He also questioned their right to exist as a corporate entity. He argued that the towns were no longer populated by native peoples but were given the "title" of Indian pueblos only by custom. In reality, he said, the towns' inhabitants were all castas who "only called themselves Indians" in order to garner jurisdictional rights and privileges.[122] Other Spanish officials echoed this sentiment as well. Even Alcalde Robledo, an individual who appears to have been sympathetic to the officials of El Niño, agreed that the town was composed of distinct castas, a claim that he leveled at the other three pueblos as well. He argued that it was relativity easy to procure the privileges reserved for individuals "truly of this category" (i.e., Indians)—one only had to reside within the district or jurisdiction of a barrio or pueblo.[123] Gómez and Robledo's attitudes illustrate that the aspersions and accusations that had been leveled at native peoples at the start of the boom had intensified by the early nineteenth century.

But Hernández and the constable Juárez responded to these charges and accusations by defending their actions on the basis of their jurisdictional prerogatives and by raising their own complaints against the improper and abusive behavior of Spanish officeholders. By vehemently protesting Gómez's excessive use of the privileges granted to him in the subdistricting articles of 1799, the native leaders used Spanish policies to deflect blame from them to Gómez. The native towns continued to retain some juridical autonomy. The redistricting ordinances mandated that the Indian pueblos keep all their rights and privileges, particularly their ability to hold elections, and have their own leaders supervise their pueblos. Zacatecas's cabildos may have even been more viable than those of Mexico City in the same period.[124] The late colonial reorganization did intrude upon aspects of indigenous autonomy, creating tensions and conditions that eventually led to their demise. But the active role of the indigenous leadership into the early nineteenth century illustrates that indigenous institutions and towns continued to operate in spite of local and viceregal attempts to undermine and dissolve them.

. . .

By 1803 Mexico's mines produced more than 67 percent of all silver in the Americas.[125] The revenues from this production were central to Spain's colonial and domestic economy and to its power in Europe, the Caribbean, and the Americas. On the eve of independence, Zacatecas was the third most prosperous mining site in New Spain. Zacatecas's reemergence as a leader in silver production after a sustained decline in the mid-eighteenth century was the product of many factors. The untold story of this late boom period is the role that indigenous peoples—migrants and natives, men and women—played in the city's economic, social, and demographic recovery.

But as they saved the city, native peoples began to suffer from the effects of centralizing reforms. Making a living became more challenging, and some of the prized labor concessions of the early years evaporated. Religious organizations continued to offer native peoples comfort and support, but some Indians might have passed a regretful sigh as they walked past the Franciscan or Augustinian convents. And it must have been disconcerting for an Indian man to bump into a Spanish official making the rounds in his pueblo in the early hours of the evening. These small but insidiously mundane changes were the first steps in the erosion of indigenous corporate rights and privileges.

The administrative policies enacted by the Spanish crown in the mid- to late eighteenth century had an unprecedented impact on individuals and local organizations and institutions throughout its Spanish American colonies, including Zacatecas's native peoples and towns. The demographic, economic, and social changes that occurred in this time frame undermined indigenous organizations and institutions in ways that were more profound than that of any other period. The production upsurge that began in the late 1760s drew migrants to the city. But declining wages and worsening work conditions may have discouraged the large number of indigenous immigrants that had arrived during previous booms. While Indians continued to flourish as a demographic group, they constituted a smaller percentage of Zacatecas's total inhabitants, while the non-Indian population more than doubled from its midcentury mark.[126] The implementation of political and religious reforms in Zacatecas brought changes to daily life as they eroded indigenous autonomy. The secularization of the native doctrinas forced indigenous peoples to worship under secular priests, while the creation of archconfraternities limited the governance opportunities these entities had provided. Spanish attempts to rid themselves of local challenges to their authority and gain greater control over the land and individuals living within the Indian towns by eradicating Indian leaders and pueblos posed a significant threat to indigenous lifeways. While these attempts were ultimately unsuccessful, the reorganization of the city in 1799 into subdistricts gave Spanish officials license to intrude in indigenous affairs. In Zacatecas, measures to make religious life, labor practices, and political systems congruent with Bourbon policies and principles significantly affected native peoples and institutions.

Yet the nature of indigenous society in this period continued to be characterized by resiliency and persistence. By the late colonial period, indigenous leaders had developed strategies to contend with changes in local and viceregal policies and practices. As the mining boom progressed, indigenous organizations continued their activities and Indian leaders looked after their modest constituent base. Yet despite high endogamy rates and the continued presence of families and Indian leaders, the overall sense in this late colonial period is one of gradual decline in indigenous organizations and institutions. Cultural and biological miscegenation are often considered the source of this decline. Yet a growing casta population in this period was matched by an equally significant increase in the indigenous population as well. Rather, a more significant factor was the altering of local practices and institutions, which left indigenous society without the resources or resiliency to withstand the sweeping changes ushered in by the independence movements and the aspirations of the new nation's creole elites.

Conclusion: From Indigenous Towns to Mestizo Barrios

Unlike towns and communities in the central highlands or southern Mexico, contemporary Zacatecas lacks an indigenous character. A UNESCO World Heritage Site, its majestic and stately rose-quartz buildings stand as symbols of the city's Spanish colonial heritage (see Figure C.1). The ruins of the Franciscan convent, along with other imposing stately churches, offer a solemn yet beautiful reminder of the city's long-term religious caretakers. On many streets the remains of mining complexes—walls, fences, and even grinding wheels—form parts of homes, businesses, and gardens. The stunning remains of the Hacienda de Bernárdez, a few miles from the center of town, lie within an exclusive, gated neighborhood. On-site artisans make silver for display and sale. A short walk from the Plaza de Armas (the main square) leads to an old mine. At night the mine serves as a popular bar and dance club. By day, visitors tour some of its interior galleries. Guides explain the production process and describe the experiences of mine laborers. Their accounts of working conditions include a discussion of native people, who are also represented by life-size figures of laboring men and boys. Save for these brief references there is little acknowledgement of the city's indigenous past. Native peoples are equally elusive. Indigenous vendors occasionally gather near the cathedral selling crafts and textiles. But these individuals are often temporary migrants from the south. In 2010 the state had the third lowest number of indigenous speakers in the country.[1] In relation to population and culture, the city shares more in common with the cultural and biological mestizaje commonly ascribed to Mexico's northern states.

The current conditions of the native population's settlements and buildings speak to the inevitable decline that overtook them and their communities, processes that contributed to Zacatecas's mestizaje in the nineteenth

FIGURE C.1. Zacatecas: Historic center. Photo taken by author in 2007.

century. Street signs, such as "Calle de Chepinque" or "Calle de Tonalá," mark the old thoroughfares of the indigenous communities. A contemporary neighborhood called Mexicapan encompasses the former site of Tlacuitlapan and its barrios. A few indigenous chapels remain. After falling into ruins in the late nineteenth century, a chapel in Mexicapan was restored in the mid-1980s (see image in Chapter 2). In spite of urban sprawl and architectural modifications, the temple of the pueblo of El Niño also survived (see Figure C.2). Both capillas have reopened for worship, with Mexicapan's chapel now recognized as a historical landmark. Time, however, has not been as kind to Zacatecas's other indigenous capillas. The temple of San Diego, home to two confraternities, was being transformed into a bar in the summer of 2007. Fortunately, the chapel's simple facade has been preserved (see Figure C.3). The back altar wall is all that remains of the Capilla de la Concepción. The site is now home to the city's livestock commission; at the same location, an indigenous cemetery was buried under a three-story parking lot. All that remain of the city's first indigenous capilla, La Santa Vera Cruz, are a few fragments that sit on private property. In short, the four Indian towns are now incorporated into the city at a level that even late colonial officials could not have envisioned.

FIGURE C.2. Chapel of El Niño. Photo taken by author in 2007.

FIGURE C.3. Facade: Temple of San Diego. Photo taken by author in 2007.

How and when did Zacatecas's native towns transform from indigenous settlements to mestizo barrios? The answers to these questions are outside of the scope of this work. My research on Zacatecas did not extend much beyond the commencement of Mexico's independence movements.[2] But during my archival investigations it appeared that the sources on native peoples became particularly thin after 1810. Had native peoples disappeared from the city? Some might have of, as I will speculate here. Had the level of biological mixing reached a point at which "Indian" as an ethnic category was no longer viable? This transformation certainly occurred, but at a slower rate than we might imagine, and definitely not during the colonial period. We can speak of major decline by 1832, the year the native pueblos ceased to exist as separate political entities. What had happened to native leaders and vecinos during that roughly twenty-year period that had left them either powerless to defend or apathetic to the loss of their juridical autonomy? Definitive conclusions should be left to future scholars of the topic. But it may be instructive to consider how viceregal events, legal and institutional practices, and population changes may have contributed to the erosion of corporate indigenous culture in the city.

External forces caused, in part, some of the weakening of indigenous identity. By 1803, Zacatecas once again counted itself among the most prosperous mining sites in New Spain, coming in third behind Guanajuato and the recently discovered site of Catorce.[3] But the independence rebellions that erupted in 1810 in the nearby Bajío and the subsequent military battles that occurred in the region severely disrupted mining production.[4] Zacatecas was not immune to the social and political chaos generated by the insurgency. Mining activity plummeted, particularly from 1810 to 1811. True, the city fared better than most others in the northern mining district, particularly Guanajuato. Tabulations from the royal mint in 1824 indicate that Zacatecas emerged from the war as the number-one silver producer in the region.[5] Yet unstable conditions and vacant or abandoned mines through the independence period may have discouraged the flow of indigenous migrants to the city.

Broadly speaking, when secession from Spain arrived, it did not serve indigenous people's interests, economically, socially, or culturally. Indians and individuals of indigenous descent still constituted 50 percent of New Spain's total population at the time of independence, but new policies slowly began to erase their legal and corporate statuses.[6] In 1821, the newly independent Mexican government eliminated all caste distinctions, including the juridical category of "Indian."[7] Over time, this policy had serious ramifications for indigenous rights and properties, facilitating the appropriation of their resources by local and national agents. As we saw in Chapter 5, the initial challenges to indigenous society in Zacatecas had already begun in the late eighteenth century, with Spaniards questioning the necessity for autonomous Indian towns and cabildos. Attempts to dissolve the native pueblos and to invalidate their corporate privileges surely continued through the early nineteenth century. Several cofradías had already been absorbed into archconfraternities by the 1780s. How much longer did cabildos survive? Documents that refer to Indian town councils become thin after 1810. The fate of indigenous institutions and organizations during the turbulent war years is unknown, but by 1832 the Indians towns had lost their political autonomy and were incorporated into the city as *barrios mineros*.[8] No doubt they remained heavily indigenous for some time, as native peoples traditionally constituted a high percentage of the mining labor force. Still, this change in nomenclature should not be taken lightly. As with their counterparts to the south, the continued persistence of Indian identities and societies depended on the extent to which their towns, institutions, organizations, practices, and networks flourished (and endured) at the local level. The loss of Indian spaces and leaders surely struck a heavy blow to the perpetuation of indigenous culture in the city, and the dissolution of their towns probably marked the end of native peoples as a corporate group in Zacatecas.

The decline of the Indian pueblos, decreasing wages, and the imposition of tribute, combined with disruptions to the mining economy, may have encouraged out-migration at the same time that it discouraged immigration. Dwindling numbers of incoming migrants and the exodus of short-term residents and possibly long-term vecinos probably contributed to a decline in the size of the city's native population. In urban centers, and other areas outside of densely populated indigenous regions, the persistence of indigenous peoples and practices depended on the development of a critical demographic mass. A large population of native peoples created internal and external circumstances that renewed the community. Larger spousal pools led to higher endogamy rates and new children, and social and cultural affinities often drew indigenous newcomers. In Zacatecas, indigenous migrants had always functioned as sources of biological and cultural regeneration for the city's native vecinos. Postindependence Zacatecas may not have proved attractive to native migrants who perhaps chose to settle in areas with a more indigenous character. On the basis of trends from nuptial requests from 1690 to 1800, native peoples probably continued to marry within the greater indigenous population in the early nineteenth century. But the dwindling spousal pool meant that more unions probably occurred with castas. From the extant marriage patterns, it would follow that the majority of these mixed marriages took place between Indians and mestizos, leading over time to Zacatecas's predominately mestizo composition.

Still, both data and archival documents suggest that the mestizaje of the city occurred much later than is usually presented in the scholarship, beginning in earnest only in the late eighteenth century. An examination of colonial-wide demographic records, most prominently censuses and marriage petitions and registers, indicates that while native peoples interacted with ethnic others, it was not at unusually high rates. Interethnic unions occurred from the moment Spaniards stepped foot in the Americas, but endogamy within the indigenous population ran fairly high in major urban centers through the colonial period.[9] No quantifiable evidence exists to indicate that native peoples would have made substantially different partner selection patterns in their informal relationships.

Moreover, records from the widespread demographic counts taken at the close of the eighteenth century illustrate an overall resurgence in the indigenous population. In cities throughout the empire Indians often numbered close to a third of the population, while mestizos averaged around 15 percent to 20 percent of their total inhabitants.[10] Though estimates, these figures do not yet suggest a mestizo population with the demographic power to cannibalize the native population. The rise of a mestizo identity was rooted in powerful ideological campaigns produced during the Mexican Revolution that continue to hold sway today.[11] In the 1920s and 1930s, intellectuals and politicians, attempting to distance themselves from European culture, articulated a Mexican identity that drew on its mestizaje, or varied racial roots: indigenous, African, and Spanish. The mestizo, or the racially mixed individual, became the biological and cultural everyman of the Mexican nation.[12] One of the many legacies of this discourse is its influence on how we perceive mestizos in the colonial period, ascribing greater numbers to them as a biological group as well as disproportionate cultural influence than was necessarily the case.[13]

In the colonial period, close affinities between mestizos and native peoples developed in the urban context. R. Douglas Cope found that for Mexico City, mestizos often "maintained strong ties" with "their parent [population]."[14] In Zacatecas, individuals described in the documents as "mestizos" often moved within indigenous spheres, frequently living in native barrios, joining indigenous parishes and confraternities, and developing personal and professional associations with indigenous people. In other words, mestizos did not necessarily draw native peoples away from indigenous culture. In 1736, for example, an indigenous man, Manuel de la Concepción, and Ana, his bride-to-be, decided to petition for marriage. Ana was a mestiza who lived in Zacatecas proper, but the couple decided to wed in Manuel's place of residence, Tonalá Chepinque. They were unable to post their banns in the pueblo's capilla because she was a registered member of Zacatecas's parish church.[15] The couple, however, eventually made their new home in Tonalá Chepinque. In this case, Ana's connections to the indigenous world became only stronger as she left her home in the Spanish city for an indigenous town and parish. This episode reminds us that interactions with mestizos (and other castas) contributed to the creation of a more inclusive urban Indian culture. Over the nineteenth century, urban native peoples surely became more influenced by Spaniards and other ethnic groups. Still, one wonders how many "Indian" traditions survive today among Zacatecas's primarily mestizo culture. In 1897, for example, the prominent historian of the city, Elías Amador, published a book exclusively devoted to the indigenous names that continued to be used in the state.[16] Even within an urban context, the process of mestizaje involved the transmission of indigenous lifeways as well as Spanish.[17]

Inevitably, the fate of Zacatecas's indigenous population eventually mirrored that of other areas of northern Mexico where a variety of local demographic and economic factors led to larger mestizo populations. In Sonora and Nueva Vizcaya, for example, small autochthonous native populations—further decimated by disease and significant changes in lifeways—had little choice but to live and marry with ethnic others in greater numbers.[18] In many mining towns or agricultural settlements, smaller populations of discrete ethnic groups led to greater levels of miscegenation. This was certainly the case in Chihuahua, where by 1785, mestizos and mulattos, constituted close to 60 percent (46 percent and 13 percent, respectively) of the total population.[19]

Despite these examples, we still cannot speak of a uniform process of mestizaje in New Spain. Cities, frontiers, and mining towns are often frequently cited in the scholarship as the great motors of miscegenation.[20] One scholar has argued that mining towns "formed the focus of" New Spain's "northern mestizaje."[21] Yet the evolution of indigenous societies in colonial Zacatecas offers an example of why we should reconsider characterizing the Mexican north as a monolithic region. Like other parts of the Americas, northern New Spain was a dynamic space that developed in response to both local conditions and viceregal practices and policies. Miscegenation occurred fairly soon at some sites and developed much later at others. Mestizaje in and of itself did not necessarily bring on immediate dramatic large-scale cultural change. Nor does it necessarily reveal the dynamic nature or the elements of continuity that persisted within refashioned ethnic groups. Examining the local processes involved in cultural changes and transformations provides a more nuanced picture of local societies, contributing to a greater understanding of this important and complex region of Spanish America.

In Zacatecas, the dissolution of the native pueblos in 1832, and Mexican laws prohibiting classifications of native people as Indians, undermined indigenous leadership, organizations, and corporate structures. Without the indigenous towns, councils, and communities it became more difficult for native peoples to be Indians, and easier for Spanish authorities, chroniclers and early historians, and even contemporary scholars, to count them among the city's many multiethnic urban vecinos. Seen in this light, it becomes easier to understand how the city lost its indigenous heritage and became a mestizo town, an inevitable process according to some scholars.[22] Still, the transformation from Indians to mestizos or towns to barrios did not occur at the moment of any given decree, but occurred in stages. Consider, for example, the ex-voto from 1832 presented in Figure C.4. The image concerns the miraculous recovery of one Simón Luján after a visit from a sacred image. The scene takes place in "Chepinque," and Luján belongs to the formerly indigenous cofradía of Nuestra Señora de la Soledad. Thus the Indian town and confraternity continued to be viable and important entities in the city. But Luján is now a ciudadano, or citizen, of the city, indeed of the greater nation, and not a local vecino. In their appearances, the mayordomo of the cofradía and the other personages in the tableaux do not appear indigenous but are clearly identifiable as nineteenth-century figures. Yet the bareness of the room seems more reminiscent of the economic

FIGURE C.4. Ex-voto to the Virgin of Solitude of Chepinque, dated 1832. Courtesy of the Museum of Spanish Colonial Art, Spanish Colonial Arts Society, Inc., Santa Fe, New Mexico (accession number 1955.69).

conditions that characterized indigenous communities. It was this combination of gradual social, material, and institutional changes that shaped evolving ethnic identities and practices in Zacatecas, and in postindependence Mexico as well.

Yet Zacatecas's contemporary mestizo composition and character should not unduly influence our perceptions of the nature of urban Indian identities and societies in the colonial period. The absence of a current indigenous presence should not detract from the large and vibrant native societies and cultures that existed for more than 250 years. Native peoples' successful re-creation of their communities and societies in Zacatecas compels us to reexamine the nature of Spanish colonialism in its urban centers. Historically, across places and time periods, cities have drawn migrant populations, especially from those subject peoples fleeing oppressive conditions or seeking improved socioeconomic situations.[23] Migrants often play key roles in the evolution of urban centers, building them, serving as the primary labor force, and revitalizing them both demographically and culturally. Migrants and subject peoples often encounter significant cultural changes in the urban environment. But ultimately cities facilitate ethnogenesis as groups and individuals exploit urban spaces and institutions to re-create social, political, and economic aspects of their home culture. Zacatecas's urban environment and mining-driven economy contributed in great measure to the persistence of indigenous culture. The consistent and pressing need for a stable labor pool created conditions of relative autonomy for both workers and the communities they established. The continued influx of migrants created a critical population mass that helped perpetuate indigenous organizations, cultures, and kin and social networks.

The case of Zacatecas forces us to reconsider assumptions that "urban Indians" did not embrace civic identities or that they quickly abandoned their ancestral identities. But can we make the same argument for other urban centers with large native populations? Is Zacatecas representative of the urban experience? Or is it an anomaly, a product of unusual circumstances and conditions? Addressing these questions proves challenging, mainly because we lack focused studies on urban native peoples. In many ways Zacatecas's unique development supports the outlier hypothesis. Evolving as it did from a previously undeveloped site meant that all its initial settlers, including the native population, were migrants. Many of these indigenous migrants did not just work for a season but settled permanently in the city. These circumstances were very different from other mining towns that received temporary coerced workers who had no intention of establishing new communities, such as Potosí. Yet recent work has highlighted the very indigenous character of San Luis Potosí during its formative years of 1591 to 1630. Like Zacatecas, multiple indigenous barrios and pueblos evolved alongside the Spanish traza.[24] Archivally driven studies of this nature will uncover more information on the civic and personal lives of native populations in mining towns as we continue to explore their experiences beyond those at mines and haciendas

From the near north to the far south, the situation of urban native peoples calls for an examination that carefully considers the local context and focuses on both change and cultural maintenance. Laura Matthew, for example, documented the persistence of a Mexica identity in native communities near Santiago de Guatemala during the colonial era among significant Maya and Spanish populations, which continues to resonate in the present day. Her study offers yet another example of the ability of native peoples to successfully transplant indigenous culture in an urban context.[25] Other studies have uncovered a strong sense of indigenous governance in Mérida's eight *barrios de indios* and in Valladolid's (Michoacán) barrios and pueblos de indios.[26] Certainly more remains to be known about Mexico City's two indigenous parcialidades, San Juan Tenochtitlán and Santiago Tlatelolco, the eight native communities that surrounded Santiago de Guatemala, as well as the Mexica, Mixtec, and Cholulteca settlements that bordered Puebla.[27] While each city created its own dynamics, it would not be surprising if it emerges that larger trends of indigence persistence were common to urban centers.

Uncovering the influence of cities on the ethnic identities and practices of immigrants and subject peoples, and in turn, examining how these groups contribute to the vitality of these urban centers, complicates our understanding of how multiracial societies were constructed in early Latin America. It also offers some context for how they continued to be forged today. Data from the 2008 US Census Bureau's American Community Survey (ACS) indicates that more than half of all Mexican migrants to the United States settled in ten major cities.[28] Three years later, a 2011 ACS count found a fourth of all Mexican migrants resided in three major metropolitan urban centers: Los Angeles (15 percent), Chicago (6 percent), and Dallas (5 percent).[29] The same census, while it accounts for the total number of immigrants—and not just those in cities—indicated that female migrants outnumbered males by 2 percent (51 percent to 49 percent). Following historical patterns, immigrants, male and female, continue to be drawn to cities and continue to have to negotiate their home customs and traditions with the sociopolitical realties of their new environments. Ironically, Zacatecas, the source of intense in-migration during the colonial period, has suffered a significant migrant exodus to the United States in recent times. In the late 1980s, the state was among the most affected by out-migration to the United States.[30] In 1995, Zacatecas ranked fourth among Mexican states with the most out-migrants. In recent years this trend has decreased, and by 2008 Zacatecas no longer counted among the top "sending states."[31]

But even with the slowdown in out-migration, large communities of new and long-standing Zacatecan immigrants continue to live in US cities. Like their colonial indigenous counterparts, they have brought their skills and talents to these urban centers, contributing to their economic development and demographic evolution. Over a third of the Mexican male immigration population labors in "construction, extraction, and transportation," while close to 40 percent of female immigrants had "service and personal care occupations."[32] And like Zacatecas's native population, many of these immigrants seek to become vecinos or citizens of these cities as they struggle to re-create a space for some of their home traditions. Their successes speak yet again to how cities facilitate ethnogenesis. In a telling title, "A Tale of Two Villages: Immigrants from Atolinga, Mexico, Build a Community More Vibrant Than the One They Used to Call Home," *Chicago Tribune* contributor Sam Quinones narrates the rise and creation of Zacatecan immigrant mutual-aid societies in Chicago and across the nation. According to Quinones, "Zacatecans have become the most organized Mexicans in the U.S.," establishing "clubs" (239 at that time) in major cities such as Los Angeles and several states, including Colorado, Texas, and New Mexico.[33] While there is no direct connection between Zacatecas's strong tradition of colonial cofradías with these contemporary civic mutual-aid societies, one cannot help drawing comparisons. The clubs constitute avenues for both recent and long-term immigrants to create personal and economic networks in new urban environments and to forge bonds with like-minded individuals who share some of their hometown preferences and practices. The proliferation of pockets of Zacatecan communities in several cities speaks to the ability of these migrants to integrate within the US urban milieu as they maintain some aspects of their local Zacatecan and greater Mexican identities.

In early modern Latin America, urban centers represented the administrative and demographic heart of Spanish rule. But these colonial epicenters depended on the presence and labor of their indigenous and other non-Spanish inhabitants. The construction of Spanish American societies reflected a series of political and social negotiations and accommodations that allowed subject peoples to participate as civic residents and to continue to develop their own identities and practices. Whether it is contemporary Los Angeles, Chicago, or Dallas, cities continue to serve as dynamic sites of personal, professional, and cultural interactions, creating sites of multiethnic populations and traditions.

Notes

INTRODUCTION

1. For production, see David A. Brading, "Mexican Silver Mining in the Eighteenth Century: The Revival of Zacatecas," in *Mines of Silver and Gold in the Americas*, ed. Peter Bakewell (Brookfield: Variorum, 1997), 307–8; for population, see José de Ribera Bernárdez, *Descripción breve de la muy noble y leal ciudad de Zacatecas* (México: Impressa por Joseph Bernando Hogal, ministro, e impressor del Real y Apostólico tribunal de la Santa Cruzada en toda esta Nueva España, 1732), 48.

2. See Archivo Histórico del Estado de Zacatecas (hereafter AHEZ), Bienes y Difuntos, box 17, *expediente* (exp.) 263, 1719, ff. 1–181. I discuss this case in greater detail in Chapter 4.

3. Preconquest indigenous mining developed in Peru, Colombia and lower Central America, and in central and western Mexico. For Mexico, see Adolfo Langenscheidts, "Las minas y la minería prehispánica," in *Minería prehispánica en la sierra de Querétaro*, ed. Adolfo Langenscheidts (México: Secretaría del Patrimonio Nacional, 1970), 45–52; Miguel León-Portilla, "Minería y metalurgia en el México antiguo," in *La minería en México: Estudios sobre su desarrollo histórico*, ed. Miguel León-Portilla, Jorge Gurría Lacroix, Roberto Moreno, and Enrique Madero Bracho (México: Universidad Nacional Autónoma de México, 1978), 7–36. For Spanish America, see Modesto Bargalló Ardévol, *La minería y la metalurgia en la América Española durante la época colonial* (México: Fondo de Cultura Económica, 1955), 24–41. In precontact Zacatecas, there is evidence of mining in the Chalchihuites area around AD 350. These mines contained many minerals, including the blue-green stone of the site's namesake, but very little evidence of silver ores. Other possible mining sites include Mazapil and Concepción de Oro. See Phil C. Weigand, "Mining and Mineral Trade in Prehispanic Zacatecas," in *Mining and Mineral Techniques in Ancient Mesoamerica*, Anthropology, ed. Phil C. Weigand and Gretchen Gwynne, 87–134. Anthropology 6 (Stony Brook: Department of Anthropology, State University of New York at Stony Brook, 1982).

4. For a social history of these two groups in the Guanajuato area, see David A. Brading, *Miners and Merchants in Bourbon Mexico, 1763–1810* (New York: Cambridge University Press, 1971); for Zacatecas, Peter Bakewell, *Silver Mining and Society in Colonial Mexico: Zacatecas, 1546–1700* (Cambridge: Cambridge University Press, 1971); Frederique Langue, *Los señores de Zacatecas: Una aristocracia minera del siglo XVIII novohispano* (México: Fondo de Cultura Económica, 1999); for Peru, John Robert Fisher, *Minas y mineros en el Perú colonial, 1776–1824* ([Lima]: Instituto de Estudios Peruanos, 1977).

5. For scholarship on mining and mining towns in Spanish America, see Robert C. West, *The Mining Community in Northern New Spain: The Parral Mining District* (Los Angeles: University of California Press, 1949); Bargalló Ardévol, *La minería y la metalurgia*; Richard L. Garner, "Zacatecas, 1750–1821: The Study of a Late Colonial Mexican City" (PhD diss., University of Michigan, 1970); Bakewell, *Silver Mining and Society*; Brading, *Miners and Merchants*; Miguel León-Portilla, Jorge Gurría Lacroix, Roberto Moreno, and Enrique Madero Bracho, eds., *La minería en México: Estudios sobre su desarrollo histórico* (México: Universidad Nacional Autónoma de México, 1978); Phillip Hadley, *Minería y sociedad en el centro minero de Santa Eulalia, Chihuahua, 1709–1750* (México: Fondo de Cultura Económica, 1979); Oscar Alatriste, *Desarrollo de la industria y la comunidad minera de Hidalgo del Parral durante la segunda mitad del siglo XVIII, 1765–1810* (México: Universidad Nacional Autónoma de México, 1983); Gilda Cubillo Moreno, *Los dominios de la plata: El precio del auge, el peso del poder: Empresarios y trabajadores en las minas de Pachuca y Zimapán, 1552–1620* (México: Instituto Nacional de Antropología e Historia, 1991); Robert Haskett, "'Our Suffering with the Taxco Tribute': Involuntary Mine Labor and Indigenous Society in Central New Spain," *Hispanic American Historical Review* 71.3 (1991): 447–75; Cheryl English L. Martin, *Governance and Society in Colonial Mexico: Chihuahua in the Eighteenth Century* (Stanford: Stanford University Press, 1996); Laura Pérez Rosales, *Minería y sociedad en Taxco durante el siglo XVIII* (México: Universidad Iberoamericana, 1996); Langue, *Los señores de Zacatecas*; Guadalupe Salazar González, *Las haciendas en el siglo XVII en la región minera de San Luis Potosí* (San Luis Potosí: Universidad Autónoma de San Luis Potosí, 2000); Alejandro Montoya, "Población y sociedad en un real de minas de la frontera norte novohispana: San Luis Potosí, de finales del siglo XVI a 1810" (PhD diss., Université de Montréal, 2004). For the Andes, see Peter Bakewell, *Miners of the Red Mountain: Indian Labor in Potosí: 1545–1650* (Albuquerque: University of New Mexico Press, 1984); Enrique Tandeter, *Coercion and Market: Silver Mining in Colonial Potosí, 1692–1826* (Albuquerque: University of New Mexico Press, 1993); Jane E. Mangan, *Trading Roles: Gender, Ethnicity, and the Urban Economy in Colonial Potosí* (Durham: Duke University Press, 2005); Nicholas A. Robins, *Mercury, Mining, and Empire: The Human and Ecological Cost of Colonial Silver Mining in the Andes* (Bloomington: Indiana University Press, 2011). For general overviews, see Peter Bakewell, ed., *Mines of Silver and Gold in the Americas* (Brookfield: Variorum, 1997); Kendall W. Brown, *A History of Mining in Latin America: From the Colonial Era to the Present* (Albuquerque: University of New Mexico Press, 2012).

6. These cities were "new" in the sense that they were not established on preconquest indigenous communities. Puebla, for example, was another significant urban center of this nature. Yet Puebla (and other sites in central Mexico) had the advantage of developing around large indigenous hinterlands. For Puebla's evolution, see Miguel Ángel Cuenya Mateos and Carlos Contreras Cruz, *Puebla de los Ángeles: Una ciudad en la historia* (Puebla: Benemérita Universidad Autónoma de Puebla, 2012), 15–37.

7. The Andean mining town of Potosí is located in contemporary Bolivia. It should not be confused with San Luis Potosí, which is located in northeastern Mexico. I will refer to these places using these exact names.

8. For Spaniards, see the many works in note 5. For global markets, see Earl J. Hamilton, *American Treasure and the Price Revolution in Spain, 1501–1650* (New York: Octagon Books, 1965); Carlos Sempat Assadourian, *El sistema de la economía colonial: Mercado interno, regiones y espacio económico* (Lima: Instituto de Estudios Peruanos, 1982); Pedro Pérez Herrero, *Plata y libranzas: La articulacíon comercial del México borbónico* (México: El Colegio de México, 1988), 113–253. Richard Von Glahn, *Fountain of Fortune: Money and Monetary Policy in China, 1000–1700* (Berkeley: University of California Press, 1996); Stanley J. Stein and Barbara H. Stein, *Silver, Trade, and War: Spain and America in the Making of Early Modern Europe* (Baltimore: John Hopkins University Press, 2000); Charles R. Boxer, "*Plata es sangre*: Sidelights on the Drain of Spanish-American Silver in the Far East, 1550–1700," in *European Entry into the Pacific: Spain and the Acapulco-Manila Galleon*, ed. Dennis Owen Flynn, Arturo Giráldez, and James Sobredo (Aldershot: Ashgate, 2001), 165–86; John Tutino, *Making a New World: Founding Capitalism in the Bajío and Spanish North America* (Durham: Duke University Press, 2011).

9. For studies on indigenous peoples and mining towns, see Bakewell, *Miners of the Red Mountain*; Haskett, "'Our Suffering with the Taxco Tribute'"; Tandeter, *Coercion and Market*; Celia Islas Jiménez, *El real de Tlalpujahua: Aspectos de la minería novohispana* (México: Instituto Nacional de Antropología e Historia, 2008), 155–94; Dana Velasco Murillo, "Laboring Above Ground: Indigenous Women in New Spain's Silver-Mining District, Zacatecas, Mexico, 1620–1770," *Hispanic American Historical Review* 93.1 (2013): 3–32; Laurent Corbeil, "Identities in Motion: The Formation of a Plural Indio Society in Early San Luis Potosí, New Spain, 1591–1630" (PhD diss., McGill University, 2015).

10. Northern New Spain was a vast region, spanning the silver mining district to the current US borderlands. For some representative studies, see Evelyn Hu-Dehart, *Missionaries, Miners, and Indians: Spanish Contact and the Yaqui Nation, 1533–1820* (Tucson: University of Arizona Press, 1981); Michael M. Swann, *"Tierra Adentro": Settlement and Society in Colonial Durango* (Boulder: Westview Press, 1982); Chantal Cramaussel, *La provincia de Santa Bárbara en la Nueva Vizcaya, 1563–1631* (Ciudad Juárez: Universidad Autónoma de Ciudad Juárez, 1990); Luis González Rodríguez, *El noroeste novohispano en la época colonial* (México: Instituto de Investigaciones Antropológicas, Universidad Nacional Autónoma de México, 1993); Martin, *Governance and Society*; Cynthia Radding, *Wandering Peoples: Colonialism, Ethnic Spaces, and Ecological Frontiers in Northwest Mexico, 1700–1850* (Durham: Duke University Press, 1997); Leslie Scott Offutt, *Saltillo, 1570–1810: Town and Region in the Mexican North* (Tucson: University of Arizona Press, 2001); Susan Deeds, *Defiance and Deference in Mexico's Colonial North: Indians Under Spanish Rule in Nueva Vizcaya* (Austin: University of Texas Press, 2003); José Cuello, *Saltillo colonial: Orígenes y formacíon de una sociedad Mexicana en la frontera norte* (Saltillo: Archivo Municipal de Saltillo y

Universidad Autónoma de Coahuila, 2004); Chantal Cramaussel, *Poblar la frontera: La provincia de Santa Bárbara en Nueva Vizcaya durante los siglos XVI y XVII* (Zamora: El Colegio de Michoacán, 2006).

11. See Susan Schroeder, "Whither Tenochtitlan: Chimalpahin and Mexico City, 1593–1631," in *City Indians in Spain's American Empire: Urban Indigenous Society in Colonial Mesoamerica and Andean South America, 1530–1810*, ed. Dana Velasco Murillo, Mark Lentz, and Margarita R. Ochoa (Brighton: Sussex Academic Press, 2012), 67.

12. See also Irene Silverblatt's discussion of how the category of "Indian" both reinforced and challenged Spanish rule in "Becoming Indian in the Central Andes of Seventeenth-Century Peru," in *After Colonialism: Imperial Histories and Postcolonial Displacements*, ed. Gyan Prakash (Princeton: Princeton University Press, 1995), 279–98.

13. Olivia Harris argues that for the purpose of collecting tribute, it was also an important "fiscal category" as well. In Zacatecas, however, "Indian" did not have such urgent fiscal connotations because the native population was exempt from tribute. See Harris, "Ethnic Identity and Market Relations: Indians and Mestizos in the Andes," in *Ethnicity, Markets and Migration in the Andes: At the Crossroads of History and Anthropology*, ed. Brooke Larson and Olivia Harris (Durham: Duke University Press, 1995), 354.

14. I do note specific ethnic affiliations whenever they appear in the documentation.

15. Karen B. Graubart, "The Creolization of the New World: Local Forms of Identification in Urban Colonial Peru, 1560–1640," *Hispanic American Historical Review* 89.3 (2009): 477–87. See also Jane E. Mangan's discussion of ethnic labels and indigenous and mestiza market women in Potosí in "A Market of Identities: Women, Trade, and Ethnic Labels in Colonial Potosí," in *Imperial Subjects: Race and Identity in Colonial Latin America*, ed. Andrew B. Fisher and Matthew D. O'Hara (Durham: Duke University Press 2009), 61–80.

16. See Graubart, "Creolization of the New World," 486–88.

17. For example, see Susan Migden Socolow, *The Merchants of Buenos Aires, 1778–1810: Family and Commerce* (Cambridge: Cambridge University Press, 1978); Francisco de Solano, ed., *Estudios sobre la ciudad iberoamericana* (Madrid: Consejo Superior de Investigaciones Científicas, 1983); Louisa Schell Hoberman and Susan Migden Socolow, eds., *Cities and Society in Colonial Latin America* (Albuquerque: University of New Mexico Press, 1986); Susan Migden Socolow, *The Bureaucrats of Buenos Aires, 1769–1810: Amor al real servicio* (Durham: Duke University Press, 1987); Angel Rama, *The Lettered City*, trans. John Charles Chasteen (Durham: Duke University Press, 1996); Richard Kagan and Fernando Marías, *Urban Images of the Hispanic World, 1493–1793* (New Haven: Yale University Press, 2000); Eugenia María Azevedo Salomao, *Espacios urbanos comunitarios durante el período virreinal en Michoacán* (Morelia: Morevallado Editores, 2003); Jay Kinsbruner, *The Colonial Spanish-American City: Urban Life in the Age of Atlantic Capitalism* (Austin: University of Texas Press, 2005); Miguel Felipe de Jesús Vallebueno Garcinava, *Civitas y urbs: La conformación del espacio urbano de Durango* (Durango: Instituto de Cultura del Estado de Durango, 2005).

18. In the period before the Spanish invasion, the Mexica capital of Tenochtitlan was among the largest cities in the world. With an estimated population of 150,000 to 200,000 people, it eclipsed Milan, Venice, and Seville in demographic size. See Michael E. Smith and Frances F. Berdan, "Archaeology and the Aztec Empire," *World Archaeology* 23.3 (1992): 354. The population of the Valley of Mexico was between one million and three million. See Charles Gibson, *Aztecs Under Spanish Rule: A History of the Indians of the Valley of Mexico, 1519–1810* (Stanford: Stanford University Press, 1964), 5. For Mexico City's preconquest urban configuration, see Alfonso Caso, *Los barrios antiguos de Tenochtitlan y Tlatelolco* (México: Memorias de la Academia Mexicana de la Historia, 1956). For preconquest social dynamics in the Valley of Mexico, see Pedro Carrasco, *Estructura político-territorial del imperio Tenochca: La triple alianza de Tenochtitlan, Tetzcoco y Tlacopan* (México: El Colegio de México y Fondo de Cultura Económica, 1996); Jorge Enrique Hardoy, *Ciudades precolombinas* (Buenos Aires: Ediciones Infinito, 1999), 136–202.

19. See James Lockhart, "Receptivity and Resistance," in *Of Things of the Indies: Essays Old and New in Early Latin American History* (Stanford: Stanford University Press, 1999), 320.

20. See Helen Nader, *Liberty in Absolutist Spain: The Habsburg Sale of Towns, 1516–1700* (Baltimore: John Hopkins University Press, 1990), 27–33; Tamar Herzog, *Defining Nations: Immigrants and Citizens in Early Modern Spain and Spanish America* (New Haven: Yale University Press, 2003); Sean F. McEnroe, *From Colony to Nationhood in Mexico: Laying the Foundations, 1560–1840* (Cambridge: Cambridge University Press, 2012), 2–14. The term also had specific usage in census records. Recorders counted households by units, listing the head as the vecino. See Nader, *Liberty in Absolutist Spain*, xv.

21. See *Real Academia Española Diccionario de Autoridades*, facs. ed., O–Z (Madrid: Editorial Gredos, 1984), 428.

22. See *Real Academia*, 428.

23. It also surely reflects the fact that 80 percent of sixteenth-century Castilians still lived in small towns, not cities. See Nader, *Liberty in Absolutist Spain*, 245n28.

24. See Ross Frank, *From Settler to Citizen: New Mexican Economic Development and the Creation of Vecino Society, 1750–1820* (Berkeley: University of California Press, 2000); Herzog, *Defining Nations*. For the use of *vecino* by various scholars for northern Mexico, see Jesús F. de la Teja and Ross Frank, *Choice, Persuasion, and Coercion: Social Control on Spain's North American Frontiers* (Albuquerque: University of New Mexico Press, 2005), 8, 19, 78–92, 97, 181–82, 195n2, and 208.

25. Peter B. Villella, for example, mentions an elite Indian who described himself as an important vecino of Singuilucan in central Mexico. See Villella, "Pure and Noble Indians, Untainted by Inferior Idolatrous Races: Native Elites and the Discourse of Blood Purity in Late Colonial Mexico," *Hispanic American Historical Review* 91.4 (2011): 644. Sean F. McEnroe discusses native peoples' adoption of the term as part of a larger Mexican identity in northern New Spain; see *From Colony to Nationhood in Mexico*, 6–14. In Zacatecas, Afro-descended individuals also identified as vecinos. For examples, see AHEZ, Notarías, Juan García Picón,

protocolos 3, ff. 125v–126v, 1736; protocolos 3, ff. 134–35, 1736. For other examples in the Americas, see Kimberly S. Hanger, "Patronage, Property and Persistence: The Emergence of a Free Black Elite in Spanish New Orleans," in *Against the Odds: Free Blacks in the Slave Societies of the Americas*, ed. Jane G. Landers (London: Frank Cass, 1996), 60; Jane G. Landers, *Black Society in Spanish Florida* (Urbana: University of Illinois Press, 1999), 8; and Jane G. Landers, "*Cimarrón* and Citizen: African Ethnicity, Corporate Identity, and the Evolution of Free Black Towns in the Spanish Circum-Caribbean," in *Slaves, Subjects, and Subversives: Blacks in Colonial Latin America*, ed. Jane Landers and Barry Robinson (Albuquerque: University of New Mexico Press, 2006), 113.

26. See Nader, *Liberty in Absolutist Spain*, 33.

27. As cited in Paul Charney, "Much too worthy. . .": Indians in Seventeenth-Century Lima," in *City Indians in Spain's American Empire: Urban Indigenous Society in Colonial Mesoamerica and Andean South America, 1530–1810*, ed. Dana Velasco Murillo, Mark Lentz, and Margarita R. Ochoa (Brighton: Sussex Academic Press, 2012), 88.

28. See Kathryn Burns, *Into the Archive: Writing and Power in Colonial Peru* (Durham: Duke University Press, 2010), 157n42; also see Rolena Adorno, "Images of *Indios Ladinos* in Early Colonial Peru," in *Transatlantic Encounters: Europeans and Andeans in the Sixteenth Century*, ed. Kenneth J. Andrien and Rolena Adorno (Berkeley: University of California Press, 1991), 232–70; Thierry Saignes, "Indian Migration and Social Change in Seventeenth-Century Charcas," in *Ethnicity, Markets and Migration in the Andes: At the Crossroads of History and Anthropology*, ed. Brooke Larson and Olivia Harris (Durham: Duke University Press, 1995), 184–85; Stuart B. Schwartz and Frank Salomon, "New Peoples and New Kinds of People: Adaptation, Readjustment, and Ethnogenesis in South American Indigenous Societies (Colonial Era)," in *The Cambridge History of the Native Peoples of the Americas*, vol. 3, *South America*, ed. Frank Salomon and Stuart B. Schwartz (Cambridge: Cambridge University Press, 1999), 454–55.

29. Apparently this sentiment remains in the contemporary period. Kevin Terraciano notes how at a 2001 conference in Mexico, indigenous peoples bemoaned the fate of native peoples who had "left their home communities to live in cities." See Terraciano, "Concluding Remarks," in *City Indians in Spain's American Empire: Urban Indigenous Society in Colonial Mesoamerica and Andean South America, 1530–1810*, ed. Dana Velasco Murillo, Mark Lentz, and Margarita R. Ochoa (Brighton: Sussex Academic Press, 2012), 221. On social death, see James H. Sweet, *Recreating Africa: Culture, Kinship, and Religion in the African-Portuguese World, 1441–1770* (Chapel Hill: University of North Carolina Press, 2003), 32–39; Orlando Patterson, *Slavery and Social Death: A Comparative Study* (Cambridge: Harvard University Press, 1982), 38–65.

30. James Lockhart, for example, argues that "the moment an individual was detached from his or her cultural, social, and geographical setting, that person usually swung quickly to the acceptance end of the spectrum" (in this case, Spanish society). See "Receptivity and Resistance," 316. See also Paul Charney, "El indio urbano: Un análisis económica y social de la población india de Lima en 1613," *Histórica* 12.1 (1988): 5–33.

31. For examples, see Karen Spalding, *De indio a campesino: Cambios en la estructura social del Perú colonial* (Lima: Instituto de Estudios Peruanos 1974): 177–78; Steve Stern, *Peru's Indian Peoples and the Challenge of Spanish Conquest: Huamanga to 1640* (Madison: University of Wisconsin Press, 1993), 158–83; Martin Minchom, *The People of Quito, 1690–1810: Change and Unrest in the Underclass* (Boulder: Westview Press, 1994), 189–90; Harris, "Ethnic Identity and Market Relations," 358.

32. On the association between urban attributes and Hispanization, see Harris, "Ethnic Identity and Market Relations," 357–59. On native peoples being "detribalized" because they no longer lived in indigenous communities, see Peter Stern, "Marginals and Acculturation in Frontier Society," in *New Views of Borderlands History*, ed. Robert H. Jackson (Albuquerque: University of New Mexico Press, 1998), 162.

33. See Christopher Lutz, *Santiago de Guatemala, 1541–1773: City, Caste, and the Colonial Experience* (Norman: University of Oklahoma Press, 1994); R. Douglas Cope, *The Limits of Racial Domination: Plebeian Society in Colonial Mexico City, 1660–1720* (Madison: University of Wisconsin Press, 1994); Robinson A. Herrera, *Natives, Europeans, and Africans in Sixteenth-Century Santiago de Guatemala* (Austin: University of Texas Press, 2003). John K. Chance's study of Antequera, Oaxaca, however, offers greater insight into the dynamics of the city's urban Indian population; see *Race and Class in Colonial Oaxaca* (Stanford: Stanford University Press, 1978).

34. For mestizos in the colonial period, see Minchom, *People of Quito*, 153–99; Berta Ares Queija, "El papel de mediadores y la construcción de un discurso sobre la identidad de los mestizos peruanos (siglo XVI)," in *Entre dos mundos: Fronteras culturales y agentes mediadores*, ed. Berta Ares Queija and Serge Gruzinski (Seville: Escuela de Estudios Hispano-americanos, 1997), 37–59; Schwartz and Salomon, "New Peoples and New Kinds of People," 477–94; Marisol de la Cadena, "Are *Mestizos* Hybrids? The Conceptual Politics of Andean Identities," *Journal of Latin American Studies* 37.2 (2005): 259–84; Joanne Rappaport, *The Disappearing Mestizo: Configuring Difference in the Colonial New Kingdom of Granada* (Durham: Duke University Press, 2014).

35. For Sarah C. Chambers's discussion of the status of mestizos in late eighteenth and nineteenth centuries Arequipa, Peru, see "Little Middle Ground: The Instability of a Mestizo Identity in the Andes, Eighteenth and Nineteenth Centuries," in *Race and Nation in Modern Latin America*, ed. Nancy P. Appelbaum, Anne S. Macpherson, and Karin Alejandra Rosemblatt (Chapel Hill: University of North Carolina Press, 2003), 33.

36. See Chambers, "Little Middle Ground," 41–42, 49; John K. Chance, "On the Mexican Mestizo," *Latin American Research Review* 14.3 (1979): 153–68. Both authors agree that not being Indian was the only shared attribute of mestizos.

37. Kathryn Burns argues that the term *montañés* did not "stick" or "enter into wider usage." See *Into the Archive*, 50–51.

38. See Stern, "Marginals and Acculturation," 160–61.

39. See Schwartz and Salomon, "New Peoples and New Kinds of People," 479–80.

40. See Ares Queija, "El papel de mediadores," 43–45. This shift reflected Spanish anxieties that some high-standing mestizos constituted potential political and social threats to Spanish rule.

41. See Claudio Esteva Fabregat, "Población y mestizaje en las ciudades de Iberoamérica: Siglo XVIII," in *Estudios sobre la ciudad iberoamericana*, ed. Francisco de Solano (Madrid: Consejo Superior de Investigaciones Científicas, 1983), 597; Magnus Mörner, *Race Mixture in the History of Latin America* (Boston: Little, Brown, 1967), 98–100.

42. For further examples of the close connections between mestizos and native peoples, see Robert C. Schwaller, "The Importance of Mestizos and Mulatos as Bilingual Intermediaries in Sixteenth-Century New Spain," *Ethnohistory* 59.4 (2012): 716–18; the examples in Aaron P Althouse, "Contested Mestizos, Alleged Mulattos: Racial Identity and Caste Hierarchy in Eighteenth-Century Pátzcuaro, Mexico," *Americas* 62.2 (2005): 157–66; Mangan, "Market of Identities," 71–76; Rappaport, *Disappearing Mestizo*, 61–87.

43. Berta Ares Queija employs the term *indianizando* to describe how the image of mestizos became associated with native peoples in late sixteenth-century Peru. See "El papel de mediadores," 44.

44. For an excellent study of the evolution of cultural identities among Nahuas and Oaxacan ethnic groups who settled near Santiago de Guatemala, see Laura E. Matthew, *Memories of Conquest: Becoming Mexicano in Colonial Guatemala* (Chapel Hill: University of North Carolina Press, 2012).

45. As John R. Wunder points out, "Acculturation has a native voice, native choices, and native strategies." See "Native American History, Ethnohistory, and Context," *Ethnohistory* 54.4 (2007): 600.

46. James Lockhart, *The Nahuas After the Conquest: A Social and Cultural History of the Indians of Central Mexico, Sixteenth Through Eighteenth Centuries* (Stanford: Stanford University Press, 1992), 57.

47. As Schwartz and Salomon point out, indigenous peoples and groups had undergone ethnic and cultural transformations prior to the Spanish invasion. See "New Peoples and New Kinds of People," 445–48.

48. See Stern, *Peru's Indian Peoples*, 165–69.

49. For Lockhart's exposition of "receptivity," see "Receptivity and Resistance," 304–32.

50. The New Conquest History reconsiders the encounters of indigenous peoples and Spaniards in the Americas from distinct perspectives and trajectories. This approach places native peoples at the center of the narrative, questions the concept of conquest as a onetime military episode, and illustrates how indigenous peoples and institutions persisted under Spanish rule. See, for example, Matthew, *Memories of Conquest*. For urban Indians in Mexico, see John K. Chance, "The Urban Indian in Colonial Oaxaca," *American Ethnologist* 3.4 (1976): 603–32; Luis Fernando Granados, "Cosmopolitan Indians and Mesoamerican Barrios in Bourbon Mexico City: Tribute, Community, Family, and Work in 1800" (PhD diss., Georgetown University, 2008); Felipe Castro Gutiérrez, ed., *Los indios y las ciudades de la Nueva España* (México: Universidad Nacional Autónoma de México, Instituto

de Investigaciones Históricas, 2010); Margarita R. Ochoa, "Gender, Power, and Authority in Indigenous Mexico City, 1700–1829" (PhD diss., University of New Mexico, 2011); Dana Velasco Murillo, Mark Lentz, and Margarita R. Ochoa, eds., *City Indians in Spain's American Empire: Urban Indigenous Society in Colonial Mesoamerica and Andean South America, 1530–1810* (Brighton: Sussex Academic Press, 2012); Corbeil, "Identities in Motion." For the Andes, see Lyn Lowry, "Forging an Indian Nation: Urban Indians Under Spanish Colonial Control (Lima, Peru, 1535–1765)" (PhD diss., University of California, Berkeley, 1991); Jacques Poloni-Simard, *El mosaico indígena: Movilidad, estratificación social y mestizaje en el corregimiento de Cuenca (Ecuador) del siglo XVI al XVIII* (Quito: Editorial Abya-Yala, Instituto Francés de Estudios Andinos, 2006); Karen B. Graubart, *With Our Labor and Sweat: Indigenous Women and the Formation of Colonial Society in Peru, 1550–1700* (Stanford: Stanford University Press, 2007).

51. Many of these histories focus on discrete native communities in central and southern Mexico composed primarily of ethnically homogenous indigenous populations. For some example of this voluminous literature for New Spain, see Gibson, *Aztecs Under Spanish Rule*; Luis Reyes García, *Cuauhtinchan del siglo XII al XVI: Formación y desarrollo histórico de un señorío prehispánico* (Wiesbaden: Franz Steiner Verlag, 1977); Nancy M. Farriss, *Maya Society Under Colonial Rule: The Collective Enterprise of Survival* (Princeton: Princeton University Press, 1984); Sarah L. Cline, *Colonial Culhuacan, 1580–1600: A Social History of an Aztec Town* (Albuquerque: University of New Mexico Press, 1986); Bernardo García Martínez, *Los pueblos de la sierra: El poder y el espacio entre los indios del norte de Puebla hasta 1700* (México: El Colegio de México, 1987); Louise M. Burkhart, *The Slippery Earth: Nahua-Christian Moral Dialogue in Sixteenth-Century Mexico* (Tucson: University of Arizona Press, 1989); Susan Schroeder, *Chimalpahin and the Kingdoms of Chalco* (Tucson: University of Arizona Press, 1991); Robert Haskett, *Indigenous Rulers: An Ethnohistory of Town Government in Colonial Cuernavaca* (Albuquerque: University of New Mexico Press, 1991); Lockhart, *Nahuas After the Conquest*; Margarita Menegus Bornemann, *Del señorío indígena a la república de indios: El caso de Toluca, 1500–1600* (México: Consejo Nacional para la Cultura y las Artes, 1994); Pedro Bracamonte y Sosa, *La memoria enclaustrada: Historia indígena de Yucatán 1750–1915* (México: Centro de Investigaciones y Estudios Superiores en Antropología Social, 1994), 23–96; Susan Kellogg, *Law and the Transformation of Aztec Culture, 1500–1700* (Norman: University of Oklahoma Press, 1995); María de los Ángeles Romero Frizzi, *El sol y la cruz: Los pueblos indios de Oaxaca colonial* (México: Centro de Investigaciones y Estudios Superiores en Antropología Social, 1996); Rebecca Horn, *Postconquest Coyoacan: Nahua-Spanish Relations in Central Mexico, 1590–1650* (Stanford: Stanford University Press, 1997); Matthew Restall, *The Maya World: Yucatec Culture and Society, 1550–1850* (Stanford: Stanford University Press, 1997); Susan Schroeder, Stephanie Wood, and Robert Haskett, eds., *Indian Women of Early Mexico* (Norman: University of Oklahoma Press, 1997); Peter Sigal, *From Moon Goddesses to Virgins: The Colonization of Yucatecan Maya Sexual Desire* (Austin: University of Texas Press, 2000); Kevin Terraciano, *The Mixtecs of Colonial Oaxaca:*

Ñudzahui History, Sixteenth through Eighteenth Centuries (Stanford: University of Stanford Press, 2001); Stephanie Wood, *Transcending Conquest: Nahua Views of Spanish Colonial Mexico* (Norman: University of Oklahoma Press, 2003); Brian Philip Owensby, *Empire of Law and Indian Justice in Colonial Mexico* (Stanford: Stanford University Press, 2008); Yanna Yannakakis, *The Art of Being In-Between: Native Intermediaries, Indian Identity, and Local Rule in Colonial Oaxaca* (Durham: Duke University Press, 2008); Caterina Pizzigoni, *The Life Within: Local Indigenous Society in Mexico's Toluca Valley, 1650–1800* (Stanford: Stanford University Press, 2012); David Tavárez, *The Invisible War: Indigenous Devotions, Discipline, and Dissent in Colonial Mexico* (Stanford: Stanford University Press, 2013); Mark Z. Christensen, *Nahua and Maya Catholicisms: Texts and Religion in Colonial Central Mexico and Yucatan* (Stanford: Stanford University Press and The Academy of American Franciscan History, 2013). For northern Mexico, see Radding, *Wandering Peoples*; Deeds, *Defiance and Deference*; José Refugio de la Torre Curiel, *Twilight of the Mission Frontier: Shifting Interethnic Alliances and Social Organization in Sonora, 1768–1855* (Stanford: Stanford University Press and The Academy of American Franciscan History, 2012); Raphael B. Folsom, *The Yaquis and the Empire: Violence, Spanish Imperial Power, and Native Resilience in Colonial Mexico* (New Haven: Yale University Press, 2014).

52. Most of the northern provinces lack the rich corpus of native-language documents of central and southern Mexico. For a discussion of the challenges confronting ethnohistorians of northern Mexico, see Radding, *Wandering Peoples*, xv–xviii; Deeds, *Defiance and Deference*, 1–11.

53. Deeds, *Defiance and Deference*, 9.

54. Even James Lockhart acknowledged that the study of native peoples could "profit greatly from further research in relevant purely Spanish sources." See Lockhart, *Nahuas After the Conquest*, 9.

CHAPTER 1. A TALE OF TWO SETTLEMENTS, 1546–1559

1. Bakewell, citing the nineteenth-century historian Elías de Amador, insists that Tolosa did not operate under his own initiative but explored the area at the request of Cristóbal de Oñate. Oñate was already a wealthy *encomendero*, or recipient of a grant of indigenous labor, of New Galicia. He eventually became one of the recognized founders of Zacatecas. See Bakewell, *Silver Mining and Society*, 7.

2. The origin of Zacatecas's discovery and foundation is the subject of distinct retellings by contemporaries, colonial chroniclers, and early historians. For examples, see José I. Dávila Garibi, *La sociedad de Zacatecas en los albores del régimen colonial: Actuación de los principales fundadores y primeros funcionarios públicos de la ciudad* (México: Antigua Librería Robredo de J. Porrúa e Hijos, 1939); Bakewell, *Silver Mining and Society*, 4–25.

3. The native peoples who originally occupied the area that became the city of Zacatecas appear in archival documents, chronicles, and contemporary scholarship as the Zacatecas, Zacateco, and Zacatecos. For issues of clarity, this study refers to them as Zacatecos.

4. Scholars define Mesoamerica as a preconquest indigenous zone with shared cultural features that encompasses central and southern Mexico, Guatemala,

Belize, Honduras, and El Salvador. For a summary of the state's preconquest indigenous groups, see Leonardo López Luján, *Nómadas y sedentarios: El pasado prehispánico de Zacatecas* (México: Instituto Nacional de Antropología e Historia, 1989).

5. See Peter F. Jiménez Betts and J. Andrew Darling, "Archaeology of Southern Zacatecas: The Malpaso, Juchipila and Valparaíso-Bolaños Valleys," in *Greater Mesoamerica: The Archaeology of West and Northwestern Mexico*, ed. Michael S. Foster and Shirley Gorenstein (Salt Lake City: University of Utah Press, 2000), 175.

6. The Loma San Gabriel culture predominated in eastern Durango and extended to parts of western Zacatecas. For a summary of the indigenous cultures of western and northwestern Mexico, see Shirley Gorenstein and Michael S. Foster, "West and Northwest Mexico: The Ins and Outs of Mesoamerica," in *Greater Mesoamerica: The Archaeology of West and Northwestern Mexico*, ed. Michael S. Foster and Shirley Gorenstein (Salt Lake City: University of Utah Press, 2000), 3–19.

7. Jiménez Betts and Darling, "Archeology of Southern Zacatecas," 160.

8. Arguments that the Chalchihuites culture extended southward are based on shared ceramic characteristics. For a summary of the debate, see Jiménez Betts and Darling, "Archaeology of Southern Zacatecas," 155–80.

9. See Manuel Gamio, *Los monumentos arqueológicos de las inmediaciones de Chalchihuites* (México: Museo Nacional de Arqueología, Historia y Etnología, 1910); J. C. Kelley, "Archeology of the Northern Frontier: Zacatecas and Durango," in *Handbook of Middle American Indians*, ed. R. Wauchope (Austin: University of Texas Press, 1971), vol. 11, pt. 2: 768–801; Phil C. Weigand, "La prehistoria del estado de Zacatecas: Una interpretación," in *Zacatecas: Anuario de Historia I* (Zacatecas: Universidad Autónoma de Zacatecas, 1978), 203–48.

10. During the colonial period, settlers called the site and the *hacienda*, or agricultural complex, La Quemada (the burned one), because of its scorched building. The hacienda was built with stones removed from the complex.

11. See Charles D. Trombold, "A Population Estimate for the Epiclassic Middle Malpaso Valley (La Quemada), Zacatecas, Mexico," *Latin American Antiquity* 16.3 (2005): 236; Ben A. Nelson, "Chronology and Stratigraphy at La Quemada, Zacatecas, Mexico," *Journal of Field Archaeology* 24.1 (1997): 85.

12. See Arturo Maldonado Romero and Peter F. Jiménez Betts, *La Quemada: Estabilización y consolidación de restos arqueológicos* (Zacatecas: Universidad Autónoma de Zacatecas, 2003), 19.

13. See Jiménez Betts and Darling, "Archaeology of Southern Zacatecas," 160.

14. Charles D. Trumbold, "A Summary of the Archaeology of the La Quemada Region," in *The Archaeology of West and Northwest Mesoamerica*, ed. Michael S. Foster and Phil C. Weigand (Boulder: Westview Press, 1985), 327–52. Archaeological evidence uncovered signs of frequent violence at the complex, including hundreds of skeletal remains. See Weigand, "Mining and Mineral Trade," 91–92.

15. See Ben A. Nelson, J. Andrew Darling, and Andrew A. Kice, "Mortuary Practices and the Social Order at La Quemada, Zacatecas, Mexico," *Latin American Antiquity* 3.4 (1992): 298–315.

16. See Nelson, Darling, and Kice, "Mortuary Practices and the Social Order at La Quemada," 299.

17. See E. Christian Wells, "Pottery Production and Microcosmic Organization: The Residential Structure of La Quemada, Zacatecas," *Latin American Antiquity* 11.1 (2000): 23–24.

18. Arturo Maldonado Romero and Peter F. Jiménez Betts argue that the site was abandoned much earlier, in the eleventh century. See *La Quemada: Estabilización y consolidación*, 19.

19. Jiménez Betts and Darling, "Archaeology of Southern Zacatecas," 167.

20. James Lockhart and Stuart B. Schwartz classify native groups into three categories: "sedentary," "semisedentary," and "nonsedentary." See *Early Latin America: A History of Colonial Spanish America and Brazil* (Cambridge: Cambridge University Press, 1983), 37–57. Matthew Restall and Kris Lane revised this scheme to distinguish two forms of sedentary, "concentrated" and "segmented," or empire or nonempire peoples. See *Latin America in Colonial Times* (Cambridge: Cambridge University Press, 2011), 12–16.

21. Ida Altman's study of New Galicia finds no evidence that "tribute was collected on a regular basis in the region at the time of contact." See *The War for Mexico's West: Indians and Spaniards in New Galicia, 1524–1550* (Albuquerque: University of New Mexico Press, 2010), 71, 84.

22. For further distinctions between the characteristics of semisedentary and nonsedentary peoples, see Restall and Lane, *Latin America in Colonial Times*, 14–15.

23. For an overview of native groups of northern Mexico, see Susan Deeds, "Legacies of Resistance, Adaptation, and Tenacity: History of the Native Peoples of Northwest Mexico," and David Frye, "The Native Peoples of Northeastern Mexico," both in *The Cambridge History of the Native Peoples of the Americas*, vol. 2, *Mesoamerica*, ed. Richard E. W. Adams and Murdo J. MacLeod (Cambridge: Cambridge University Press, 2000), pt. 2, 44–88 and 89–135, respectively.

24. Chichimec derives from the Nahuatl *chichimecatl*. For translations and interpretations, see Frances Karttunen, *An Analytical Dictionary of Nahuatl* (Norman: University of Oklahoma Press, 1992), 48. For a repudiation of the ethnic homogeneity of indigenous groups of northern Mexico, see Edward H. Spicer, *Cycles of Conquest: The Impact of Spain, Mexico, and the United States on the Indians of the Southwest, 1533–1960* (Tucson: University of Arizona Press, 1962). For the vilification of groups who choose to live outside "state" areas, see James C. Scott, *The Art of Not Being Governed: An Anarchist History of Upland Southeast Asia* (New Haven: Yale University Press, 2009).

25. On the different meanings that Spaniards associated with the term, see Charlotte M. Gradie, "Discovering the Chichimecas," *Americas* 51.1 (1994): 67–88. On the processes by which Spaniards identified and named northern indigenous groups, see Chantal Cramaussell, "De cómo los españoles clasificaban a los indios: Naciones y encomiendas en la Nueva Vizcaya central," in *Nómadas y sedentarios en el norte de México: Homenaje a Beatriz Braniff*, ed. Marie-Areti Hers, José Luis Mirafuentes, Mara de los Dolores Soto, and Miguel Vallebueno (México: Universidad Nacional Autónoma de México, 2000), 275–303.

26. For further studies on native peoples north of Mexico City, see Isauro Rionda Arreguín, ed., *Comunidades indígenas en Guanajuato: Pasado y presente*

de los chichimecas (Guanajuato: Archivo General del Gobierno del Estado de Guanajuato, 1996); Beatriz Braniff and Marie-Areti Hers, "Herencias chichimecas," *Arqueología* 19 (1998): 55–80; Carlos Viramontes Anzures, *De chichimecas, pames y jonaces: Los recolectores-cazadores del semidesierto de Querétaro* (México: Instituto Nacional de Antropología e Historia, 2000); see also the various essays in Marie-Areti Hers et al., eds., *Nómadas y sedentarios en el norte de México*.

27. See Radding, *Wandering Peoples*, xvi–xviii; Deeds, *Defiance and Deference*, 1–11.

28. Indigenous accounts include the Florentine Codex (see note 33) and the copious writings of the Amecamecan Domingo de San Antón Muñón Chimalpahin Quauhtlehuanitzin. For the latter, see Arthur Anderson and Susan Schroeder, eds. and trans., *Codex Chimalpahin: Society and Politics in Mexico Tenochtitlan, Tlatelolco, Texcoco, Culhuacan, and Other Nahua Altepetl in Central Mexico: The Nahuatl and Spanish Annals and Accounts Collected and Recorded by Don Domingo de San Antón Muñón Chimalpahin Quauhtlehuanitzin* (Norman: University of Oklahoma Press, 1997); James Lockhart, Susan Schroeder, and Doris Namala, eds. and trans., *Annals of His Time: Don Domingo de San Antón Muñón Chimalpahin Quauhtlehuanitzin* (Stanford: Stanford University Press, 2006). For mestizo chroniclers, see Diego Muñoz Camargo, *Historia de Tlaxcala*, ed. Germán Vázquez (Madrid: Historia 16, [1585] 1986); Hernando de Alvarado Tezozomoc, *Crónica mexicana* (Barcelona: Linkgua Ediciones, [1598] 1992); and Fernando de Alva Ixtlilxochitl, *Historia de la nación chichimeca* (Barcelona: Linkgua Ediciones, [1640] 1985).

29. The most prominent colonial chroniclers of New Galicia include Alonso de la Mota y Escobar, *Descripción geográfica de los reinos de Nueva Galicia, Nueva Vizcaya y Nuevo León* (México: Editorial Pedro Robredo, [c. 1600] 1940); Domingo Lázaro de Arregui, *Descripción de la Nueva Galicia* (Sevilla: Escuela de Estudios Hispano-Americanos de la Universidad de Sevilla, [1621] 1946); Antonio Tello, *Crónica miscelánea y conquista espiritual y temporal de la Sancta provincia de Xalisco en el Nuevo Reino de la Galicia y Nueva Vizcaya y descubrimiento del Nuevo Mexico, escrito por fray Antonio Tello en 1653* (Guadalajara: Tip. de "La República Literaria" de Ciro L. de Guevara y Ca., [1650] 1890); José A. Arlegui, *Crónica de la provincia de n.s.p.s Francisco de Zacatecas* (México: J. Bernardo de Hogal, [1737] 1960); and Matías de la Mota Padilla, *Historia de la conquista del reino de la Nueva Galicia* (Guadalajara: Talleres Gráficos de Gallardo y Álvarez del Castillo, [1742] 1920).

30. See Altman, *War for Mexico's West*, 18–19.

31. However, the Spanish settler Domingo Lázaro de Arregui's 1621 chronicle offers, at times, a surprisingly impartial ethnography. See *Descripción de la Nueva Galicia*, 26–38.

32. Mota y Escobar, *Descripción geográfica*, 31–36.

33. The *Historia general de las cosas de Nueva España* (also known as the Florentine Codex) comprises twelve books on a variety of aspects of native culture in Nahuatl and Spanish. Indigenous elites composed the native-language sections of the book under the guidance of the Spanish friar Bernardino de Sahagún between 1540 and 1585. The Florentine Codex's description of the "Çacachichimeca"

probably reflects the conflation of the lifeways of several of the area's indigenous groups. See Sahagún, *The Florentine Codex: General History of the Things of New Spain*, vol. 10, *The People*, trans. Arthur J. O. Anderson and Charles E. Dibble (Santa Fe: School of American Research, 1975), 171–75.

34. See Gonzalo de las Casas, *La guerra de los chichimecas*, ed. José Fernando Ramírez and Luis González Obregón (México: Editor Vargas Rea, 1944); Pedro de Ahumada Sámano, *Relación sobre la rebelión de los indios zacatecas* (México: Editor Vargas Rea, [1562] 1954). See also Carlos Sempat Assadourían, *Zacatecas: Conquista y transformación de la frontera en el siglo XVI* (México: El Colegio de México, 2008).

35. José del Refugio Gasca, *Timbres y laureles zacatecanos: Escritos en verso* (Zacatecas: Impr. Económica de M. Ruiz de Esparza, 1902), 15.

36. Scholarly debate exists over whether Zacatecos or other ethnic groups, or both, immediately occupied La Quemada after its collapse. See Jiménez Betts and Darling, "Archaeology of Southern Zacatecas," 167.

37. See Peter Gerhard, *The North Frontier of New Spain* (Norman: University of Oklahoma Press, 1993), 158.

38. Salvador Vidal, *Estudio histórico de la ciudad de Zacatecas* (México: Arcimiaga, 1955), 2.

39. Estimates place the postconquest Zacateco population (c. 1620 to 1625) at 1,500. See Frye, "Native Peoples of Northeastern Mexico," 112.

40. Other groups listed by Las Casas include Pames, Guamares, and Guachachiles. See *La guerra de los Chichimecas*, 22, 24.

41. In 1519, the Zacatecos occupied an estimated sixty thousand square kilometers of territory. See Frye, "Native Peoples of Northeastern Mexico," 112.

42. There is no record of the language(s) spoken by the Zacatecos. H. R. Harvey claimed that Zacateco was a Nahua language and had a Uto-Aztecan linguistic base. See "The *Relaciones geográficas, 1579–1586*: Native Languages," in *Handbook of Middle American Indians*, ed. Robert Wauchope (Austin: University of Texas Press, 1972), 12:300. Miguel Othón de Mendizábal argued that Zacateco, like many indigenous languages in New Galicia, shared similarities with Nahuatl because of frequent interactions with central Mexicans. See Miguel Othón de Mendizábal, *Obras completas* (México: La Cooperativa de Trabajadores de los Talleres Gráficos de la Nación, Tolosa y Enrico Martínez 1946), 2:206. For challenges to this idea, see Altman, *War for Mexico's West*, 16, 235–36n49.

43. Vidal claims that they lived in small huts on the summit of the Bufa. See *Estudio histórico*, 2. A similar description of diet and living habits appears in Tello, *Crónica miscelánea*, 107–11.

44. New York Public Library, Obadiah Rich Collection (hereafter NYPL, ORC), Simancas, Cartas de Nueva Galicia, f. 267, 1550–51.

45. See Sahagún, *Florentine Codex*, 173–74.

46. See "[Minas del Fresnillo II]," as transcribed in René Acuña, *Relaciones geográficas del siglo XVI: Nueva Galicia* (México: Universidad Nacional Autónoma de México, Instituto de Investigaciones Antropológicas, 1982), 121.

47. See Susan Deeds, "Double Jeopardy: Indian Women in Jesuit Missions," in *Indian Women*, 257. Lázaro de Arregui also briefly mentions indigenous women's

roles in his 1621 account. See *Descripción de la Nueva Galicia*, 36. For gender complementarity in central and southern Mexico, see Susan Kellogg, "From Parallel and Equivalent to Separate but Unequal: Tenochca Mexica Women, 1500–1700," in *Indian Women*, 123–43; Lisa Mary Sousa, "Women and Crime in Colonial Oaxaca: Evidence of Complementary Gender Roles in Mixtec and Zapotec Societies," in *Indian Women*, 199–214.

48. Deeds, "Double Jeopardy," 257–58; Deeds, *Defiance and Deference*, 46; Sahagún, *Florentine Codex*, 171–75.

49. For the Cazcanes and the Zacatecos, see Altman, *War for Mexico's West*, 279n60.

50. The Mixton War figures among the largest battles that took place in New Spain, second only to the siege of Tenochtitlan. The conflict occurred in the southern part of the state in the Juchipila Valley. For an account of the war, including indigenous perspectives, see Altman, *War for Mexico's West*, 121–83; on the conflict, see Arthur Scott Aiton, *Antonio de Mendoza, First Viceroy of New Spain* (Durham: Duke University Press, 1927); Philip Wayne Powell, *Soldiers, Indians, and Silver: The Northward Advance of New Spain, 1550–1600* (Berkeley: University of California Press, 1969); *Tenamaxtli y Guaxicar: Las raíces profundas de la rebelión de Nueva Galicia* (Zamora: Colegio de Michoacán; Guadalajara: Secretaría de Cultura de Jalisco, 1996), 127–40.

51. See Altman, *War for Mexico's West*, 126–46.

52. For indigenous perspectives of the conquest of Tenochtitlan, see Matthew Restall, *The Seven Myths of the Spanish Conquest* (New York: Oxford University Press, 2003); Kevin Terraciano, "Three Texts in One: Book XII of the Florentine Codex," *Ethnohistory* 57.1 (2010): 51–72; William F. Connell, *After Moctezuma: Indigenous Politics and Self-Government in Mexico City, 1524–1730* (Norman: University of Oklahoma Press, 2011); Connell, "Alliance Building and the Restoration of Native Government in the Altepetl of Mexico Tenochtitlan, 1521–1565," in *City Indians*, 8–31. For indigenous allies, see Laura E. Matthew and Michel R. Oudijk, *Indian Conquistadors: Indigenous Allies in the Conquest of Mesoamerica* (Norman: University of Oklahoma Press, 2007); and Matthew, *Memories of Conquest*.

53. Guzmán eventually became governor of New Galicia as well. Ultimately, he ended his career—after a yearlong prison stint in Mexico City—exiled in Spain and shadowed by accusations of mismanagement, abuse of power, and mistreatment of native peoples.

54. For a complete account of Guzmán's destructive campaign in this area, see Altman, *War for Mexico's West*, 20–56.

55. There is little information on the fourth founder, Baltasar Temiño de Bañuelos, a native of Burgos. The three other founders were of Basque descent. See José Manuel Azcona Pastor, *Possible Paradises: Basque Emigration to Latin America* (Reno: University of Nevada Press, 2004), 162–64. For more on the Ibarras, see J. Lloyd Mecham, *Francisco de Ibarra and Nueva Vizcaya* (New York: Greenwood Press, 1968); for Juanes de Tolosa, see José Enciso Contreras and Ana Hilda Reyes Veyna, *Juanes de Tolosa descubridor de las minas de Zacatecas, información de méritos y servicios* (Zacatecas: Tribunal Superior de Justicia de Zacatecas, 2002).

56. The founders of Zacatecas fit the social profile that James Lockhart outlines for the men who invaded Peru. They had been in the Indies for several years and had family connections in the Americas. See *The Men of Cajamarca: A Social and Biographical Study of the First Conquerors of Peru* (Austin: University of Texas Press, 1972), 22–26.

57. See Bret Blosser, "'By the Force of their Lives and the Spilling of Blood': Flechero Service and Political Leverage on a Nueva Galicia Frontier," in *Indian Conquistadors*, 289–316; Altman, *War for Mexico's West*.

58. See Robert C. West, "Early Silver Mining in New Spain, 1531–1555," in *In Quest of Mineral Wealth: Aboriginal and Colonial Mining and Metallurgy in Spanish America*, ed. Alan K. Craig and Robert C. West (Baton Rouge: Geoscience Publications, Department of Geography and Anthropology, Louisiana State University, 1994), 122–23. For an example from central Mexico, see Archivo General de Indias (hereafter AGI), Justicia, ff. 13–16v, 1564.

59. Accounts do not agree on the ethnicity of the Indians that informed Tolosa of the ores at Zacatecas.

60. See Arlegui, *Crónica de la provincia*, 35.

61. Gasca, *Timbres y laureles zacatecanos*, 7.

62. Francisco Frejes claimed that "there was no war with the Indians in the conquest of Zacatecas." See his *Memoria de la conquista de Zacatecas que para la historia general del estado escribió el R. P. Fr. Francisco Frexes del Colegio de N. S. De Guadalupe* (Zacatecas: Imprenta a cargo de Pedro Piña, 1834), 9. See also Gasca, *Timbres y laureles zacatecanos*, 8.

63. See "[Minas de San Demetrio]," 106–7; "[Minas del Fresnillo II]," 121, as transcribed in Acuña, *Relaciones geográficas*.

64. Eugo B. Sego identifies a Zacateco barrio in a map of Chalchihuites but provides no other information on this ethnic group. See *Aliados y adversarios: Los colonos tlaxcaltecas en la frontera septentrional de Nueva España* (San Luis Potosí: El Colegio de San Luis, 1998), 282. San Andrés (de Teul) was located fifteen miles from Chalchihuites. Santa Clara was nine miles further.

65. Biblioteca Nacional, Mexico City, Archivo del Fondo Franciscano (hereafter BNM, AFF), box 58, folder 1160, no. 1, 1622.

66. Francisco Frejes, *Historia breve de la conquista de los estados independientes del imperio mexicano* (Guadalajara: Tip. de S. Banda, Exconvento de Sta. María de Gracia, 1878), 191; Frye, "Native Peoples of Northeastern Mexico," 113–14.

67. Frye, "Native Peoples of Northeastern Mexico," 113–14.

68. For an overview of the frontier wars of 1550 to 1590, see Philip Wayne Powell, "Spanish Warfare Against the Chichimecas in the 1570s," *Hispanic American Historical Review* 24.4 (1944): 580–604; and Powell, *Soldiers, Indians, and Silver*, 57–119; Alberto Carrillo Cázares, *El debate sobre la guerra chichimeca, 1531–1585: Derecho y política en Nueva España* (San Luis Potosí: El Colegio de San Luis, 2000), 1:39–221.

69. Connell, "Alliance Building and the Restoration," 8–31.

70. For the activities around peacemaking, see Philip Wayne Powell, "Peacemaking on North America's First Frontier," *Americas* 16.3 (1960): 221–50; and Powell, *Soldiers, Indians, and Silver*, 204–23.

71. AGI, Contaduría 851, 1590–1604.

72. See "Relación de Nuestra Señora de los Zacatecas, sacada de la información que, por mandado del Consejo, en ella se hizo el año de 1608" (hereafter Anonymous, "Relación"), as transcribed in *Pedro de Valencia, obras completas*, ed. Jesús Paniagua Pérez and Rafael González Cañal, Humanistas Españoles (Salamanca: Secretariado de Publicaciones de la Universidad de León, 1995), 5:298–99; AGI, Contaduría 851, 1590–1604. A ducat, or *ducado*, was the equivalent of eleven silver reales. If the number given by the royal official in 1608 is to be believed, maintaining the peace was costing the crown 444,000 reales a year. Yet this sum paled in comparison to that of the financial and human toll exacted by the war. In 1561, property losses alone from "Chichimec" incursions totaled from seven hundred thousand to eight hundred thousand ducados. Estimates of human casualities in the period from Zacatecas's founding in 1546 to 1561 included two hundred Spaniards and more than two thousand indigenous allies and settlers. See Powell, *Soldiers, Indians, and Silver*, 61–62.

73. See AGI, Contaduría, 851, 1590–1603; Powell, "Peacemaking," 226–28.

74. Although Zacatecas did not come under direct assault, men were expected to take an active role in leading campaigns against "Chichimecs" in nearby areas. See Powell, *Soldiers, Indians, and Silver*, 65.

75. See "[Minas de San Demetrio]," as transcribed in Acuña, *Relaciones geográficas*, 108.

76. Las Casas's account makes clear that that the supply trains bringing goods to Zacatecas formed the target of these attacks, not the mining camp itself. See *La guerra de los chichimecas*, 47–48.

77. Measurements were very imprecise in this period. The actual distance of a league could vary by place or official. I follow Barbara E. Mundy's approximation of 4.3 kilometers, or 2.7 miles. See *The Mapping of New Spain: Indigenous Cartography and the Maps of the Relaciones Geográficas* (Chicago: University of Chicago Press, 1996), 57.

78. Las Casas, *La guerra de los chichimecas*, 47; Bakewell, *Silver Mining and Society*, 22.

79. Powell, *Soldiers, Indians, and Silver*, 74.

80. Powell, *Soldiers, Indians, and Silver*, 74–75.

81. NYPL, ORC, Simancas, Cartas de Nueva Galicia, f. 267, 1551.

82. NYPL, ORC, Simancas, Cartas de Nueva Galicia, f. 262v, 1549.

83. The complete title of his account was *Relación hecha por D. Pedro de Ahumada sobre la rebelión de los indios zacatecos y guachichiles y de la alteración en que pusieron el reino de la Galicia, 1562*. See also Powell, "Spanish Warfare Against the Chichimecas," 587.

84. Deeds, *Defiance and Deference*, 24.

85. The year 1548 marked the discovery of three rich mines, assuring the town, under the shadow of abandonment, of its survival and prosperity.

86. For indigenous draft labor, see Tandeter, *Coercion and Market*; Bakewell, *Miners of the Red Mountain*; Silvio Arturo Zavala, *El servicio personal de los indios en la Nueva España* (México: Colegio de México, Centro de Estudios Históricos, 1984); Susan Deeds, "Rural Work in Nueva Vizcaya: Forms of Labor

Coercion on the Periphery," *Hispanic American Historical Review* 69.3 (1989): 425–49; Haskett, "'Our Suffering with the Taxco Tribute.'"

87. See Gradie, "Discovering the Chichimecas," 69.
88. See Bakewell, *Miners of the Red Mountain*, 182–83.
89. See Weigand, "Mining and Mineral Trade," 94.
90. Altman, *War for Mexico's West*, 85.
91. Gerhard, *North Frontier*, 158.
92. Sites include Mexico City, northern Mexico, Central America, and Peru. See Bakewell, *Miners of the Red Mountain*, 184–85.
93. West, "Early Silver Mining in New Spain," 131.
94. Haskett, "'Our Suffering with the Taxco Tribute,'" 465–67.
95. Altman, *War for Mexico's West*, 86.
96. AHEZ, Libro de Cabildo, 1, f. 21, 1563.
97. For mining and the Afro-descended population, see Kris Lane, "Africans and Natives in the Mines of Spanish America," in *Beyond Black and Red: African-Native Relations in Colonial Latin America*, ed. Matthew Restall (Albuquerque: University of New Mexico Press, 2005), 159–84; Dana Velasco Murillo and Pablo Miguel Sierra Silva, "Mine Workers and Weavers: Afro-Indigenous Labor Arrangements and Interactions in Puebla and Zacatecas, 1600-1700," in *City Indians*, 104–27.
98. See Velasco Murillo and Sierra Silva, "Mine Workers and Weavers," 110.
99. Among other health problems, mining caused silicosis, pneumonia, and tuberculosis. For the hazards associated with mining, see Brown, *A History of Mining*, 62–63.
100. Miners also used blacks sparingly in Potosí, Bakewell argues, because of similar fears that they would die from the area's cold climate. See *Miners of the Red Mountain*, 56. For Mota y Escobar, *Descripción geográfica*, 122, 151.
101. Peter Bakewell, "Notes on the Mexican Silver Mining Industry in the 1590s," in *Mines of Silver and Gold in the Americas*, ed. Peter Bakewell (Brookfield: Variorum, 1997), 195; Engel Sluiter, *Gold and Silver in Spanish America, c. 1572–1648* (Berkeley: University of California Press, 1998), appendix 3, "Zacatecas y congregaciones de minas della."
102. See Silvio Arturo Zavala, *Los esclavos indios en Nueva España* (México: Colegio Nacional, 1967).
103. The province of Nueva Vizcaya was the site of more cases of coerced labor. Much of this draft or enslaved labor worked on tasks related to mining production. See, for example, José Cuello, "The Persistence of Indian Slavery and Encomienda in the Northeast of Colonial Mexico, 1577-1723," *Journal of Social History* 21.4 (1988): 683–700; Deeds, "Rural Work in Nueva Vizcaya"; Chantal Cramaussel, "La tributación de los indios en el septentrión novohispano," in *Indios, españoles y mestizos en zonas de frontera, siglos XVII–XX*, ed. José Marcos Medina Bustos and Esther Padilla Calderón (Hermosillo: Colegio de Sonora y Colegio de Michoacán, 2013), 19–52.
104. See Altman, *War for Mexico's West*, 84.
105. Gasca, *Timbres y laureles zacatecanos*, 8; Bakewell, *Silver Mining and Society*, 15; Gerhard, *North Frontier*, 158.

106. See West, "Early Silver Mining in New Spain," 123.

107. Peter Bakewell argues that by the early 1550s, indigenous slaves in Zacatecas "formed an insignificant portion of the labor force." See "Zacatecas: An Economic and Social Outline of a Silver Mining District, 1547–1700," in *Provinces of Early Mexico*, ed. Ida Altman and James Lockhart (Los Angeles: UCLA Latin American Center, 1976), 215.

108. Bakewell, *Silver Mining and Society*, 122.

109. Ignacio del Río, "Sobre la aparición del trabajo libre asalariado en el norte de Nueva España, siglos XVI y XVII," in *Estudios históricos sobre la formación del norte de México*, ed. Ignacio del Río (México: Universidad Nacional Autónoma de México, 2009), 27–46.

110. There is a robust literature on the Tlaxcalans in northern New Spain. For example, see David B. Adams, *Las colonias tlaxcaltecas de Coahuila y Nuevo León en la Nueva España: Un aspecto de la colonización del norte de México* (Saltillo: Archivo Municipal de Saltillo, 1991); Andrea Martínez Baracs, "Colonizaciones tlaxcaltecas," *Historia Mexicana* 43.2 (1993): 195–250; Eugene B. Sego, *Aliados y adversarios*; Leslie Scott Offutt, "Defending Corporate Identity on the Northern New Spanish Frontier: San Esteban de Nueva Tlaxcala, 1780–1810," *Americas* 64.3 (2008): 351–75; Sean F. McEnroe, *From Colony to Nationhood in Mexico*.

111. It is unknown what percentage short-term laborers accounted for of the total indigenous workforce. Peter Bakewell argues for frequent indigenous movement between Zacatecas and the south. See Bakewell, "Zacatecas: An Economic and Social Outline," 215. In the early 1550s enough Indians were returning to their home communities to compel the oidor Martínez de la Marcha to order Spanish masters to provide their native laborers with sufficient food for the journey home. I have yet to find evidence that seasonal workers continued to fulfill tribute and draft-labor obligations in their communities of origin. Thierry Saignes found evidence for the Andes that many native migrants retained ties to their home communities. See "Indian Migration and Social Change," 176–79, 183.

112. For concessions to military allies, see Matthew and Oudijk, *Indian Conquistadors*; Matthew, *Memories of Conquest*.

113. See José Enciso Contreras, *Ordenanzas de Zacatecas del siglo XVI y otros documentos normativos neogallegos* (Zacatecas: Ayuntamiento de Zacatecas, 1998), 47.

114. For the defection of draft laborers from their communities, see Bakewell, *Miners of the Red Mountain*; Deeds, "Rural Works in Nueva Vizcaya"; Haskett, "'Our Suffering with the Taxco Tribute'"; Stern, *Peru's Indian Peoples*; Radding, *Wandering Peoples*.

115. Haskett, speaking particularly of Taxco, argues that repartimiento labor in central Mexico "touched the heartland of indigenous society far more directly and much more profoundly than did the labor needs of mines in the North." See "'Our Suffering with the Taxco Tribute,'" 474.

116. Lockhart and Schwartz, *Early Latin America*, 37–39.

117. Haskett, "'Our Suffering with the Taxco Tribute,'" 459.

118. Deeds, "Rural Work in Nueva Vizcaya," 436.

119. Tarascans transported wood to the mines of Taxco. By the sixteenth century they occupied two wards in the central Mexican town. See Haskett, "'Our Suffering with the Taxco Tribute,'" 450–51. In Zacatecas, they established barrios in the city and in several adjacent mining towns. See Gerhard, *North Frontier*, 85.

120. Mota y Escobar, *Descripción geográfica*, 145; Bakewell, "Zacatecas: An Economic and Social Outline," 215. This was not the first infiltration of central Mexicans to the greater area. Weigand cites two "waves" of contact, in the form of trade and colonization, between central Mexico and the Chalchihuites area (c. 350 and 800 C.E.). There is also speculation that La Quemada served as a trading nexus between the central areas and the far north. See Weigand, "Mining and Mineral Trade," 94.

121. See Felipe Castro-Gutiérrez, *Los tarascos y el imperio español, 1600–1740* (México: Universidad Nacional Autónoma de México and Universidad Michoacana de San Nicolás de Hidalgo, 2004), 47–48. Kendall Brown argues that *lazadores*, or labor recruiters, brought native peoples to the mines against their will. See *A History of Mining*, 66.

122. The late eighteenth-century Zacatecan chronicler José Bezanilla Mier y Campa claimed that Spaniards brought Mexicas to "civilize" the Zacatecos by serving as model Indians. But it is more likely that Mexicapan's early residents derived from the initial wage-seeking commoners from central Mexico or the Indians that Tolosa brought in his train. See *Muralla zacatecana de doce preciosas piedras, erigidas en doce sagrados títulos, y contempladas en el patrocinio y patronato de su augustísima patrona y señora María Santísima, para el día ocho de cada mes: por don Joseph Mariano Estevan de Bezanilla Mier y Campa* (México: El Ilustrador Católico, 1909), 22; also Gerhard, *North Frontier*, 158.

123. Martínez de la Marcha dictated a series of ordinances to regulate silver production and labor practices on April 20, 1550. About a week later, on April 27, he promulgated another set of measures directed mainly at the activities and treatment of indigenous laborers. See AGI, Guadalajara 5, ramo 12, 1550. My work draws from transcribed material in Enciso Contreras, *Ordenanzas de Zacatecas*. For the first set, see "Ordenanzas de minas"; for the second, see "Este es un traslado."

124. Bakewell notes that in preconquest times the status of yanacona was hereditary and held by individuals who worked for, but were not part of, an *ayllu*, a traditional indigenous community. See Bakewell, *Miners of the Red Mountain*, 33–60.

125. See Castro Gutiérrez, "El origen y conformación de los barrios de indios," in *Los indios y las ciudades*, 119.

126. See Altman, *War for Mexico's West*, 2010.

127. For example, in 1579, the archbishop of Guadalajara ordered the city's new clerics to take care in instructing the city's "naborías y esclavos" in the Catholic faith. Note the early date and how he distinguishes between *naborías* and slaves. See AHEZ, Libro de Cabildo, 1, f. 84, 1589. The term *peón* also appears sporadically throughout the eighteenth century, when it simply referred to a day laborer.

128. For naborías, see Lockhart and Schwartz, *Early Latin America*, 71; Peter Bakewell argues that over time a naboría in Zacatecas denoted a "full-time

employee" of a Spaniard. See "Notes on the Mexican Silver," 184; "Zacatecas: An Economic and Social Outline," 217.

129. See "Este es un traslado," 47.

130. AHEZ, Libro de Cabildo, 3, f. 69v, 1621.

131. In 1559 the archbishop forbade native peoples from participating in monastery construction without the Audiencia's consent. See AHEZ, Libro de Cabildo, 1, f. 10v, 1560, and f. 60, 1576.

132. AHEZ, Libro de Cabildo, 2, f. 16, 1587.

133. AHEZ, Libro de Cabildo, 2, f. 121v, 1596.

134. AHEZ, Libro de Cabildo, 1, f. 44, 1575. See also Libro de Cabildo, 3, f. 69, 1621; ff. 219–219v, 1630; f. 244v, 1632; f. 293, 1634.

135. AHEZ, Libro de Cabildo, 2, f. 244, 1609.

136. In his 1609 visita of the area, the visitador Gaspar de la Fuente received several complaints from native peoples of mistreatment from Spanish miners and overseers in the hinterland mining towns of Ramos, Fresnillo, and Mazapil. See "Relación de lo hecho por el señor licenciado Gaspar de la Fuente, oidor de esta Real Audiencia, Visitador General de este reino del tiempo que anduvo en la visitas de él," as transcribed by Jean-Pierre Berthe in *Sociedades en construcción: La Nueva Galicia según las visitas de oidores, 1606–1616*, ed. Jean-Pierre Berthe, Thomas Calvo, and Águeda Jiménez Pelayo (Guadalajara: Universidad de Guadalajara, Centre Français d'Études Mexicaines et Centraméricaines, 2000), 120–30.

137. AHEZ, Libro de Cabildo, 4, f. 4; ff. 10–11, 1637.

138. Chapter 5 examines the resurgence of repartimiento-like practices in Zacatecas proper in the late colonial period. See AHEZ, Intendencia, box 1, exp. 3, various loose leaf, 1790.

139. This included placing metal and wood chips in the furnace and carrying metals anywhere other than to the lavadero.

140. See "Este es un traslado," 44.

141. See Bakewell, *Silver Mining and Society*, 126.

142. Miners offering wages greater than those stipulated by the ordinances would receive a fine of ten pesos per indigenous worker. See "Este es un traslado," 50.

143. To be exact, a *real y medio* per day. See "Ordenanzas de minas," 38.

144. For a discussion of the value of silver tailings to indigenous mine laborers, see Bakewell, *Silver Mining and Society*, 125; Ann Zulawski, "Wages, Ore Sharing, and Peasant Agriculture: Labor in Oruro's Silver Mines, 1607–1720," *Hispanic American Historical Review* 67.3 (1987): 405–20; Tandeter, *Coercion and Market*, 88–94.

145. Native peoples also called these furnaces *tochinombos* and in the Andes, *guayras*. See West, "Aboriginal Metallurgy and Metalworking in Spanish America," 14–15.

146. Violation of these measures included such penalties as fines, removal of hornos and bellows, and confiscation of any metals. Native peoples also faced the threat of the lash. See "Ordenanzas de minas" and "Este es un traslado," 25–51.

147. Spanish and indigenous interactions in Zacatecas illustrate Jose Moya's argument that "high levels of social inequality . . . have been generally lower during periods of labor scarcity . . . and in regions where free immigration played a

more significant role than slavery or conquest." See "Introduction," *The Oxford Handbook of Latin American History*, ed. Jose Moya (New York: Oxford University Press, 2011), 4–5.

148. Prospectors discovered the silver veins of La Albarrada on March 1, San Bernabé on June 4, and Pánuco on November 1, 1548. See Bakewell, *Silver Mining and Society*, 14.

149. Gerhard, *North Frontier*, 158.

150. See AGI, Justicia, 167, f. 15, 1564.

151. Frejes, *Historia breve*, 193.

152. Little is known about Pánuco or Veta Grande, as only a small number of colonial documents exist for the two sites. Today, the towns languish in poverty and obscurity, the product of a lack of economic development and infrastructure, as well as population loss—a not uncommon fate of many mining towns.

153. Gasca, *Timbres y laureles zacatecanos*, 88; Frejes, *Historia breve de la conquista*, 195. All that remains of this chapel are the ruins of its facade.

154. NYPL, ORC, Simancas, Cartas de Nueva Galicia, f. 261, 1549.

155. See J. H. Parry, *The Audiencia of New Galicia in the Sixteenth Century: A Study in Spanish Colonial Government* (Cambridge: Cambridge University Press, 1948).

156. For the evolution of Guadalajara, see Eric Van Young, *Hacienda and Market in Eighteenth-Century Mexico: The Rural Economy of the Guadalajara Region, 1675–1820* (Lanham: Rowman and Littlefield Publishers, Inc, 2006).

157. NYPL, ORC, Simancas, Cartas de Nueva Galicia, f. 261, 1549.

158. NYPL, ORC, Simancas, Cartas de Nueva Galicia, ff. 264–67, 1551.

159. In this comment, the visitador specifically compared production at Zacatecas to that of Culiacán. See NYPL, ORC, Simancas, Cartas de Nueva Galicia, f. 262v, 1549.

160. See NYPL, ORC, Simancas, Cartas de Nueva Galicia, f. 272, 1551.

161. See West, "Early Silver Mining in New Spain," 123.

162. See Gerhard, *North Frontier*, 89.

163. NYPL, ORC, Simancas, Carta de Nueva Galicia, ff. 264–67, 1551.

164. Bakewell, *Silver Mining and Society*, appendix 2, 268.

165. AHEZ, Libro de Cabildo, 1, f. 10, 1560; Gerhard, *North Frontier*, 158.

166. Local historians have identified San Francisco as the first barrio inhabited by native peoples and the oldest in the city. The site was located just above the Franciscan convent and directly south of the chapel at Bracho. Bezanilla Mier y Campa claims that the first indigenous community founded in the city was that of Mexicapan, located about a half mile east of San Francisco. See *Muralla zacatecana*, 22.

167. Robert Haskett argues that native migrants who had been forced from their communities often "coped by settling in separate districts within their new towns." See *Indigenous Rulers*, 13.

168. Lockhart, *Nahuas After the Conquest*, 21.

169. Claudia Magaña, *Panorámica de la ciudad de Zacatecas y sus barrios en la época virreinal* (Zacatecas: Gobierno del Estado de Zacatecas, 1998); Gerhard, *North Frontier*, 158.

170. See "Ordenanzas de minas," 38.

171. In other areas of New Spain, the Spanish cabildo or clergy allocated land for urban Indian communities. See Carlos Paredes Martínez, "Convivencia y conflictos: La ciudad de Valladolid y sus barrios de indios, 1541–1809," in *Los indios y las ciudades*, 49.

172. See Archivo Parroquial de Zacatecas (hereafter APZ), Varios, box 201, *carpeta* (folder) 4, 1630.

173. AHEZ, Casas and Solares, box 1, exp. 53, 1747.

174. APZ, Varios, box 201, carpeta 4, 1631.

175. Frejes, *Historia breve*, 195.

176. AHEZ, Criminales, box 5, exp. 8, ff. 1–2v, 1700.

177. Scarcity, price gouging, and shortages of basic foodstuffs lingered in the city well into the early seventeenth century. For an example, see AHEZ, Libro de Cabildo, 2, ff. 192v–193, 1606.

178. As a measure of grain the *almud* could vary by region from one half (as in this case) to one twelfth of a *fanega* (2.57 bushels). Martínez de la Marcha ordered buyers to pay native peoples two tomines (two-eighths of a peso) for the three almudes of grain. See "Este es un traslado," 47.

179. See Archivo General de la Nación, México (hereafter AGN), General de Partes, 2, exp. 1258, 1580; for another example, see AGN, General de Partes, 2, exp. 1318, 1580.

180. González appears to have been a successful trader. He owned mules, and on one business trip to Zacatecas he brought tobacco worth up to 352 pesos and 4 reales (one real was an eighth of a peso). For the complete case see AHEZ, Poder Judicial Civil, box 16, exp. 10, 1722.

181. Bakewell, "Zacatecas: An Economic and Social Outline," 227.

182. See "[Minas del Fresnillo II]," 121.

183. See "Este es un traslado," 48.

184. See "Este es un traslado," 50.

185. For the urban layout of cities in the Americas, see Joanne Rappaport and Tom Cummins, *Beyond the Lettered City: Indigenous Literacies in the Andes* (Durham: Duke University Press, 2012), 221–25.

186. For municipal councils in Spain, see Antonio Muro Orejón, "El ayuntamiento de Sevilla modelo de los municipios americanos," *Anales de la Universidad Hispalense* 20 (1960): 69–85; Antonio Domínguez Ortiz, *El antiguo régimen: Los Reyes católicos y los Austrias* (Madrid: Alianza Editorial, 1973), 194–212; Nader, *Liberty in Absolutist Spain*; José Manuel de Bernardo Ares, "El régimen municipal en la corona de Castilla," *Studia Historica, Historia Moderna* 15 (1996): 23–61; Helen Nader, "The Spain That Encountered Mexico," in *The Oxford History of Mexico*, ed. William. H. Beezley and Michael Meyer (New York: Oxford University Press, 2010), 11–44.

187. See Eugenio del Hoyo, "La Diputación de Mineros en las minas ricas de los zacatecas, democracia corporativa," in *Primera libro de actas de cabildo de las minas de los zacatecas, 1557–1586* (Zacatecas: Ayuntamiento de la ciudad de Zacatecas, 1991), 4–22.

188. See Del Hoyo, "La Diputación de Mineros," 17.

189. AHEZ, Libro de Cabildo, 1, f. 6, 1557.
190. AHEZ, Libro de Cabildo, 1, f. 7v, 1559.
191. AHEZ, Libro de Cabildo, 1, f. 7v, 1559.
192. Bakewell, "Introduction," *Mines of Silver and Gold*, xvi.
193. Bakewell, *Silver Mining and Society*, 268.

CHAPTER 2. ETHNIC COHESION AND COMMUNITY FORMATION, 1560–1608

1. See Ahumada Sámano, *Relación sobre la rebelión*.
2. AHEZ, Libro de Cabildo, 1, ff. 28–28v, 1566.
3. AHEZ, Libro de Cabildo, 1, f. 13, 1561.
4. APZ, Disciplinar, box 145, carpeta 1, f. 97, 1566.
5. By 1561 cabildo records mention the Spanish confraternities of Santa Vera Cruz, Nuestra Señora de la Concepción, and Santísimo Sacramento (the latter founded circa 1551). See AHEZ, Libro de Cabildo, 1, f. 8, 1559; f. 13, 1561. For Spanish confraternities, see Lara Mancuso, *Cofradías mineras: Religiosidad popular en México y Brasil, siglo XVIII* (México: El Colegio de México, Centro de Estudios Históricos, 2007), 84–85 and 102–7.
6. Cortés founded the Caballeros de la Cruz (Knights of the Cross) in Mexico City in 1526. See Brian Larkin, "Confraternities and Community: The Decline of the Communal Quest for Salvation in Eighteenth-Century Mexico City," in *Local Religion in Colonial Mexico*, ed. Martin Austin Nesvig (Albuquerque: University of New Mexico, 2006), 194. For an overview of cofradía development, see Dagmar Bechtloff, *Las cofradías en Michoacán durante la época de la colonia: La religión y su relación política y económica en una sociedad intercultural* (Zinacantepec: El Colegio de Michoacán, 1996), 13–77.
7. For postconquest indigenous communities, see Haskett, *Indigenous Rulers*, 16.
8. See http://whp.uoregon/dictionaries/nahuatl/index.lasso. The Franciscan Alonso de Molina's sixteenth-century *Vocabulario* (published in Mexico City in 1571) translates *tlacuitlapampa* as *detras de algo*, or "behind something." See *Vocabulario en lengua castellana y mexicana* (Madrid: Ediciones Cultura Hispánica, Colección de Incunables Americanos Siglo XVI Volumen IV, 1944), f. 120, facs.
9. Bezanilla Mier y Campa, *Muralla zacatecana*, 20.
10. See AHEZ, Libro de Cabildo, 1, f. 23, 1563.
11. See AHEZ, Libro de Cabildo, 1, f. 23, 1563.
12. See AHEZ, Libro de Cabildo, 1, f. 21v, 1563.
13. See Biblioteca Pública del Estado de Jalisco (hereafter BPEJ), box 1, exp. 4, ff. 1–14, 1567.
14. Bakewell, *Silver Mining and Society*, 43.
15. Both repúblicas would ultimately include Africans and individuals of African descent.
16. For the evolution of indigenous urbanization patterns, see Francisco de Solano, "Urbanización y municipalización de la población indígena," in *Estudios sobre la ciudad*, 241–68. For theories and realities behind the repúblicas, see Cope, *Limits of Racial Domination*, 3–26 and 171n3.

17. These laws formed part of the *Recopilación de leyes de los reynos de las Indias*. See Juan Manzano, ed., *Recopilación de leyes de los reynos de las Indias* (Madrid: Ediciones Cultura Hispánica, Madrid, 1973). See also the 1512 Leyes de Burgos for earlier policies governing the treatment and care of the native population; AGI, Biblioteca, GR-174, ff. 1–14v, 1512, facs.; Taylor, *Drinking, Homicide, and Rebellion*, 16–17.

18. Indian towns commonly developed at the borders of Spanish cities and mining centers. For Potosí, see Bakewell, *Miners of the Red Mountain*, 98–99. In Taxco, there were three barrios: Teteltzingo, Cantarranas, and Tenango. See Haskett, "'Our Suffering with the Taxco Tribute,'" 450. By the seventeenth century, Valladolid had at least thirteen indigenous communities. See Carlos Paredes Martínez, "Convivencia y conflictos: La ciudad de Valladolid y sus barrios de Indios, 1541–1809," in *Los Indios y las ciudades*, 47–48. For Indian towns near Santiago de Guatemala, see Matthew, *Memories of Conquest*; Herrera, *Natives, Europeans, and Africans*; Lutz, *Santiago de Guatemala*. For Oaxaca, see Chance, *Race and Class*. For Mexico City, see Gibson, *Aztecs Under Spanish Rule*. For Lima, see Paul Charney, *Indian Society in the Valley of Lima, Peru, 1532–1824* (Lanham: University Press of America, 2001).

19. AHEZ, Intendencia, box 1, exp. 20, 1796.

20. AHEZ, Libro de Cabildo, 2, f. 8, 1587.

21. Zavala, *El servicio personal*, 325–26.

22. Carlos Paredes Martínez argues that urban native settlers had little say in determining the location of their communities, with Spaniards relegating them to the outskirts of the urban core. See "Convivencia y conflictos," 43–44.

23. Zavala, *El servicio personal*, 325–26.

24. See Clara Bargellini, *La arquitectura de la plata: Iglesias monumentales del centro-norte de México, 1640–1750* (México: Universidad Nacional Autónoma de México, 1991), 265. In 1608, a crown official claimed that the Franciscan convent was founded in 1558, the year commonly given for the order's establishment in the city. See Anonymous, *Relación*, 300.

25. APZ, Disciplinar, box 145, carpeta 1, f. 97, 1566.

26. San Francisco eventually evolved into the racially mixed community of La Pinta.

27. See Bezanilla Mier y Campa, *Muralla zacatecana*, 22.

28. Mexicapan never evolved into an indigenous town but eventually "merged" and became a barrio of Tlacuitlapan. See Gerhard, *North Frontier*, 158.

29. As late as 1806, the Spanish cabildo, in reference to a building close to the area, observed that the hospital "was somewhat distant and removed from the center of the city." See AHEZ, Criminales, box 2, f. 213v, 1806.

30. See Gerhard, *North Frontier*, 158.

31. See Lockhart, *Nahuas After the Conquest*, 16. For Zacatecas, I have yet to find the term *tlaxilacalli* in any archival documents or to uncover native-language documentation that notes how indigenous peoples described their communities.

32. See Bakewell, *Silver Mining and Society*, 45–46.

33. Spaniards gave the name of the Vera Cruz to a hospital and chapel they built fairly soon after the establishment of Zacatecas. These institutions should not be confused with the indigenous confraternity of the Vera Cruz. The hospital of San Francisco served native peoples. In 1608 an anonymous crown official claimed that the indigenous hospital had existed for only four years. Archival records indicate that hospital San Francisco dates to the 1560s. Other studies and sources do not offer further clarity. See Bakewell, *Silver Mining and Society*, 45; Anonymous, *Relación*, 300–301.

34. See Archivo Histórico de la Arquidiócesis de Guadalajara (hereafter AAG), Zacatecas, box 1, unmarked exp., January 31, 1654.

35. As with most of the communities around southern Guadalajara, the Tonaltecos fell to the rapaciousness of Nuño de Guzmán and his company in the 1530s. At the time of Zacatecas's founding the community had shrunk to half of its precontact size (from 11,000 to 5,110). See Gerhard, *North Frontier*, 153–56.

36. For the Tarascans, see Magaña, *Panorámica de la ciudad*, 97; for both groups, see Gerhard, *North Frontier*, 158.

37. Bakewell translates *Chepinque* as "wet in the dry time." See "Zacatecas: An Economic and Social Outline," 204. Molina lists *chapanqui*, defining it as "something very wet." There is also an entry for *chichipini*, which means to "drizzle or distill something liquid." See Molina, *Vocabulario*, ff. 19, 20.

38. Not only did native peoples have access to this precious resource, but many individuals made a living collecting and distributing water to individuals in the city center. See AHEZ, Libro de Cabildo, 2, f. 11v, 1587.

39. AHEZ, Libro de Cabildo, 1, f. 8v, 1559.

40. AHEZ, Libro de Cabildo, 2, f. 244v, 1609.

41. APZ, Varios, box 201, carpeta 4, 1631. The lot for sale contained two living quarters.

42. AHEZ, Bienes y Difuntos, box 1, exp. 13, 1601–1737.

43. AHEZ, Criminales, box 2, exp. 32, f. 1, 1667.

44. See AAG, box 1, Zacatecas, ff. 1–33v, 1628–1634.

45. AHEZ, Bienes y Difuntos, box 1, exp. 13, 1602–1737.

46. Mota y Escobar, *Descripción geográfica*, 33.

47. Garner, *Zacatecas, 1750–1821*, 43.

48. Bakewell, *Silver Mining and Society*, 126.

49. Mangan, *Trading Roles*, 27.

50. See Bartolomé Arzáns de Orsúa y Vela, *Historia de la villa imperial de Potosí*, ed. Lewis Hanke and Gunnar Mendoza (Providence: Brown University Press, 1965), 1:42–43.

51. See AHEZ, Libro de Cabildo, 1, f. 47v, 1575.

52. BPEJ, box 1, exp. 4, ff. 1–14, 1567. For indigenous women in the marketplace, see Kimberly Gauderman, *Women's Lives in Colonial Quito: Gender, Law, and Economy in Spanish America* (Austin: University of Texas Press, 2003), 92–123; Mangan, *Trading Roles*.

53. AGI, Guadalajara 230, legajo 1, f. 99, 1577.

54. BPEJ, box 1, exp. 4, ff. 1–14, 1567.

55. See "Este es un traslado," 47–48.

56. AHEZ, Criminales, box 1, exp. 13, 1619.
57. See the special issue of *Ethnohistory*, "A Language of Empire, a Quotidian Tongue: The Uses of Nahuatl in New Spain," 59.4 (2012).
58. See "[Minas del Fresnillo II]," 122.
59. Lázaro de Arregui, *Descripción de la Nueva Galicia*, 34. Gerhard states that Nahuatl "was widely if imperfectly spoken as a second language by many of the native groups in Nueva Galicia." See *North Frontier*, 49.
60. BPEJ, box 1, exp. 4, ff. 1–14, 1567.
61. See, for example, Schwaller, "Importance of Mestizos," 713–38; Yanna Yannakakis, "Introduction: How Did They Talk to One Another? Language Use and Communication in Multilingual New Spain," *Ethnohistory* 59.4 (2012): 667–74.
62. AHEZ, Libro de Cabildo, 1, f. 70, 1577.
63. AHEZ, Libro de Cabildo, 2, f. 240v, 1609; Libro de Cabildo, 3, f. 13v, 1619.
64. AHEZ, Libro de Cabildo, 1, f. 22, 1563.
65. AHEZ, Libro de Cabildo, 2, f. 252v, 1609.
66. AHEZ, Libro de Cabildo, 2, f. 244v, 1609.
67. See "Este es un traslado," 51.
68. Anonymous, *Relación*, 294.
69. See Yannakakis, "Introduction," 668. For the important role of cultural intermediaries, see Yannakakis, *The Art of Being In-Between*.
70. Kevin Terraciano notes how Nahuatl "facilitated communication" between distinct ethnic groups in Oaxaca's multilingual Mixteca region. See *Mixtecs of Colonial Oaxaca*, 45.
71. For the acquisition of Nahuatl by Spaniards, see Martin Nesvig, "Spanish Men, Indigenous Language, and Informal Interpreters in Postcontact Mexico," *Ethnohistory* 59.4 (2012): 739–64.
72. AHEZ, Bienes y Difuntos, box 1, exp. 13, f. 1v, 1602–1737.
73. Ranches and agricultural haciendas existed and some native peoples tended their own milpas, but few urban Indians engaged full-time in farming or agriculture.
74. Kendall Brown argues that in Potosí mine workers were organized in parishes according to ethnic groups so that they could find support from workers of similar ethnic backgrounds. He states, "Throughout the colonial period, the parishes provided an ethnic anchor for the transitory workers, a cultural refuge that slowed Hispanization and preserved ethnic differences." See, *History of Mining*, 82.
75. AHEZ, Libro de Cabildo, 1, f. 16, 1562.
76. For the activities of male laborers at mining complexes, see Bakewell, *Silver Mining and Society*, 134–49; Tandeter, *Coercion and Market*. For a general description of extraction and refining, see Bargalló Ardévol, *La minería y la metalurgia*, 87–90; Jaime J. Lacueva Muñoz, *La plata del rey y de sus vasallos: Minería y metalurgia en México (siglos XVI y XVII)* (Madrid: Consejo Superior de Investigaciones Científicas, 2010), 33–56 and 89–135.
77. For Indian women and silver-mining production in Zacatecas, see Velasco Murillo, "Laboring Above Ground."
78. Bakewell, *Miners of the Red Mountain*, 104, 141.

79. BNM, AFF, box 58, folder 1160, no. 5, ff. 1–2, 1623.
80. BNM, AFF, box 58, folder 1160, no. 2, ff. 1–2, 1623.
81. For ordinances concerning urban native peoples, see Zavala, *El servicio personal*, 403–10, 455–68.
82. Mota y Escobar, *Descripción geográfica*, 146.
83. AHEZ, Libro de Cabildo, 1, f. 77v, 1577.
84. AHEZ, Libro de Cabildo, 3, f. 116, 1623; Libro de Cabildo, 2, f. 244v, 1609.
85. Anonymous, *Relación*, 297.
86. Pablo Miguel Sierra Silva notes a similar shift from African to Indian textile laborers in Puebla. See Velasco Murillo and Sierra Silva, "Mine Workers and Weavers," 112–13.
87. The actual percentage for Zacatecas-Pánuco was 89 percent. The total numbers for four of these centers represent information taken from two smaller sites counted as one. For example, statistics from Fresnillo and San Demetrio were entered together. For the complete table, see Bakewell, "Notes on the Mexican Silver," 195; Sluiter, "Zacatecas y congregaciones de minas della," appendix 3.
88. See Gerhard, *North Frontier*, 158–59.
89. See Bakewell, "Notes on the Mexican Silver Mining," 195.
90. Eighteen centers appear on the inventory, but only fifteen had information. See Bakewell, "Notes on the Mexican Silver Mining," 196; for percentages, see p. 184.
91. Bakewell, "Notes on the Mexican Silver Mining," 197.
92. See Zavala, *El servicio personal*, 323. For the complete chart, see Sluiter, "Zacatecas y congregaciones de minas della," appendix 3.
93. Charcas and La Habana asked for two hundred slaves, but also one hundred additional native laborers (they had eighty-three at the time). See Sluiter, "Zacatecas y congregaciones de minas della," appendix 3.
94. AHEZ, Libro de Cabildo, 4, ff. 10–11, 1637.
95. Slave sales appear in several extant notarial books. For an example, see AHEZ, Notarías, Juan García Picón, 1734–1755.
96. Schwaller, "Importance of Mestizos and Mulatos," 719–21; See Mónica Blanco, Alma Parra, and Ethelia Ruiz Medrano, *Breve historia de Guanajuato* (México: Fondo de Cultura Económica, 2000), 66.
97. For a discussion of the various meanings of the term *barrio* in relation to indigenous communities, see Castro Gutiérrez, "Origen y conformación," 106–7.
98. Jose Moya's argument that "the rural population in Afro-America lacked the basic economic and social security that Indian villages and communal land tenure provided in Indo-America" applies to urban African and casta populations as well. See "Introduction," 2–3.
99. Nicole Von Germeten argues that Afro-descended peoples also utilized confraternities to develop solidarity and corporate group identities. See *Black Blood Brothers: Confraternities and Social Mobility for Afro-Mexicans* (Gainesville: University Press of Florida, 2006). Herman L. Bennett examines how urban slaves used church institutions, particularly marriage, to create Afro-Mexican identities

and communities in Mexico City. See *Africans in Colonial Mexico: Absolutism, Christianity, and Afro-Creole Consciousness, 1570–1640* (Bloomington: Indiana University Press, 2003). In Zacatecas, from 1635 to the mid-seventeenth century, a cofradía of mulattos, San Juan de la Penitencia, operated from the parish church. See Mancuso, *Cofradías mineras*, 107–12.

100. See Lockhart, *Nahuas After the Conquest*, 218–19.

101. For scholarship on cofradía development in the periphery and urban areas, see Gary W. Graff, "Spanish Parishes in Colonial New Granada: Their Role in Town-Building on the Spanish-American Frontier," *Americas* 33.2 (1976–1977): 336–51; Nancy M. Farriss, *Maya Society Under Colonial Rule*; Asunción Lavrin, "La congregación de San Pedro: Una cofradía urbana del México colonial, 1604–1730," *Historia Mexicana* 29.4 (1980): 562–601; John Chance and William Taylor, "Cofradías and Cargos: An Historical Perspective on the Mesoamerican Civil-Religious Hierarchy," *American Ethnologist* 12.1 (1985): 1–26; Albert Meyers, "Religious Sodalities in Latin America: A Sketch of Two Peruvian Case Studies," in *Manipulating the Saints: Religious Brotherhoods and Social Integration in Post-conquest Latin America*, ed. Albert Meyers and Diane Elizabeth Hopkins (Hamburg: Wayasbah, 1988): 1–21; Alicia Bazarte Martínez, *Las cofradías de españoles en la ciudad de México (1526–1860)* (México: Universidad Autónoma Metropolitana, 1989); Bechtloff, *Las cofradías en Michoacán*; Paul Charney, "A Sense of Belonging: Colonial Indian Cofradías and Ethnicity in the Valley of Lima, Peru," *Americas* 54.3 (1998): 379–407; María del Pilar Martínez López-Cano, Gisela von Wobeser, and Juan Guillermo Muñoz, eds., *Cofradías, capellanías, y obras pías en la América colonial* (México: Universidad Nacional Autónoma de México, 1998), 17–117; Mangan, *Trading Roles*, 2005; and Mancuso, *Cofradías mineras*.

102. James Lockhart's explanation for this phenomenon is that lay brotherhoods flourished "where the strong mechanisms of the altepetl or its equivalent were lacking." See *Nahuas After the Conquest*, 219. Other scholars note a similar trend among other urban Indian populations in the Andes. According to Albert Meyers, confraternities served as institutions that allowed "dominated" groups to function in urban centers. See "Religious Sodalities," 18. Paul Charney argues that native people in Lima and its hinterlands utilized cofradías to redefine their homogenized "indio" classification into a corporate ethnic identity, whereas in Potosí, Jane Mangan notes, sodalities "quickly became important unifying groups for urban indigenous residents." See "Sense of Belonging," 381; see also Mangan, *Trading Roles*, 154.

103. Felipe Castro Gutiérrez, "Conflictos y fraudes electorales en los cabildos indígenas de Michoacán colonial," *Journal of Iberian and Latin American Studies* 4.2 (1998): 45.

104. Recall that a Spanish confraternity, also called La Vera Cruz, slightly predated its indigenous counterpart.

105. See, for example, Gasca, *Timbres y laureles zacatecanos*, 159.

106. Bakewell, *Silver Mining and Society*, 44.

107. AAG, Visitas, box 1, ff. 70v–74, 1707.

108. There is a significant corpus of work on the effects of Spanish missionary efforts in northern New Spain. For some examples, see Ignacio del Río, *Conquista*

y aculturación en la California jesuítica (México: Universidad Nacional Autónoma de México, 1984); Robert H. Jackson, *Indian Population Decline: The Missions of Northwestern New Spain, 1687–1840* (Albuquerque: University of New Mexico Press, 1994); Cecilia Sheridan, *Anónimos y desterrados: La contienda por el sitio que llaman de Quauyla: Siglos XVI–XVIII* (México: Centro de Investigaciones y Estudios Superiores de Antropología Social, 2000), 131–212; Charlotte M. Gradie, *The Tepehuan Revolt of 1616: Militarism, Evangelism, and Colonialism in Seventeenth-Century Nueva Vizcaya* (Salt Lake City: University of Utah Press, 2000); Deeds, *Defiance and Deference.*

109. For the establishment of hospitals in New Spain, see Josefina Muriel, *Hospitales en la Nueva España, fundaciones del siglo XVI* (México: Universidad Nacional Autónoma de México, 1990), especially 115–38; for indigenous hospitals, 175–76.

110. The Dominicans may have established an indigenous hospital near the carnicería in the early seventeenth century that fell into disuse and later was reinstated by the friars of San Juan de Dios following their arrival to the city in 1608. See Anonymous, *Relación*, 300n49.

111. In Guanajuato, a mining town with a large migrant native population, hospitals developed that represented distinct ethnic groups, such as Nahuas, Otomís, Tarascans, and Mazahuas. See Castro Gutiérrez, "Origen y conformación," 111–12.

112. Fragments of the hospital's records were found in the confraternity book of the Vera Cruz. See APZ, Disciplinar, box 145, carpeta 1, loose-leaf, 1564.

113. The storing of the hospital's records with the sodality's illustrates the close connection between the two organizations.

114. The majority of hospital confraternities developed in the mid-sixteenth century, before 1580. See Chance and Taylor, "Cofradías and Cargos," 8–9.

115. See Bargellini, *La arquitectura de la plata*, 265.

116. APZ, Disciplinar, box 145, carpeta 1, f. 97v, 1566. The migrant Tarascan population also came to the city with a tradition of hospitals and cofradías. See Laura Gemma Flores García and Carlos Paredes Martínez, "El cabildo, hospital y cofradía de indios de Pátzcuaro: Ámbitos de poder y conflictos en el siglo XVII," in *Autoridad y gobierno indígena en Michoacán: Ensayos a través de su historia*, ed. Carlos Paredes Martínez and Marta Terán (Zamora: El Colegio de Michoacán, 2003), 185–215.

117. For the 1566 membership list, see APZ, Disciplinar, box 145, carpeta 1, ff. 4–5v, 1566.

118. Bargellini bases these claims on a manuscript, *Libro de cofradía de San Francisco*, which I did not have access to, located at the cathedral archives. See *La arquitectura de la plata*, 265.

119. Zacatecas's indigenous cofradías may have been more exclusive than those of other regions. Flores García and Paredes Martínez claim that confraternities in Pátzcuaro were open to individuals of any ethnoracial identity, but that ultimately they remained indigenous. See "El cabildo, hospital y cofradía," 195.

120. Lockhart, *Nahuas After the Conquest*, 219.

121. For confraternities in the periphery, see Chance and Taylor, "Cofradías and Cargos."

122. See Jonathan Truitt, "Courting Catholicism: Nahua Women and the Catholic Church in Colonial Mexico City," *Ethnohistory* 57.3 (2010): 416, and especially 435–38 (for their role in cofradías).

123. In Pátzcuaro, for example, a group of around four to six indigenous women cared for the sick at the hospital. See Flores García y Paredes Martínez, "El cabildo, hospital y cofradía," 194.

124. APZ, Disciplinar, box 145, carpeta 1, ff. 1, 4–5v, 1566.

125. Although much later (1660–1720), for trends in indigenous naming patterns for Mexico City, see Cope, *Limits of Racial Domination*, 58–67.

126. *Çemmac* is Nahuatl for "in one hand." *Michuani* means "someone who is an owner of fish" or a "fisherman."

127. The constitution stipulated the doubling of dues for deceased members who could no longer be counted on for alms. See APZ, Disciplinar, box 145, carpeta 1, f. 97v, 1566.

128. As such, cofradías in Zacatecas followed the pattern Nancy Farriss noted for Mayan communities in that they were "corporate without being egalitarian." See *Maya Society Under Colonial Rule*, 271.

129. In this period, most native commoners had a Spanish first name and an indigenous second name, which often functioned as a surname. For naming patterns, see Lockhart, *Nahuas After the Conquest*, 117–30.

130. Other cofradías sometimes used three books, keeping separate logs for expenses and collections.

131. This argument is based on material from a sixteenth-century manuscript, *El primer libro de gobierno*. Unfortunately, I have not had access to this book. However, I received this information from John Sullivan, a noted scholar of the city.

132. APZ, Disciplinar, box 145, carpeta 1, f. 53v, 1618.

133. APZ, Disciplinar, box 145, carpeta 1, f. 3, f. 51v, 1641, 1643, 1644.

134. APZ, Disciplinar, box 145, carpeta 1, f. 97v, 1566.

135. The appearance of membership lists in the account book could suggest that by this period the confraternity kept all its records in one book. I believe that these are temporary lists.

136. APZ, Disciplinar, box 145, carpeta 1, ff. 27v–28, 1634; f. 3, 1633.

137. Susan Schroeder argues that cofradías in central Mexico "were in a way the altepetl writ small, for they fostered an enduring sense of identity and solidarity." See "Whither Tenochtitlan," 79.

138. APZ, Disciplinar, box 145, carpeta 1, f. 99, 1577; APZ, Procesos Eclesiásticos, box 165, carpeta 1, 1625. We lack details of the types of leadership positions for hospitals in Zacatecas. They may have been similar to those of Pátzcuaro where the leadership pool included, among others, a mayordomo, fiscal, and notary. See Flores García y Paredes Martínez, "El cabildo, hospital y cofradía," 194.

139. APZ, Disciplinar, box 145, carpeta 1, f. 11, 1621.

140. See Lockhart, *Nahuas After the Conquest*, 124.

141. AHEZ, Libro de Cabildo, 7, f. 115v, 1689.

142. As of 1626, a continued association existed between the hospital and the cofradía, but the collection of separate dues indicates that they remained independent organizations.

143. APZ, Disciplinar, box 145, carpeta 1, ff. 97–97v, 98, 1566.

144. For a transcript of an abridged version of the constitution, see Flores García and Paredes Martínez, "El cabildo, hospital y cofradía," 203.

145. Sporadic record keeping for Zacatecas makes it difficult to determine the regularity of elections. However, the presence of mayordomos in various documents throughout the colonial period speaks to the stability of the office, if not the process. In contrast, Lockhart argues that in central Mexico native people held elections intermittently, on random dates, and at times under duress. See *Nahuas After the Conquest*, 225.

146. Haskett discusses the important connections between cabildo and cofradía office holders. Yet he argues that "religious offices" ultimately "did not overshadow high secular posts." See *Indigenous Rulers*, 121–23.

147. In a petition regarding alms collection the mayordomos implied that other confraternities had haciendas and goods to support them. APZ, box 165, carpeta 1, loose-leaf, 1600.

148. The four Spanish cofradías were the Santa Vera Cruz, Nuestra Señora de la Concepción, Santísimo Sacramento, and Santo Entierro de Cristo. In her list of confraternities, Lara Mancuso does not enter a founding date for Nuestra Señora de la Concepción, but it appears in cabildo records by 1559. See AHEZ, Libro de Cabildo, 1, f. 8, 1559. For Mancuso, *Cofradías mineras*, 84–85.

149. APZ, Disciplinar, box 165, carpeta 1, loose-leaf, 1619.

150. See APZ, Procesos Eclesiásticos, box 165, carpeta 1, 1625; APZ, Disciplinar, box 145, carpeta 1, ff. 97–98, 1566 and f. 99, 1577.

151. Collaboration between civil and religious authorities was fairly commonplace. William Connell cites an example from Mexico City where cofradía and cabildo leaders joined together to petition colonial authorities for the return of certain privileges after the uprising of 1692. See *After Moctezuma*, 282n101.

152. AHEZ, Notarias, Juan Picón, protocolos 2, ff. 95v–98, 1735.

153. AHEZ, Notarias, Juan Picón, protocolos 2, ff. 95v–98, 1735.

154. See APZ, Guía de Cofradías. Lara Mancuso argues that the vecinos of El Niño formed the indigenous branch of this Spanish cofradía. This assertion is difficult to prove given the lack of documentation for this organization. See *Cofradías mineras*, 100.

155. Lockhart, *Nahuas After the Conquest*, 54.

156. AHEZ, Libro de Cabildo, 3, f. 218v, 1630.

157. For more on these rock fights, see Dana Velasco Murillo, "'For the Last Time, Once and for All': Indians, Violence, and Local Authority in the Colonial City, Zacatecas, Mexico, 1587–1628," *Ethnohistory* 63.1 (2016): 62–63.

158. Castro Gutiérrez cites Guanajuato as another example of a mining town with a migrant native population that used the church for social organization in the absence of official political institutions. See "Origen y conformación," 111–12. For the Andes, see also Saignes, "Indian Migration and Social Change," 187.

159. APZ, Procesos Eclesiásticos, box 165, carpeta 1, 1625.
160. AAG, Visitas, box 1, libro 3, ff. 70v–74, 1707.
161. As mentioned earlier, Meyers and Charney arrive at similar conclusions for Peru. However, Meyers viewed cofradías as instruments of assimilation more than ethnic consolidation.
162. See Graubart, "Creolization of the New World," 479.
163. For the complete case, see BPEJ, box 1, exp. 4, ff. 1–14, 1567.
164. AHEZ, Libro de Cabildo, 1, f. 18v, 1563.
165. AHEZ, Libro de Cabildo, 2, ff. 2v–3, 1586.
166. AHEZ, Libro de Cabildo, 2, ff. 5–7, 1587. As a city, Zacatecas could elect up to eight regidores. For the evolution of Spanish government in mining towns, see John Lloyd Mecham, "The *Real de Minas* as a Political Institution: A Study of a Frontier Institution in Colonial Spanish America," *Hispanic American Historical Review* 7.1 (1927): 45–83.
167. A 1608 anonymous account from an official offers insights into conditions in the city at the beginning of the seventeenth century. See Anonymous, *Relación*, 291–301.
168. For Puebla's claims to being "the second city of New Spain" in the early seventeenth century, see Frances L. Ramos, *Identity, Ritual and Power in Colonial Puebla* (Tucson: University of Arizona Press, 2012), 1–22. In 1621, Lázaro de Arregui considered that "without a doubt" Zacatecas was the third most important city in New Spain. See *Descripción de la Nueva Galicia*, 125.
169. Gerhard, *North Frontier*, 158.
170. As Nancy Farris argues for the Yucatec Maya, "the *cofradía* in its modified form *was* the community." See *Maya Society Under Colonial Rule*, 266.

CHAPTER 3. THE CREATION OF INDIAN TOWNS AND OFFICIALS, 1609–1650

1. A native of Toledo, de la Fuente received his appointment in August 1601 and probably sailed to the Americas in September 1602. By 1603 he assumed his position as one of the Audiencia's four judges. He died within a year of the completion of his visita in September 1610. See Berthe, *Sociedades en construccion*, 95–99.
2. The visitador made an initial shorter stop of twenty-seven days in Zacatecas within a few weeks of the start of his trip. For a transcription of the complete inspection, see *Relación de lo hecho*, 105–54.
3. See *Relación de lo hecho*, 107.
4. See AHEZ, Libro de Cabildo, 2, f. 244, 1609.
5. *Saçemi* is Nahuatl for *ça* (once and only) and *çemi* (for always, forever). See Bakewell, "Zacatecas: An Economic and Social Outline," 216. For the fights themselves, see Velasco Murillo, "'For the Last Time.'"
6. See *Relación de lo hecho*, 133. In his 1550 ordinances, Martínez de la Marcha referred to "indios alguaciles" (constables). These native peoples should not be confused for local indigenous leaders, but the overseers of repartimiento Indians brought by individual Spaniards to work at the mines. See "Ordenanzas de minas," 38.

7. For Valladolid, see Paredes Martínez, "Convivencia y conflictos," 50. For Chiapas, see Gudrun Lenkersdorf, "Los cabildos de naturales en la provincia de Chiapas, de la posconquista temprana a las ordenanzas del oidor-visitador Axcoeta en 1573," in *Gobierno y economía en los pueblos indios del México colonial*, ed. Francisco González-Hermosillo Adams (México: Instituto Nacional de Antropología e Historia, 2001), 184.

8. The initiative of Zacatecas's native population to establish municipal representation differed from that of other cities. For Valladolid, Paredes Martínez argues that some of the indigenous barrios were established at the request of religious officials. See "Convivencia y conflictos," 49.

9. Lockhart, *Nahuas After the Conquest*, 36.

10. For Spanish opposition, see Lenkersdorf, "Los cabildos de naturales."

11. For scholarship on indigenous cabildos, see Charles Gibson, *Tlaxcala in the Sixteenth Century* (Stanford: Stanford University Press, 1952), 89–123; *Aztecs Under Spanish Rule*, 166–93, 395–98; Cline, *Colonial Culhuacan*, 35–58; Francisco González-Hermosillo Adams, "Historiografía de los cabildos indios," *Historias* 26 (1991): 25–53; Haskett, *Indigenous Rulers*; Lockhart, *Nahuas After the Conquest*, 28–58; Horn, *Postconquest Coyoacan*, 44–66; Restall, *Maya World*, 61–83; González-Hermosillo Adams, *Gobierno y economía*, 113–43, 181–231; Terraciano, *Mixtecs of Colonial Oaxaca*, 182–97; Paredes Martínez and Terán, *Autoridad y gobierno*; Andrea Martínez Baracs, *Un gobierno de indios: Tlaxcala, 1519–1750* (México: Fondo de Cultura Económica, 2008); Connell, *After Moctezuma*; Paredes Martínez, "Convivencia y conflictos," 50–54; Mark Lentz, "Batabs of the Barrio: Urban Maya Rulers, Merida, Yucatan, 1670–1806," in *City Indians*, 172–98.

12. See Gibson, *Aztecs Under Spanish Rule*, 32; *Tlaxcala in the Sixteenth Century*, 165.

13. For royal policies on the creation of indigenous cabildos in the Americas, see Luise M. Enkerlin Pauwells, "El cabildo indígena de Pátzcuaro: Un espacio de poder en decadencia durante la primera mitad del siglo XVIII," in *Gobierno y economía*, 243–45. For the initial establishment of offices, see Peter Villella, *Indigenous Elites and Creole Identity in Colonial Mexico, 1500–1800* (Cambridge: Cambridge University Press, 2016), 34–37.

14. For the development of Tlaxcala's cabildo, see Baber, "Empire, Indians," 19–44.

15. See Haskett, *Indigenous Rulers*, 138–41; Kellogg, *Law and the Transformation of Aztec Culture*, 24; Lockhart, *Nahuas After the Conquest*, 28–41, 112; Enkerlin Pauwells, "El cabildo indígena de Pátzcuaro," 241.

16. In Zacatecas, colonial authorities often used the terms *barrio* and *pueblo* interchangeably when describing indigenous communities. But by the 1650s, the word *pueblo* mainly referred to the Indian towns, whereas Spaniards and native peoples employed *barrio* to describe smaller units within the pueblo or ethnic neighborhoods. For the use of these terms in central Mexico, see Lockhart, *Nahuas After the Conquest*, 44.

17. See AHEZ, Libro de Cabildo, 2, f. 244, 1609.

18. See AHEZ, Libro de Cabildo, 2, f. 256v, 1609.

19. See Haskett, *Indigenous Rulers*, 21.

20. AHEZ, Libro de Cabildo, 2, f. 256v, 1609.

21. Native peoples could request the appointment and dismissal of Indian fiscales. For an example, see AGI, Guadalajara, 56, no foliation, 1627.

22. AHEZ, Libro de Cabildo, 2, f. 244, 1609; AHEZ, Libro de Cabildo, 3, f. 258, 1633.

23. See, for example, Enkerlin Pauwells, "El cabildo indígena de Pátzcuaro," 246–47.

24. See, for example, the dispute that arose between native officials and residents in Cholula in Francisco González-Hermosillo Adams, "Macehuales versus señores naturales: Una mediación franciscana en el cabildo indio de Cholula ante el conflicto por el servicio personal (1553–1594)," in *Gobierno y economía*, 113–43.

25. See Nader, *Liberty in Absolutist Spain*, xv.

26. See Baber, "Empire, Indians," 29–32.

27. See Enkerlin Pauwells, "El cabildo indígena de Pátzcuaro," 244–45.

28. This practice was common in central Mexico. See Horn, *Postconquest Coyoacan*, 58–59. But even within larger town councils, the rotation of positions helped ease tensions in areas where the Spanish creation of *cabeceras* (head towns) and *sujetos* (subject communities) among previously equal and autonomous entities disrupted the traditional balance of power. See Lockhart, *Nahuas After the Conquest*, 33, 37.

29. Paredes Martínez also documents the rotation of offices by barrios. See "Convivencia y conflictos," 51–52.

30. AHEZ, Libro de Cabildo, 3, f. 6v, 1615.

31. Zacatecas's Indian towns are not referred to by the term *cabecera* until the late colonial period, but they followed the cabecera and sujeto model of central Mexico. For an example of the former, see AGI, Guadalajara, 348, no. 4, ff. 1025v–1026v, 1772.

32. AHEZ, Libro de Cabildo, 5, f. 79, 1654, and f. 175, 1657.

33. Not all confraternities participated in indigenous government. The cofradía of Santísima Trinidad, dissolved by 1686, never appears in election records or in viceregal inspections from the early eighteenth century. See AHEZ, Libro de Cabildo, 6, f. 314, 1686; AAG, Visitas Pastorales, box 1, ff. 174–174v, 1728. Also missing is evidence of the development of governance in the barrio of Mexicapan, often cited as the oldest indigenous settlement in the city. I believe that Mexicapan and Tlacuitlapan frequently operated as one sociopolitical unit. Two eighteenth-century maps of Zacatecas illustrate the communities side by side.

34. AHEZ, Libro de Cabildo, 5, f. 175, 1659.

35. AHEZ, Libro de Cabildo, 5, f. 79, 1654, and f. 152v, 1656.

36. AHEZ, Libro de Cabildo, 6, f. 5v, 1674.

37. APZ, Mandatos, box 187, carpeta 17, loose-leaf, 1661.

38. AHEZ, Libro de Cabildo, 6, f. 1v, 1673.

39. AHEZ, Libro de Cabildo, 7, ff. 115–115v, 1689.

40. This example illustrates how the city's indigenous cabildos followed the central Mexican tradition of using offices to represent geographic districts. See Haskett, *Indigenous Rulers*.

41. AHEZ, Libro de Cabildo, 11, ff. 81–84, 1713.

42. AHEZ, Libro de Cabildo, ff. 4–7, 1737. Although El Niño gained juridical autonomy, it continued to be linked with Chepinque because the two communities belonged to the same religious parish. In the eighteenth century, for example, clerics recorded marriage petitions for both communities in the same book.

43. Franciscans, for example, promoted the formation of cabildos in Cholula; see González-Hermosillo Adams, "Macehuales versus señores naturales," 115.

44. For central Mexico, see Lockhart, *Nahuas After the Conquest*, 55. For Michoacán, see Flores García and Paredes Martínez, "El cabildo, hospital y cofradía," 187.

45. The lack of election results for this period is sheer bad luck, and not an indication that elections were not held. Notaries often recorded indigenous elections on the first few pages of the libros de cabildo. Often, these opening fojas were missing or badly damaged.

46. For of one these memoriales, see AHEZ, Libro de Cabildo, 7, ff. 2v–6, 1686.

47. Lockhart, *Nahuas After the Conquest*, 30.

48. Haskett, *Indigenous Rulers*, 23.

49. Confraternity mayordomos appear alongside other principales on the election records often enough to suggest that they had a voice in the process. For an example, see AHEZ, Libro de Cabildo, 7, f. 115v, 1689.

50. APZ, Disciplinar, box 145, carpeta 1, f. 7, 1617.

51. The indigenous alcaldes assumed the responsibility of building fences for the city's bull fights. AHEZ, Libro de Cabildo, 3, f. 61v, 1631. For the activities allowed to indigenous leaders by the Leyes de Indias (the laws governing the Americas established by the Spanish crown), see Enkerlin Pauwells, "El cabildo indígena de Pátzcuaro," 250–51.

52. AHEZ, Bienes y Difuntos, box 1, exp. 13, 1602–1729.

53. AHEZ, Bienes y Difuntos, box 24, exp. 335, 1729; AHEZ, Notarias, Juan Picón, protocolos 2, ff. 95v–98, 1735.

54. Zacatecas's indigenous cabildos could not count on some of the more traditional forms of corporate income used in central and western Mexico, such as the sale of natural resources. In Pátzcuaro, for example, the crown granted the Indian cabildos proceeds from the sale of fish from the region's lake. For the former, see Gibson, *Tlaxcala in the Sixteenth Century*, 121; for the latter, see Flores García and Paredes Martínez, "El cabildo, hospital y cofradía," 189–90.

55. See, for example, AAG, Visitas, ff. 170–72; 174–74v, 1728. The pueblo of San Josef, for example, counted on funds from a ranch, and other towns collected prison fines. For a detailed inventory of the ranch and its holdings, see APZ, Cofradías, box 141, exp. 1, ff. 9–39, 1800. The ranch had been in the community's possession since at least 1703.

56. It is difficult to say which task occupied more of the protector's attention. Sporadic rebellions occurred around the Zacatecas area through the seventeenth century.

57. AHEZ, Libro de Cabildo, 9, ff. 4–5v, 1698.

58. APZ, Mandatos, box 187, carpeta 17, loose-leaf, 1661.

Notes to Chapter 3

59. AHEZ, Libro de Cabildo, 7, unnumbered folio [47?], 1688.

60. The position of gobernador appears to have been a periodic office in others area as well. Kevin Gosner argues that it is uncertain whether the office was consistently exercised in Chiapas. See "Las élites de indígenas en los altos de Chiapas (1524–1714)," *Historia Mexicana* 33.4 (1984): 414.

61. AHEZ, Libro de Cabildo, 22, ff. 5–8, 1733.

62. In election results, the alcalde was always named before the gobernador. For an example, see AHEZ, Libro de Cabildo, 10, f. 295, 1710.

63. AHEZ, Libro de Cabildo, 9, f. 249, 1704.

64. Lockhart, *Nahuas After the Conquest*, 49–51.

65. AHEZ, Libro de Cabildo, 13, ff. 200–202, 1720.

66. AHEZ, Libro de Cabildo, ff. 4–7, 1737.

67. AHEZ, Libro de Cabildo, 10, ff. 371–73, 1711.

68. Haskett argues for the participation of elders as a preconquest governance accommodation. This was probably true for Zacatecas as well. See *Indigenous Rulers*, 22.

69. AHEZ, Libro de Cabildo, 8, f. 61, 1694.

70. The first mention of a *topil* occurs in 1660. Alguaciles appear with frequency after 1673. See AHEZ, Libro de Cabildo, 5, f. 181, 1660, and 6, f. 1v, 1673.

71. AHEZ, Libro de Cabildo, 7, ff. 328–328v, 1691.

72. Ministros first appeared in 1685 in San Josef, and in other pueblos by the 1720s. San Josef always maintained a greater number and type of officials than the other towns. Although mandones and fiscales appear more frequently after 1740, sources indicate that fiscales evolved fairly soon after that establishment of Indian alcaldes, and I suspect that mandones did as well. See AHEZ, Libro de Cabildo, 6, f. 80, 1685; f. 5, 1739; and 8, f. 131v, 1695.

73. AHEZ, Libro de Cabildo, 7, f. 115, 1689.

74. See AHEZ, Libro de Cabildo, 10, f. 178, 1709. For the importance of notaries in central Mexico, see Lockhart, *Nahuas After the Conquest*, 41.

75. AHEZ, Libro de Cabildo, 14, ff. 281–83, 1723, and 15, ff. 134–36, 1724.

76. See Charles Thomson, *The Ordinances of the Mines of New Spain Translated from the Original Spanish, with Observations upon the Mines and Mining Associations* (London: Printed for J. Booth, 1825), 108–9.

77. See AHEZ, Libro de Cabildo, 7, ff. 328–328v, 1691.

78. See AHEZ, Libro de Cabildo, 7, unnumbered folio [46?], 1688.

79. See AHEZ, Libro de Cabildo, 10, f. 176, 1709.

80. For the role of mandones in Michoacán, see Castro Gutiérrez, "Conflictos y fraudes electorales," 46.

81. See Pedro Nolasco Pérez, *Los obispos de la Orden de la Merced en América (1601–1926): Documentos del Archivo General de Indias* (Santiago de Chile: Imprenta Chile 1927), 62–63.

82. AGI, Guadalajara, 56, 1627.

83. See AAG, Visitas, book 3, ff. 70–74v, 1707. For connections to colonial authorities, see Velasco Murillo, "'For the Last Time.'" 63.

84. By contrast, sixteenth-century Tlaxcala had a gobernador, four alcaldes, twelve regidores, several alguaciles, and a multitude of minor officials. See Gibson, *Tlaxcala in the Sixteenth Century*, 112, 116. In the early seventeenth century Pátzcuaro's cabildo had a similar composition to that of Tlaxcala. But instead of four alcaldes, there were only two. See Enkerlin Pauwells, "El cabildo indígena de Pátzcuaro," 246.

85. For example, in 1695, San Josef's council had three fiscales. Chepinque had two mandones in 1739. In 1740, Tlacuitlapan possessed a ministro, teniente, and justicia mayor. See AHEZ, Libro de Cabildo, 8, f. 131, 1695.

86. It is difficult to establish a date for when this transition occurred. There is a gap in the reporting of election results for the period 1634–1651. Native peoples certainly controlled their elections by the time Spanish council minutes reappear in 1652. See AHEZ, Libro de Cabildo, 5, f. 17v, 1652.

87. The information on indigenous elections in Zacatecas is rather rich compared to other areas, such as Chiapas. For the latter, see Lenkersdorf, "Los cabildos de naturales," 185–87. The process is well documented for Michoacán; see Castro Gutiérrez, "Conflictos y fraudes," 47–50.

88. These chapels took some time to build. For example, as of May 1621, the confraternity of the Vera Cruz had yet to finish its capilla, sixty-five years after its official founding in 1566. See APZ, Disciplinar, box 145, carpeta 1, f. 11, 1621.

89. AHEZ, Libro de Cabildo, 11, f. 168, 1713.

90. AHEZ, Libro de Cabildo, 13, ff. 2–4v, 1719. Church construction began in 1710 and was finished by 1728. See APZ, Cofradías, box 141, f. 80v, 1710; AAG, Visitas Pastorales, box 2, f. 148v, 1728.

91. For an example of this process, see AHEZ, Libro de Cabildo, 7, f. 329, 1690.

92. For evidence of curate assistance with elections, see AHEZ, Libro de Cabildo, 13, ff. 3–5, 1724, and ff. 4–7, 1737.

93. In Michoacán, the eligible voting pool ranged from ten to twelve in large towns like Pátzcuaro to forty people or "all the heads of family" in smaller communities. See Castro Gutiérrez, "Conflictos y fraudes," 50.

94. AHEZ, Libro de Cabildo, 21, ff. 3–5, 1732.

95. AHEZ, Libro de Cabildo, 11, f. 3, 1712.

96. AHEZ, Libro de Cabildo, 5, f. 17v, 1652; AHEZ, Libro de Cabildo, 9, ff. 213–15, 1702.

97. AHEZ, Libro de Cabildo, 7, ff. 328–28v, 1691.

98. See Castro Gutiérrez, "Conflictos y fraudes," 56.

99. AHEZ, Libro de Cabildo, 9, ff. 119–21, 1701, and 15, ff. 3–5, 1724.

100. AHEZ, Libro de Cabildo, ff. 4–7, 1737.

101. AHEZ, Libro de Cabildo, 41, f. 3, 1748, and 44, f. 3, 1750.

102. See Lenkersdorf, "Los cabildos de naturales," 190.

103. AHEZ, Libro de Cabildo, 6, ff. 44v–45. Felipe Castro Gutiérrez argues that in Michoacán, religious officials and corregidores often intimidated native leaders by attending their elections. See "Conflictos y fraudes," 56–57.

104. AHEZ, Libro de Cabildo, 5, f. 175, 1657.

105. AHEZ, Libro de Cabildo, 13, ff. 2–4v, 1719.
106. For examples, see AHEZ, Libro de Cabildo, 3, f. 120v, 1624, and f. 208, 1630.
107. AHEZ, Libro de Cabildo, 5, f. 175, 1657.
108. Bakewell, *Miners of the Red Mountain*, 33–60; Haskett, "'Our Suffering with the Taxco Tribute,'" 459.
109. APZ, Disciplinar, box 145, carpeta 1, f. 97, 1566. The Mexica probably continued to dominate leadership positions well after this time.
110. Ethnic identity was unmarked for the other years so the possibility remains that even more Mexicas held office in Tonalá. See AHEZ, Libro de Cabildo, 2, f. 267, 1611; 2, f. 276, 1612; 2, f. 294, 1613; 3, f. 35v, 1619.
111. *Criollo* is a very fluid word, deriving its meaning according to time frame and geographic context. In this case, it clearly refers to a native person born in the town. See AHEZ, Libro de Cabildo, 7, f. 328, 1691.
112. This phenomenon occurred in the Valley of Mexico as well. See Lockhart, *Nahuas After the Conquest*, 51; Horn, *Postconquest Coyoacan*, 57–58; Cline, *Colonial Culhuacan*, 53.
113. Indigenous election results are recorded throughout the Spanish council minutes. Citations that encompass multiple entries are listed by book(s) instead of individual fojas. Extant entries can be located on the first few pages of each individual year. See AHEZ, Libros de Cabildo, 1–9, various fojas, 1610–1700.
114. AHEZ, Libros de Cabildo, 1–9, various fojas, 1610–1700.
115. AHEZ, Libro de Cabildo, 7, f. 44v, 1688.
116. AHEZ, Libro de Cabildo, 8, f. 130, 1695.
117. AHEZ, Libro de Cabildo, 7, f. 4v, 1686, and 8, f. 9, 1693.
118. AHEZ, Libro de Cabildo, 8, f. 130, 1694.
119. AHEZ, Libro de Cabildo, 21, ff. 3–5, 1732.
120. Still, as Felipe Castro Gutiérrez points out, the majority of positions on the council were achieved via elections. This was in direct contrast to posts on the Spanish cabildo. Aside from the alcalde ordinario, Spanish offices were hereditary and long term. See "Conflictos y fraudes," 42.
121. The use of terms such as *don*, *principal*, and *cacique* to describe indigenous leaders in Zacatecas first appears in the records in the 1690s, a time period that coincides with more developed and mature municipal councils. For examples, see AHEZ, Libro de Cabildo, 7, ff. 256–58v; 8, f. 209, 1696; 9, ff. 4–5v, 1698; and 10, f. 4, 1708.
122. AHEZ, Libro de Cabildo, 7, f. 168, 1689.
123. See AHEZ, Libro de Cabildo, 10, f. 49v, 1708.
124. The 1734 *Real Academia* defines *ladino* as "one who could express himself with astuteness and accuracy in a language." See website Nuevo diccionario histórico de español, s.v. "Ladino," http://web.frl.es/DA.html.
125. In 1612, for example, Juan Jiménez and Diego Sánchez, each described as "mexicano vecino," received their appointments from the Spanish cabildo via the city's interpreter Pedro Francisco Granado. See AHEZ, Libro de Cabildo, 2, f. 276, 1612.

126. Baltasar García had served as alcalde several years earlier in 1619. See AHEZ, Libro de Cabildo, 3, f. 35v, 1619, and f. 120v, 1624.

127. Haskett, *Indigenous Rulers*, 138–41.

128. The leadership pool was drawn from the native pueblos, which remained heavily indigenous through the eighteenth century. Marriage records, for example, offer one indication of the presence of other ethnic groups in the Indian pueblos. Nuptial petitions from the four towns indicate that over a hundred-year period, 1680–1780, only thirty-seven non-Indians resided in the pueblos when they made their requests. See APZ, Matrimonios, Informaciones, Indios, Negros, y Castas (hereafter Matrimonios, IINC), 1681–1780.

129. AHEZ, Libro de Cabildo, 7, f. 368, 1692.

130. AHEZ, Libro de Cabildo, 7, ff. 328–28v, 1691.

131. AHEZ, Libro de Cabildo, 8, f. 211, 1696.

132. APZ, Mandatos, box 187, carpeta 16, loose-leaf, ff. 1v–2, 1661.

133. AHEZ, Libro de Cabildo, 7, f. 329, 1691.

134. In Pátzcuaro, for example, Spanish-indigenous alliances often influenced the actions of the city's native cabildos. See Castro Gutiérrez, "Conflictos y fraudes," 45–46, 51.

135. AHEZ, Libro de Cabildo, 4, ff. 81–81v, 1640, and 5, f. 94v, 1650.

CHAPTER 4. INDIOS AND VECINOS

1. See Ribera Bernárdez, *Descripción breve*, 48.

2. AAG, Justicia, Cofradías, Zacatecas, box 1, exp. 44, 1628–1734.

3. AHEZ, Poder Judicial Civil, box 4, exp. 4, ff. 1–47v, 1702–1705.

4. AHEZ, Bienes y Difuntos, box 17, exp. 263, ff. 1–181, 1719.

5. AHEZ, Bienes y Difuntos, box 1, exp. 13, ff. 1–15v, 1602–1629, and box 24, exp. 335, ff. 1–2v 1729.

6. See Lockhart and Schwartz, *Early Latin America*, 122.

7. Schwartz and Salomon argue that a similar population dynamic of communities composed of long-term and migrant "Indians" played a significant role in the persistence of indigenous identities in the Andes. See "New Peoples and New Kinds of People," 455.

8. For production decline in this period, see Bakewell, *Silver Mining and Society*, 221–26 and 231–36.

9. Bakewell, *Silver Mining and Society*, 231–36.

10. See AHEZ, Libro de Cabildo, 4, f. 4, 1637.

11. See AGN, Reales Cedulas, vol. 1, exp. 261, ff. 497–497v, 1641.

12. The exact toll of this epidemic is unknown, but the outbreaks could take a severe demographic toll. From 1576 to 1577, typhus, according to one viceregal official, claimed two thousand mine workers. Bakewell argues that this estimate is too high. See Bakewell, *Silver Mining and Society*, 126–27.

13. The nature of this contagion is unknown, but plague appeared in Mexico City from 1633 to 1634. See Peter Gerhard, *A Guide to the Historical Geography of New Spain*, revised edition (Norman: University of Oklahoma Press, 1993), 23; for Zacatecas, see AHEZ, Libro de Cabildo, 4, f. 4, 1637.

14. For Zacatecas, see AHEZ, Libro de Cabildo 3, ff. 199v–200v, 1629. For Mexico, and a comprehensive description of epidemics in New Spain, see Gerhard, *Guide to the Historical Geography*, 23.

15. AHEZ, Notarias, Felipe Espinosa, box 2, exp. 143, ff. 123–24, 1656.

16. AHEZ, Notarias, Felipe Espinosa, box 1, exp. 19, ff. 121–121v, 1653.

17. AHEZ, Indios, box 1, exp. 4, ff. 1–2, 1642.

18. We also need to consider that individuals with fewer economic means often lacked the resources to uproot themselves.

19. See AHEZ, Poder Judicial Civil, box 1, exp. 57, ff. 1–1v, 1666.

20. APZ, Libro de Matrimonios, box 67, carpeta 2, exp. 194, ff. 98v–99, 1742.

21. For the important role of women in Mexica family units, see María de Jesús Rodríguez, "Mujer y familia en la sociedad mexica," in *Presencia y transparencia: La mujer en la historia de México*, ed. Carmen Ramos-Escandón (México: El Colegio de México, Programa Interdisciplinario de Estudios de la Mujer, 1987), 28–32.

22. See Pilar Gonzalbo Aizpuru, "Nuevo mundo, nuevas formas familiares," in *Género, familia y mentalidades en América Latina* (San Juan: Universidad de Puerto Rico, 1997), 34.

23. For family structure in Zacatecas, see Francisco García Gonzáles, *Familia y sociedad en Zacatecas: La vida de un microcosmos minero novohispano, 1750–1830* (Zacatecas: Universidad Autónoma de Zacatecas, 2000). García Gonzáles's analysis focuses on a census from 1823. For studies of the family in the colonial period, see Pilar Gonzalbo Aizpuru, ed., *Familias novohispanas, siglos XVI–XIX* (México: El Centro de Estudios Históricos, Colegio de México, 1990), 389–402. Pilar Gonzalbo Aizpuru, "Con amor y reverencia: Mujeres y familias en el México colonial," in *Educación, familia y vida cotidiana en México virreinal*, ed. Pilar Gonzalbo Aizpuru (México: El Colegio de México, 2013), 69–88; Chantel Cramaussel, "El mestizaje, las familias pluriétnicas de la villa de San Felipe El Real de Chihuahua y la sorpresiva multiplicación de los mulatos en el septentrión novohispano del siglo XVIII," in *Familias pluriétnicas y mestizaje en la Nueva España y el Río de la Plata*, ed. David Carbajal López (Guadalajara: Universidad de Guadalajara, 2014), 17–45. Pilar Gonzalbo Aizpuru, *Familia y orden colonial* (México: El Centro de Estudios Históricos, Colegio de México, 1998); Deborah E. Kanter, *Hijos del Pueblo, Gender, Family and Community in Rural Mexico, 1730–1850* (Austin: University of Texas Press, 2008). For Brazil, see Elizabeth Anne Kuznesof, *Household Economy and Urban Development: São Paolo, 1765 to 1836* (Boulder: Westview Press, 1986); Linda Lewin, *Surprise Heirs I: Illegitimacy, Patrimonial Rights, and Legal Nationalism in Luso-Brazilian Inheritance, 1750–1821* (Stanford: Stanford University Press, 2003); Alida C. Metcalf, *Family and Frontier in Colonial Brazil: Santana de Parnaíba, 1580–1822* (Austin: University of Texas Press, 2005).

24. See Corbeil, "Identities in Motion," 181–82.

25. See AAG, Padrones, 1656.

26. AHEZ, Criminales, box 5, exp. 8, ff. 1–2v, 1711.

27. For the former, see Velasco Murillo, "Laboring Above Ground," 21–31; for the latter, see Teresa C. Vergara, "Growing Up Indian: Migration, Labor, and Life

in Lima (1570–1640)," in *Raising an Empire: Children in Early Modern Iberia and Colonial Latin America*, ed. Ondina E Gonzáles and Bianca Premo (Albuquerque: University of New Mexico Press, 2007), 75–106.

28. AHEZ, Notarias, Felipe Espinosa, box 2, exp. 162, ff. 1–2, 1656.

29. For example, see AHEZ, Notarías, Felipe Espinosa, box 2, ff. 99–100, 1673.

30. Orphans appear sporadically throughout the documentation, making it difficult to garner what percentage of the population they constituted. Mining zones, and the north in general, had a reputation for high rates of illegitimacy. See Thomas Calvo, "The Warmth of the Hearth: Seventeenth-Century Guadalajara Families," in *Sexuality and Marriage in Colonial Latin America*, ed. Asunción Lavrin (Lincoln: University of Nebraska Press, 1989), 302–5; Chantal Cramaussel, "Ilegítimos y abandonados en la frontera norte: Parral y San Bartolomé en el siglo XVII," *Colonial Latin American Historical Review* 4.4 (1995): 405–39. But other studies have noted overall lower rates of illegitimacy among the indigenous population. See Nara Milanich, "Historical Perspectives on Illegitimacy and Illegitimates in Latin America," in *Minor Omissions: Children in Latin American History and Society*, ed. Tobias Hecht (Madison: University of Wisconsin Press, 2002), 74; Cramaussel, "Ilegítimos y abandonados," 415, 420. For Zacatecas, indigenous orphans do not appear with great frequency in the sources.

31. AAG, Padrones, exp. 6, 1669.

32. For colonial policies regarding women's labor and their roles in the workforce, see Julia Tuñón Pablos, *Mujeres en México: Una historia olvidada* (México: Grupo Editorial Planeta, 1987), 55–56.

33. AHEZ, Libro de Cabildo, 3, ff. 262v–265v, 1633.

34. AHEZ, Criminales, box 2, exp. 32, 1667.

35. See AHEZ, Poder Judicial Civil, box 1, exp. 56, ff. 1–2v, 1666; AHEZ, Poder Judicial Civil, box 1, exp. 57, ff. 1–1v, 1666.

36. See Velasco Murillo, "Laboring Above Ground."

37. Bakewell also believes that the migratory nature of the Indian population "facilitated . . . the settlement of whole families in the refining works." See Bakewell, "Economic and Social Outline," 217; Velasco Murillo, "Laboring Above Ground," 10–11.

38. BNM, AFF, box 58, folder 1160, no. 1, f. 2, 1622.

39. For another example, see AAG, Padrones, exp. 7, 1671.

40. APZ, Libro de Matrimonios, box 67, carpeta 2, exp. 194, ff. 143v–144, 1732.

41. See François Giraud, "Mujeres y familia en Nueva España," in *Presencia y transparencia*, 69.

42. This time frame appears to follow suit with other areas in northern Mexico, such as nineteenth-century Sonora, where children commonly began working around the ages of eight or nine. See Laura M. Shelton, "Like a Servant or Like a Son? Circulating Children in Northwestern Mexico, 1790–1850," in *Raising an Empire*, 219–37.

43. For examples, see AHEZ, Criminales, box 5, exp. 8, ff. 1–2v, 1711; AHEZ, Bienes y Difuntos, box 10, exp. 161, ff. 1–5, 1709.

44. For indigenous children, see Dorothy Tanck de Estrada, "Indian Children in Early Mexico," in *Children in Colonial America*, ed. James Marten (New York: New York University Press, 2007), 13–32. For studies on children in Spanish America, see González and Premo, *Raising an Empire*; Bianca Premo, *Children of the Father King: Youth, Authority and Legal Minority in Colonial Lima* (Chapel Hill: University of North Carolina Press, 2005); Hecht, *Minor Omissions*, 3–138.

45. APZ, Mandatos, box 187, carpeta 16, unmarked exp., 1661.

46. Adoption of children often served as a guise for indentured labor. Parents could procure needed funds or pay off debts. See Martin, *Governance and Society*, 61.

47. See AHEZ, Poder Judicial Civil, box 37, exp. 4, ff. 1–2v, 1761. The resolution of this case is unknown.

48. Bakewell, *Silver Mining and Society*, 124.

49. Magaña argues that the Afro-descent population initially settled this barrio. See *Panorámica de la ciudad*, 106.

50. In Zacatecas, individuals from Asia were labeled "chinos," as opposed to "indios chinos," a term often used to refer to an indigenous person of mixed racial descent. The city's Asian population remained relatively small. For examples, see AHEZ, Notarias, Felipe Espinosa, box 2, exp. 188, ff. 153v–154, 1656; AHEZ, Notarias, Felipe Espinosa, box 2, exp. 237, f. 200, 1656.

51. AHEZ, Libro de Cabildo, 5, f. 175, 1657.

52. These figures reflect the number of petitions. A few couples submitted two requests.

53. In 1622, a Franciscan census recorded 804 adult men and women for Tlacuitlapan and several adjacent haciendas de minas. It did not include the town's large number of children. See BNMFF, box 58, folder 1160, no. 1, 1622.

54. I have not found any population figures for El Niño. Spanish officials may have included its vecinos with those of Tonalá Chepinque.

55. To clarify, "migrants" refers to those individuals who arrived from areas outside of Zacatecas's greater jurisdictional boundaries. I did not count as significant migrations the internal movements between the Spanish traza, the four Indian towns, the mining camps of Veta Grande and Pánuco, or the haciendas and ranches located within six leagues (or about sixteen miles) from the city.

56. For demographic analysis using marriage petitions for Nueva Galicia and Nueva Vizcaya, see Robert McCaa, "Marriage, Migration, and Settling Down: Parral (Nueva Vizcaya), 1770–1788," in *Migration in Colonial Spanish America*, ed. David J. Robinson (Cambridge: Cambridge University Press, 1990), 212–37; David A. Brading and Celia Wu, "Population Growth and Crisis: Leon, 1720–1860," *Journal of Latin American Studies* 5.1 (1973): 1–36; Marcello Carmagnani, "Demografía y sociedad: La estructura de los centros mineros del norte de México, 1600–1720," *Historia Mexicana* 21.3 (1972): 419–59.

57. For a discussion of migration trends in northern Mexico, see Michael M. Swann, "Migration, Mobility, and the Mining Towns of Colonial Northern Mexico," in *Migration in Colonial Spanish America*; McCaa, "Marriage, Migration, and Settling Down."

58. The majority of the nonresident Indians came from towns and pueblos near the mining complex of Ojocaliente, located about twenty-one miles southeast of Zacatecas. See APZ, Matrimonios, IINC, 1681–90.

59. See APZ, Matrimonios, IINC, 1681–90.

60. APZ, Matrimonios, IINC, box 67, carpeta 2, exp. 194, ff. 78v–79, 1739.

61. APZ, Matrimonios, IINC, box 3, carpeta 9, f. 39, 1718.

62. APZ, Matrimonios, IINC, box 63, carpeta 2, f. 72, 1720.

63. See Deeds, *Defiance and Deference*, 2003; Juliana Barr, *Peace Came in the Form of a Woman: Indians and Spaniards in the Texas Borderlands* (Chapel Hill: University of North Carolina Press, 2007).

64. Radding, *Wandering Peoples*, 168.

65. See APZ, Matrimonios, IINC, 1681–1740.

66. For an analysis of early seventeenth-century indigenous marriage patterns among discrete ethnic affiliations, see Laurent Corbeil's study of San Luis Potosí, "Identities in Motion," 202–9.

67. During that decade, for example, the endogamy rate of the male Indian population in the city was 80 percent, only slightly lower than the overall 87 percent for men and women. Both the criollo (native-born) and migrant male population had the same endogamy rate of 82 percent. These numbers do not include two Indians who identified as vecinos of the city but did not list a place of origin. Both these men married mestizas. Endogamy rates were even higher in the Indian towns. Records from 1681 to 1690 indicate that only one vecino of an Indian town married a non-Indian, a mestiza. See APZ, Matrimonios, IINC, 1681–1690.

68. See Gonzalbo Aizpuru, "Nuevo mundo, nuevas formas familiares," 18–19. However, there is debate on the topic. Susan Kellogg argues that the Mexica were "not necessarily" endogamous. See *Law and the Transformation*, 163. Moreover, the Mexica and their descendants were not the only ethnic group present in city.

69. APZ, Matrimonios, IINC, box 62, carpeta 10, f. 56, 1718.

70. James Lockhart argued that native peoples who labored in northern mining districts went from being "somewhat Hispanized in the sixteenth century" to having descendants in the eighteenth century who "were no longer Indians at all." See *Provinces of Early Mexico*, 196.

71. For the complete inspection, see AAG, Visitas, ff. 170–72; 174–74v, 1728.

72. AHEZ, Libro de Cabildo, 2, f. 220v, 1608.

73. See APZ, Cofradías, box 141, exp. 1, ff. 9–39, 1800.

74. The word appears as *tenanchi*, a variant of the Nahuatl *temachtia*, or teacher. For the term, see Karttunen, *Analytical Dictionary*, 221.The exact nature of these jobs is unclear. For examples, see APZ, Disciplinar, box 141, carpeta 3, ff. 106, 108v, and 127, 1756–58, and box 145, carpeta 7, f. 41, 1731. By 1758, San Josef also had an official female cook.

75. See APZ, Cofradías, box 141, exp. 1, ff. 9–39, 1800.

76. For micropatriotism in central Mexico, see Horn, *Postconquest Coyoacan*, 20–21.

77. AHEZ, Libro de Cabildo, 10, f. 354, 1710. Having a job in the Spanish city, however, did not necessarily mean social advancement. The executioner claimed that the Spanish cabildo had not paid him his salary in two years. He petitioned the

council to pay him all or at least part of the money owed to him because he had no other resources and lacked funds for such basic necessities as clothing.

78. AHEZ, Ayuntamiento, Indios, box 1, ff. 1–27, 1702. The indigenous soldiers were paid five pesos and armed with *escopetas* (shotguns), bows, arrows, horses, powder, and shot.

79. AHEZ, Notarías, Juan García Picón, protocolos 2, ff. 95v–98, 1735.

80. See AAG, Justicia, Cofradías, Zacatecas, box 1, exp. 44, 1628–1734.

81. AAG, Justicia, Cofradías, Zacatecas, box 1, exp. 44, f. 21v, 1628–1734.

82. A dispute in 1708 between a newly arrived priest and San Josef's confraternity and principales led to a permanent rupture with the Dominicans. See Chapter 5.

83. In the Andes, workers also constructed chapels in the interior of the mines. See Brown, *History of Mining*, 74.

84. For the conflation of church and personal property, see Lockhart, *Nahuas After the Conquest*, 229–35.

85. Schwartz and Solomon, "New Peoples and New Kinds of People," 456.

86. See Linda A. Curcio-Nagy, *The Great Festivals of Mexico City: Performing Power and Identity* (Albuquerque: University of New Mexico Press, 2004), 17–18.

87. AAG, Justicia, Cofradías, Zacatecas, box 1, exp. 44, f. 4, 1628–1734.

88. Conflicts between Spaniards and native peoples over religious precedence were not uncommon (although they rarely led to threats of rioting). For Pátzcuaro, see Flores García and Paredes Martínez, "El cabildo, hospital y cofradía," 194–95. For Mexico City, see Connell, *After Moctezuma*, 234–35n61; Matthew O'Hara, *A Flock Divided: Race, Religion, and Politics in Mexico, 1749–1857* (Durham: Duke University Press, 2009), 144–56.

89. According to San Josef's leaders, the origin of this conflict stemmed from Miguel Francisco's overseer's threat to remove the Santo Cristo from the mine.

90. See Velasco Murillo, "'For the Last Time,'" 62–63.

91. AAG, Justicia, Cofradías, Zacatecas, box 1, exp. 44, f. 11v, 1628–1634.

92. AAG, Zacatecas, box 1, unmarked exp., 1654.

93. AAG, Visitas, box 3, unmarked exp., 1707.

94. Lockhart, *Nahuas After the Conquest*, 208.

95. This episode also illustrates their capability to organize and unify for a common cause. For an examination of how ritual conflicts often masked political discord, see Ramos, *Identity, Ritual, and Power*, 132–52.

96. But not all Indian towns successfully limited outsiders, for example, see Chance's discussion of the urban Indian town of Jalatlaco, which abutted Antequera, Oaxaxa, in *Race and Class*, 152–53.

97. AHEZ, Casas and Solares, box 1, exp. 53, 1747.

98. See APZ, Matrimonios, IINC, 1681–1780.

99. See APZ, Matrimonios, IINC, 1681–1780.

100. Cuernavaca, for example, had a large mestizo population. See Haskett, *Indigenous Rulers*, 1991.

101. AHEZ, Libro de Cabildo, 10, ff. 278–81v, 1709.

102. AHEZ, Libro de Cabildo, 10, ff. 283–85, 1709. The cabildo minutes described Bartolomé, and the aforementioned Nicolás, as both "Indio" and "Indio ladino." Both men presented their petitions in Spanish.

103. AHEZ, Casas and Solares, box 1, exp. 15, 1689.
104. AHEZ, Casas and Solares, box 1, exp. 32, ff. 1–3v, 1661–1719.
105. AHEZ, Libro de Cabildo, 10, f. 278, 1709.
106. AHEZ, Notarías, Juan García Picón, protocolos 3, ff. 35–36, 1736. The Spanish owner was unable to sell the couple the plot because of complaints from a priest. The incident reminds us that while urban centers were multiethnic sites, pockets of segregation existed. In this case, certain area remained closed to non-Spaniards.
107. AHEZ, Notarías, Juan García Picón, protocolos 2, ff. 82v–83v, 1735; book 3, ff. 112v–113, 1736; book 3, ff. 84–85v, 1736.
108. The retention of lands by indigenous communities depended on the number of Spaniards present in the area. In communities near large Spanish clusters, such as Coyoacan, land loss was significant, whereas in more removed areas such as Oaxaca, large tracts of arable land were preserved throughout the colonial period. For the former, see Horn, *Postconquest Coyoacan*, 229–31; for the latter, see Terraciano, *Mixtecs of Colonial Oaxaca*, 226.
109. AHEZ, Bienes y Difuntos, box 1, exp. 13, ff. 1–15v, 1602–1737; AHEZ, Bienes y Difuntos, box 24, exp. 335, ff. 1–2v, 1737.
110. AHEZ, Bienes y Difuntos, box 1, exp. 13, f. 11, 1602–1737.
111. See AHEZ, Casas and Solares, box 1, exp. 32, ff. 1–3v, 1661–1719.
112. See Horn, *Postconquest Coyoacan*, 111–65. For scholarship on indigenous land tenure in central and southern Mexico, see Cline, *Colonial Culhuacan*, 125–59; Gibson, *Aztecs Under Spanish Rule*, 257–99; Lockhart, *Nahuas After the Conquest*, 141–76; Terraciano, *Mixtecs of Colonial Oaxaca*, 198–220. For northern New Spain, see François Chevalier, *Land and Society in Colonial Mexico: The Great Hacienda* (Berkeley: University of California Press, 1966); Susan Deeds, "Land Tenure Patterns in Northern New Spain," *Americas*, 41. 4 (1985), 446–61.
113. Olivia Harris, for example, connects Andean urban living with acculturative experiences, arguing that the term "urban Indians" is an "oxymoronic concept." See "Ethnic Identity and Market Relations," 357–58.
114. For Matías Ramírez, see AHEZ, Libro de Cabildo, 10, f. 5, 1708; 10, f. 176, 1709; 10, f. 294, 1710; 10, f. 371, 1711; 11, f. 3, 1712. For María, see APZ, Matrimonios, IINC, box 3, carpeta 5, ff. 110–13, 1712.
115. On the origins of the term *ladino*, see Adorno, "Images of *Indios Ladinos*," 234–35.
116. See Schwartz and Salomon, "New Peoples and New Kinds of People," 455.
117. In current usage *mineros* or miners refers to mine workers. But in colonial Zacatecas the term was reserved for owners of refining mills—the means of production. Even individuals who owned mines but no mills did not always receive this designation. See Bakewell, "Zacatecas, an Economic and Social Outline," 207. But the meaning of *minero* in colonial Spanish America often depended on local context. In the Andes, Susan Ramírez notes that *minero* applied to individuals who worked below ground; see "Ethnohistorical Dimensions of Mining and Metallurgy in Sixteenth-Century Northern Peru," in *In Quest of Mineral Wealth*, 98.
118. The majority of Indians in Zacatecas, according to Bakewell, "had no means of gathering the capital needed to pay for these means of production" and were relegated to manual labor jobs. See Bakewell, "Introduction," xvi.

119. West, "Early Silver Mining," 123–24.
120. For the complete case, see AHEZ, Bienes y Difuntos, box 25, exp. 343, ff. 1–27, 1730.
121. AHEZ, Bienes y Difuntos, box 17, exp. 263, ff. 1–181, 1719.
122. This appears to be the case with Los Remedios, which in between bursts of productivity yielded very few "metals of high quality."
123. AHEZ, Bienes y Difuntos, box 25, exp. 343, f. 1, 1730.
124. Karen Spalding describes patronage ties between native peoples and non-Indians, as opposed to those "of traditional indigenous society," as another sign of acculturation. This position is representative of other works that depict the evolution of ethnic identity in terms of an "either or model." See Spalding, *De indio a campesino*, 178.
125. AHEZ, Bienes y Difuntos, box 25, exp. 343, ff. 1–10v, 1730.
126. See AHEZ, Poder Judicial Civil, box 26, exp. 8, ff. 1–2v, 1736.
127. See Thomas Calvo, "Warmth of the Hearth," 302–5.
128. Ann Zulawski, citing a study by Luis Miguel Glave, notes the high presence of indigenous female orphans in La Paz in a 1684 census of domestic servants. See "Social Differentiation, Gender, and Ethnicity: Urban Indian Women in Colonial Bolivia, 1640–1725," *Latin American Research Review* 25.2 (1990): 94–95; Teresa C. Vergara also documents the presence of large numbers of indigenous orphans in early seventeenth-century Lima. See "Growing Up Indian," 75–106.
129. Mexico City, Lima, and Havana were among the major Spanish American cities with foundling homes and orphanages. In Spain, charitable institutions existed in Seville and Valencia. See Ann Twinam, "The Church, the State, and the Abandoned: *Expósitos* in Late Eighteenth-Century Havana," in *Raising an Empire*, 163–86.
130. See AHEZ, Poder Judicial Civil, box 4, exp. 4, ff. 1–47v, 1702–1705.
131. It is possible that María served and continued to act as wet nurse after Joseph arrived at Andrea's home.
132. Children received *expósito* designations if both parents failed to appear on their baptismal records. See Twinam, "Church, the State, and the Abandoned," 164.
133. *Calidad* is a term that remains fluid and open to interpretation based on context. For a discussion of *calidad* in northern Mexico, see Robert McCaa, "Calidad, Class, and Marriage in Colonial Mexico: The Case of Parral, 1788–90," *Hispanic American Historical Review* 64.3 (1984): 477–501, especially 478n3; see also Pilar Gonzalbo Aizpuru, "La vida familiar y las movibles fronteras sociales en el siglo XVIII novohispano," in *Educación, familia y vida cotidiana en México virreinal: Trayectoria de Pilar Gonzalbo Aizpuru*, ed. Pilar Gonzalbo Aizpuru (México: El Centro de Estudios Históricos, El Colegio de México, 2013). Also David Tavárez's useful summary of the various attributes that could figure in the construction of calidad: "Legally Indian: Inquisitorial Readings of Indigenous Identity in New Spain," in *Imperial Subjects*, 81–82. For another perspective, see Patricia Seed, "Social Dimensions of Race: Mexico City, 1753," *Hispanic American Historical Review* 62.4 (1982): 569–606.
134. *Jacal*, from the Nahuatl *xacalli*, was associated with "temporary" dwellings in the Mixteca Alta. See Terraciano, *Mixtecs of Colonial Oaxaca*, 201–2. In

Zacatecas, the term perhaps initially referred to short-term living accommodations but eventually became synonymous with permanent indigenous residences.

135. Jane Mangan argues that in some contexts "daily activities were indicative of ethnicity." In Zacatecas, mine labor was usually associated with indigenous peoples. See "Market of Identities," 67–68.

136. Aaron P. Althouse argues that in Pátzcuaro, identifying as mestizo "remained the best available avenue for racial improvement" for individuals of African descent. See "Contested Mestizos," 167. In Zacatecas, native peoples had no compelling reasons to pass as mestizo. Moreover, in her work on the Andes, Karen Spalding raises the point that "passing" from Indian to Spaniard was not a viable or even a desired outcome of the native population. See Spalding, *De indio a campesino*, 181–85. I do, however, agree with Cope that social advancement was about access to patronage networks. See *Limits of Racial Domination*, 106-24.

137. For a study of the tensions between self and communal identification, see Tavárez, "Legally Indian," 81–100; see also Althouse, "Contested Mestizos," 151–75.

138. See Tavárez who cites Cope, "Legally Indian," 82–83.

139. See Adorno, "Images of *Indios Ladinos*," 235–59.

140. Schwartz and Salomon, "New Peoples and New Kinds of People," 443.

141. See Schwartz and Salomon, "New Peoples and New Kinds of People," 448.

142. Olivia Harris, for example, suggests that native peoples who left their communities, adopted European dress, and acquired a trade or skill had "[abandoned] their ethnic affiliation." See "Ethnic Identity and Market Relations," 357–58.

143. Irene Silverblatt draws a similar conclusion. However, while she states that native peoples were "fluent in both imperial and local worlds," she stresses processes of Hispanization rather than biculturalism. See "Becoming Indian," 290–91. Thierry Saignes suggests that urban fluency on the part of the native population had implications beyond the colonial era. He argues that it may have been the skills that native peoples developed navigating the heavily commercialized areas of Potosí and Oruro that account for why these regions continue to retain a strong sense of ethnic identity and community resources. See "Indian Migration and Social Change," 190.

CHAPTER 5. REVIVAL AND SURVIVAL

1. See AHEZ, Criminales, box 17, exp. 13, f. 4, 1806.

2. AHEZ, Criminales, box 17, exp. 13, f. 1, 1806.

3. By 1821, Gerhard estimates that there were two million Indians and individuals of indigenous descent in New Spain. This figure represents a substantial increase from the 1620 nadir of less than one million but pales in comparison to the estimated twenty-two million at 1519. See Gerhard, *Guide to the Historical Geography*, 22–28; for the latter, see Woodrow Borah, *New Spain's Century of Depression* (Berkeley: University of California Press, 1951), 3. For general population trends in the late eighteenth century, see Esteva Fabregat, "Población y mestizaje," 551–604.

4. Claudio Esteva Fabregat based his analysis on Antonio de Alcedo's 1789 *Diccionario geográfico-histórico de las Indias Occidentales o América*. See "Población y mestizaje," 578.
5. See Chance, *Race and Class*, 151.
6. Esteva Fabregat, "Población y mestizaje," 580.
7. Gerhard, *North Frontier*, 158–59.
8. For the Bourbon Reforms in New Spain, see Richard L. Garner and Spiro E. Stefanou, *Economic Growth and Change in Bourbon Mexico* (Gainesville: University Press of Florida, 1993); Ignacio del Río, *La aplicación regional de las Reformas borbónicas en Nueva España: Sonora y Sinaloa, 1768–1787* (México: Universidad Nacional Autónoma de México, Instituto de Investigaciones Históricas, 1995); Horst Pietschmann, *Las reformas borbónicas y el sistema de intendencias en Nueva España: Un estudio político administrativo* (México: Fondo de Cultura Económica, 1996). For general overviews, see Gabriel B. Paquette, *Enlightenment, Governance, and Reform in Spain and Its Empire, 1759–1808* (Basingstoke: Palgrave Macmillan, 2008); Gabriel B. Paquette, ed., *Enlightened Reform in Southern Europe and Its Atlantic Colonies, c. 1750–1830* (Burlington: Ashgate, 2009).
9. See Brading, "Mexican Silver Mining," 307–8.
10. See Gerhard, *North Frontier*, 159.
11. For indigenous migration, see Ann M. Wightman, *Indigenous Migration and Social Change: The Forasteros of Cuzco, 1570–1720* (Durham: Duke University Press, 1990); Larson, Harris, and Tandeter, eds., *Ethnicity, Markets, and Migration*; Karen Powers, *Andean Journeys: Migration, Ethnogenesis, and the State in Colonial Quito* (Albuquerque: University of New Mexico Press, 1995); Radding, *Wandering Peoples*; Robinson, *Migration in Colonial Spanish America*.
12. AAG, Visitas Pastorales, box 4, f. 16, 1752.
13. See Swann, "Migration, Mobility, and the Mining Towns," 150–51.
14. The number of children in Zacatecas accelerated citywide in the early independence period. In his analysis of two neighborhoods of the 1827 census, Francisco García González concluded that there was a substantial presence of children under the age of ten. See *Familia y sociedad*, 190.
15. APZ, Matrimonios, IINC, box 67, carpeta 2, exp., 194, ff.143v–144, 1731–1781.
16. These numbers do not include information on one indigenous male who listed a place of origin I have yet to locate.
17. Place of origin may have had some bearing on migrants and their length of tenure in a community. In his study of Parral from 1770 to 1788, Robert McCaa found that long-distance migrants were among the least likely to develop long-term roots in their new towns. See "Marriage, Migration, and Settling Down," 232–34.
18. APZ, Libro de Matrimonios, box 67, carpeta 2, exp. 194, ff. 95v–96, 1731–1781.
19. For an overview of Bourbon policies and approaches from the early to the middle century, see Francisco A. Eissa-Barroso and Ainara Vazquez, eds., *Early Bourbon Spanish America: Politics and Society in a Forgotten Era (1700–1759)* (Leiden: Brill, 2013).

20. See O'Hara, *Flock Divided*, 103; Brian Larkin, *The Very Nature of God: Baroque Catholicism and Religious Reform in Bourbon Mexico City* (Albuquerque: University of New Mexico Press, 2010), 240–42; Karen Melvin, *Building Colonial Cities of God: Mendicant Orders and Urban Culture in New Spain, 1570–1800* (Stanford: Stanford University Press, 2012), 55–65.

21. See Christoph Rosenmüller, "'The Indians . . . Long for Change': The Secularization of Regular Parishes in Mid Eighteenth-Century New Spain," in *Early Bourbon Spanish America*, 143.

22. See Lockhart, *Nahuas After the Conquest*, 350–51.

23. Deeds, *Defiance and Deference*, 182–83.

24. See Gerhard, *North Frontier*, 157.

25. By 1558, only one permanent chapel had been constructed. See also AHEZ, Libro de Cabildo, 1, f. 8v, 1559.

26. For examples, see AHEZ, Libro de Cabildo, 1, f. 7, f. 8v, 1559; Libro de Cabildo, 1, f. 84, 1579; and Libro de Cabildo, 1, f. 32v, 1578.

27. Some of these personal enterprises included exploiting vacant or abandoned mining sites or the smelting of ores in their private furnaces—common practices in Potosí as well. For the latter, see Tandeter, *Coercion and Market*, 85–144.

28. Gibson documents similar conflicts for the Valley of Mexico; see *Aztecs Under Spanish Rule*, 105–11.

29. In 1707, for example, secular clerics tried to claim jurisdiction over the indigenous and casta populations in the city and at adjacent mining haciendas. Parish priests warned mine owners not to allow their servants to congregate with the priests of the indigenous pueblos and complained to viceregal officials that the clerics of Tlacuitlapan administered to Indians, castas, and other vagrants who lived in barrios and mines outside of their congregation. Tlacuitlapan's clerics responded by showing directives from 1584, 1589, and 1655 that authorized them to minister to mine workers of any ethnic group outside the indigenous pueblo. However, parish priests insisted that these documents granted them permission to teach, correct, and punish but not to administer sacraments. Bishop Diego de Camacho ruled in favor of the priests of Tlacuitlapan, granting them continued jurisdiction over all the Indians who lived in barrios and mines adjacent to the pueblos. This episode is telling in that it suggests that individuals—indigenous or otherwise—felt more connected to the orders than to clerics randomly assigned to them by colonial authorities. See AAG, Visitas, book 3, unmarked exp., 1707.

30. AAG, Zacatecas, box 1, unmarked exp., ff. 1–12, 1708.

31. AAG, Zacatecas, box 2, umarked exp., ff. 1–7v, 1702–1716.

32. San Josef continued to have problems with the Dominicans even after authorities removed them from their custody. See AHEZ, Libro de Cabildo, 10, f. 4, 1708; AAG, Zacatecas, box 2, umarked exp., ff. 1–7v, 1702–1716.

33. According to Christoph Rosenmüller, very few native communities protested secularization. The Spanish elite, he claims, were the most vehement opponents. See "'The Indians . . . Long for Change,'" 156.

34. AHEZ, Poder Judicial Civil, box 53, exp. 25, 1801.

35. See AGI, Guadalajara, 56, unmarked, no pagination, 1627.

36. APZ, Mandatos, Circulares, box 187, carpeta 1, loose-leaf, 1835.

37. The reduction of feast days reflected not only the growing power of miners in the nineteenth century but also the continuation of eighteenth-century practices of reducing the number of feast days and the pageantries associated with them. See Curcio-Nagy, *Great Festivals*, 107–11.

38. AHEZ, Libro de Cabildo, 1, f. 84, 1579.

39. For cofradías and the reform movements of the late colonial period, see Larkin, "Confraternities and Communities," 197–207.

40. See Larkin, "Confraternities and Communities," 199–200.

41. APZ, Disciplinar, box 145, carpeta 2, loose-leaf, 1563. As of 1830, a continued association remained between the two confraternities. AAG, Zacatecas, box 1, loose-leaf, 1830; for the merger, see Mancuso, *Cofradías mineras*, 86.

42. AGI, Guadalajara, 543, ff. 372v–379, 1798.

43. See AGI, Guadalajara, 543, ff. 372v–379, 1798.

44. AAG, Zacatecas, box 3, unnumbered exp., ff. 1–12, 1771–1787.

45. For example, see AAG, Gobierno, Zacatecas, box 4, unmarked exp., 1791–1810.

46. AAG, Visitas, book 3, unmarked exp., 1707.

47. A reference to the cofradía appears in an ex-voto from 1832. See the comments in the conclusion.

48. Personal communication, Judith Medina Reynosa, July 15, 2007.

49. See Mancuso, *Cofradías mineras*, 84, 116.

50. Matthew D. O'Hara documents the various indigenous responses to the religious reforms in Mexico City. See *Flock Divided*, especially 91–156.

51. High mercury prices, insolvent miners, heavy crown taxes on mineral production, and inadequate draining techniques were some of the main causes of the mid-eighteenth-century production decline. See Brading, "Mexican Silver Mining," 307–8.

52. Gerhard, *North Frontier*, 159.

53. In general, these jobs reflected those typically held by native peoples. For Antequera, from 1793 to 1797, Chance documented the top four indigenous jobs as weaver, mason, hatter, and baker. The Zacatecas data also confirm that few Indians worked in elite or high-status artisan jobs, which follows Chance's arguments that native peoples had experienced relatively little "occupational mobility" from a century earlier. See "Urban Indian," 626–27, 622. See also, for example, lists for Quito from 1768 in Minchom, *People of Quito*, 183–86. The diversity of the urban indigenous workforce in 1800 is documented in detail by Luis Fernando Granados. See "Cosmopolitan Indians," 426–97.

54. An informal survey of the records does not suggest that women were traveling to the city with their fiancés. See APZ, Matrimonios, IINC, 1771–1780.

55. See APZ, Matrimonios, IINC, box 76, carpeta 8, ff. 59–60, 1777.

56. See APZ, Matrimonios, IINC, box 75, carpeta 8, ff. 33–34, 1773.

57. See George F. Lyon, *Journal of a Residence and Tour in the Republic of Mexico in the Year 1826: With Some Account of the Mines of that Country* (London: John Murray, Albemarle Street, 1828), 2:286. Early seventeenth-century

accounts from the Andes note the presence of indigenous women and children in mining-related activities. Both searched for ore. Some women participated in ore trading and smelting. See Bakewell, *Miners of the Red Mountain*, 104, 141. Jane Mangan argues that Andean women played a role in the rescate trade by collecting the ores from their husbands at the mines. See *Trading Roles*, 32.

58. García González, *Familia y sociedad*, 126–30.

59. See Richard L. Garner, "Prices and Wages in Eighteenth-Century Mexico," in *Essays on the Price History of Eighteenth-Century Latin America*, ed. Lyman L. Johnson and Enrique Tandeter (Albuquerque: University of New Mexico Press, 1990), 73–108; for Zacatecas, in particular, 93–98, 100–102.

60. For some examples of wages received by hacienda workers, see AHEZ, Poder Judicial Civil, box 51, exp. 29, various fojas, 1798; Poder Judicial Civil, box 61, exp. 4, various fojas, 1820–1821.

61. Brading, "Mexican Silver Mining," 311.

62. Garner, *Zacatecas, 1750–1821*, 322.

63. See John M. Monteiro, "Labor Systems," in *The Cambridge Economic History of Latin America*, vol. 1, *The Colonial Era and the Short Nineteenth Century*, ed. Victor Bulmer-Thomas, John H. Coatsworth, and Roberto Cortés Conde (Cambridge: Cambridge University Press, 2006), 227.

64. See Martin, *Governance and Society*, 50–56.

65. See Brígida von Mentz, "Coyuntura minera y protesta campesina en el centro de Nueva España, siglo XVIII," in *La minería mexicana: De la colonia al siglo XX*, ed. Inés Herrera Canales (México: Instituto de Investigaciones Dr. José María Luis Mora, 1998), 23–45.

66. See Doris Ladd, *The Making of a Strike: Mexican Silver Workers' Struggles in Real de Monte, 1766–1775* (Lincoln: University of Nebraska Press, 1988).

67. Brading, "Mexican Silver Mining," 310–11.

68. See Lyon, *Journal of a Residence*, 286.

69. David Brading quotes a mine worker's complaint to the viceroy: "In addition to the fact that in the mine of the Quebradilla they do not pay us in the customary fashion, they are destroying us by giving us our salary in goods." See "Mexican Silver Mining," 318.

70. Kendall Brown argues that some laborers in New Spain could earn as much as "20 reales per day" beyond their set wages. See *History of Mining*, 66.

71. See, for example, Eric Van Young's discussion of the decline of real wages in nearby Guadalajara in *Hacienda and Market*, 248–59; on wage stagnation during the eighteenth century, see Richard L. Garner, "Prices and Wages," 76.

72. While we lack information on living conditions in the late colonial period, Harry E. Cross has worked extensively on rural living standards for Zacatecas in the nineteenth century. See "Dieta y nutrición en el medio rural de Zacatecas y San Luis Potosí (siglos XVIII and XIX)," *Historia Mexicana* 31.1 (1981): 101–16; Cross, "Living Standards in Rural Nineteenth-Century Mexico: Zacatecas (1820–1880)," *Journal of Latin American Studies* 10.1 (1978): 1–19.

73. AHEZ, Intendencia, Gobierno, box 1, exp. 20, 1796.

74. AHEZ, Intendencia, box 1, exp. 3, 1790.

75. The documents suggest that Emiterio's son worked for the charcoal maker as well, suggesting a cycle of indentured servitude. See AHEZ, Poder Judicial Civil, box 53, exp. 25, ff. 1–3v, 1801.

76. I offer thanks to Juan Valencia Rojas for providing me with some transcribed material from this census.

77. Frédérique Langue argues that in 1781, mestizos constituted 48 percent of the laboring population. See "Trabajadores y formas de trabajo en las minas zacatecanas del siglo XVIII," *Historia Mexicana* 40.3 (1991): 467.

78. See Brown, *History of Mining*, 85.

79. Brading cites a quote from Lucas Alamán in which the Mexican statement claims that the majority of Guanajuato's workers were mulattos and mestizos. But he made these comments in 1826, and hence at some distance from the late eighteenth century. See *Miners and Merchants*, 146.

80. For population figures, see Martin, *Governance and Society*, 210.

81. APZ, Matrimonios, IINC, 1751–1760.

82. Four petitioners listed vecino status in a location outside of Zacatecas. I was unable to identify the location of one town. See APZ, Matrimonios, IINC, 1751–1760.

83. See Bakewell, *Silver Mining and Society*, 56.

84. AGI, Guadalajara, 248, N. 4, ff. 1025v–1026v, 1772.

85. AGI, Guadalajara, 248, N. 4, ff. 1025v–1026v, 1772.

86. AGI, Guadalajara, 248, N. 4, ff. 1027–1027v, 1772.

87. AAG, Zacatecas, box 3, unmarked exp., 1775–1780, ff. 1–4, 1777.

88. AAG, Zacatecas, box 3, unmarked exp., 1771–1782.

89. AAG, Visitas Pastorales, box 7, 1798–1799.

90. AAG, Zacatecas, box 3, unmarked exp., 1770.

91. See AGI, Guadalajara, 543, ff. 372v–379, 1798.

92. See AGI, Guadalajara, 543, ff. 372v–379, 1798.

93. See Van Young, *Hacienda and Market*, 29.

94. For Guadalajara's population, see Van Young, *Hacienda and Market*, 30–31; for Zacatecas, see Gerhard, *North Frontier*, 158–59.

95. See Brading, *Miners and Merchants*, 340–42.

96. See Gerhard, *Guide to the Historical Geography*, 122.

97. See Tutino, *Making a New World*.

98. See AHEZ, Intendencia, Zacatecas, box 2, exp. 1, loose-leaf, 1799. On the basis of Royal Treasury figures, the spike in tribute collection in 1799 suggests that Branciforte enacted the measure in 1798 during his last year in office. For tribute figures, see John J. TePaske and Herbert S. Klein, *Ingresos y egresos de la Real Hacienda de Nueva España* (México: Instituto Nacional de Antropología e Historia, Colección Fuentes, 1986–1988), "Zacatecas summary," vol. 2, n.p.

99. Tribute, however, had doubled from 1800, when the total collected was 12,745 pesos. This dramatic increase suggests that it may have taken time to implement the new tax. Resistance to the new measure was more than likely. For royal

treasury figures, see Carlos Maríchal, *Bankruptcy of Empire: Mexican Silver and the Wars between Spain, Britain, and France (1760–1810)* (New York: Cambridge University Press, 2007), 70.

100. See "Ordenanzas de la división de la muy noble y leal ciudad de Nuestra Señora de los Zacatecas," as transcribed in Ernesto Lemoine Villicaña, "Miscelánea zacatecana: Documentos históricos-geográficos de los siglos XVII al XIX," *Boletín del Archivo General de la Nación* 5.2 (1964): 284–315.

101. "Ordenanzas de la división," 284.

102. "Ordenanzas de la división," 303.

103. For 1799, see AHEZ, Intendencia, Zacatecas, box 2, exp. 1, loose-leaf, 1799; for 1806, see Intendencia, Zacatecas, box 2, exp. 3, loose-leaf, 1806.

104. See AHEZ, Intendencia, Gobierno, box 1, exp. 20, loose-leaf, 1796.

105. AHEZ, Intendencia, Gobierno, box 1, exp. 20, loose-leaf, 1796.

106. See "Ordenanzas de la división," 284.

107. AHEZ, Intendencia, Zacatecas, box 2, exp. 3, loose-leaf, 1806.

108. AHEZ, Criminales, box 18, exp. 13, ff. 7–8v, 1806.

109. "Ordenanzas de la división," 303–4.

110. AHEZ, Criminales, box 18, exp. 13, ff. 9–11v, 1806.

111. AHEZ, Intendencia, Zacatecas, box 2, exp. 24, loose-leaf, 1804.

112. For the case, see AHEZ, Poder Judicial Civil, box 36, exp. 15, 1759.

113. For other examples, see AHEZ, Libro de Cabildo, ff. 59–82, 1742–1743; Libro de Cabildo, ff. 1–25v, 1752.

114. For example, for Tlacuitlapan, see AHEZ, Intendencia, Zacatecas, box 1, exp. 18, loose-leaf, 1800. For San Josef, see AHEZ, Intendencia, Zacatecas, box 2, exp. 24, loose-leaf, 1804. Indigenous elections probably continued through the independence period.

115. In his testimony, Carrion himself appeared to recognize his tenuous position of authority, admitting that he was part of the watch but not a formal official. See AHEZ, Criminales, box 17, exp. 13, f. 2v, 1806.

116. AHEZ, Criminales, box 17, exp. 13, f. 16, 1806.

117. AHEZ, Criminales, box 17, exp. 13, f. 15v, 1806.

118. AHEZ, Criminales, box 17, exp. 13, f. 9v, 1806.

119. The cabildos of Pátzcuaro, Uruapan, and several other communities in Michoacán were dissolved in retribution for their violent reactions to the Bourbon Reforms. See Castro Gutiérrez, "Conflictos y fraudes electorales," 62. See also *Nueva ley y nuevo rey: Reformas borbónicas y rebelión popular en Nueva España* (Zamora: El Colegio de Michoacán, 1996), 115–275.

120. AHEZ, Criminales, box 17, exp. 13, f. 7v, 1806.

121. Gómez's incarceration had occurred in the public jail in the Spanish center. I have yet to uncover the archival materials for the prior detention of a Spanish alcalde in El Niño. Gómez refers to the case in his complaint. See AHEZ, Criminales, box 17, exp. 13, f. 7v, 1806.

122. AHEZ, Criminales, box 17, exp. 13, f. 7v, 1806.

123. AHEZ, Criminales, box 17, exp. 13, ff. 9v–10, 1806.

124. For the decline of indigenous government in Mexico City, see Gibson, *Aztecs Under Spanish Rule*, 191–93.

125. See Brading, "Revival of Zacatecas," 303.

126. In 1754 the combined population of non-Indians in Zacatecas was 11,300. By 1799, that figure had more than doubled to 23,500. See Gerhard, *North Frontier*, 159.

CONCLUSION

1. According to the 2010 Mexican census, Zacatecas ranked third in the nation (behind the states of Aguascalientes and Colima) for the fewest native-language speakers. The registered 4,924 individuals constituted less than 1 percent of the total population. The most common languages were Huichol and Nahuatl. Zacatecas also had the third-smallest population of individuals who identified as "indigenous" on the census (2.9 percent), regardless of whether they spoke a native language. See John P. Schmal, "Essays and Research on Indigenous Mexico," http://www.somosprimos.com.

2. For a study of urban indigenous society during the postindependence period, see Andrés González Lira, *Comunidades indígenas frente a la ciudad de México: Tenochtitlan y Tlatelolco, sus pueblos y barrios, 1812–1919* (México: El Colegio de México, 1983), 21–76.

3. Catorce belonged to the jurisdiction of San Luis Potosí. For Zacatecas, see Brading, "Revival of Zacatecas," 308, 318; Mariana Terán Fuentes, "Por lealtad al rey, a la patria y a la religión: Los años de transición en la provincia de Zacatecas, 1808–1814," *Mexican Studies/Estudios Mexicanos* 24.2 (2008): 293–97.

4. See Anne Staples, "Mexican Mining and Independence: The Saga of Enticing Opportunities," in *The Birth of Modern Mexico, 1780–1824*, ed. Christon I. Archer (Wilmington: Scholarly Resources, 2003), 151–64.

5. Arturo Burnes Ortiz, *La minería en la historia económica de Zacatecas (1546–1876)* (Zacatecas: Universidad Autónoma de Zacatecas, 2008), 124–25.

6. The growing indigenous population of the late colonial period was matched by a rise in the number of *castas*, the latter also constituting a third of New Spain's population by 1821. See Gerhard, *Guide to the Historical Geography*, 25.

7. See O'Hara, *Flock Divided*, 188–91.

8. Magaña, *Panorámica de la ciudad de Zacatecas*, 87.

9. See Lutz, *Santiago de Guatemala*, 129–32; for Antequera, Oaxaca, see Chance, *Race and Class*, 169–71.

10. Chance, "On the Mexican Mestizo," 154–62; Esteva Fabregat, "Población y mestizaje."

11. Chance, "On the Mexican Mestizo," 165–66.

12. Rick Anthony López, *Crafting Mexico: Intellectuals, Artisans, and the State After the Revolution* (Durham: Duke University Press, 2010), 127–47. For the development of mestizo identities in the postcolonial Andes, see Fiona Wilson, "Indians and Mestizos: Identity and Urban Popular Culture in Andean Peru," *Journal of Southern African Studies*, 26.2 (June 2000): 239–53.

13. Magnus Mörner argues that the emergence of mestizos as a significant demographic group dates to the mid-seventeenth century. See *Race Mixture*, 98. His impressionistic arguments are not borne out by the demographic data. Esteva Fabregat believes, however, that the mestizo population was higher than the counts

indicate. See "Población y mestizaje," 554. See also Schwartz and Salomon, "New Peoples and New Kinds of People," 478–79; de la Cadena, "Are *Mestizos* Hybrids?" 264–65.

14. Cope identifies two "parent populations," Indian and African. See *Limits of Racial Domination*, 82–84.

15. See APZ, Libro de Matrimonio, box 67, exp. 194, ff. 64v–65, 1736.

16. See Elías Amador, *Nombres indígenas todavía en uso en el estado de Zacatecas* (Zacatecas: Tip. del Hospicio de Niños en Guadalupe, 1897).

17. For the influence of native culture on Spaniards in other areas of New Spain, see Solange Alberro, *Del gachupín al criollo, o de cómo los españoles de México dejaron der serlo* (México: El Colegio de México, 1992), 55–98. In frontier zones, it was not uncommon for Spaniards or other ethnic groups to integrate into indigenous society. See the various examples in Stern, "Marginals and Acculturation," 174–78. Biological miscegenation among the Spanish population was also common. Anthony Pagden argues that "by the beginning of the eighteenth century, there were few criollo families who were entirely without Indian blood." See "Identity Formation in Spanish America," in *Colonial Identity in the Atlantic World, 1500–1800*, ed. Nicholas Canny and Anthony Pagden (Princeton: Princeton University Press, 1987), 69.

18. Radding, *Wandering Peoples*, 137–38, 164; Deeds, *Defiance and Deference*, 129.

19. Martin, *Governance and Society*, 44.

20. For examples, see Bakewell, *Miners of the Red Mountain*, 49; Harris, "Ethnic Identity and Market Relations," 354.

21. Stern, "Marginals and Acculturation," 165.

22. Felipe Castro Gutiérrez argues that "sooner or later" urban indigenous barrios evolved into mestizo suburbs in the most "marginal and impoverished sections" of the city. See "El origen y conformación," 122.

23. For example, for the crucial role of migrants in the construction of European societies, see Robert Bartlett, *The Making of Europe: Conquest, Colonization, and Cultural Change, 950–1350* (Princeton: Princeton University Press, 1993), and the various case studies in Bert De Munck and Anne Winter, eds., *Gated Communities? Regulating Migration in Early Modern Cities* (Farnham: Ashgate Publishing, 2012).

24. Laurent Corbeil's work focuses on indigenous people's daily experiences, economic transactions, and personal and social relationships. See "Identities in Motion." In addition, Fernando Serrano is completing a dissertation on native communities in the Guanajuato area at the University of California, Los Angeles.

25. Matthew, *Memories of Conquest*, particularly 132–77.

26. For Mérida, the eight barrios were Santiago, San Cristóbal, Santa Ana, Santa Catalina, San Juan, Santa Lucía, San Sebastián, and La Mejorada. See Lentz, "Batabs of the Barrio." For Valladolid, see Paredes Martínez, "Convivencia y conflictos," 50–54.

27. Pablo Miguel Sierra Silva speaks of several native communities that bordered Puebla, including the Mexica settlements of San Francisco, Analco, El Alto,

as well as a Mixtec community, Yancuitlalpan, and Santiago, a neighborhood of people from nearby Cholula. See Velasco Murillo and Sierra Silva, "Mine Workers and Weavers." Eight indigenous barrios—La Merced, Santo Domingo, San Antonio, San Gerónimo, Santiago, San Francisco, Santa Cruz, and Espíritu Santo—encircled Santiago de Guatemala.

28. For a complete list of cities and figures, see Aaron Terrazas, "Mexican Immigrants in the United States," *Migration Information Source* (2010), http://www.migrationpolicy.org/article/mexican-immigrants-united-states-0.

29. This information derives from the US Census Bureau's 2011 ACS. See Sierra Stoney and Jeanne Batalova, "Mexican Immigrants in the United States," *Migration Information Source* (2013), http://www.migrationpolicy.org/article/mexican-immigrants-united-states.

30. See Richard C. Jones, *Ambivalent Journey: U.S. Migration and Economic Mobility in North-Central Mexico* (Tucson: University of Arizona Press, 1995), 51–52.

31. Zacatecas came in fourth behind Guanajuato, Michoacán, and Jalisco. See Terrazas, "Mexican Immigrants in the United States."

32. See Stoney and Batalova, "Mexican Immigrants in the United States."

33. See Sam Quinones, "A Tale of Two Villages: Immigrants from Atolinga, Mexico, Build a Community More Vibrant Than the One They Used to Call Home," *Chicago Tribune*, July 22, 2001, http://articles.chicagotribune.com/2001-07-22/features/0107210271_1_restaurant-mexican-chicago-area/4.

Glossary

alcabala   Merchandise duties; sales tax.
alcalde   First-instance judge and town council member.
alcalde mayor   Chief magistrate of a designated jurisdiction.
alcalde ordinario   A municipal judge.
alguacil mayor   A town constable.
almotacén   An inspector of weights and measures.
almude   A measurement, used for maize; three almudes equals approximately eight bushels.
altepetl   Nahuatl term. The preconquest indigenous state; the basic organizing structural unit of central Mexican indigenous society.
amparo   Protection provided to indigenous peoples by colonial officials.
antiguo   An elder with important standing in the community.
aposento   Living quarters or small storage building.
apurandero/a   Individual, usually an older woman, assigned to carry off and rewash ore after its initial mixture with quicksilver.
arroba   A measurement equal to fifty pounds.
audiencia   The crown appointed high court of a district.
aviador   A creditor who supplied miners with goods or financed their projects.
barretero   A laborer who excavated ore from a mine with a crowbar or a pick.
barrio   A smaller unit, neighborhood, or community within a city.
barrios de indios   Indigenous neighborhoods; in this study, those communities that had yet to receive "town" status.
cabecera   The seat of a larger municipal unit.
cabildo   A municipal town council.
cacique   Taíno term. An Indian ruler.
cafre   In this study, an enslaved Asian, usually from the Philippines.
calidad   Assessment of an individual's social standing drawn from myriad factors, including, but not limited to, ethnicity, place of origin and residence, occupation, civil status, and social networks.
calpolli   Nahuatl term. Constituent political units.
camino   A road.
capilla   A small chapel.
carbón   Charcoal; used in the smelting process.
carcel pública   The public jail.
carnicería   Slaughterhouse or butcher shop.
casa de fundación   Assay office or foundry house where the amount of refined silver was registered for taxation.
casa del cabildo   The town hall.

casta Individual of diverse racial ancestry.
caudal An individual's resources or wealth.
cendradilla Small cupel furnace used to smelt crushed ore.
Chichimec Nahuatl term. Deprecating and homogenizing term for nonempire peoples of northern Mexico who did not practice sedentary agriculture.
chinos Term given to individuals of Asian descent living in New Spain.
ciudad A population center that had achieved the municipal status of city.
coatequitl Nahuatl term. A system of preconquest rotational draft labor in which native peoples worked on public works projects for and within their communities under local supervision.
cocolitzli Nahuatl term. Illness or plague.
cofradía A confraternity or religious lay brotherhood.
comarca In general terms, a border or district; in this study, a mining zone near the city.
compañía A group of individuals who owned a mine in partnership.
corregidor The highest-ranking Spanish official in the city.
coyote/coyota An individual of indigenous and African descent.
criollo An individual who is native born or indigenous to an area.
cuadrilla Labor gang at mines or refining plants.
cuartel During Zacatecas's intendancy period, from 1786 to 1810, a subdistrict within a city.
demanda A criminal or civil suit.
diezmo A concessionary tax of one-tenth that the crown granted to silver produced from an official hacienda de minas.
diputado Municipal officer or representative.
doctrina A religious parish.
don/doña Spanish honorific title.
donativo A collection of charitable money for the crown.
encomendero An individual with rights to indigenous labor and tribute.
escribano A notary.
escriptura de ventas Bill of sale.
estancia An outlying settlement.
expósito An orphan.
extramuros Literally, "outside the walls." Refers to an area outside the jurisdiction of the Spanish city.
ex-voto An offering to a religious figure in thanks for their intercession.
factor A purchasing agent.
fiscal A religious or civil functionary.
gobernador An indigenous governor.
hacienda de minas In general, a silver-refining plant; also called a hacienda de beneficio.
hermandad A lay brotherhood.
hijos Literally "sons," but in this study the corporate members of a town or confraternity.
horno (hornillo) Small cylindrical furnace used to smelt crushed ore.

hospital   A hospital.
huehuetque   Nahuatl term. Male community elders.
huerta   An orchard or farm.
iglesia mayor   The principal church of a town or city.
ingenio   Stamp mill to crush, process, and refine ores.
jacal   Nahuatl loanword. A humble, temporary dwelling. In Zacatecas, the term became associated with permanent indigenous residences.
juez   In this study, used only in the pueblo of San Josef for a few years; appears to be a synonym for *regidor*.
justicia mayor   In this study, a lower-level functionary of an Indian town council.
ladino/a   Term used to describe a native person who had Spanish-language fluency. In this study, it also refers to bicultural individuals.
lavadero   A washer used to separate ore from waste in the smelting process.
libro de cabildo   The minutes of the town council's proceedings.
libro de cofradía   The minutes or records of a confraternity.
libro de matrimonios   Parish book of marriage petitions.
lobo/a   An individual of black and Indian ancestry.
mandón   An officer on an indigenous municipal council with some involvement in mining production.
matlazahuatl   Nahuatl term. A widespread illness or epidemic; in this study, most likely typhus.
mayordomo   A confraternity foreman.
memoriales   In this study, notes from indigenous elections that were submitted to the Spanish town council.
merced   A Spanish land grant.
mestizaje   Biological or cultural miscegenation.
mestizo/a   An individual of Spanish and Indian ancestry.
milpa   Nahuatl loanword. A maize field.
mina   A mine.
minero   An owner of a mine or refining mill.
moreno/a   An individual with some African ancestry.
morisco/a   An individual of mixed ancestry, possibly Spanish and African.
motín   A riot.
naboría   Arawak term for an Indian dependent. However, the meaning varied according to time periods and regions. In central Mexico and the Yucatán, *naboría* or *indio de servicio*, referred to an Indian dependent in the permanent service of a Spaniard. In this study, a free wage worker.
Nahuatl   The predominate language spoken by the native population of central Mexico.
nahuatlato   Nahuatl term. Literally "Nahuatl speaker"; often generically applied to translators of indigenous languages.
natural   A term used to indicate an individual native to a place; often used to refer to an indigenous person.
oidor   A judge of the viceregal court (Audiencia).
originario(a)   Denotes an individual who is native to a location.

padrino Fictive kin; a godfather.
padrón An ecclesiastical census.
partida In silver mining, a worker's share of precious metals.
peninsular An individual living in the Americas who was born in Spain.
pepena Nahuatl term. A labor agreement in which native peoples kept a certain percentage of the ore that they extracted.
plata del rescate Silver produced outside of an official hacienda de minas, usually by native peoples from pepenas.
plaza pública The main square of a town.
poblador A settler.
postura The authorized price assigned by authorities to an item.
pregonero A town crier.
principal An important indigenous community leader who did not have a formal position on the town council.
pueblo A settlement with the municipal status of a town.
quinto A tax of one-fifth due to the Spanish crown on precious metals.
ranchería In Potosí, an Indian neighborhood; in northern New Spain, a small, semisedentary indigenous settlement.
realengas Vacant or unappropriated land.
real de minas Designation for a municipality dedicated to mining.
Real Hacienda The royal treasury.
reclutador An individual hired to recruit indigenous men for mine work. Also known as a *sacagentes*.
regidor A member of the municipal town council.
regidor mayor The head councilman.
repartimiento A system of forced draft labor implemented in New Spain.
repasador An individual who refined silver.
repúblicas de indios y españoles Separate republics for Indians and Spaniards mandated by the crown; theoretically maintained through separate living spaces and sets of laws.
rescate In this study; unrefined and usually unregistered silver ores traded by native peoples.
saçemis Nahuatl loanword. Informal, ritualized fights between native peoples.
sonsacar A practice in which a miner enticed a native person with higher wages to leave a work site before completing his original contract.
soplillo An indigenous blowpipe used to blast air in furnaces and aid in the smelting process.
sujeto A subject community within a larger jurisdictional unit.
tameme Nahuatl term. An indigenous porter or carrier; often an enslaved individual.
tenatero Nahuatl loanword. An individual who carried ores out of the mines.
tequío Nahuatl loanword. An agreement to produce a certain amount of ore for specific wages.
tianguiz Nahuatl loanword. The marketplace.
tlatoani Nahuatl term. The hereditary ruler of an altepetl.

tlaxilacalli Nahuatl term. The constituent part of a preconquest indigenous state (altepetl).
tomines Three-eighths of a peso.
topile Nahuatl term. Constable.
traza The Spanish administrative, economic, and demographic sections of an urban center.
vagabundo An individual with no fixed occupation or residence; in this study, the term could also refer to a laborer working without a contract.
varas A form of measurement (about thirty-three inches).
vecino/a A property-owning individual with rights within the town; a resident or householder of a population center.
verdugo The town executioner.
villa An urban settlement. In theory, a villa had anywhere from two thousand to four thousand vecinos and hence was larger than a town, but smaller than a city.
visitador The judge and inspector of the high court of a district.
xacalli Nahuatl term. A house.
yanacona Quechua loanword. Indigenous free wage laborer in the Andes.

Bibliography

Archives
Archivo General de las Indias (AGI), Seville, Spain
Archivo General de la Nación (AGN), Mexico City, México
Archivo Histórico de la Arquidiócesis de Guadalajara (AAG), Guadalajara, México
Archivo Histórico del Estado de Zacatecas (AHEZ), Zacatecas, México
Archivo Parroquial de Zacatecas (APZ), Zacatecas, México
British Library (BL), London, England
Biblioteca Nacional (BNM), Mexico City, México
Biblioteca Pública del Estado de Jalisco (BPEJ), Guadalajara, México
New York Public Library, Obadiah Rich Collection (NYPL, ORC), New York City, United States

Consulted Works
Acuña, René. *Relaciones geográficas del siglo XVI: Nueva Galicia.* México: Universidad Nacional Autónoma de México, Instituto de Investigaciones Antropológicas, 1982.
Adams, David B. *Las colonias tlaxcaltecas de Coahuila y Nuevo León en la Nueva España: Un aspecto de la colonización del norte de México.* Saltillo: Archivo Municipal de Saltillo, 1991.
Adams, Richard E. W., and Murdo J. MacLeod, eds. *Mesoamerica.* Vol. 2 of *The Cambridge History of the Native Peoples of the Americas.* Cambridge: Cambridge University Press, 2000.
Adorno, Rolena. "Images of *Indios Ladinos* in Early Colonial Peru." In *Transatlantic Encounters: Europeans and Andeans in the Sixteenth Century,* edited by Kenneth J. Andrien and Rolena Adorno, 232–70. Berkeley: University of California Press, 1991.
Ahumada Sámano, Pedro de. *Relación sobre la rebelión de los indios zacatecas.* Biblioteca de Historiadores Mexicanos. México: Vargas Rea, [1562] 1954.
Aiton, Arthur Scott. *Antonio de Mendoza, First Viceroy of New Spain.* Durham: Duke University Press, 1927.
Alatriste, Oscar. *Desarrollo de la industria y la comunidad minera de Hidalgo del Parral durante la segunda mitad del siglo XVIII (1765–1810).* México: Universidad Nacional Autónoma de México, 1983.
Alberro, Solange. *Del gachupín al criollo, o de cómo los españoles de México dejaron de serlo.* México: El Colegio de México, 1992.
———. *Inquisición y sociedad en México, 1571–1700.* México: Fondo de Cultura Económica, 1988.

Alessio Robles, Vito. *Francisco de Urdiñola y el norte de la Nueva España*. México: [Imprenta Mundial], 1931.

Althouse, Aaron P. "Contested Mestizos, Alleged Mulattos: Racial Identity and Caste Hierarchy in Eighteenth-Century Pátzcuaro, Mexico." *Americas* 62.2 (2005): 151–75.

Altman, Ida. *The War for Mexico's West: Indians and Spaniards in New Galicia, 1524–1550*. Albuquerque: University of New Mexico Press, 2010.

Altman, Ida, and James Lockhart. *Provinces of Early Mexico: Variants of Spanish American Regional Evolution*. Los Angeles: UCLA Latin American Center Publications, 1976.

Alva Ixtlilxochitl, Fernando de. *Historia de la nación chichimeca*. Barcelona: Linkgua Ediciones, [1640] 1985.

Alvarado Tezozomoc, Hernando de. *Crónica mexicana*. Barcelona: Linkgua Ediciones, [1598] 1992.

Amador, Elías. *Nombres indígenas todavía en uso en el estado de Zacatecas*. Zacatecas: Tip. del Hospicio de Niños en Guadalupe, 1897.

Anderson, Arthur, and Susan Schroeder, eds. *Codex Chimalpahin: Society and Politics in Mexico Tenochtitlan, Tlatelolco, Texcoco, Culhuacan, and Other Nahua Altepetl in Central Mexico: The Nahuatl and Spanish Annals and Accounts Collected and Recorded by Don Domingo de San Antón Muñón Chimalpahin Quauhtlehuanitzin*. 2 vols. Norman: University of Oklahoma Press, 1997.

Angeles Romero Frizzi, María de los. *El sol y la cruz: Los pueblos indios de Oaxaca colonial*. México: Centro de Investigaciones y Estudios Superiores en Antropología Social, 1996.

Ares Queija, Berta. "El papel de mediadores y la construcción de un discurso sobre la identidad de los mestizos peruanos (siglo XVI)." In *Entre dos mundos: Fronteras culturales y agentes mediadores*, edited by Berta Ares Queija and Serge Gruzinski, 37–59. Seville: Escuela de Estudios Hispanoamericanos, 1997.

Arlegui, José A. *Crónica de la provincia de n.s.p.s Francisco de Zacatecas*. México: J. Bernardo de Hogal, 1960.

Arzáns de Orsúa y Vela, Bartolomé. *Historia de la villa imperial de Potosí*. Vol. 1. Edited by Lewis Hanke and Gunner Mendoza. Providence: Brown University Press, 1965.

Azcona Pastor, José Manuel. *Possible Paradises: Basque Emigration to Latin America*. Reno: University of Nevada Press, 2004.

Azevedo Salomao, Eugenia María. *Espacios urbanos comunitarios durante el período virreinal en Michoacán*. Morelia: Morevallado Editores, 2003.

Baber, R. Jovita. "Empire, Indians, and the Negotiation for the Status of City in Tlaxcala, 1521–1550." In *Negotiation within Domination: New Spain's Indian Pueblos Confront the Spanish State*, edited by Ethelia Ruiz Medrano and Susan Kellogg, 19–44. Boulder: University Press of Colorado, 2010.

Bakewell, Peter. "Introduction," *Mines of Silver and Gold in the Americas*, edited by Peter Bakewell, xiii–xxiv. Brookfield: Variorum, 1997.

———. *Miners of the Red Mountain: Indian Labor in Potosí, 1545–1650*. Albuquerque: University of New Mexico Press, 1984.

———, ed. *Mines of Silver and Gold in the Americas*. Brookfield: Variorum, 1997.

———. "Notes on the Mexican Silver Mining Industry in the 1590s." In *Mines of Silver and Gold in the Americas*, edited by Peter Bakewell, 171–98. Brookfield: Variorum, 1997.

———. *Silver Mining and Society in Colonial Mexico: Zacatecas, 1546–1700*. Cambridge: Cambridge University Press, 1971.

———. "Zacatecas: An Economic and Social Outline of a Silver Mining District, 1547–1700." In *Provinces of Early Mexico*, edited by Ida Altman and James Lockhart, 199–229. Los Angeles: UCLA Latin American Center, 1976.

Bargalló Ardévol, Modesto. *La minería y la metalurgia en América española durante la época colonial*. México: Fondo de Cultura Económica, 1955.

Bargellini, Clara. *La arquitectura de la plata: Iglesias monumentales del centronorte de México, 1640–1750*. México: Universidad Nacional Autónoma de México, 1991.

Barr, Juliana. *Peace Came in the Form of a Woman: Indians and Spaniards in the Texas Borderlands*. Chapel Hill: University of North Carolina Press, 2007.

Bartlett, Robert. *The Making of Europe: Conquest, Colonization, and Cultural Change, 950–1350*. Princeton: Princeton University Press, 1993.

Bazarte Martínez, Alicia. *Los cofradías de españoles en la ciudad de México (1526–1860)*. México: Universidad Autónoma Metropolitana, 1989.

Bechtloff, Dagmar. *Las cofradías en Michoacán durante la época de la colonia: La religión y su relación política y económica en una sociedad intercultural*. Zinacantepec: El Colegio de Michoacán, 1996.

Bennett, Herman L. *Africans in Colonial Mexico: Absolutism, Christianity, and Afro-Creole Consciousness, 1570–1640*. Bloomington: Indiana University Press, 2003.

Bernardo Ares, José Manuel de. "El régimen municipal en la corona de Castilla." *Studia Historica, Historia Moderna* 15 (1996): 23–61.

Berthe, Jean-Pierre, "El licenciado Gaspar de la Fuente y su visita tierra adentro, 1608–1609." In *Sociedades en construcción: La Nueva Galicia según las visitas de oidores, 1606–1616*, edited by Jean-Pierre Berthe, Thomas Calvo, and Águeda Jiménez Pelayo, 95–154. Guadalajara: Universidad de Guadalajara, Centre Français d'Études Mexicaines et Centraméricaines, 2000.

Bezanilla Mier y Campa, José Mariano Estevan de. *Muralla zacatecana de doce preciosas piedras, erigidas en doce agrados títulos, y contempladas en el patrocinio y patronato de su augustísima patrona y señora María Santísima, para el día ocho de cada mes: Por Don Joseph Mariano Estevan de Bezanilla Mier y Campa*. México: El Ilustrador Católico, [1788] 1909.

Blanco, Mónica, Alma Parra, and Ethelia Ruiz Medrano. *Breve historia de Guanajuato*. México: Fondo de Cultura Económica, 2000.

Blosser, Bret. "'By the Force of their Lives and the Spilling of Blood': Flechero Service and Political Leverage on a Nueva Galicia Frontier." In *Indian Conquistadors: Indigenous Allies in the Conquest of Mesoamerica*, edited by Laura Matthew and Michel R. Oudijk, 289–317. Norman: University of Oklahoma Press, 2007.

Borah, Woodrow. *New Spain's Century of Depression*. Berkeley: University of California Press, 1951.

Boxer, Charles R. "*Plata es Sangre*: Sidelights on the Drain of Spanish-American Silver in the Far East, 1550–1700." In *European Entry into the Pacific: Spain and the Acapulco-Manila Galleon*, edited by Dennis Owen Flynn, Arturo Giráldez, and James Sobredo, 165–86. Aldershot: Ashgate, 2001.

Bracamonte y Sosa, Pedro. *La memoria enclaustrada: Historia indígena de Yucatán, 1750–1915*. México: Centro de Investigaciones y Estudios Superiores en Antropología Social, 1994.

Brading, David A. "Mexican Silver Mining in the Eighteenth Century: The Revival of Zacatecas." In *Mines of Silver and Gold in the Americas*, edited by Peter Bakewell, 303–19. Brookfield: Variorum, 1997.

———. *Miners and Merchants in Bourbon Mexico, 1763–1810*. New York: Cambridge University Press, 1971.

Brading, David, and Celia Wu. "Population Growth and Crisis: Leon, 1720–1860." *Journal of Latin American Studies* 5.1 (1973): 1–36.

Braniff, Beatriz, and Marie-Areti Hers. "Herencias chichimecas." *Arqueología* 19 (1998): 55–80.

Brown, Kendall W. *A History of Mining in Latin America: From the Colonial Era to the Present*. Albuquerque: University of New Mexico Press, 2012.

Burkhart, Louise M. *The Slippery Earth: Nahua-Christian Moral Dialogue in Sixteenth-Century Mexico*. Tucson: University of Arizona Press, 1989.

Burnes Ortiz, Arturo. *La minería en la historia económica de Zacatecas, 1546–1876*. Zacatecas: Universidad Autónoma de Zacatecas, 2008.

Burns, Kathryn. *Into the Archive: Writing and Power in Colonial Peru*. Durham: Duke University Press, 2010.

Bustamante, José María. *Descripción de la serranía de Zacatecas*. México: Imp. de Galván a cargo de M. Arévalo, 1834.

Cadena, Marisol de la. "Are *Mestizos* Hybrids?: The Conceptual Politics of Andean Identities." *Journal of Latin American Studies* 37.2 (2005): 259–84.

Calvo, Thomas. "The Warmth of the Hearth: Seventeenth-Century Guadalajara Families." In *Sexuality and Marriage in Colonial Latin America*, edited by Asunción Lavrin, 287–313. Lincoln: University of Nebraska Press, 1989.

Carmagnani, Marcello. "Demografía y sociedad: La estructura de los centros mineros del norte de México, 1600–1720." *Historia Mexicana* 21.3 (1972): 419–59.

Carrasco, Pedro. *Estructura político-territorial del imperio Tenochca: La triple alianza de Tenochtitlan, Tetzcoco y Tlacopan*. México: El Colegio de México y Fondo de Cultura Económica, 1996.

Carrillo Cázares, Alberto. *El debate sobre la guerra chichimeca, 1531–1585*. Vol. 1 of *Derecho y política en la Nueva España*. San Luis Potosí: El Colegio de San Luis Potosí y El Colegio de Michoacán, 2000.

Casas, Gonzalo de las. *La guerra de los chichimecas*. Edited by José Fernando Ramírez and Luis González Obregón. México: Editor Vargas Rea, 1944.

Caso, Alfonso. *Los barrios antiguos de Tenochtitlan y Tlatelolco*. México: Academia Mexicana de la Historia, 1956.

Castro Gutiérrez, Felipe. "Conflictos y fraudes electorales en los cabildos indígenas de Michoacán colonial." *Journal of Iberian and Latin American Studies* 4.2 (1998): 41–68.

———, ed. *Los indios y las ciudades de la Nueva España*. México: Universidad Nacional Autónoma de México, Instituto de Investigaciones Históricas, 2010.

———. *Nueva ley y nuevo rey: Reformas borbónicas y rebelión popular en Nueva España*. Zamora: El Colegio de Michoacán, 1996.

———. "El origen y conformación de los barrios de indios." In *Los indios y las ciudades de Nueva España*, edited by Felipe Castro Gutiérrez, 105–22. México: Universidad Nacional Autónoma de México, 2010.

———. *Los tarascos y el imperio español, 1600–1740*. México: Universidad Nacional Autónoma de México and Universidad Michoacana de San Nicolás de Hidalgo, 2004.

Chambers, Sarah C. "Little Middle Ground: The Instability of a Mestizo Identity in the Andes, Eighteenth and Nineteenth Centuries." In *Race and Nation in Modern Latin America*, edited by Nancy P. Applebaum, Anne S. Macpherson, and Karin Alejandra Rosemblatt, 32–55. Chapel Hill: University of North Carolina Press, 2003.

Chance, John K. "On the Mexican Mestizo." *Latin American Research Review* 14.3 (1979), 153–68.

———. *Race and Class in Colonial Oaxaca*. Stanford: Stanford University Press, 1978.

———. "The Urban Indian in Colonial Oaxaca." *American Ethnologist* 3.4 (1976): 603–32.

Chance, John K., and William Taylor. "Cofradías and Cargos: An Historical Perspective on the Mesoamerican Civil-Religious Hierarchy." *American Ethnologist* 12.1 (1985): 1–26.

Charney, Paul. *Indian Society in the Valley of Lima, Peru, 1523–1824*. Lanham: University Press of America, 2001.

———. "El indio urbano: Un análisis económica y social de la población india de Lima en 1613." *Histórica* 12.1 (1988): 5–33.

———. "Much too worthy . . . Indians in Seventeenth-century Lima." In *City Indians in Spain's American Empire: Urban Indigenous Society in Colonial Mesoamerica and Andean South America, 1521–1810*, edited by Dana Velasco Murillo, Mark Lentz, and Margarita Ochoa, 87–103. Brighton: Sussex Academic Press, 2012.

———. "A Sense of Belonging: Colonial Indian Cofradías and Ethnicity in the Valley of Lima, Peru." *Americas* 54.3 (1998): 379–407.

Chevalier, François. *Land and Society in Colonial Mexico: The Great Hacienda*. Berkeley: University of California Press, 1966.

Chimalapahin Cuauhtlehuantzin, Domingo Francisco de San Antón Muñón. *Annals of His Time: Don Domingo de San Antón Muñón Chimalpahin Quauhtlehuanitzin*. Edited by James Lockhart, Susan Schroeder, and Doris Namala. Stanford: Stanford University Press, 2006.

Christensen, Mark Z. *Nahua and Maya Catholicisms: Texts and Religion in Colonial Central Mexico and Yucatan*. Stanford: Stanford University Press and Academy of American Franciscan History, 2013.

Cline, Sarah L. *Colonial Culhuacan, 1580–1600: A Social History of an Aztec Town*. Albuquerque: University of New Mexico Press, 1986.

Connell, William F. *After Moctezuma: Indigenous Politics and Self-Government in Mexico City, 1524–1730*. Norman: University of Oklahoma Press, 2011.

———. "Alliance Building and the Restoration of Native Government in the Altepetl of Mexico Tenochtitlan, 1521–1565." In *City Indians in Spain's American Empire: Urban Indigenous Society in Colonial Mesoamerica and Andean South America, 1530–1810*, edited by Dana Velasco Murillo, Mark Lentz, and Margarita Ochoa, 8–31. Brighton: Sussex Academic Press, 2012.

Contreras, José Enciso. *Ordenanzas de Zacatecas del siglo XVI y otros documentos normativos neogallegos*. Zacatecas: Ayuntamiento de Zacatecas, 1998.

Contreras, José Enciso, and Ana Hilda Reyes Veyna. *Juanes de Tolosa descubridor de las minas de Zacatecas, información de méritos y servicios*. Zacatecas: Tribunal Superior de Justicia de Zacatecas, 2002.

Cope, R. Douglas. *The Limits of Racial Domination: Plebian Society in Colonial Mexico City, 1660–1720*. Madison: University of Wisconsin Press, 1994.

Corbeil, Laurent. "Identities in Motion: The Formation of a Plural Indio Society in Early San Luis Potosí, New Spain, 1591–1630." PhD diss., McGill University, 2015.

Cramaussel, Chantal. "De cómo los españoles clasificaban a los indios: Naciones y encomiendas en la Nueva Vizcaya central. In *Nómadas y sedentarios en el norte de México: Homenaje a Beatriz Braniff*, edited by Marie-Areti Hers, José Luis Mirafuentes, Mara de los Dolores Soto, and Miguel Vallebueno, 275–303. México: Universidad Nacional Autónoma de México, 2000.

———. "Ilegítimos y abandonados en la frontera norte: Parral y San Bartolomé en el siglo XVII." *Colonial Latin American Historical Review* 4.4 (1995): 405–39.

———. "El mestizaje, las familias pluriétnicas de la villa de San Felipe El Real de Chihuahua y la sorpresiva multiplicación de los mulatos en el septentrión novohispano durante el siglo XVIII." In *Familias pluriétnicas y mestizaje en la Nueva España y el Río de la Plata*, edited by David Carbajal López, 17–45. Guadalajara: Universidad de Guadalajara, 2014.

———. *Poblar la frontera: La provincia de Santa Bárbara en Nueva Vizcaya durante los siglos XVI y XVII*. Zamora: El Colegio de Michoacán, 2006.

———. *La provincia de Santa Bárbara en la Nueva Vizcaya, 1563–1631*. Ciudad Juárez: Universidad Autónoma de Ciudad Juárez, 1990.

———. "La tributación de los indios en el septentrión novohispano." In *Indios, españoles, mestizos en zonas de frontera, siglos XVII–XX*, edited by José Marcos Medina Bustos and Esther Padilla Calderón, 19–52. Hermosillo: El Colegio de Sonora y El Colegio de Michoacán, 2013.

Cross, Harry E. "Dieta y nutrición en el medio rural de Zacatecas y San Luis Potosí (siglos XVIII and XIX)." *Historia Mexicana* 31.1 (1981): 101–16.

———. "Living Standards in Rural Nineteenth-Century Mexico: Zacatecas (1820–1880)." *Journal of Latin American Studies* 10.1 (1978): 1–19.

Cubillo Moreno, Gilda. *Los dominios de la plata—El precio del auge, el peso del poder: Empresarios y trabajadores en las minas de Pachuca y Zimapán, 1552–1620*. México: Instituto Nacional de Antropología e Historia, 1991.

Cuello, José. "The Persistence of Indian Slavery and Encomienda in the Northeast of Colonial Mexico, 1577–1723." *Journal of Social History* 21.4 (1988): 683–700.

———. *Saltillo colonial: Orígenes y formación de una sociedad Mexicana en la frontera norte*. Saltillo: Archivo Municipal de Saltillo y Universidad Autónoma de Coahuila, 2004.

Cuenya Mateos, Miguel Ángel, and Carlos Contreras Cruz. *Puebla de los Ángeles: Una ciudad en la historia*. Puebla: Benemérita Universidad Autónoma de Puebla, 2012.

Curcio-Nagy, Linda Ann. *The Great Festivals of Colonial Mexico City: Performing Power and Identity*. Albuquerque: University of New Mexico Press, 2004.

Dávila Garibi, José I. *La sociedad de Zacatecas en los albores del régimen colonial: Actuación de los principales fundadores y primeros funcionarios públicos de la ciudad*. México: Antigua Librería Robredo de J. Porrúa e Hijos, 1939.

Deeds, Susan. *Defiance and Deference in Mexico's Colonial North: Indians Under Spanish Rule in Nueva Vizcaya*. Austin: University of Texas Press, 2003.

———. "Double Jeopardy: Indian Women in Jesuit Missions of Nueva Vizcaya." In *Indian Women of Early Mexico*, edited by Susan Schroeder, Stephanie Wood, and Robert Haskett, 255–72. Norman: University of Oklahoma Press, 1997.

———. "Land Tenure Patterns in Northern New Spain." *Americas* 41.4 (1985): 446–61.

———. "Legacies of Resistance, Adaptation, and Tenacity: History of the Native Peoples of Northwest Mexico." In *Mesoamerica*, vol. 2 of *The Cambridge History of the Native Peoples of the Americas*, edited by Richard E. W. Adams and Murdo J. MacLeod, pt. 2, 44–88. Cambridge: Cambridge University Press, 2000.

———. "Rural Work in Nueva Vizcaya: Forms of Labor Coercion on the Periphery." *Hispanic American Historical Review* 69.3 (1989): 425–49.

De Munck, Bert, and Anne Winter, eds. *Gated Communities? Regulating Migration in Early Modern Cities*. Farnham: Ashgate Publishing, 2012.

Domínguez Ortiz, Antonio. *El antiguo régimen: Los Reyes Católicos y los Austrias*. Madrid: Alianza, Editorial, 1973.

Eissa-Barroso, Francisco A., and Ainara Vázquez Varela. *Early Bourbon Spanish America: Politics and Society in a Forgotten Era (1700–1759)*. Leiden: Brill, 2013.

Enkerlin Pauwells, Luise M. "El cabildo indígena de Pátzcuaro: Un espacio de poder en decadencia durante la primera mitad del siglo XVIII." In *Gobierno y economía en los pueblos indios del México colonial*, edited by Francisco González-Hermosillo Adams, 241–66. México: Instituto Nacional de Antropología e Historia, 2001.

Enrique Hardoy, Jorge. *Ciudades precolombinas*. Buenos Aires: Ediciones Infinito, 1999.

Esteva Fabregat, Claudio. "Población y mestizaje en las ciudades de Iberoamérica: Siglo XVIII." In *Estudios sobre la ciudad iberoamericana*, edited by Francisco de Solano, 551–604. Madrid: Consejo Superior de Investigaciones Científicas, 1983.

Farriss, Nancy M. *Maya Society Under Colonial Rule: The Collective Enterprise of Survival*. Princeton: Princeton University Press, 1984.

Fisher, John Robert. *Minas y mineros en el Perú colonial, 1776–1824*. Lima: Instituto de Estudios Peruanos, 1977.

Flores García, Laura Gemma, and Carlos Paredes Martínez. "El cabildo, hospital y cofradía de indios de Pátzcuaro: Ámbitos de poder y conflictos en el siglo XVII." In *Autoridad y gobierno indígena en Michoacán: Ensayos a través de su historia*, edited by Carlos Paredes Martínez and Marta Terán, 185–215. Zamora: El Colegio de Michoacán, 2003.

Folsom, Raphael B. *The Yaquis and the Empire: Violence, Spanish Imperial Power, and Native Resilience in Colonial Mexico*. New Haven: Yale University Press, 2014.

Foster, Michael S., and Shirley Gorenstein, eds. *Greater Mesoamerica: The Archeology of West and Northwestern Mexico*. Salt Lake City: University of Utah Press, 2000.

Frank, Ross. *From Settler to Citizen: New Mexican Economic Development and the Creation of Vecino Society, 1750–1820*. Berkeley: University of California Press, 2000.

Frejes, Francisco. *Historia breve de la conquista de los estados independientes del imperio mexicano*. Guadalajara: Tip. de S. Banda, Exconvento de Sta. María de Gracia, 1878.

———. *Memoria de la conquista de Zacatecas que para la historia general del estado escribió el R.P. Fr. Francisco Frexes del Colegio de N.S. de Guadalupe*. Zacatecas: Imprenta á cargo de Pedro Piña, 1834.

Frye, David. "The Native Peoples of Northeastern Mexico." In *The Cambridge History of the Native Peoples of the Americas*, vol. 2, *Mesoamerica*, edited by Richard E. W. Adams and Murdo J. MacLeod, pt. 2, 89–135. Cambridge: Cambridge University Press, 2000.

Gamio, Manuel. *Los monumentos arqueológicos de las inmediaciones de Chalchihuites*. México: Museo Nacional de Arqueología, Historia y Etnología, 1910.

García González, Francisco. *Familia y sociedad en Zacatecas: La vida de un microcosmos minero novohispano, 1750–1830*. Zacatecas: Universidad Autónoma de Zacatecas, 2000.

García Martínez, Bernardo. *Los pueblos de la sierra: El poder y el espacio entre los indios del norte de Puebla hasta 1700*. México: El Colegio de México, 1987.

Garner, Richard L. "Prices and Wages in Eighteenth-Century Mexico." In *Essays on the Price History of Eighteenth-Century Latin America*, edited by Lyman L. Johnson and Enrique Tandeter, 73–108. Albuquerque: University of New Mexico Press, 1990.

———. "Zacatecas, 1750–1821: The Study of a Late Colonial Mexican City." PhD diss., University of Michigan, 1970.

Garner, Richard L., and Spiro E. Stefanou. *Economic Growth and Change in Bourbon Mexico*. Gainesville: University Press of Florida, 1993.

Gauderman, Kimberly. *Women's Lives in Colonial Quito: Gender, Law, and Economy in Spanish America*. Austin: University of Texas Press, 2003.

Gerhard, Peter. *A Guide to the Historical Geography of New Spain*. Revised ed. Norman: University of Oklahoma Press, 1993.

———. *The North Frontier of New Spain*. Norman: University of Oklahoma Press, 1993.

Gibson, Charles. *Aztecs Under Spanish Rule: A History of the Indians of the Valley of Mexico, 1519–1810*. Stanford: Stanford University Press, 1964.

———. *Tlaxcala in the Sixteenth Century*. Stanford: Stanford University Press, 1952.

Giraud, François. "Mujeres y familia en Nueva España." In *Presencia y transparencia: La mujer en la historia de México*, edited by Carmen Ramos-Escandón, 65–81. México: Colegio de México, Programa Interdisciplinario de Estudios de la Mujer, 1987.

Gonzalbo Aizpuru, Pilar. "Con amor y reverencia: Mujeres y familias en el México colonial." In *Educación, familia y vida cotidiana en México virreinal*, edited by Pilar Gonzalbo Aizpuru, 69–88. México: El Colegio de México, 2013.

———. *Familia y orden colonial*. México: El Centro de Estudios Históricos, Colegio de México, 1998.

———. "Nuevo mundo nuevas formas familiares." In *Género, familia y mentalidades en América Latina*, edited by Pilar Gonzalbo Aizpuru, 13–38. San Juan: Universidad de Puerto Rico, 1997.

———, ed. "Perspectivas sobre historia de la familia en México." In *Familias novohispanas, siglos XVI–XIX*. México: El Centro de Estudios Históricos, El Colegio de México, 1990.

———. "La vida familiar y las movibles fronteras sociales en el siglo XVIII novohispano." In *Educación, familia y vida cotidiana en México virreinal: Trayectoria de Pilar Gonzalbo Aizpuru*, edited by Pilar Gonzalbo Aizpuru, 89–103. México: El Centro de Estudios Históricos, El Colegio de México, 2013.

Gonzáles, Ondina E., and Bianca Premo, eds. *Raising an Empire: Children in Early Modern Iberia and Colonial Latin America*. Albuquerque: University of New Mexico Press, 2007.

González Hermosillo Adams, Francisco, ed. *Gobierno y economía en los pueblos indios del México colonial*. México: Instituto Nacional de Antropología e Historia, 2001.

———. "Historiografía de los cabildos indios." *Historias* 26 (1991): 25–53.

———. "Macehuales versus señores naturales: Una mediación franciscana en el cabildo indio de Cholula ante el conflicto por el servicio personal (1553–1594)." In *Gobierno y economía en los pueblos indios del México colonial*. Edited by Francisco González-Hermosillo Adams, 241–66. México: Instituto Nacional de Antropología e Historia, 2001.

González Rodríguez, Luis. *El noroeste novohispano en la época colonial*. México: Instituto de Investigaciones Antropológicas, Universidad Nacional Autónoma de México, 1993.

Gorenstein, Shirley, and Michael S. Foster. "West and Northwest Mexico: The Ins and Outs of Mesoamerica." In *Greater Mesoamerica: The Archeology of West and Northwestern Mexico*, edited by Michael S. Foster and Shirley Gorenstein, 3–19. Salt Lake City: University of Utah Press, 2000.

Gosner, Kevin. "Las élites de indígenas en los altos de Chiapas (1524–1714)." *Historia Mexicana* 33.4 (1984): 405–23.

Gradie, Charlotte M. "Discovering the Chichimecas." *Americas* 51.1 (1994): 67–88.

———. *The Tepehuan Revolt of 1616: Militarism, Evangelism, and Colonialism in Seventeenth-Century Nueva Vizcaya*. Salt Lake City: University of Utah Press, 2000.

Graff, Gary W. "Spanish Parishes in Colonial New Granada: Their Role in Town-Building on the Spanish-American Frontier." *Americas* 33.2 (1976–1977): 336–51.

Granados, Luis Fernando. "Cosmopolitan Indians and Mesoamerican Barrios in Bourbon Mexico City: Tribute, Community, Family, and Work in 1800." PhD diss., Georgetown University, 2008.

Graubart, Karen B. "The Creolization of the New World: Local Forms of Identification in Urban Colonial Peru, 1560–1640." *Hispanic American Historical Review* 89.3 (2009): 471–99.

———. *With Our Labor and Sweat: Indigenous Women and the Formation of Colonial Society in Peru, 1550–1700*. Stanford: Stanford University Press, 2007.

Hadley, Phillip. *Minería y sociedad en el centro minero de Santa Eulalia, Chihuahua, 1709–1750*. México: Fondo de Cultura Económica, 1979.

Hamilton, Earl J. *American Treasure and the Price Revolution in Spain, 1501–1650*. New York: Octagon Books, 1965.

Hanger, Kimberly S. "Patronage, Property and Persistence: The Emergence of a Free Black Elite in Spanish New Orleans." In *Against the Odds: Free Blacks in the Slave Societies of the Americas*, edited by Jane Landers, 44–64. London: Frank Cass, 1996.

Harris, Olivia. "Ethnic Identity and Market Relations: Indians and Mestizos in the Andes." In *Ethnicity, Markets and Migration in the Andes: At the Crossroads of History and Anthropology*, edited by Brooke Larson and Olivia Harris, 351–90. Durham: Duke University Press, 1995.

Harvey, H. R. "The *Relaciones geográficas*, 1579–1586: Native Languages." In *Handbook of Middle American Indians*, edited by Robert Wauchope, vol. 12. Austin: University of Texas Press, 1972.

Haskett, Robert. *Indigenous Rulers: An Ethnohistory of Town Government in Colonial Cuernavaca*. Albuquerque: University of New Mexico Press, 1991.

———. "'Our Suffering with the Taxco Tribute': Involuntary Mine Labor and Indigenous Society in Central New Spain." *Hispanic American Historical Review* 71.3 (1991): 447–75.

Hecht, Tobias, ed. *Minor Omissions: Children in Latin American History and Society*. Madison: University of Wisconsin Press, 2002.

Herrera, Robinson A. *Natives, Europeans, and Africans in Sixteenth-Century Santiago de Guatemala*. Austin: University of Texas Press, 2003.

Herzog, Tamar. *Defining Nations: Immigrants and Citizens in Early Modern Spain and Spanish America*. New Haven: Yale University Press, 2003.

Hoberman, Louisa Schell, and Susan Migden Socolow, eds. *Cities and Society in Colonial Latin America*. Albuquerque: University of New Mexico Press, 1986.

Horn, Rebecca. *Postconquest Coyoacan: Nahua-Spanish Relations in Central Mexico, 1590–1650*. Stanford: Stanford University Press, 1997.
Hoyo, Eugenio del. "La Diputación de Mineros en las minas ricas de los Zacatecas, democracia corporativa." In *Primera libero de actas de cabildo de las minas de los Zacatecas, 1557–1586*. Zacatecas: Ayuntamiento de la Ciudad de Zacatecas, 1991.
Hu-DeHart, Evelyn. *Missionaries, Miners, and Indians: Spanish Contact with the Yaqui Nation of Northwestern New Spain, 1533–1820*. Tucson: University of Arizona Press, 1981.
Islas Jiménez, Celia. *El real de Tlalpujahua: Aspectos de la minería novohispana*. México: Instituto Nacional de Antropología e Historia, 2008.
Jackson, Robert H. *Indian Population Decline: The Missions of Northwestern New Spain, 1687–1840*. Albuquerque: University of New Mexico Press, 1994.
Jesús Rodríguez, María de. "Mujer y familia en la sociedad Mexica." In *Presencia y transparencia: La mujer en la historia de México*. Edited by Carmen Ramos-Escandón, 21–38. México: Colegio de México, Programa Interdisciplinario de Estudios de la Mujer, 1987.
Jiménez Betts, Peter F., and J. Andrew Darling. "Archaeology of Southern Zacatecas: The Malpaso Juchipila and Valparaíso-Bolaños Valleys." In *Greater Mesoamerica: The Archaeology of West and Northwestern Mexico*, edited by Michael Foster and Shirley Gorenstein. Salt Lake City: University of Utah Press, 2000.
Jiménez Pelayo, Águeda. *Haciendas y comunidades indígenas en el sur de Zacatecas: Sociedad y economía colonial, 1600–1820*. México: Instituto Nacional de Antropología y Historia, 1989.
Jones, Richard C. *Ambivalent Journey: U.S. Migration and Economic Mobility in North-Central Mexico*. Tucson: University of Arizona Press, 1995.
Kagan, Richard, and Fernando Marías. *Urban Images of the Hispanic World, 1493–1793*. New Haven: Yale University Press, 2000.
Kanter, Deborah E. *Hijos del Pueblo, Gender, Family and Community in Rural Mexico, 1730–1850*. Austin: University of Texas Press, 2008.
Karttunen, Frances. *An Analytical Dictionary of Nahuatl*. Norman: University of Oklahoma Press, 1992.
Kelley, J. C. "Archeology of the Northern Frontier: Zacatecas and Durango." In *Handbook of Middle American Indians*, edited by R. Wauchope, 11:768–801. Austin: University of Texas Press, 1971.
Kellogg, Susan. "From Parallel and Equivalent to Separate but Unequal: Tenochca Mexica Women, 1500–1700." In *Indian Women of Early Mexico*, edited by Susan Schroeder, Stephanie Wood, and Robert Haskett, 123–44. Norman: University of Oklahoma Press, 1997.
———. *Law and the Transformation of Aztec Culture, 1500–1700*. Norman: University of Oklahoma Press, 1995.
Kinsbruner, Jay. *The Colonial Spanish-American City: Urban Life in the Age of Atlantic Capitalism*. Austin: University of Texas Press, 2005.
Kuznesof, Elizabeth Anne. *Household Economy and Urban Development: São Paolo, 1765 to 1836*. Boulder: Westview Press, 1986.

Lacueva Muñoz, Jaime J. *La plata del rey y de sus vasallos: Minería y metalurgia en México (siglos XVI y XVII)*. Madrid: Consejo Superior de Investigaciones Científicas, 2010.

Ladd, Doris. *The Making of a Strike: Mexican Silver Workers' Struggles in Real de Monte, 1766–1775*. Lincoln: University of Nebraska Press, 1988.

Landers, Jane G. *Black Society in Spanish Florida*. Urbana: University of Illinois Press, 1999.

———. "*Cimarrón* and Citizen: African Ethnicity, Corporate Identity, and the Evolution of Free Black Towns in the Spanish Circum-Caribbean." In *Slaves, Subjects, and Subversives: Blacks in Colonial Latin America*, edited by Jane Landers and Barry Robinson, 111–46. Albuquerque: University of New Mexico Press, 2006.

Lane, Kris. "Africans and Natives in the Mines of Spanish America." In *Beyond Black and Red: African-Native Relations in Colonial Latin America*, edited by Matthew Restall, 159–84. Albuquerque: University of New Mexico Press, 2005.

Langenscheidts, Adolfo. "Las minas y la minería prehispánica." In *Minería prehispánica en la sierra de Querétaro*, edited by Adolfo Langenscheidts. México: Secretaría del Patrimonio Nacional, 1970.

Langue, Frederique. *Los señores de Zacatecas: Una aristocracia minera del siglo XVIII novohispano*. México: Fondo de Cultura Económica, 1999.

———. "Trabajadores y formas de trabajo en las minas zacatecanas del siglo XVIII." *Historia Mexicana* 40.3 (1991): 463–506.

Larkin, Brian. "Confraternities and Community: The Decline of the Communal Quest for Salvation in Eighteenth-Century Mexico City." In *Local Religion in Colonial Mexico*, edited by Martin Austin Nesvig, 189–213. Albuquerque: University of New Mexico Press, 2006.

———. *The Very Nature of God: Baroque Catholicism and Religious Reform in Bourbon Mexico City*. Albuquerque: University of New Mexico Press, 2010.

Larson, Brooke, Olivia Harris, and Enrique Tandeter, eds. *Ethnicity, Markets, and Migration in the Andes: At the Crossroads of History and Anthropology*. Durham: Duke University Press, 1995.

Lavrin, Asunción. "La congregación de San Pedro: Una cofradía urbana del México colonial 1604–1730." *Historia Mexicana* 29.4 (1980): 562–601.

Lázaro de Arregui, Domingo. *Descripción de la Nueva Galicia*. Seville: Escuela de Estudios Hispanoamericanos de la Universidad de Sevilla, [1621] 1946.

Lemoine Villicaña, Ernesto. "Miscelánea zacatecana: Documentos histórico-geográficos de los siglos XVII al XIX." *Boletín del Archivo General de la Nación* 5.2 (1964): 284–315.

Lenkersdorf, Gudrun. "Los cabildos de naturales en la provincia de Chiapas, de la posconquista temprana a las ordenanzas del oidor-visitador Axcoeta en 1573." In *Gobierno y economía en los pueblos indios del México colonial*, edited by Francisco González-Hermosillo Adams, 181–92. México: Instituto Nacional de Antropología e Historia, 2001.

Lentz, Mark. "Batabs of the Barrio: Urban Maya Rulers, Mérida, Yucatan, 1670–1806." In *City Indians in Spain's American Empire: Urban Indigenous Society* in *Colonial Mesoamerica and Andean South America, 1530–1810*, edited by Dana Velasco Murillo, Mark Lentz, and Margarita R. Ochoa, 172–98. Brighton: Sussex Academic Press, 2012.

León-Portilla, Miguel. "Minería y metalurgia en el México antiguo," in *La minería en México: Estudios sobre su desarollo histórico*, edited by Miguel León-Portilla, Jorge Gurría Lacroix, Roberto Moreno, and Enrique Madero Bracho. México: Universidad Nacional Autónoma de México, 1978.

Lewin, Linda. *Surprise Heirs I: Illegitimacy, Patrimonial Rights, and Legal Nationalism in Luso-Brazilian Inheritance, 1750–1821*. Stanford: Stanford University Press, 2003.

Lira González, Andrés. *Comunidades indígenas frente a la ciudad de México: Tenochtitlan y Tlatelolco, sus pueblos y barrios, 1812–1919*. México: El Colegio de México, 1983.

Lockhart, James. *The Men of Cajamarca: A Social and Biographical Study of the First Conquerors of Peru*. Austin: University of Texas Press, 1972.

———. *The Nahuas After the Conquest: A Social and Cultural History of the Indians of Central Mexico, Sixteenth Through Eighteenth Centuries*. Stanford: Stanford University Press, 1992.

———. "Receptivity and Resistance." In *Of Things of the Indies: Essays Old and New in Early Latin American History*, 304–32. Stanford: Stanford University Press, 1999.

Lockhart, James, and Stuart B. Schwartz. *Early Latin America: A History of Colonial Spanish America and Brazil*. Cambridge: Cambridge University Press, 1983.

López, Rick Anthony. *Crafting Mexico: Intellectuals, Artisans, and the State after the Revolution*. Durham: Duke University Press, 2010.

López Luján, Leonardo. *Nómadas y sedentarios: El pasado prehispánico de Zacatecas*. México: Instituto Nacional de Antropología e Historia, 1989.

Lowry, Lyn. "Forging an Indian Nation: Urban Indians Under Spanish Colonial Control (Lima, Peru, 1535–1765)." PhD diss., University of California, Berkeley, 1991.

Lutz, Christopher. *Santiago de Guatemala, 1541–1773: City, Caste, and the Colonial Experience*. Norman: University of Oklahoma Press, 1994.

Lyon, George F. *Journal of a Residence and Tour in the Republic of Mexico in the Year 1826: With Some Account of the Mines of that Country*. Vol. 2. London: John Murray, Albemarle Street, 1828.

Magaña, Claudia. *Panorámica de la ciudad de Zacatecas y sus barrios en la época virreinal*. Zacatecas: Gobierno del Estado de Zacatecas, 1998.

Mancuso, Lara. *Cofradías mineras: Religiosidad popular en México y Brasil, siglo XVIII*. México: El Colegio de México, Centro de Estudios Históricos, 2007.

Mangan, Jane E. "A Market of Identities: Women, Trade, and Ethnic Labels in Colonial Potosí." In *Imperial Subjects: Race and Identity in Colonial Latin America*, edited by Andrew B. Fisher and Matthew D. O'Hara, 61–80. Durham: Duke University Press, 2009.

———. *Trading Roles: Gender, Ethnicity, and the Urban Economy in Colonial Potosí*. Durham: Duke University Press, 2005.

Manzano, Juan. *Recopilación de leyes de los reynos de las Indias*. Madrid: Ediciones Cultura Hispánica, 1973.

Maríchal, Carlos. *Bankruptcy of Empire: Mexican Silver and the Wars Between Spain, Britain, and France, 1760–1810*. New York: Cambridge University Press, 2007.

Martin, Cheryl English L. *Governance and Society in Colonial Mexico: Chihuahua in the Eighteenth Century*. Stanford: Stanford University Press, 1996.

Martínez Baracs, Andrea. "Colonizaciones tlaxcaltecas." *Historia Mexicana* 43.2 (1993): 195–250.

———. *Un gobierno de indios: Tlaxcala, 1519–1750*. México: Fondo de Cultura Económica, 2008.

Martínez López-Cano, María del Pilar, Gisela von Wobeser, and Juan Guillermo Muñoz, eds. *Cofradías, capellanías, y obras pías en la América colonial*. México: Universidad Nacional Autónoma de México, 1998.

Matthew, Laura E. *Memories of Conquest: Becoming Mexicano in Colonial Guatemala*. Chapel Hill: University of North Carolina Press, 2012.

Matthew, Laura E., and Michel R. Oudijk. *Indian Conquistadors: Indigenous Allies in the Conquest of Mesoamerica*. Norman: University of Oklahoma Press, 2007.

McCaa, Robert. "*Calidad, Clase*, and Marriage in Colonial Mexico: The Case of Parral, 1788–90." *Hispanic American Historical Review* 64.3 (1984): 477–501.

———. "Marriage, Migration, and Settling Down: Parral (Nueva Vizcaya), 1770–1788." In *Migration in Colonial Spanish America*, edited by David J. Robinson, 212–37. Cambridge: Cambridge University Press, 1990.

McEnroe, Sean F. *From Colony to Nationhood in Mexico: Laying the Foundations, 1560–1840*. Cambridge: Cambridge University Press, 2012.

Mecham, John Lloyd. *Francisco de Ibarra and Nueva Vizcaya*. New York: Greenwood Press, 1968.

———. "The *Real de Minas* as a Political Institution: A Study of a Frontier Institution in Colonial Spanish America." *Hispanic American Historical Review* 7.1 (1927): 45–83.

Melvin, Karen. *Building Colonial Cities of God: Mendicant Orders and Urban Culture in New Spain, 1570–1800*. Stanford: Stanford University Press, 2012.

Mendizábal, Miguel Othón de. *Obras completas*. México: La Cooperativa de Trabajadores de los Talleres Gráficos de la Nación, Tolosa y Enrico Martínez, 1946.

Menegus Bornemann, Margarita. *Del señorío indígena a la república de indios: El caso de Toluca, 1500–1600*. México: Consejo Nacional para la Cultura y las Artes, 1994.

Metcalf, Alida C. *Family and Frontier in Colonial Brazil: Santana de Parnaíba, 1580–1822*. Austin: University of Texas Press, 2005.

Meyers, Albert. "Religious Sodalities in Latin America: A Sketch of Two Peruvian Case Studies. In *Manipulating the Saints: Religious Brotherhoods and Social Integration in Postconquest Latin America*, edited by Albert Meyers and Diane Hopkins, 1–21. Hamburg: Wayasbah, 1988.

Milanich, Nara. "Historical Perspectives on Illegitimacy and Illegitimates in Latin America." In *Minor Omissions: Children in Latin American History and Society*, edited by Tobias Hecht, 72–101. Madison: University of Wisconsin Press, 2002.

Minchom, Martin. *The People of Quito, 1690–1810: Change and Unrest in the Underclass*. Boulder: Westview Press, 1994.

Molina, Alonso de. *Vocabulario en lengua castellana y mexicana*. Vol. 4 of *Colección de incunables americanos siglo XVI*. Facsimile ed. Madrid: Ediciones Cultura Hispánica, 1944.

Monteiro, John M. "Labor Systems." In *The Cambridge Economic History of Latin America*, vol. 1, *The Colonial Era and the Short Nineteenth Century*, edited by Victor Bulmer-Thomas, John H. Coatsworth, and Robero Cortés Conde, 185–233. Cambridge: Cambridge University Press, 2006.

Montoya, Alejandro. "Población y sociedad en un real de minas de la frontera norte Novohispana: San Luis Potosí, de finales del siglo XVI a 1810." PhD diss., Université de Montréal, 2004.

Mörner, Magnus. *Race Mixture in the History of Latin America*. Boston: Little, Brown, 1967.

Mota Padilla, Matías de la. *Historia de la conquista del reino de la Nueva Galicia*. Guadalajara: Talleres Gráficos de Gallardo y Álvarez del Castillo, 1920.

Mota y Escobar, Alonso de la. *Descripción geográfica de los reinos de Nueva Galicia, Nueva Vizcaya y Nuevo León*. México: Editorial Pedro Robredo, [1600] 1940.

Moya, Jose. "Introduction." In *The Oxford Handbook of Latin American History*, edited by Jose Moya, 1–24. New York: Oxford University Press, 2011.

Mundy, Barbara E. *The Mapping of New Spain: Indigenous Cartography and the Maps of the Relaciones Geográficas*. Chicago: University of Chicago Press, 1996.

Muñoz Camargo, Diego. *Historia de Tlaxcala*, edited by Germán Vázquez. Madrid: Historia 16, [1585] 1986.

Muriel, Josefina. *Hospitales en la Nueva España, fundaciones del siglo XVI*. México: Universidad Nacional Autónoma de México, 1990.

Muro Oregón, Antonio. "El ayuntamiento de Sevilla: Modelo de los municipios americanos." *Anales de la Universidad Hispalense* 20 (1960): 69–85.

Nader, Helen. *Liberty in Absolutist Spain: The Habsburg Sale of Towns, 1516–1700*. Baltimore: John Hopkins University Press, 1990.

———. "The Spain That Encountered Mexico." In *The Oxford History of Mexico*, edited by William H. Beezley and Michael Meyer, 11–44. New York: Oxford University Press, 2010.

Nelson, Ben A. "Chronology and Stratigraphy at La Quemada, Zacatecas, Mexico." *Journal of Field Archaeology* 24.1 (1997): 85–109.

Nelson, Ben A., J. Andrew Darling, and Andrew A. Kice. "Mortuary Practices and the Social Order at La Quemada, Zacatecas, Mexico." *Latin American Antiquity* 3.4 (1992), 298–315.

Nesvig, Martin. "Spanish Men, Indigenous Language, and Informal Interpreters in Postcontact Mexico." *Ethnohistory* 59.4 (2012): 739–64.

Nolasco Pérez, Pedro. *Los obispos de la Orden de la Merced en América, 1601–1926*. Santiago de Chile: Documentos del Archivo General de Indias, 1927.

Ochoa, Margarita R. "Gender, Power, and Authority in Indigenous Mexico City, 1700–1829." PhD diss., University of New Mexico, 2011.

Offutt, Leslie Scott. "Defending Corporate Identity on the Northern New Spanish Frontier: San Esteban de Nueva Tlaxcala, 1780–1810." *Americas* 64.3 (2008): 351–75.

———. *Saltillo, 1770–1810: Town and Region in the Mexican North*. Tucson: University of Arizona Press, 2001.

O'Hara, Matthew D. *A Flock Divided: Race, Religion, and Politics in Mexico, 1749–1857*. Durham: Duke University Press, 2009.

Olague, Jesus Flores. *Breve historia de Zacatecas*. México: El Colegio de México, 1997.

Owensby, Brian Philip. *Empire of Law and Indian Justice in Colonial Mexico*. Stanford: Stanford University Press, 2008.

Pagden, Anthony. "Identity Formation in Spanish America." In *Colonial Identity in the Atlantic World, 1500–1800*, edited by Nicholas Canny and Anthony Pagden, 51–93. Princeton: Princeton University Press, 1987.

Paquette, Gabriel B. *Enlightened Reform in Southern Europe and Its Atlantic Colonies, c. 1750–1830*. Burlington: Ashgate, 2009.

———. *Enlightenment, Governance, and Reform in Spain and Its Empire, 1759–1808*. Basingstoke: Palgrave Macmillan, 2008.

Paredes Martínez, Carlos. "Convivencia y conflictos: La ciudad de Valladolid y sus barrios de Indios, 1541–1809." In *Los indios y las ciudades de Nueva España*, edited by Felipe Castro Gutiérrez, 35–55. México: Universidad Nacional Autónoma de México, 2010.

Paredes Martínez, Carlos, and Marta Terán, eds. *Autoridad y gobierno indígena en Michoacán*. Vols. 1–2. Zamora: El Colegio de Michoacán, 2003.

Parry, J. H. *The Audiencia of New Galicia in the Sixteenth Century: A Study in Spanish Colonial Government*. Cambridge: Cambridge University Press, 1948.

Patterson, Orlando. *Slavery and Social Death: A Comparative Study*. Cambridge: Harvard University Press, 1982.

Pérez Herrero, Pedro. *Plata y libranzas: La articulación comercial del México borbónico*. México: El Colegio de México, 1988.

Pérez Rosales, Laura. *Minería y sociedad en Taxco durante el siglo XVIII*. México: Universidad Iberoamericana, 1996.

Pietschmann, Horst. *Las reformas borbónicas y el sistema de intendencias en Nueva España: Un estudio político administrativo*. México: Fondo de Cultura Económica, 1996.

Pizzigoni, Caterina. *The Life Within: Local Indigenous Society in Mexico's Toluca Valley, 1650–1800*. Stanford: Stanford University Press, 2012.

Pollard, Helen Perlstein. "Del estado Tarasco a los cabildos indígenas coloniales." In *Autoridad y gobierno indígena en Michoacán*, edited by Carlos Paredes Martínez and Marta Terán, 49–60. Zamora: El Colegio de Michoacán, 2003.

Poloni-Simard, Jacques. *El mosaic indígena: Movilidad, estratificación social y mestizaje en el corregimiento de Cuenca (Ecuador) del siglo XVI al XVII*. Quito: Editorial Abya-Yala, Instituto Francés de Estudios Andinos, 2006.
Powell, Philip Wayne. "Peacemaking on North America's First Frontier." *Americas* 16.3 (1960): 221–50.
———. *Soldiers, Indians, and Silver: The Northward Advance of New Spain, 1550–1600*. Berkeley: University of California Press, 1969.
———. "Spanish Warfare Against the Chichimecas in the 1570s." *Hispanic American Historical Review* 24.4 (1944): 580–604.
Powers, Karen. *Andean Journeys: Migration, Ethnogenesis, and the State in Colonial Quito*. Albuquerque: University of New Mexico Press, 1995.
Premo, Bianca. *Children of the Father King: Youth, Authority, and Legal Minority in Colonial Lima*. Chapel Hill: University of North Carolina Press, 2005.
Radding, Cynthia. *Wandering Peoples: Colonialism, Ethnic Spaces, and Ecological Frontiers in Northwest Mexico, 1700–1850*. Durham: Duke University Press, 1997.
Rama, Angel. *The Lettered City*. Translated by John Charles Chasteen. Durham: Duke University Press, 1996.
Ramírez, Susan. "Ethnohistorical Dimensions of Mining and Metallurgy in Sixteenth-Century Northern Peru." In *In Quest of Mineral Wealth: Aboriginal and Colonial Mining and Metallurgy in Spanish America*, edited by Alan K Craig, and Robert C West. Baton Rouge: Department of Geography and Anthropology, Louisiana State University, 1994.
Ramos, Frances L. *Identity, Ritual, and Power in Colonial Puebla*. Tucson: University of Arizona Press, 2012.
Rappaport, Joanne. *The Disappearing Mestizo: Configuring Difference in the Colonial New Kingdom of Granada*. Durham: Duke University Press, 2014.
Rappaport, Joanne, and Tom Cummins. *Beyond the Lettered City: Indigenous Literacies in the Andes*. Durham: Duke University Press, 2012.
Real Academia Española. *Diccionario de autoridades*. Facsimile ed., O–Z. Madrid: Editorial Gredos, 1984.
Refugio Gasca, José del. *Timbres y laureles zacatecanos: Escritos en verso*. Zacatecas: Imprenta Economía de Mariano Ruiz de Esparza, 1902.
"Relación de nuestra Señora de los Zacatecas, sacada de la información que, por mandado del Consejo, en ella se hizo el año de 1608." In *Pedro de Valencia, obras completas*, edited by Jesús Paniagua Pérez and Rafael González Cañal, 291–301, Humanistas Españoles 5. Salamanca: Secretariado de Publicaciones de la Universidad de León, 1995.
Restall, Matthew. *The Maya World: Yucatec Culture and Society, 1550–1850*. Stanford: Stanford University Press, 1997.
———. *The Seven Myths of the Spanish Conquest*. New York: Oxford University Press, 2003.
Restall, Matthew, and Kris Lane. *Latin America in Colonial Times*. Cambridge: Cambridge University Press, 2011.
Reyes García, Luis. *Cuauhtinchan del siglo XII al XVI: Formación y desarrollo histórico de un señorío prehispánico*. Wiesbaden: Franz Steiner Verlag, 1977.

Ribera Bernárdez, José de. *Descripción breve de la muy noble y leal ciudad de Zacatecas*. México: Impressa por Joseph Bernando Hogal, ministro, e impressor del Real y Apostólico Tribunal de la Santa Cruzada en toda esta Nueva España, 1732.

Río, Ignacio del. *La aplicación regional de las Reformas borbónicas en Nueva España: Sonora y Sinaloa, 1768–1787*. México: Universidad Nacional Autónoma de México, Instituto de Investigaciones Históricas, 1995.

———. *Conquista y aculturación en la California jesuítica*. México: Universidad Nacional Autónoma de México, 1984.

———. "Sobre la aparición del trabajo libre asalariado en el Norte de Nueva España, siglos XVI y XVII." In *Estudios históricos sobre la formación del Norte de México*, edited by Ignacio del Río, 27–46. México: Universidad Nacional Autónoma de México, 2009.

Rionda Arreguín, Isauro, ed. *Comunidades indígenas en Guanajuato: Pasado y presente de los chichimecas*. Guanajuato: Archivo General del Gobierno del Estado de Guanajuato, 1996.

Robins, Nicholas A. *Mercury, Mining and Empire: The Human and Ecological Cost of Colonial Silver Mining in the Andes*. Bloomington: Indiana University Press, 2011.

Robinson, David J., ed. *Migration in Colonial Spanish America*. Cambridge: Cambridge University Press, 1990.

Romero, Arturo Maldonado, and Peter F. Jiménez Betts. *La Quemada: Estabilización y consolidación de restos arqueológicos*. Zacatecas: Universidad Autónoma de Zacatecas, 2003.

Rosenmüller, Christoph. "'The Indians . . . Long for Change': The Secularization of Regular Parishes in Mid Eighteenth-Century New Spain." In *Early Bourbon Spanish America: Politics and Society in a Forgotten Era (1700–1759)*, edited by Francisco A. Eissa-Barroso and Ainara Vázquez Varela, 143–63. Leiden: Brill, 2013.

Sahagún, Bernardino de. *The Florentine Codex: General History of the Things of New Spain*. 13 vols. Sante Fe: School of American Research, 1950–1982.

Saignes, Thierry. "Indian Migration and Social Change in Seventeenth-Century Charcas." In *Ethnicity, Markets, and Migration in the Andes: The Crossroads of History and Anthropology*, edited by Brooke Larson and Olivia Harris, 167–95. Durham: Duke University Press, 1995.

Salazar González, Guadalupe. *Las haciendas en el siglo XVII en la región minera de San Luis Potosí*. San Luis Potosí: Universidad Autónoma de San Luis Potosí, 2000.

Schroeder, Susan. *Chimalpahin and the Kingdoms of Chalco*. Tucson: University of Arizona Press, 1991.

———. "Whither Tenochtitlan?: Chimalpahin and Mexico City, 1593–1631." In *City Indians in Spain's American Empire: Urban Indigenous Society in Colonial Mesoamerica and Andean South America, 1530–1810*, edited by Dana Velasco Murillo, Mark Lentz, and Margarita Ochoa, 63–86. Brighton: Sussex Academic Press, 2012.

Schroeder, Susan, Stephanie Wood, and Robert Haskett, eds. *Indian Women of Early Mexico*. Norman: University of Oklahoma Press, 1997.

Schwaller, Robert C. "The Importance of Mestizos and Mulatos as Bilingual Intermediaries in Sixteenth-Century New Spain." *Ethnohistory* 59.4 (2012): 713–38.
Schwartz, Stuart B., and Frank Salomon. "New Peoples and New Kinds of People: Adaptation, Readjustment, and Ethnogenesis in South American Indigenous Societies (Colonial Era)." In *The Cambridge History of the Native Peoples of the Americas*, vol. 3, *South America*, edited by Frank Salomon and Stuart B. Schwartz, 443–501. Cambridge: Cambridge University Press, 1999.
Scott, James C. *The Art of Not Being Governed: An Anarchist History of Upland Southeast Asia*. New Haven: Yale University Press, 2009.
Seed, Patricia. "Social Dimensions of Race: Mexico City, 1753." *Hispanic American Historical Review* 62.4 (1982): 569–606.
Sego, Eugene B. *Aliados y adversarios: Los colonos tlaxcaltecas en la frontera septentrional de Nueva España*. San Luis Potosí: El Colegio de San Luis, 1998.
Sempat Assadourian, Carlos. *El sistema de la economía colonial: Mercado interno, regiones y espacio económico*. Lima: Instituto de Estudios Peruanos, 1982.
———. *Zacatecas: Conquista y transformación de la frontera en el siglo XVI*. México: El Colegio de México, 2008.
Shelton, Laura M. "Like a Servant or Like a Son? Circulating Children in Northwestern Mexico, 1790–1850." In *Raising an Empire: Children in Early Modern Iberia and Colonial Latin America*, edited by Ondina E Gonzáles and Bianca Premo, 219–37. Albuquerque: University of New Mexico Press, 2007.
Sheridan, Cecilia. *Anónimos y desterrados: La contienda por el sitio que llaman de Quauyla: Siglos XVI–XVIII*. México: Centro de Investigaciones y Estudios Superiores de Antropología Social, 2000.
Sigal, Peter. *From Moon Goddesses to Virgins: The Colonization of Yucatecan Maya Sexual Desire*. Austin: University of Texas Press, 2000.
Silverblatt, Irene. "Becoming Indian in the Central Andes of Seventeenth-Century Peru." In *After Colonialism: Imperial Histories and Postcolonial Displacements*, edited by Gyan Prakash, 279–98. Princeton: Princeton University Press, 1995.
Sluiter, Engel. *Gold and Silver in Spanish America c. 1572–1648*. Berkeley: University of California Press, 1998.
Smith, Michael E., and Frances F. Berdan, "Archaeology and the Aztec Empire." *World Archaeology* 23.3 (1992): 353–67.
Socolow, Susan Migden. *The Bureaucrats of Buenos Aires, 1769–1810: Amor al real servicio*. Durham: Duke University Press, 1987.
———. *The Merchants of Buenos Aires, 1778–1810: Family and Commerce*. Cambridge: Cambridge University Press, 1978.
Solano, Francisco de, ed. *Estudios sobre la ciudad iberoamericana*. Madrid: Consejo Superior de Investigaciones Científicas, 1983.
———. "Urbanización y municipalización de la población indígena." In *Estudios sobre la ciudad iberoamericana*, edited by Francisco de Solano, 241–68. Madrid: Consejo Superior de Investigaciones Científicas, 1983.
Sousa, Lisa Mary. "Women and Crime in Colonial Oaxaca: Evidence of Complementary Gender Roles in Mixtec and Zapotec Societies." In *Indian Women of Early Mexico*, edited by Susan Schroeder, Stephanie Wood, and Robert Haskett, 199–216. Norman: University of Oklahoma Press, 1997.

Spalding, Karen. *De indio a campesino: Cambios en la estructura social del Perú colonial*. Lima: Instituto de Estudios Peruanos, 1974.

———. *Huarochirí: An Andean Society Under Inca and Spanish Rule*. Stanford: Stanford University Press, 1984.

Spicer, Edward H. *Cycles of Conquest: The Impact of Spain, Mexico, and the United States on the Indians of the Southwest, 1533–1960*. Tucson: University of Arizona Press, 1962.

Staples, Anne. "Mexican Mining and Independence: The Sage of Enticing Opportunities." In *The Birth of Modern Mexico, 1780–1824*, edited by Christon I. Archer, 151–64. Wilmington: Scholarly Resources, 2003.

Stein, Stanley J., and Barbara H Stein. *Silver, Trade, and War: Spain and America in the Making of Early Modern Europe*. Baltimore: John Hopkins University Press, 2000.

Stern, Peter. "Marginals and Acculturation in Frontier Society." In *New Views of Borderlands History*, edited by Robert H. Jackson, 157–88. Albuquerque: University of New Mexico Press, 1998.

Stern, Steve. *Peru's Indian Peoples and the Challenge of Spanish Conquest: Huamanga to 1640*. Madison: University of Wisconsin Press, 1993.

Super, John C. *La vida en Querétaro durante la colonia, 1531–1810*. México: Fondo de Cultura Económica, 1983.

Swann, Michael M. "Migration, Mobility, and the Mining Towns of Northern Mexico." In *Migration in Colonial Spanish America*, edited by David J. Robinson, 143–81. Cambridge: Cambridge University Press, 1990.

———. *Tierra Adentro: Settlement and Society in Colonial Durango*. Boulder: Westview Press, 1982.

Sweet, James H. *Recreating Africa: Culture, Kinship, and Religion in the African-Portuguese World, 1441–1770*. Chapel Hill: University of North Carolina Press, 2003.

Tanck de Estrada, Dorothy. "Indian Children in Early Mexico." In *Children in Colonial America*, edited by James Marten, 13–32. New York: New York University Press, 2007.

Tandeter, Enrique. *Coercion and Market: Silver Mining in Colonial Potosí, 1692–1826*. Albuquerque: University of New Mexico Press, 1993.

Tavárez, David. "Legally Indian: Inquisitorial Readings of Indigenous Identity in New Spain." In *Imperial Subjects: Race and Identity in Colonial Latin America*, edited by Andrew B. Fisher and Matthew D. O'Hara, 81–100. Durham: Duke University Press, 2009.

———. *The Invisible War: Indigenous Devotions, Discipline, and Dissent in Colonial Mexico*. Stanford: Stanford University Press, 2013.

Taylor, William B. *Drinking, Homicide, and Rebellion in Colonial Mexican Villages*. Stanford: Stanford University Press, 1979.

Teja, Jesús F. de la, and Ross Frank. *Choice, Persuasion, and Coercion: Social Control on Spain's North American Frontiers*. Albuquerque: University of New Mexico Press, 2005.

Tello, Antonio. *Crónica miscelánea y conquista espiritual y temporal de la Sancta provincia de Xalisco en el Nuevo Reino de la Galicia y Nueva Vizcaya y descu-*

brimiento del Nuevo México, escrito por fray Antonio Tello en 1653. Guadalajara: Tip. de "La República Literaria" de Ciro L. de Guevara y Ca., [1650] 1890.

TePaske, John J., and Herbert S. Klein. *Ingresos y egresos de la Real Hacienda de Nueva España*. Vol. 2. México: Instituto Nacional de Antropología e Historia, Colección Fuentes, 1986–1988.

Terán Fuentes, Mariana. "Por lealtad al rey, a la patria y a la religión: Los años de transición en la provincia de Zacatecas: 1808–1814." *Mexican Studies/Estudios Mexicanos* 24.2 (2008): 289–323.

Terraciano, Kevin. "Concluding Remarks." In *City Indians in Spain's American Empire: Urban Indigenous Society in Colonial Mesoamerica and Andean South America, 1530–1810*, edited by Dana Velasco Murillo, Mark Lentz, and Margarita Ochoa, 221–32. Brighton: Sussex Academic Press, 2012.

———. *The Mixtecs of Colonial Oaxaca: Ñudzahui History, Sixteenth Through Eighteenth Centuries*. Stanford: Stanford University Press, 2001.

———. "Three Texts in One: Book XII of the Florentine Codex." *Ethnohistory* 57.1 (2010): 51–72.

Thomson, Charles. *The Ordinances of the Mines of New Spain Translated from the Original Spanish, with Observations Upon the Mines and Mining Associations*. London: Printed for J. Booth, 1825.

Torre Curiel, José Refugio de la. *Twilight of the Mission Frontier: Shifting Interethnic Alliances and Social Organization in Sonora, 1768–1855*. Stanford: Stanford University Press and Academy of American Franciscan History, 2013.

Trombold, Charles D. "A Population Estimate for the Epiclassic Middle Malpaso Valley (La Quemada), Zacatecas, Mexico." *Latin American Antiquity* 16.3 (2005): 235–53.

———. "A Summary of the Archeology of the La Quemada Region." In *The Archeology of West and Northwest Mesoamerica*, edited by Michael S. Foster and Phil C. Weigand, 327–52. Boulder: Westview Press, 1985.

Truitt, Jonathan. "Courting Catholicism: Nahua Women and the Catholic Church in Colonial Mexico City." *Ethnohistory* 57.3 (2010): 415–44.

Tuñón Pablos, Julia. *Mujeres en México: Una historia olvidada*. México: Grupo Editorial Planeta, 1987.

Tutino, John. *Making a New World: Founding Capitalism in the Bajío and Spanish North America*. Durham: Duke University Press, 2011.

Twinam, Ann. "The Church, the State, and the Abandoned: *Expósitos* in Late Eighteenth-Century Havana." In *Raising an Empire: Children in Early Modern Iberia and Colonial Latin America*, edited by Ondina E Gonzáles and Bianca Premo, 163–86. Albuquerque: University of New Mexico Press, 2007.

Vallebueno Garcinava, Miguel Felipe de Jesús. *Civitas y urbs: La conformación del espacio urbano de Durango*. Durango: Instituto de Cultura del Estado de Durango, 2005.

Van Young, Eric. *Hacienda and Market in Eighteenth-Century Mexico: The Rural Economy of the Guadalajara Region, 1675–1820*. Lanham: Rowman and Littlefield, 2006.

Velasco Murillo, Dana. "'For the Last Time, Once and for All': Indians, Violence, and Local Authority in the Colonial City, Zacatecas, Mexico, 1587–1628." *Ethnohistory* 63.1 (2016): 47–70.

———. "Laboring Above Ground: Indigenous Women in New Spain's Silver Mining District, Zacatecas, Mexico, 1620–1770." *Hispanic American Historical Review* 93.1 (2013): 3–32.

Velasco Murillo, Dana, Mark Lentz, and Margarita Ochoa, eds. *City Indians in Spain's American Empire: Urban Indigenous Society in Colonial Mesoamerica and Andean South America, 1530–1810*. Brighton: Sussex Academic Press, 2012.

Velasco Murillo, Dana, and Pablo Sierra Silva. "Mine Workers and Weavers: Afro-Indigenous Labor Arrangements and Interactions in Puebla and Zacatecas, 1600–1700." In *City Indians in Spain's American Empire: Urban Indigenous Society in Colonial Mesoamerica and Andean South America, 1530–1810*, edited by Dana Velasco Murillo, Mark Lentz, and Margarita R. Ochoa, 104–27. Brighton: Sussex Academic Press, 2012.

Vergara, Teresa C. "Growing Up Indian: Migration, Labor, and Life in Lima (1570–1640)." In *Raising an Empire: Children in Early Modern Iberia and Colonial Latin America*, edited by Ondina E Gonzáles and Bianca Premo, 75–106. Albuquerque: University of New Mexico Press, 2007.

Vidal, Salvador. *Estudio histórico de la ciudad de Zacatecas*. México: Arcimiaga, 1955.

Villella, Peter B. *Indigenous Elites and Creole Identity in Colonial Mexico, 1500–1800*. Cambridge: Cambridge University Press, 2016.

———. "'Pure and Noble Indians, Untainted by Inferior Idolatrous Races': Native Elites and the Discourse of Blood Purity in Late Colonial Mexico." *Hispanic American Historical Review* 91.4 (2011): 633–63.

Viramontes Anzures, Carlos. *De Chichimecas, pames y jonaces: Los recolectores-cazadores del semidesierto de Querétaro*. México: Instituto Nacional de Antropología e Historia, 2000.

Von Germeten, Nicole. *Black Blood Brothers: Confraternities and Social Mobility for Afro-Mexicans*. Gainesville: University Press of Florida, 2006.

Von Glahn, Richard. *Fountain of Fortune: Money and Monetary Policy in China, 1000–1700*. Berkeley: University of California Press, 1996.

Von Mentz, Brígida. "Coyuntura minera y protesta campesina en el centro de Nueva España, siglo XVIII." In *La minería mexicana: De la colonia al siglo XX*, edited by Inés Herrera Canales, 23–45. México: Instituto de Investigaciones Dr. José María Luis Mora, 1998.

Wauchope, Robert, and Howard F. Cline, eds. *Handbook of Middle American Indians*. Vol. 12 of *Guide to Ethnohistorical Sources*. Austin: University of Texas Press, 1971.

Weigand, Phil C. "Mining and Mineral Trade in Prehispanic Zacatecas." In *Mining and Mineral Techniques in Ancient Mesoamerica*, edited by Phil C. Weigand and Gretchen Gwynne, 87–134. Anthropology 6. Stony Brook: Department of Anthropology, State University of New York, Stony Brook, 1982.

———. "La prehistoria del estado de Zacatecas: Una interpretación." *Anuario de Historia* 1 (1978): 203–48.

———. *Tenamaxtli y Guaxicar: Las raíces profundas de la rebelión de Nueva Galicia*. Zamora: El Colegio de Michoacán; Guadalajara: Secretaría de Cultura de Jalisco, 1996.

Weigand, Phil C., and Acelia García de Weigand. *Los orígenes de los caxcanes y su relación con la guerra de los nayaritas: Una hipótesis*. Zapopan: El Colegio de Jalisco, 1995.

Wells, E. Christian: "Pottery Production and Microcosmic Organization: The Residential Structure of La Quemada, Zacatecas." *Latin American Antiquity* 11.1 (2000): 21–43.

West, Robert C. "Aboriginal Metallurgy and Metalworking in Spanish America." In *In Quest of Mineral Wealth: Aboriginal and Colonial Mining and Metallurgy in Spanish America*, edited by Alan K. Craig and Robert C. West, 5–20. Baton Rouge: Geoscience Publications, Department of Geography and Anthropology, Louisiana State University, 1994.

———. "Early Silver Mining in New Spain, 1531–1555." In *In Quest of Mineral Wealth: Aboriginal and Colonial Mining and Metallurgy in Spanish America*, edited by Alan K. Craig and Robert C. West, 119–35. Baton Rouge: Geoscience Publications, Department of Geography and Anthropology, Louisiana State University, 1994.

———. *The Mining Community in Northern New Spain: The Parral Mining District*. Los Angeles: University of California Press, 1949.

Wightman, Ann M. *Indigenous Migration and Social Change: The Forasteros of Cuzco, 1570–1720*. Durham: Duke University Press, 1990.

Wilson, Fiona. "Indians and Mestizos: Identity and Urban Popular Culture in Andean Peru." *Journal of Southern African Studies* 26.2 (June 2000): 239–53.

Wood, Stephanie. *Transcending Conquest: Nahua Views of Spanish Colonial Mexico*. Norman: University of Oklahoma Press, 2003.

Wunder, John R. "Native American History, Ethnohistory, and Context." *Ethnohistory* 54.4 (2007): 591–604.

Yannakakis, Yanna. *The Art of Being In-Between: Native Intermediaries, Indian Identity, and Local Rule in Colonial Oaxaca*. Durham: Duke University Press, 2008.

———. "Introduction: How Did They Talk to One Another? Language Use and Communication in Multilingual New Spain." *Ethnohistory* 59.4 (2012): 667–74.

Zavala, Silvio Arturo. *El servicio personal de los indios en la Nueva España*. México: El Colegio de México, Centro de Estudios Históricos, 1984.

———. *Los esclavos indios en Nueva España*. México: El Colegio Nacional, 1967.

Zulawski, Ann L. "Social Differentiation, Gender, and Ethnicity: Urban Indian Women in Colonial Bolivia, 1640–1725." *Latin American Research Review* 25.2 (1990), 93–113.

———. "Wages, Ore Sharing, and Peasant Agriculture: Labor in Oruro's Silver Mines, 1607–1720." *Hispanic American Historical Review* 67.3 (1987): 405–30.

Index

Page numbers followed by "f" or "t" indicate material in figures or tables. Please also see the glossary, beginning on page 269.

acculturation: association with ladino, 115; and urban Indians, 6–7, 10–11, 148, 157
Acosta, Mathías de, 121
African/Afro-descended residents: in mining jobs, 41, 68, 126, 175–76; relations with Indians, 135; residential patterns, 51, 56, 127–29; and slave labor in the mines, 35–36; in urban/domestic labor, 68, 127–29 (127t–129t); utilizing church institutions, confraternities, 238–39n99
Aguascalientes, 49
Aguilar, Pedro de, 125
Aguirre, Ana de, 61, 123
Ahumada Sámano, Pedro de, 25, 33, 53
Alba, María, 165
alcaldes: *alcalde mayor* (magistrate), 49–50; *alcalde ordinario* (municipal judge), 49, 84; authorized for Zacatecas, 92–93, 187; election of, 104, 106–9 (108t); holding multiple terms, 110–13 (111t); Indians as, 80, 89, 92–93, 95t, 97, 110, 113–14; language of, 115; low compensation for, 109; non-Indians as, 113, 191; protecting community from abuse, 116; relationship with governor, 101–3; rights and duties of, 94, 101–2, 246n51; rotation of, 95, 98t; Spaniards as, 135, 159–60, 187–88, 191, 193–95; under Spanish supervision, 93–94; in Tlacuitlapan, 109–11 (111t), 129. See also *cabildos*
alguaciles, 101, 104, 192
altepetl (indigenous ethnic state): absence of as organizing mechanism, 54–55, 71–72; influence on confraternity and community development, 82, 85, 90, 100, 139, 239n102, 241n137; as model for governance practices, 95, 100, 103
Althouse, Aaron P., 258n136
Altman, Ida, 222n21
Alva Ixtlilxochitl, Fernando de, 10

Alvarado, Pedro de, 27, 28
Amador, Elías, 205
amalgamation process, 67, 149
Amaya, María de, 148
Antonio García, Joseph, 118
archconfraternities: creation of, 169–70; impact on community autonomy, 170, 197, 203. See also *cofradías*
Arellano, Roque de, 128, 130t
Ares Queija, Berta, 218n43
Argüello, Cristóbal de, 53
Arlegui, José de, 30
Artacha, Pedro de, 127–28 (128f)
Arzáns Orsúa y Veloa, Bartolomé de, 61–62
Audiencia, New Galicia: 45; appeals to by Indian leaders, 80, 102, 114; authorization of indigenous government by, 107; authorization of Spanish government by, 49–50, 84
Augustinian order, 58–59; *cofradías* sponsored by, 80, 81t; and indigenous sociopolitical autonomy, 143–44, 170; secularization of Indian parishes, 166–68

Bachiller, Alonso Fernández, 84
Bajío: migration to Zacatecas from, 185; rebellion (Independence), 202; regional development, 49, 186
Bakewell, Peter, 220n1, 228n100, 229nn107, 111, 230–31n128, 252n37, 256n118
Baltazar, Juan, 143
Bañuelos, Baltasar de, 53, 84–85, 225n55
barreteros (excavators), 67; formation of confraternity for, 170
barrios/pueblos: *barrios mineros* under Mexico, 203; elections in, 106–10 (108t); growth between traza and towns, 47–48, 127, 180–82, 188; incorporation of pueblos into city, 187–92, 197, 205–6;

barrios/pueblos (continued)
Indians conducting rounds, 139; Lomas del Calvario, 47–48; Mexicapan, 47, 48, 58, 60; San Francisco, 47, 48, 58, 71, 91; San Josef, 47, 48, 89; Tlacuitlapan, 47, 54, 58, 62f, 71–72, 89, 181t; Tonalá (San Agustín), 47, 59, 89, 91; transition of barrios to pueblos, 94–100 (100f)
Basílico, Juan, 112
Bennett, Herman L., 238–39n99
booms. *See* mining booms/busts
Bourbon Reforms: definition of, 161; influences on indigenous sociopolitical autonomy, 187–88, (188f), 195; influences on labor practices, 177; influences on religious life, 166–67, 168–70; intendancy system, 186–87
Bracho, El, 44–45, 47–48
Brading, David, 171, 262n69
Branciforte, Marquis de, 186–87
Brown, Kendall, 237n74, 262n70
Bufa mountain, 25, 44–45
buhíos, 61
busts. *See* mining booms/busts

Caballeros, Don Bonifacio, 194–95
Cabañas, Juan Cruz Ruiz de, 169–70
cabecera (head town), 95–96, 98t, 100, 245nn28, 31
cabildos (municipal councils), 49–50, 116; as adaptation of altepetl structure, 100; alcalde versus governor position in, 101–3; Chepinque and San Josef, 78, 99, 104, 138; and cofradías, 54, 78–80, 99; combining with preconquest practices, 6–7; composition of, 101, 104, 112–13; development of, 101–6; dissolution of, 191, 193, 196, 203, 205; during economic busts, 120–21; elections for, 97f, 98, 107; El Niño, 99, 138; factionalization within, 109; indigenous, authority of, 118; indigenous, dissolution of, 191; indigenous, expansion of, 95–96, 101, 104, 106; indigenous, rise of, 59, 90–91, 93–95, 101, 106, 146; *mandones* serving on, 105, 247n72; and *mayordomos*, 54, 102, 104; officials in, 101, 103–7; power sharing among, 95–98 (97t); records/minutes of, 84, 90, 101; required for official town status, 94; rights under Spanish law, 114, 116, 145–47; Tlacuitlapan (San Francisco), 97t, 104, 109, 129, 138; Tlaxcala, 59, 91; Tonalá (San Agustín), 138; Tonalá Chepinque, 98t, 114, 138; using interpreters, 64–65, 115; vecindad and land-tenure, 147. *See also alcaldes*
cacique, use of title, 110
calidad (social standing), 154, 257n133
Camacho, Diego de, 144, 260n29
capillas (chapels), 200, 201f; and cofradías, 138, 183; consolidation under Bourbon reforms, 170; first permanent, 45, 62 (62f); in haciendas, 67; town meetings at, 54, 107
Carrasco, Joseph, 118, 154
Carreño, Alonso, 64
carriers, long-distance, 17, 32, 41
Casa de Fundación, 43
casa del cabildo (town hall), 50, 54, 56, 62
Casillas, Juan Marcos, 140
castas/castazation: demographic growth, 132, 135, 170–72, 179–80; lack of corporate rights, 82, 191
Castro Gutiérrez, Felipe, 39, 242n158, 248n103, 249n120, 266n22
caudal, 154
Cazcanes, 23; as interpreters, 64–65; role in Mixton War, 20, 27
cendradillas, 43
Chalchihuites culture, 20
Chambers, Sarah C., 9
Chance, John K., 160, 261n53
chapels. *See capillas*
Charcas, 69
Charney, Paul, 239n102
Chepinque barrio/pueblo, 96–99 (98t), 104; cofradía, 183; elections in, 107; incorporated into third district, 187; joint cabildo with San Josef, 99, 104; map, 100 (100f); population, 133t. *See also* Tonalá Chepinque
Chiametla, 69
Chichimecs, 23–25
Chihuahua, 179, 185
children: labor abductions of, 123, 253n46; as migrants, 125 (125t), 164 (164t); orphans, 122; at San Josef, 124–25 (125t); in Tlacuitlapan, 182; working in mines, 252n42
chinos (Asians), 128, 129t, 130t, 253n50
Cholula, 55, 208
"cihuatepixque (women in charge of people)," 73
ciudadano: definitions of, 7–8
coatequitl work system, 37
cocoliztli (illness), 120

cofradías (confraternities), 53–54, 76f; as adoption of Spanish institution, 70; chapels housing, 138; as civic/governance institutions, 75–82 (80t, 81t); closures/mergers of, 169–70; female members of, 73; mixture of Indian ethnicities in, 71–73, 82; and mutual-aid "clubs" in United States, 209; similarities to tlaxilacalli, 73; statue dispute between San Josef and Vera Cruz, 117–18, 139–44; in Tlacuitlapan, 72. See also *altepetl*; individual *cofradías*
Colotlán, 139
Compostela: mint of, 33, 46; site of Audiencia, 33, 45
Connell, William, 242n151
Contreras, Pedro Gómez de, 50
Cope, R. Douglas, 204
Corral, Doña Ana del, 66
Cortés, Francisco, 28, 34
Cortés, Hernán, 28
Cosme, Juana, 178
Costantino, Miguel and Miguel Álvarez, 48
Coyote, Angel, 95
coyote(a) (of Indian/African descent), 163, 179t
criollo(a) (native born), 110, 249n111; marriage patterns, 184 (184t), 254n67; as status marker, 113–15
Cross, Harry E., 262n72
cuadrilla, 42, 67
cuarteles mayores/menores (districts), 187–88 (188f), 193
Cuatitlán, 88
Cuernavaca, 101
Cuzco, 10

Deeds, Susan, 14
de Guzmán, Juan, 40
de la Borda, José, 177
de la Concepción, Manuel, 204
de la Cruz, Buenaventura, 88–89, 92
de la Cruz, Ignacia, 149, 151
de la Cruz, Jerónimo, 105
de la Cruz, Joseph, 1–2, 12, 118, 149–53, 155
de la Cruz, Juana, 124 (124t)
de la Cruz, Magdalena, 121–22, 130
de la Cruz, Manuel, 169
de la Fuente, Gaspar: and indigenous governance, 87–89, 92–93; inspection of Zacatecas district, 40, 60, 231n136
de la Fuente, Juan, 144–45

de la Rodríguez, Miguel, 135
de las Casas, Gonzalo, 25
de las Nieves, Dominga, 135
de la Trinidad, Agustín, 112
de la Trinidad, Antonio, 111–12 (111t)
de la Vega, Inca Garcilaso, 10
de los Reyes, officeholders named, 108, 112
de los Santos, Anastasio, 118, 145–47
Díaz de Cisneros, Eugenio, 56
Diego, Juan, 111
Diputación de Minería, 50, 84
diputados (representatives), 50
Domingo, Francisco, 60
Domingo, García, 61
Dominican order: *cofradías* sponsored by, 80, 81t; conflicts with native towns, 143, 168
don, use of title, 110
draft labor. See forced/draft labor practices
Duarte, Juan, 126, 127t
Dulce Nombre de Jesús cofradía, 81t
Durán, Roque Antonio, 135

economic booms and busts. See mining booms/busts
elections in pueblos, 106–10 (108t)
Elías, Alejandro Dolores, 173
elites/nobles, 110
El Niño barrio/pueblo, 81t, 201f; arrest of José Ramón Gómez, 159–60, 193–96; cabildo established in, 138; cofradía, 169; dissolution of cofradía, 169; Dominican/Augustinian dispute over, 143–44; elections in, 107–8; endogamy in, 183t; growth of, 98t; hospital in, 139; incorporation of, 96, 187; marriage petitions in, 162–63; migrant petitioners to, 163–66 (163t–165t); placed in fourth district, 187, 188f, 193; and Tonalá Chepinque, 59, 99, 104, 138
encomiendas, 37, 39, 41
endogamy rates, 136–38 (137t), 183 (183t), 254n67
epidemics, 37–38, 40, 120, 160, 250n12
escribanos (notaries), 101
Espinosa, Melchor, 102
Esteban, Pedro, 139
Esteva Fabregat, Claudio, 160, 265–66n13
ethnic cohesion, 66–70
excavation labor, 41
expósitos (orphans), 122, 153, 257n132
ex-votos, 141, 206 (206f)

Farriss, Nancy, 241n128, 243n170
feast days, 81, 169, 261n37
Fernández Moreno, Joseph, 187
Ferrer Sanchez, Vicente, 140
fiscales, indigenous, 105–6, 247n72; on cabildos, 104; as hacienda overseers, 92–93, 245n21
Flores, María Magdalena, 125–26
food: agricultural complexes, 48–49, 135, 174, 185–86, 205; bakers, confectioners, 172; daily rations, 42, 176; in markets, 63; need to import, 48–49; San Juan del Mezquital community, 30; sedentary agriculture, 20, 23, 26; slaves doing agricultural work, 68; women cultivating crops and cooking, 26, 41, 68; women selling food in haciendas, 67, 151, 174
forced/draft labor practices: complaints regarding, 40, 88, 114; preferred over slave labor, 69; required for public works projects, festivals, 39–40; requiring sedentary populations, 23, 34; Spaniards moving away from, 35; Zacatecas residents exempt from, 37, 94, 178
foundry work, 41
Franciscan order: cofradías sponsored by, 72, 80, 81t; custodianship of Indians, 47, 58, 82, 168–69, 260n29; and indigenous sociopolitical organization, 71–72; secularization of Indian parishes, 166–68
Francisco, Juan, 113
free-wage labor in Zacatecas, 34–35, 37; as an advantage, 46; competition for, 42; delayed, reduced wages, 39; encouraging native migrants, 51; and freedom to leave or change employer, 41–42, 51; *indios libres*, 39–44; use of contracts, 41–42
Frejes, Francisco, 44, 226n62
Fresnillo, 49

Gamboa, Mateo de, 111, 114, 125
García, Baltasar, 113
García, Diego, 108
García, Flores, 240n119
García, Inés, 63
García, Joseph Antonio, 145–47
García, Lorenzo, 112
García, Nicolás, 145
García de Ortega, Ruy, 53
García González, Francisco, 259n14
Gasca, José del Refugio, 25
Gerhard, Peter, 237n59, 258n3

gobernadores (governors), 102, 247n60, 248n84
Gómez, José Ramón, 159–60, 193–96
Gomez, Juan, 128 (128f)
González, Antonia, 145
González, Bartolomé, 145
González, Juan (El Niño), 99
González, Juan (Jalpa), 49
González, Lucas, 145
González, Nicolasa, 147
Gosner, Kevin, 247n60
Granados, Pedro Francisco, 64
gran mortandad (epidemic), 120
Graubart, Karen, 5
Guachichiles, 23, 32–33
Guachinango mines, 46
Guadalajara: composition of mining labor force, 69; migration to Zacatecas from, 72, 134, 164, 185; regional development of, 185; as site of Audiencia, 45, 185
Guamán Poma de Ayala, Felipe, 9
Guanajuato: composition of mining labor force, 263n79; development of indigenous organizations in, 240n111, 242n158; migration to Zacatecas from, 134, 164; silver production in, 186, 202
Guerra de los chichimecas, 32
Gutiérrez del Campo, Alonso, 53
Guzmán, Juan de, 88
Guzmán, Nuño Beltrán de, 28, 225n53, 236n35

Hacienda de Bernárdez, 178–79
Hacienda de la Polvorista, 180
hacienda de minas, 66–67, 122–27, 145; ethnic composition of, 124t; families in, 122–27; female owners/residents of, 66, 68–69; living conditions in, 61, 69; Ruiz de Quiroga, Pedro, 126 (126t); Spanish-owned, 145; in Tlacuitlapan, 181t; women's labor in, 67, 124–25, 151, 174
Harris, Olivia, 214n13, 258n142
Harvey, H. R., 224n42
Haskett, Robert, 113, 229n115, 232n167, 247n68
hereditary rulers, 91
Hernández, Mateo, 107, 108t, 111t
Hernández, Pedro (of Huexotzinco), 77
Hernández, Perfecto, 159, 193–94, 196
Hernández de Herrera, Miguel, 53
Historia general de las cosas de Nueva España (Sahagún), 25

holidays, illegal work on, 41
hospitals, 58–59, 138–39; and indigenous community formation, 71, 76–77
huehuetque/antiguos (elders), 104
huerta (commercial farm), 126, 127t
Huidobro, Juan de, 53

Ibarra, Diego de, 32–33, 50
Ibarra, Francisca de, 140
Ibarra, Francisco de, 114, 125
Ibarra, Miguel de, 29
indianizando, 218n43
"Indians," use of term, 4–5
Indian towns, of Zacatecas, 19f, 89–90, 100f, 190f
indigenous residents of Zacatecas, 47; as "acculturated," 148; *barrios mineros* under Mexico, 203; and Catholic Church, 142–44; commoners filling leadership roles, 110; conducting neighborhood rounds, 139; at disadvantage in courts, 154; *don, principal, cacique* titles for, 249n121; ethnic identity of alcaldes, 95t; indigenous names among current, 205; languages spoken by, 63–66; long-term roots of, 60, 121; as mature urban Indian culture, 148–56; merchants and traders, 48; as mine owners, 149–50; no hereditary nobility, 91, 94, 110; permanent versus itinerant, 61–62; petition for self-rule, 54, 89, 92–95; policing non-Indians, 159–60, 193–96; population fluctuations of, 132–33 (133t), 160, 161–62; practicing "fission, readaptation, and recombination," 156–57; preconquest government, 95; preferred for labor, 119–20; purchasing lots, 47–48, 60–61; relations with Spanish officials, 114; participating in processions, 112; settlements around mines, 44–45, 57; as slaves, 27, 36, 41, 46; as stabilizing or destabilizing force, 162; as well-suited to mine work, 35; work relations among, 69–70. See also Zacatecas; Zacatecos
indio ladino/criollo/acholizado, 8–9
indios libres (free wage laborers), 39–44
"indios vecinos": Spanish appeals for, 58
intendancies, 186
interpreters, 64–66, 162; Nahuatlatos, 61

jacales (huts), 44
jacal/xacalli, 61

Jacobo, Diego, 77
Jalisco: migrants arriving to Zacatecas from, 72, 184
Jerónima, María, 127–28 (128f)
Jerónima Martínez, Antonia, 135
Jesuits, 25, 166–67
Jesús Nazareno cofradía, 96, 138, 169
Jiménez, Francisco, 64–65
Jiménez, Juan Bautista, 123
José, Nicolás, 108, 113
Joseph, Marcos, 192
Juana Ana, 60–61
Juan Antonio, 103
Juan Bautista, 61
Juárez, Gabriel, 128 (128f)
Juárez, Máximo, 159
juez, 105
justicias mayores, 104

Kellogg, Susan, 254n68

labor, types of, 34, 66–70. See also free-wage labor; slave labor
ladino(a) (bilingual, bicultural), 149, 151–52, 155–56; as ethnic descriptor, 113, 115, 149
La Habana, 69
land/property ownership, indigenous: cofradías buying land, 139; houses, 118, 145–46; indigenous, 60–61; mines, haciendas, 50, 149–52, 175
languages in Zacatecas, 63–66
Langue, Frédérique, 263n77
La Quemada, 25, 221n10, 224n36
lavadero (washer), 41, 67
lawsuits, 118
Lázaro de Arregui, Domingo, 243n168
León, Diego de (El Tarasco), 149–53
León, María Josefa, 1–2, 12, 118, 149–53
Limpia Concepción cofradía, 80t–81t; of Tlacuitlapan, 72, 80t, 138, 169; of Tonalá Chepinque, 80, 81t, 170
lobo(a) (of mixed black and indigenous ancestry), 145
Lockhart, James, 216n30, 220n54, 226n56, 239n102, 242n145, 254n70
Loma San Gabriel Culture, 20
Lomas del Calvario barrio, 47–48
López, Sebastián, 108
Los Remedios mine, 1, 149–51, 257n122
Luján, Simón, 206
Lyon, George F., 174, 177

Mancuso, Lara, 242n154
mandones (mine foremen), 99, 105–6, 247n72; on cabildos, 105–6, 108 (108t)
Mangan, Jane, 239n102, 258n135
Mariana, 123, 127–28 (128f)
marketplace, 62–63; women in, 67. See also *tianguiz*
marriage: during economic booms, busts, 162–64, 171–72 (171t); ethnoracial composition of, 135–38 (137t), 165–66, 171–72 (171t), 183, 203; of immigrants, 165; and Indian women in labor force, 172–75; of natives/vecinos, 180, 181t, 184, 204–5; records of, 123–24, 131–33
Martín (of Chalco), 77
Martín, Diego, 105
Martín, Francisco, 121
Martín, Juan, 108, 113
Martín, Nicolás, 108
Martínez, Andrés, 104–5
Martínez, Pedro, 108
Martínez de la Marcha, Hernando, 230n123; confining sales to tianguiz, 63; description of Zacatecos, 26, 33; migrants declared free-wage laborers, 39, 41–42; ordinances against vagabonds, 49; reporting on mines, 45–46; requiring all merchants to sell maize, 48; setting of wages, 42
matlazahuatl (epidemic), 160
Matthew, Laura, 208
mayordomos (confraternity foremen): authority and responsibilities of, 78, 79–81, 91; ethnicity of, 54, 58, 74, 77–78, 206; petitions against Spanish confraternities, 79; selection of, 53–54, 78–79; serving on cabildos, 102, 104; and Vera Cruz statue dispute, 117–18, 139–44
Mazapil, 87
McCaa, Robert, 259n17
Mendoza, Andrés de, 135
Mendoza, Antonio de, 27
Mérida, Mexico, 208
mestizaje (miscegenation): challenges to, 10, 205; in urban areas, 9
mestizo(a), 113, 132; absence of "shared" corporate or cultural identity, 9–10, 70, 82; affiliations with Indians, 10, 137, 145, 170, 180, 204–5; marriage patterns, 171t; in mining jobs, 178–79 (179t); population patterns, 172, 204
mexicano. See Nahuatl

Mexicapan barrio/pueblo, 47, 48, 58, 60
Mexicas: as contemporary identity, 208; endogamy and, 254n68; leadership positions of, 95, 110; as mythical, 25; role of women among, 251n21; in Tenochtitlan, 215n18; in Tlacuitlapan, 58; in Tonalá, 95–96; as vecinos, 83
Mexico, independent government of: eliminating caste distinctions, 202–3, 205–6; rise of mestizo identity, 204
Meyers, Albert, 239n102, 243n161
Michoacán, 3f, 49; decline in migration to Zacatecas, 184–85; migrants arriving to Zacatecas from, 65, 72, 88, 134, 164
micropatriotism, 7–8, 139
Mier y Campa, José Bezanilla, 230n122, 232n166
migrants/migration from Zacatecas, 120, 208–9
migrants/migration to Zacatecas, 203, 207, 253n55; children, 125, 164 (164t); commoners not nobles, 77; to El Niño and Tonalá Chepinque, 162–66 (163t–165t); ethnicity of, 55, 72, 126, 132, 134–35, 184–85; free-wage labor as incentive to, 39, 46, 50–51; Nahuatl speakers, 64–65, 75; non- and semisedentary peoples, 20, 23–26, 31, 34, 37; from other provinces, 134t; Purépecha speakers, 64; voluntary, 34, 37–38, 51; women, 163–66 (163t–165t), 173–74 (174t), 184t–185t. See also indigenous residents of Zacatecas; mining booms/busts
migration to United States, 208–9
Miguel (*mayordomo* of Vera Cruz), 77
Miguel, Francisco, 92–93
military campaigns, participation in, 139
minero (miner, mine owner), 149, 256n117
mining, silver: disputes over rights, 150; need for skilled labor, 37; occupations in, 175t, 176t; ongoing discoveries in Zacatecas, 34, 47; ore separation, 41; preconquest, 211n3; reinvestment in, revitalization of, 171; rescate silver, 43; smelting, 41, 43, 149, 260n27, 262n57; tailings (*pepena* or *partida*), 42–43, 176–78; tasks of, 41. See also *hacienda de minas*
mining booms/busts, 60, 135–37 (137t), 150, 156, 164; boom (1550s), 41–42,

45–46, 48–49; boom (1570s–1635), 85, 91–92, 119; bust (1635–1670), 118, 119–21, 131; boom (1670–1690), 118, 132, 133–34, 136; bust (1690–1705), 118, 131; boom (1705–1732), 1, 117–18, 131–33, 145, 147–50, 161, 189; bust (1732–1767), 161–66, 171, 184, 186; boom (1767–1809), 171–78, 180–88, 189t, 196–97, 202; bust (1810–1811), 202; boom (1824), 202
ministros, 104
Mixton War, 20, 27, 29–31, 225n50
montañés (mestizos), 10
Monteiro, John, 177
Montejo, Francisco de, 28
Morales, Matheo de, 121
Morales, Teresa de, 66
Moran, Josepha, 152
Moreno, Josef María, 194
Mörner, Magnus, 265n13
Mota y Escobar, Alonso de la, 24, 26, 35
motín (riot): and El Niño, 143–44; and San Josef, 117, 142
Moya, Jose, 231–32n147, 238n98
mulatto(a): in labor force, 126, 172, 173t; marriage patterns of, 171t; in mining jobs, 175, 176t, 178–79 (179t); population of Zacatecas, 92t, 132
municipal councils. See *cabildos*
Murguía, Antonio Martínez de, 135
mutual-aid societies, US, 209

naboría (servant, dependent), 39, 230n127, 230–31n128
Nahuatl (*mexicano*): in Catholic religious functions, 115, 162; interpreters, 64; ledgers, minutes kept in, 5–6, 90; as lingua franca of Zacatecas, 64–66, 75, 83, 115; during migrant booms, 162
Namiguemaculichema, 33
New Conquest History, 11, 218n50
New Galicia (Nueva Galicia): de la Fuente's tour of, 87–88, 92; discovery of silver in, 17; early history of, 24, 28–29; indigenous auxiliaries in, 59; migration to Zacatecas from, 134t; slavery in, 36; warfare within, 31, 33
New Spain (Nueva España): indigenous autonomous towns in, 90; migration to Zacatecas from, 134t; northern silver mining district map, 3f
Nicolás, Juan, 143

Nieves, 69
non- and semisedentary peoples, 20; classifications of, 23–26; Spanish warfare with, 31–33
nonmining occupations, 172, 173t
notaries, 104–5
Nuestra Señora de la Asunción cofradía, 72, 80t, 81t, 105, 138
Nuestra Señora de la Soledad cofradía, 81t, 99, 138, 170, 183, 206
Nueva Vizcaya, 3f; labor patterns in, 38, 69, 228n103; migrants to Zacatecas from, 134t, 165t; mining activities in, 33, 40; population patterns of, 205
Nuin, María Josefa, 173, 185

Oñate, Cristóbal de, 28, 32–33, 50
orphans (*expósitos*), 122, 153, 257n132
Othón de Mendizábal, Miguel, 224n42

Pablo Miguel, 61
Pagden, Anthony, 266n17
Palencia, Pedro Ortiz de, 50
Pánuco, Zacatecas, 48, 136
Paola, Hilaria, 135
parcialidades (autonomous clusters), 47
Paredes Martínez, Carlos, 235n22, 240n119, 244n8
partida/pepena (metal sharing), 42–43; attempts to eliminate, 176–78
"patrician Indians," 44
Pátzcuaro, 246n54, 248n84
Pedregoso barrio, 127–28 (128f)
Pedro Miguel, 109
Pedro Sebastián, 109
Philip II, 84
Philip III, 87
Pizarro brothers, 28
plan of Zacatecas, 100f, 190f
plata del rescate (silver not from registered mine), 43, 262n57, 272
population of Indian towns, 133t, 183t, 184–86, 189
Portugal, Bernardo, 189, 190f
Potosí: housing arrangements of, 61; labor arrangements of, 13, 34, 39, 67
precious metals, 28–29. See also mining, silver
pregoneros, 65
principales, 103
Proaño, Diego Hernández de, 50
processions, 81, 112, 142

pueblos de indios (autonomous indigenous towns), 5, 90, 187. *See also* El Niño; San Josef; Tlacuitlapan; Tonalá Chepinque
Purépecha, 6, 63–64, 83, 134

Querétaro: migrants to Zacatecas from, 134, 186
Quicama, 33
Quinones, Sam, 209

Radding, Cynthia, 136
Raja Peñas Cristo statue, 117–18, 139–44
Ramírez, Cristóbal, 124 (124t)
Ramírez, Matías, 113, 148
Ramírez, Susan, 256n117
rancherías, 25–26
Real, Francisco, 109
Real de Monte labor uprisings, 177
realengas (unappropriated lands), 145
regidor, 105
Rendón, Francisco, Intendant of Zacatecas, 187
Rentería, Juan de, 53
repartimiento service, 37–38, 39, 40
repúblicas de indios y españoles, 55; as imperial policy by 1530s, 56–57; in Zacatecas, 57–59
Reyes, Miguel, 109
Reyes, Miguel de los, 105
Reynoso, Pedro, 92–93
Ribera Bernárdez, Joseph de, 117, 143
Rivera, Francisco de, 77, 143
Robledo, Josef de, 195–96
Rodríguez, Andrea, 118, 153–56
Rodríguez, Isabel, 121
Rodríguez, José Manuel, 185
Romero Rodríguez, Francisco, 137
rotation of offices, 95–96 (95t)
Ruiz, Pedro, 77
Ruiz de Quiroga, Pedro, 126 (126t)

sacagentes (labor recruiters), 38
saçemis (rock fights), 81, 88–89, 116, 143
Saenz, Antonio, 125
Saenz, Josef, 145
Sahagún, Bernardino de, 25, 26
Saignes, Thierry, 258n143
Salas, Antonio de, 84
Saldaña, Beatriz de, 127–28 (128f)
Salomon, Frank, 156, 250n7
San Agustín. *See* Tonalá (San Agustín) barrio/pueblo
San Bernabé mine, 44

Sánchez, Miguel Francisco, 140
Sánchez, Pedro, 164
San Diego cofradía, 81t, 138–39, 170, 200, 201f; assets of, 80, 139, 184
San Francisco barrio/pueblo, 47, 48, 58, 71, 91, 95. *See also* Tlacuitlapan (San Francisco) barrio/pueblo
San Josef barrio/pueblo, 247n72; civil status of population, 122–23 (123t); cofradía, 170, 183–84; complaints of abuse, 80; dispute over statue, 117–18, 139–44; and Dominican order, 168; on donated land, 48; elections in, 107; endogamy in, 183t; governorship of, 103; joint cabildo with Chepinque, 104; map, 100 (100f); petition against forced labor in, 114; placed in fourth district, 187, 188f, 193; population, 133, 183t; properties of, 183–84; property disputes in, 147; Tarascan neighborhood in, 96; Tlaxcalan population in, 47, 95–96; and Tonalá, 96–97, 99
San Luis Potosí: indigenous communities of, 207–8; migration to Zacatecas from, 134, 184
San Miguel, 134
San Nicolás cofradía, 139, 169
Santa Vera Cruz, indigenous cofradía of, 71–73; allowing women, children, 73; alms collection, 79; building of chapel, 248n88; constitution of, 84; ethnic diversity of, 73–74; first indigenous cofradía, 53–54, 170; leadership of, 77–78; membership rolls, 73–74; merging with Limpia Concepción, 169; use of Nahuatl by, 75, 76f; written records of, 74–75
Santa Vera Cruz, Spanish cofradía of, 236n33; conflict with San Josef, 117–18, 139–44
Santiago de Guatemala, 208
Santiago Tlatelolco, Mexico City, 208
Santísimo Sacramento cofradía, 170
Santo Cristo de Raja Peñas statue, 117–18, 139–44
Santo Niño de Atocha shrine, 141f
Schwartz, Stuart B., 156, 250n7
secession from Spain, 202
secular priests, 167–70, 183, 197, 260n29
silver. *See* mining, silver
Silverblatt, Irene, 258n143
slave labor, African: in mining labor force, 35–36, 68–69; in nonmining labor force, 68, 126–27 (127t); petitions for, 35, 120;

population of Zacatecas, 92; royal ordinances on, 41
slave labor, indigenous, 17, 29, 34, 36; ban of, 36, 46; royal ordinances on, 41
smelting, 41, 43, 149, 260n27, 262n57
"social utility" rhetoric, 177
solarero(a): meaning of, 5
Sonora, Mexico, 136, 205
sonsacar, 42
Soto, Francisco, 63, 64, 82–83
Soto, Hernando de (Zacatecas *mayordomo*), 53
Sotomayor, Joaquín de, 100f, 189
Spalding, Karen, 257n124, 258n136
Spanish American societies, 209
Spanish language: interpreters/translators, 64–66, 75, 113; need for fluency in, 83, 104–5, 113, 152–53; notaries in, 104; source documents, 14, 90. See also *ladino*
statues/effigies, 141. See also Santo Cristo de Raja Peñas statue

Tacuba, 90
tailings (silver), 42. See also *partida/pepena*
"Tale of Two Villages, A" (Quinones), 209
tamemes (indigenous porters), 17, 32, 36
Tarahumara people, 26
Tarascans, 47, 59, 65, 72, 95, 96, 151
tarasca/Purépecha, 63–64
Tecuexes, 47, 59, 65, 96
temachti grande (head teacher), 138
temachti menores (assistant instructors), 138
tenateros (carriers), 67
tenientes, 101, 104
Tenochtitlan, 28, 90–91, 215n18
Tepehuanes, 31
Tepeques, 31
tequío, 42
Terraciano, Kevin, 216n29, 237n70
Texcoco/Texcocans, 55, 58–59, 88, 90, 95, 110
tianguiz (market), 45, 48, 62–63. See also marketplace
timacehualtin (we commoners), 5
titlaca (we people), 5
Tlacuitlapan barrio/pueblo: alcalde position, 109–11 (111t), 129; cabildo in, 97t, 104, 138; and Catholic Church, 144; chapel in, 183; clerics in, 260n29; incorporated into second district, 187; map, 100 (100f); Mexica in, 110; population, 133t, 183t; properties of, 184; town structure of, 96t
Tlaltenango, 17–18

tlatoani, 103
Tlaxcala/Tlaxcalans, 248n84; city of, 90–91, 97, 110, 248; as "friendly," 37; helping suppress rebellion, 139; protesting forced labor, 88; in San Josef, 47, 96; in Tlacuitlapan, 47, 58; in Tonalá, 59, 95. See also San Josef
tlaxilacalli (neighborhood), 55, 235n31
Tolosa, Juan (Juanes) de: expedition to future site of Zacatecas, 17, 29, 220n1; Franciscans and, 71; indigenous allies of, 29, 44, 230n122; initial contact with Zacatecos, 30; in Mixton War, 29
Toluca, 55
Tonalá (San Agustín) barrio/pueblo, 91; alcaldes in, 110–11 (111t); cabildo in, 138; Calle de Tonalá, 138, 200; early settlers in, 59; founding of, 47, 89; Mexica and Tlaxcala in, 95–96; power sharing within/around, 96–99, 98t
Tonalá Chepinque: alcaldes in, 111 (111t), 113; alguaciles in, 112; cabildo in, 98t, 114, 138; and Calle de Tonalá, 138; cofradías in, 80, 81t; endogamy in, 183t; hospitals in, 139; joining in suppressing rebellion, 139; Limpia Concepción cofradía, 72, 80t–81t, 138, 169–70; marriage petitions in, 162–63; migrant petitioners to, 163–66 (163t–165t); population, 183t; previously "pueblo de Tlaxcala," 59; processions for dead, 170; property disputes in, 145–47; purchasing land, 139; San Josef split from, 99. See also Chepinque
Tonalatecos, 59, 72, 88, 96
topiles (constables), 104
translators, 64–66
traza (city center), 5, 45, 56
tribute collection, 23, 37–38, 214n13; exemption of, in Zacatecas, 4, 19, 37, 94, 102, 135, 260n111; reinstatement in Zacatecas, 186–87, 203, 263–64nn98–99
Trinidad, Antonio de, 107
Truitt, Jonathan, 73
Trujillo, Peru, 5
tunal, 61

United States, Mexican migrants to, 208
urban development, 44
"urban Indians," 6; approaches to, 10–11; cultural fluency of, 148–49; definition of, 4
urban labor, 66–70

urban living as "social death," 9
Urquiola, Joseph de, 151
Ursua, Martín de, 150, 152

vagabondage, 42
Valladolid, Michoacán, 208
Vanegas, Emiterio Seledonio, 178
Vázquez, Maria Estafana, 173
Vázquez Macias, Diego, 140
vecinos: importance of status, 115, 152–53; initially squatters, 47; and interethnic interactions, 147–56; land sales only to, 144–46; meaning of, 7–8, 83; open to Indians, Africans, and Spaniards, 8; qualifications for, 92–93, 148
Velasco, Luis de, 31
Ventura, Nicolás, 145
verdugo (executioner), 139
Veta Grande, 44, 48, 136
villa (city), 90, 273
Villareal, Joseph de, 129t
Villella, Peter B., 215n25
visitador, 40, 87–89, 92–93, 231n136
Von Germeten, Nicole, 238n99

wages, 42
weight limits for laborers, 41
women: as cofradía members, 73, 138; as emigrants to United States, 208–9; gender roles among Zacatecos, 26; as immigrants, 163–66 (163t–165t), 173–74 (174t), 184t–185t; in Indian labor force, 172–75; jobs held by, 66–68, 123–26; labor in haciendas de minas, 67, 124–25, 151, 174; as mining co-owners, 151; not working below ground, 151; single/widowed, 67–68, 73, 122–23 (123t), 153–54, 175; unlawful forced labor of, 41
Wunder, John R., 218n45

Xochimilco, 90

yanaconas, 39
Yannakakis, Yanna, 65
Young, Eric Van, 185

Zacatecas, 100f, 190f, 200f; as an official town, 49–50, 84; building of chapel, 45; current conditions in, 199, 200f–201f, 207; draft laborers migrating to, 38; emigration from, 120, 208–9; establishment of cabildo, 49–50; forced to offer wages, 4, 34–35; founding of, 2, 6–7, 17–18, 28–33; growth of barrios around, 47–48; growth of honorific titles, 112; imported food a necessity, 48; increase in castas workers, 179; Indians gaining more responsibility, 48; informal economy in, 43; itinerant laborers, 48; little slave labor at, 68–69; as a *minas*, 45, 49, 84; native communities as parishes, 51, 91; native communities as pueblos, 90–91, 139; near ruins of earlier civilization, 23; need to attract permanent labor, 37; no hereditary nobility in, 91; plan of, 100f, 190f; population figures, 91–92 (92t), 117, 184–86, 189t, 203; replacing war with diplomacy, 31–32; sale of public offices, 56; size and ethnic makeup in 1550s, 46–47, 52; Tolosa's expedition to, 17, 29, 220n1; as UNESCO World Heritage Site, 199. *See also* indigenous residents of Zacatecas; mining booms/busts
Zacatecas, Felipe, 192
Zacatecos: attempts to avoid Spaniards, 18, 29–30; causing relatively little disruption, 50; considered uncivilized, 20; diet, 24, 26; dispersed around Zacatecas, 30–31; "friendly Indians" among, 32; gender roles, 26; language of, 224n42; in Mixton War, 27; as nonsedentary, 2, 26; organized into "rancherías," 25–26; raids by, 32; relocating away from Zacatecas, 33; size of population, 3, 18, 25; Spanish chroniclers on, 20–26; too few for labor support, 3, 18, 50
Zaldaña, Ana María de, 137
Zamora, Bartolomé de, 124
Zulawski, Ann, 257n128
Zumalde, Gregorio de, 140, 142
Zúñiga y Avellaneda, Félix de, 84

The authorized representative in the EU for product safety and compliance is:
Mare Nostrum Group
B.V Doelen 72
4831 GR Breda
The Netherlands

www.ingramcontent.com/pod-product-compliance
Lightning Source LLC
Chambersburg PA
CBHW031901220426
43663CB00006B/712